Taxation of
Farmers and Landowners

Taxation of Farmers and Landowners

Fifth Edition

Oliver Stanley   MA (Oxon)

BARRISTER; CHAIRMAN, RATHBONE BROTHERS PLC
FORMERLY ONE OF HM SENIOR INSPECTORS OF TAXES

Butterworths
London, Dublin and Edinburgh
1993

United Kingdom	Butterworth & Co (Publishers) Ltd, 88 Kingsway, LONDON WC2B and 4 Hill Street, EDINBURGH EH2 3JZ
Australia	Butterworths Pty Ltd, SYDNEY, MELBOURNE, BRISBANE, ADELAIDE, PERTH, CANBERRA and HOBART
Canada	Butterworths Canada Ltd, TORONTO and VANCOUVER
Ireland	Butterworth (Ireland) Ltd, DUBLIN
Malaysia	Malayan Law Journal Sdn Bhd, KUALA LUMPUR
New Zealand	Butterworths of New Zealand Ltd, WELLINGTON and AUCKLAND
Puerto Rico	Equity de Puerto Rico, Inc, HATO REY
Singapore	Malayan Law Journal Pte, Ltd, SINGAPORE
USA	Butterworth Legal Publishers, AUSTIN, Texas; BOSTON Massachusetts; CLEARWATER, Florida (D & S Publishers); ORFORD, New Hampshire (Equity Publishing); ST PAUL, Minnesota; and SEATTLE, Washington

A CIP Catalogue record for this book is available from the British Library.

First edition 1981
Second edition 1984
Third edition 1987
Fourth edition 1991

ISBN 0 406 02133 3

Typeset by Phoenix Photosetting, Chatham, Kent
Printed and bound in Great Britain by
Mackays of Chatham PLC, Chatham, Kent

Preface

This book attempts a comprehensive survey of United Kingdom taxes to which farmers and landowners are likely to be liable. It sets out to expound the law and practice of income tax; corporation tax; capital gains tax; inheritance tax; value added tax; stamp duty, community charge and council tax. It includes an introductory summary of National Insurance Contributions.

This book is selective in approach, omitting or summarising certain topics, and concentrating on those of particular relevance. It includes several chapters on tax planning – the arrangement of affairs so as to reduce taxes to their legal min· · mum. As tax planning is a subject of great complexity, these chapters are of aι elementary nature, but I hope they will help the reader to reconcile the demands of the Exchequer with the economics of his farm or estate.

When the first edition of this book was written 13 years ago, I had in mind that the reader might be a farmer or a landowner with little previous knowledge of taxation. On the other hand, the book was also intended for farmers' and landowners' professional advisers: lawyers, accountants, surveyors and land agents, who, I wrote, would find the latter parts of the book more relevant than the earlier. My experience with the first four editions has been that the book has been found to be most useful to professional a 'visers.

This book is substantially based on my experience as Chief Executive of Rathbone Brothers plc, an organisation which has set itself to advise land-owning and farming clients during the last 20 years. It is also based on my experience as Chief Taxation Adviser to the Country Landowners Association between 1975 and 1983, and I am grateful to members of that Association and to my clients · who, one way or another, have helped provide material and who have indicated the tax problems which farmers and landowners face. I hope that this book will add to all readers' understanding of taxation, help them to protect their lands and businesses, and help preserve the countryside for our enjoyment. I believe that life in the English countryside can be enriching and rewarding in the best sense, and if this book contributes in a small way to preserving the countryside, that would make it worthwhile.

Since publication of the first edition there have been dramatic changes in the economics of agriculture. The profitability of farming has fallen into decline. Average farm incomes in 1992 were half of what they had been in real terms ten years ago. It is notorious that there is world over-production of basic foodstuffs, although a short visit to a primitive and backward country makes this difficult to believe. The economics of agriculture in Britain are now substantially regulated by the authorities in the European Economic Community, and a sense of help-lessness has settled over the whole industry. As profitability has declined, so have land values. Lower profits have made the financing of taxation more difficult, and many farmers have been obliged to contemplate sales in whole or part, triggering liability to capital gains tax which is totally unrelieved by farming losses sustained over many years. However, agriculture has certainly benefited from the important alleviations accorded by the Conservative administration since 1979, so that the pressures of taxation now seem secondary to the pressure exerted on many farmers by their bank managers. In particular, the new 1992 inheritance tax reliefs at the rate of 100% for owner–occupied land and 50% for tenanted land have reduced the threat of inheritance tax, and have substantially changed tax planning and tax financing techniques.

Much of this book has been re-written since the fourth edition to take account of this particular change in the law and practice, and its important secondary effects on tax planning, eg, as to the balance and emphasis of different taxes. All these changes are dealt with in this edition.

In the fourth edition, additional space was allocated to capital gains tax and value added tax and the tax consequences of alternative non-agricultural forms of land use were examined in some detail for the first time. These sections have been retained and expanded in this edition. Despite the changes in the relative importance of different taxes since this book was first written, the layout and structure have been left unchanged, so as to assist readers familiar with the earlier editions and because, I have been told, the structure is generally a helpful one.

I am grateful to all my collaborators, particularly colleagues in Rathbone Brothers plc, who have helped to correct errors and supply material. I am also grateful to many professional readers of the book, who have written to correct errors and to report their experiences in practice, many of which have been incorporated in the text.

Both I and my publishers have tried to make this book as up to date as possible, including the 1993 changes enacted in the Finance Act 1993.

July 1993
Oliver Stanley

Contents

Chapter 8   Inheritance tax   143

Chapter 9   Value Added Tax   167

Chapter 10   Stamp duty   191

Chapter 11   Community charge and council tax   195

Chapter 19   Procedure: tax returns; assessment; collection   315

Appendices   331

Index   345

Table of statutes

References in this Table to Statutes are to Halsbury's *Statutes* of England (Fourth Edition) showing the volume and page at which the annotated text of the Act may be found.

Table of cases

Chapter 1

Introduction and outline

1.1 INTRODUCTION AND OUTLINE

The purpose of this book is to bring together all aspects of tax law and practice, affecting farmers and country landowners in Britain. By 'farmers' is meant those carrying on the trade or business of farming whether as tenants; as owner occupiers; or via a farming partnership or company. By 'country landowners' is meant those not carrying on such a business, but owning a landed estate, which may comprise one or more tenanted farms. In practice, these classes overlap. The same individual may be at one and the same time an owner of some land, and a tenant of other land. He may have some land 'in hand', that is, be farming it himself, and have some land occupied by his tenants.

This book concentrates on those features of the tax system of special relevance to farmers and landowners and does not attempt to be a comprehensive review of the tax system as a whole. Features of the UK tax system not directly applicable tend to be briefly summarised and some specialised aspects are omitted altogether.

Almost all of the contents of this book will be relevant to the affairs of a farmer, and to his professional advisers, be they solicitors, accountants, chartered surveyors, valuers or land agents. The only parts not of immediate interest will be those describing taxation of rentals and the fiscal effects of obtaining vacant possession of land, included in chapters 4 and 5.

Both farmers and country landowners are exceptionally vulnerable to capital taxation in the respective forms described below. There are several reasons for this; first, farmers and landowners seem to represent a class including 'vast aggregations of inherited wealth', the obvious target of attack by past Labour governments.

However, there is an economic as well as a political vulnerability. Farmers hold their capital in relatively illiquid assets: land, buildings, stocks, plant, crops etc, and in order to pay capital taxation they are obliged to realise assets and convert them into cash. This conversion may trigger off a second tax, capital gains tax, and in any case, farms and farmlands are not usually capable of partial realisation, to pay capital taxation representing a percentage of their total value.

Again, substantial arguments can be mounted in favour of capital taxation on death. The argument here falls into two parts: there are those who argue that what an heir receives should be more severely taxed because it comes to him as 'bounty', and therefore his acceptance of taxation will be readier. Again, it is sometimes contended that inheritance has a greater capacity for taxation because it is value which has not been earned by the recipient personally but by his forebears at some distant time in the past.

Whatever the true merits of these arguments, they have encouraged capital based taxation which could have been severely damaging to farms and farmlands had it not been for the fact that it has brought with it a range of reliefs (see chapters 7 and 8). Generally, these reliefs operate by reducing the capital base by some percentage of value or, alternatively, allowing a period of time during which capital taxes may be paid by instalments.

Both categories of relief are notoriously imperfect. The first category emphasises the importance and the difficulty of the valuation of land; the second transforms a tax on capital into a tax on income, in so far as it intends net post income tax profits to be the source out of which capital tax instalments become payable.

Agriculture has long been an industry whose profitability is capable of close regulation by national and international pricing mechanisms. In recent years, the profitability of farming has declined as a consequence of common agricultural policies, reductions to European Economic Community budgets, world food surpluses, and other reasons too general to be explained here. Income taxes have diminished in importance more or less proportionately with the diminution of incomes. Capital taxes however, have not. Although the price of farmland has ceased to rise, its dramatic rises in recent years can create substantial capital taxation liabilities on sales or on a death. The profits and cash flow available to finance capital taxation have become manifestly inadequate.

Farming and land ownership are both long-term activities in which, tradi- tionally, businesses passed down the generations from father to son, each transfer capable of creating liabilities to inheritance tax. It is worth comparing the position of, say, manufacturing industries in Britain constituted in quoted or unquoted companies whose fragmented ownership parts, that is their stocks and shares, can change hands so much more readily in small value units.

Farming seems to be an activity not susceptible to being undertaken on a scale which the investing public can be invited to subscribe. This may be because the profitability has traditionally been low, or it may be that in farming ownership and management are indivisible elements. Whatever the reason, farmers have not accepted the shelter of the private limited liability company with any enthusi- asm. The fiscal disadvantages of incorporation are sometimes used to explain the reluctance to incorporate, but whatever the reason, the industry has suffered from its reluctance.

Those who are attacked may be excused for defending themselves. One way in which the country landowner can theoretically do that is to seek to become a farmer. For that reason, owners and their advisers will be interested in those parts of this book which describe their present fiscal posture; and those parts which describe the tax regime of farmers, to which they aspire. Since 1979, distinct and measurable progress has been made in equalising the tax regimes of the two classes. However, this progress has been slow, allegedly because of political constraints. Hence discrepancies and disadvantages remain on the statute, exer- cising considerable influence. Two examples will suffice at this stage: for inheri- tance tax, agricultural property relief for let land is still given at a lower rate, 50% as against 100%; for capital gains tax, roll-over relief (see section **7.4**) is denied for let land.

Vacant possession is often not readily achievable. Farm tenants have been granted rights of tenure, under the Agricultural Holdings Act 1948, as amended. All yearly tenancies as a general rule continue in force from year to year, unless voluntarily surrendered, or terminated by a valid notice to quit. Twelve months' notice is required, and the tenant has one month in which to serve a counter- notice. In such circumstances, the issue is adjudicated by the Agricultural Land Tribunal, which can grant possession to the landlord in the interests of good husbandry; sound estate management; or hardship. There are certain circum- stances in which a tenant loses the right to serve a counter-notice, eg failure to pay rent, bankruptcy, etc.

Until 1976, a landlord could obtain possession on the death of a tenant, but the Agriculture (Miscellaneous Provisions) Act 1976 Pt II accorded security of tenure for up to three generations in England and Wales. (In Scotland, security of tenure has long been in force.) Eligible successors apply to the Agricultural Land Tribunal for grant of a tenancy. To be eligible, a successor may be wife, husband, brother, sister or child of the deceased, deriving his principal source of livelihood for not less than five years from work on the particular farm. Disputes between the parties are adjudicated by the Agricultural Land Tribunal.

One result has been to put the landlord and tenant system into some jeopardy. Few landlords have been willing to grant new tenancies, so creating a famine, and there is evidence of uneconomically high rents being tendered to secure any tenancies offered. Prophets have forecast the doom of the individual landlord,

Percentage of Agricultural Acreage by Tenure and Size Group
(England and Wales)

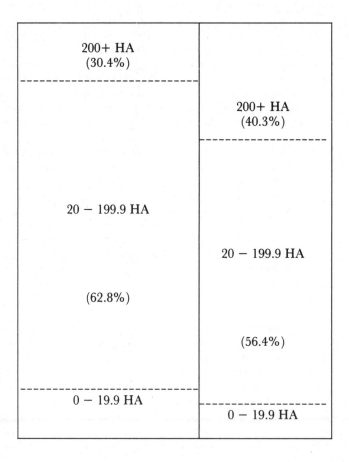

Owner Occupied*   Let*
60.2%   39.8%

100%

200+ HA
(30.4%)

200+ HA
(40.3%)

20 – 199.9 HA

20 – 199.9 HA

(62.8%)

(56.4%)

0 – 19.9 HA

0 – 19.9 HA

0%

* In 1991, the respective percentages are 64% owner occupied and 36% let.

Source: Ministry of Agriculture, Fisheries and Food.
        Agricultural Statistics, United Kingdom, 1983.

with his function as supplier of capital passing to the financial institutions for whom exclusion from possession is less significant.

Another view is that the tenancy succession law was misconceived, and needs amendment, as attempted in the Agricultural Holdings Act 1984. Broadly, the effect of this Act is to limit security of tenure to one generation for new tenancies only, that is, those contracted after the passing of the Act. As a quid pro quo for this concession, amendments have been made to the basis on which farm rents are arbitrated, using a revised formula designed to avoid oppressively high rents during a period of abnormal scarcity. The formula takes account of the productive capacity of a particular farm, as well as market conditions generally. Hopefully, both changes will increase the supply of let land, which was the expressed government intention. It is fair to add that the Bill aroused considerable controversy and misgivings, varying from the view that it did not go far enough, to the view that it would have the precisely opposite effect from that intended.

Some attempts have been made to deregulate and provide a better framework. However, it is important to note that existing tenancies are unaffected by these attempts, and it therefore follows that it must be a long time before the new regime makes a serious impact on the current situation.

It is unlikely that the grant of inheritance tax reliefs to owners of tenanted land will successfully induce additional lettings. One view is that a free and vigorous market will not emerge until tenancy law is more drastically changed; certainly, several years will need to elapse before judgments can be made. Some owners who might have let their land, have become owner-occupiers, and others have set up partnerships and joint ventures with those who might have become tenants. These business arrangements will not be reversed overnight (see section **17.4**).

This book is arranged in the following sequence: the first three chapters describe respectively the income tax treatment of farm profits; farm stocks and agricultural rents. The next chapter compares and contrasts the treatments of farmers and country landowners and describes certain tax features common to both.

Partnerships and companies are examined in a single chapter and the two capital taxes in separate chapters without differentiating the treatment of the two categories although that differentiation should emerge and is summarised in section **15.6:14**.

Various forms of taxation which have a lesser but still important incidence are briefly summarised and the liabilities and reliefs applicable to both woodlands and to the countryside are allotted separate chapters.

All taxes are described, but general knowledge of the scope and outline of each has been assumed. For those readers without the necessary background knowledge, the appropriate standard references have been provided. By confining description of the scope of each tax to a mere summary, space has been created to treat those aspects of the law and practice relevant to agriculture in more detail.

Thereafter, this book advances into the territory of tax planning for both farmers and country landowners. The general principles of tax planning are summarised so as to concentrate upon those particular strategies, which are relevant. The content has been influenced by the fact that farming is a small scale activity in Britain.

One of the purposes of the tax-planning chapters (15 to 18) is to alert farmers, landowners and their advisers to the fact that much can be done by those prepared to work patiently at the task. Agriculture is a vocation which breeds conservatism, and landowners have not all done their homework since capital taxation has been imposed. Although inheritance tax has been on the statute book for almost twenty years, many farmers and landowners have still taken no steps to provide for it.

Yet, they represent a class most vulnerable to capital taxation, because agriculture is a capital intensive industry, offering a broader base towards progressive capital taxation than many other industries in Britain. It has been calculated that the average return is 2.7% compared with 15.7% for industry as a whole (see *Capital for Agriculture*, Centre for Agricultural Strategy, University of Reading, 1978).

The corollary of this is that income yields are low. In particular, this is true of rental yields from tenanted lands. In recent years, it has been assumed that *gross* yields run at the rate of some 4% to 5%, at a time when gilt edged stocks have been yielding 12% plus. One explanation is that farm rents are reviewed under the Agricultural Holdings Acts at three-yearly intervals (five years in Scotland), so there is always considerable delay while rents catch up with prices and inflation. Another is that the price of farmland has been rising dramatically in recent years, due partly to institutional buying and the fact that it is a commodity in limited supply. These low yields mean that the profits and cash flows available to finance taxation become inadequate. Again, farming and landownership are relatively illiquid activities, and this illiquidity creates an inflexibility which makes tax planning more difficult.

Another problem is that the structure of the British farming industry is currently changing in response to changing government policies for national food production, for agricultural subsidy withdrawal, to establish alternative land use, and to protect the so called 'rural environment'.

Individual farmers and landowners have been finding these changes puzzling, difficult and disheartening. The difficulties have been compounded by the influence of taxation, particularly capital taxation, which represents an obstacle in the way of change. It is not so much that the tax system is unfair, but that it is ill-adapted to the changing direction of agriculture and land ownership.

These different factors operating together have driven farmers and landowners to seek via their representative organisations, special reliefs from taxation. Some of the reliefs described below are peculiar to agriculture, others are available to all 'small businesses', of which farming is undoubtedly one. So valuable are these reliefs that any farmer who fails to secure his entitlement, or fails to maximise the value of a particular relief, can be said to be offering to pay a 'voluntary' tax.

However (and this is a truism), the scope for securing relief, and for performing tax-planning exercises will vary according to the family and farming circumstances of the individual. As an obvious example, those with an ample and timely supply of offspring, who intend to make the family farm their careers, tend to be better placed than those without, and this book cannot remedy so grave a defect.

Because farming is a very long-term activity, the urge to retain land and houses in the family is often strong. Those who currently own often see themselves as having an obligation to their forebears to pass on their inheritance to their children. Often they see themselves as quasi-trustees, and for this reason and because land is an historical form of wealth, landowners have tended to settle land upon trust for their descendants. This book does not embark upon any detailed exposition of trust law, but limits itself to those aspects directly relevant to the readership.

Chapter 14 entitled 'The Countryside and the National Heritage' has special relevance. In practice, it is often income from landownership or farming which is applied by owners to support or subsidise the existence of a country mansion house and surrounding parklands, which may be part of our national heritage, or which contain works of art which so qualify. The future of the heritage has been the subject of much recent debate. One thing is clear: taxation, particularly capital taxation, exerts an enormous influence. Individual owners have sought and won vital reliefs from capital taxes, but no such general relief has been accorded for income tax, and there is only one specialised and limited concession. When houses are open to the public, income tax treatment can be crucial. This contentious topic is discussed in section **14.5**, and generally this book concentrates upon the practical aspects, and the decisions facing owners, who sometimes feel that to take advantage of the reliefs offered by the State is to make themselves into hostages; striking a bargain with a party – the State – which is capable of changing the terms after the bargain has been made.

The tax-planning chapters of this book, chapters 15 to 18, disclose how much more room for manoeuvre the farmer has had than his landowner counterpart. The farmer's principal tactic was to secure relief by reduction of the value of his land from vacant possession value to that of tenanted value. That required the most scrupulous attention to detail by professional advisers, and there were many traps for the unwary, but the rewards were not trivial. At the time of writing, it is customary to suggest that tenanted land is worth some 50% to 60% of the comparable land with vacant possession, although this is a percentage which varies substantially from time to time, in different areas of the country, and with differing qualities and quantities of land. It has been a strategy with many secondary effects, variations and refinements, and once the relief has been secured, preservation of it needed to be kept in mind and this need remains.

Another important tax-planning strategy involves the tax treatment of farm finance. This is described in chapter 16. Because agriculture is a capital intensive industry, one might expect outside borrowing to play a large part. The reverse is true: the industry is largely financed by individual owners out of their retained profits. Finance is important in the defence mechanism it can offer for preserving intact a farm or estate in life or on death. Taxes have to be paid in cash, and borrowing can be cheaper than selling.

Life assurance has, over the years, become an important aid in this kind of tax planning, and some of the most relevant forms are described in section **16.4**.

Tax planning is not a once-and-for-all-time exercise capable of being performed and forgotten. On the contrary, the taxation effects require attention, whenever a farm is bought, sold, expanded in size, merged, reduced and upon all similar occasions. Land is a very flexible commodity capable of being dealt with in a variety of ways. Special tax reliefs require special attention, involving consideration of the different methods by which an end can be achieved. Some reliefs operate retrospectively after the event giving rise to the tax, even after a tax year has been closed, or a death has occurred. These aspects are described in section **18.3**.

Finally, certain administrative aspects often assume great importance. The timing of tax demands and payments can be critical in an era when borrowing costs are high, and rents are low. Payment by instalment procedures need to be carefully considered; these are described in chapter 19.

Generally, this book also contemplates farmland and agriculture as potential investment media. Taxation may be regarded as one of the hazards facing a new entrant to farming, or an existing farmer-tenant, who aspires to own his land. Other investors – potentially at least – are trustees of private trusts with substantial portfolios, and institutional investors, and those buying simply to secure tax reliefs.

During the period since the fourth edition of this book, the general trends discussed in the Introduction to that edition have continued. Firstly, agriculture: the profitability of farming in Britain has continued to decline in consequence of Common Market agricultural policies; world food surpluses; and alleged over-production of basic food stuffs.

Estimates made in the autumn of 1990, based on government statistics, showed that farm incomes had declined by 9% per annum in real terms since the early 1980s. Earnings from lowlands, cereal and livestock farms were 85% less in 1989/90 than they had been in 1982/83. Annual investment in farming fixed capital was less than half of what it had been six years earlier in 1983. In consequence approximately 60,000 farming jobs had been lost during that decade. It is claimed that farm values have fallen by 50%, comparing 1993 with the 1980's peak. But a glimmer of hope has recently been created by the 23.6% devaluation of the green pound and the fall in UK interest rates. It is too soon to predict an upturn, merely a respite!

Reduced profits have certainly produced corresponding reductions in the pressure of taxation, but when tax bills do arise, for example on the sales of land, or on rearrangements amongst the family, the cashflow available to finance the tax bill is often inadequate. This decline of economic potential has led to an extraordinary and much criticised phenomenon: State payments to farmers simply for taking their land out of food production: the 'set-aside scheme' (see chapter 17).

The fiscal consequences of set-aside need study, as clearly there is a danger that the value received may be eroded by increased taxes.

In this book, set-aside is treated as one form of diversification or new activity (or inactivity!); an 'alternate land use', which perhaps offers an ironic comment on the principle involved. The incidence of income tax, capital gains tax and inheritance tax may all be affected (see chapter 17).

There are, of course, more positive forms of alternative use of farmland: for non-food crops, and for countryside, sporting, and recreational activities. It is a truism that the countryside has become the playground of town dwellers and the industry has begun to recognise that providing this playground with desirable amenities can be a reasonably profitable alternative to growing food. Among those amenities must be included caravans, holiday cottages and farm shops.

'Alternative use' covers a variety of other possibilities. There have been some notorious and expensive miscalculations; for example, the architecturally satisfying conversion of disused and redundant milking parlours into rural craftsmen's workshops, which then remain vacant as had been the parlours before. The critical issue is whether taking land out of agricultural use is a proper step. First, there is the fundamental question: will the alternative use produce a reasonable return on capital, bearing in mind the additional cost of conversion? Secondly – but a question often capable of being overlooked – is it prudent to forfeit the taxation reliefs which attach to a farming business or to agricultural land, and which may be irrevocably lost once the land use has been changed?

Yet another recourse has been the increased sale of farmland for development. It is obvious that as towns encroach on the countryside in Britain, more farmland is capable of becoming developed into residential estates. Unfortunately, this trend has coincided with an unexpected and unwelcome rise in the rate of capital gains tax from 30% to 40%. Thus a sale destined to supply badly needed fresh capital or to reduce expensive borrowing may be severely eroded by capital gains tax. This can be very frustrating, and can act as a disincentive to positive action.

It is notorious that capital gains tax has a lock-in effect discouraging sales badly needed to reduce borrowing costs.

Another predictable phenomenon has been the continuing decline of the traditional landlord and tenant system, in course of being replaced by less formal more 'egalitarian' arrangements between a landowner and the former tenant. With farming capital as costly as it has become there is not the same incentive for a landowner to obtain vacant possession of additional land so as to farm it himself. On the contrary, the idea of someone else providing the necessary working capital so that an owner can receive an annual rental income seems now a much more attractive one. Unfortunately tenanted land has still not attracted the same tax reliefs has owner occupied land, so here again, increased taxes represent a threat.

Neither agriculture nor taxes are static. The shape and weight of the UK system has also changed since the last edition. The reductions in marginal rates of income tax and inheritance tax from 60% to 40% have diminished the importance of those two taxes, relative to capital gains tax, the effective rate of which has been increased to 40%. The system of indexation for capital gains tax: that is, relief for inflationary gains has, however, been significantly improved. Even so, capital gains tax now seems the biggest single menace to farmers and landowners. That is because it taxes abruptly in one year value increases which may have accrued over a lifetime of business activity, realised by a single disposal.

Farming and landowning are relatively illiquid activities, and this illiquidity creates an inflexibility which makes capital gains tax planning more difficult. It is not now an easy tax to reduce or defer, particularly since the hold-over relief for the capital gains tax arising on gifts (as opposed to sales) of assets has been narrowed in scope. In landowning families, systematic lifetime gifts of land have always been a useful method of passing value down generations and these have been constrained.

In addition, value added tax at 17½% is continuing to make greater impact on farmers since the important changes made in 1989 to harmonise with the rules in other European Community countries and to comply with a decision of the European Court of Justice on 21 June 1988. Sales of new non-residential buildings; assignments and surrenders of tenancies and sporting rights have been brought within the charge (chapter 9).

The Finance Act 1993 signals new increases in personal taxation, not all of which are immediately apparent. The most important is the change in dividend tax which will affect many farmers and landowners, whose investment incomes are applied to support their farming businesses, or to pay for their ordinary living costs.

The system of advance corporation tax (ACT) and tax credits on dividends was designed to avoid shareholders' double taxation on company profits. Insofar as profits are taxed once on the company to corporation tax, and then again on the shareholders as income tax on their dividends, earnings from one economic activity are being taxed twice. This is alleviated by the tax credit on dividends allowed to shareholders, but under the new rules, that credit is reduced from 25% to 20% and the burden of double taxation is correspondingly increased.

The rate of tax credit applicable to companies has now been disengaged from the rate of tax credit applicable to shareholders. Although the company's tax credit and the higher rate taxpayers credit is to be at 20%, the basic rate taxpayer's tax credit will be at 25%. Once an anomaly of this kind is admitted in the tax system, it is capable of being developed by future administrations, so that the way is open for a different government, for example, to erode the value of the shareholders' tax credit, reducing it ultimately to nil.

The purpose of advance corporation tax as a mechanism to avoid double taxation seems to have been completely disregarded. The famous level playing field has been tilted. By reducing the credit on dividends, there has been recreated a selective investment income surcharge, under which the rate of tax on dividend income has been increased by 5%, by comparison to the rate of tax on what used to be called 'earned income' and interest on deposits, loans and loan stock. This is a concealed income tax rate increase. To achieve it, the government has gone to extraordinary lengths: destroying the rate symmetry that previously existed between the shareholder and the company, and opening up a route for future distortions.

Chapter 2

Farming profits and losses

2.1 GENERAL SCHEME OF INCOME TAX

2.1:1 Introduction

It is notorious that income tax is an obscure subject for farmers. One way of overcoming the difficulty is to examine how it arises, and this may serve as a helpful introduction to taxation for those without previous knowledge, for whom this preliminary section is intended.

Some of the complexities flow from the fact that income tax is a part of a larger system of law, and relies upon general legal principles. Another is that it necessarily involves abstract ideas such as 'income' and 'capital'. Another is that it has grown up piecemeal over the years, and is always in a state of flux. Another is that in an attempt to be 'fair' it tries to cater for many different taxpayers' personal and business circumstances. Yet another is that changes in taxation are made by Parliament for economic or social reasons, rather than to improve the tax system itself.

This book does not attempt any overall summary of UK taxation, but outlines certain features fundamental to the system:

(a) the source of taxation law;
(b) the classification of taxes;
(c) the Schedular principle;
(d) the annual nature of taxation;
(e) key administrative aspects.

2.1:2 Sources of tax law

Tax law is created by Parliament and interpreted by the courts. Government of the day decides its policy, and invents or varies national taxation to implement or assist that policy. Parliament is required to re-impose income tax each year (see Provisional Collection of Taxes Act 1968), so that the elected representatives of taxpayers may have their say, and this has provided an opportunity to make annual changes.

Another source of tax law is the orders or regulations made by government; and another is the precedent rules laid down by judges in the High Court, when deciding a particular piece of litigation between the Inland Revenue and a taxpayer, who has appealed against assessment to taxation.

2.1:3 The classification of taxes

Taxes in the UK referred to in this book may be classified as follows:

1. Taxes on *income*, for example, income tax, corporation tax.
2. Taxes upon *capital*, eg capital gains tax, inheritance tax.
3. Taxes on *expenditure*, eg value added tax, stamp duty.

There is no comprehensive definition of 'income', nor any single method of distinguishing between income and capital gains. 'Income' is used to mean profits in money or money's worth derived from an identifiable source, rather than a mere receipt.

In order to differentiate between income and capital, an analogy with a growing tree has frequently been used. Capital has been compared with the tree; and income with its annual and seasonal growing fruits, which may be taken without destruction of the tree itself. This image is used to visualise income as having a quality of recurrence, and capital as being of a once-and-for-all-time nature.

2.1:4 The Schedular principle

The income tax Schedules referred to throughout this book represent a classification of income tax according to the nature of the source from which the income is received:

Schedule A Rents and other receipts from land and buildings (TA 1988 Pt II).

Schedule B Repealed.

Schedule C Interest on British and foreign government securities (TA 1988 Pt III).

Schedule D Income from trades and professions; interest and other income, classified again into various Cases (TA 1988 Pt IV):

Case I Profits of a trade, eg farming carried on in the UK (see section **2.2**).

Case II Profits of a profession or vocation.

Case III Interest, annuities or other annual payments, eg savings bank interest.

Case IV Income arising from overseas securities.

Case V Income arising from overseas possessions (see section **17.6**), eg land abroad, or a trade carried on abroad.

Case VI Annual profits or gains not falling under any other Case, or any other Schedule (see section **5.6**).

Schedule E Income from offices and employments, pensions and social security benefits, often taxed under PAYE (TA 1988 Pt V).

Schedule F Income tax charged on company dividends, and other distributions by companies to shareholders (TA 1988 Pt VI) (see section **6.3**).

The various Schedules are mutually exclusive, so that the same profit or income can be taxed only once under its appropriate Schedule. The Cases of Schedule D, however, are subject to a different rule: the Inland Revenue may decide under which Case a given item of income should be taxed. But the same item cannot be taxed under more than one Case.

2.1:5 The annual nature of income tax

Income tax is an annual tax, annually re-imposed by Parliament. The income tax year runs from 6 April until the following 5 April, and it is helpful to visualise the system as a chain of separate tax years with each 6 April as the link date. The introduction of an autumn Budget will not change the income tax year. Rates of charge to tax, reliefs granted and all the other rules may vary from one year to another, so that it is always important to state the year or years to which any provision applies and for which any piece of income is to be taxed.

There are different rules for allocating income to different years depending upon which Schedule or Case is involved. Income is allocated to a particular tax year in accordance with *the basis of assessment* of that class of income. The basis of assessment for any income tax year is the period of time to be adopted in allocating income to be assessed for that year. The income arising in that period of time becomes the income of that tax year.

In some cases, for example for wages under Schedule E, the basic period coincides with the tax year. This is known as the *current year* basis. The treatment of farming profits is more complicated. In the normal course the basis period for any tax year is the 12 months' accounting period ending in the preceding tax year. Suppose a farmer makes up his accounts to 31 December each year. Then the accounts ending on 31 December 1993 will form the basis period ending in 1993–94 and will be the basis period for the tax year 1994–95. It is worth noting that there are currently proposals for simplifying this treatment.

There are special rules for varying the basis described above (TA 1988 s 60). The years in which a farming business commences and ceases are treated on a current year basis. Since farming profits tend to fluctuate, there can be wide differences in the amounts chargeable to income tax as between one year and another. In a progressive tax system, with rates rising according to a scale, fluctuating profits can be taxed more heavily than consistent profits. To alleviate the hardship to farmers, a system of profit averaging may be adopted, under which a farmer has the right to elect for a different basis of assessment if certain tests are satisfied and if it is beneficial to him (TA 1988 s 96). The topic is discussed below (see section **2.5**).

2.1:6   Key administrative aspects

The assessment and collection of income and capital taxation is entrusted to the Commissioners of Inland Revenue, usually referred to as the Board. The day to day work is carried out by HM Inspectors of Taxes, and by Collectors of Taxes, who respectively make assessments and collect the tax so assessed.

Value added tax is administered by the Board of Customs and Excise, and local rates are levied by local authorities (see section **9.1** and Chapter 11). Liability to all forms of taxation can be disputed in the courts (see Chapter 19).

2.2   THE TRADE OF FARMING

There is a special tax regime for the profits of a trade carried on in the United Kingdom: Sch D Case I. Whether or not a person is carrying on a trade is a question of fact, but the word 'trade' includes the idea of exchanging goods or services for a reward.

The question also arises as to what 'farming' means for taxation purposes. 'Farm land' 'means land in the United Kingdom wholly or mainly occupied for the purposes of husbandry . . . and "farming" shall be construed accordingly' (TA 1988 s 832(1)). In the absence of more specific definition, the word has its ordinary meaning. It is safe to assume that 'farming' means the production and sale of cereals (arable); the production and sale of milk and associated products (dairy); and the production and sale of animals (livestock). To be a farmer, it is not necessary to engage in all these activities, but on the other hand, if all are performed by others, so that the only function retained is the mere ownership of land, then no trade is being carried on. This is so, when an owner grants a tenancy or a licence to someone else to farm on his land. The income then arises to him, not because of his activity, but because of his ownership.

The expression 'agriculture' is similarly not defined. The expression is used primarily in the context of 'agricultural land' (CAA 1968 s 69) and means land, houses or other buildings in the UK occupied wholly or mainly for the purposes of husbandry (see section **5.2:5**).

The expression 'agricultural purposes' is used several times in connection with inheritance tax (see chapter 8). 'Agricultural purposes' is not statutorily defined, nor is the expression 'agriculture' itself. Some help may be obtained from IHTA 1984 s 115(2) which provides that: 'agricultural property means agricultural land or pasture and includes woodland and any building used in connection with the intensive rearing of livestock or fish if the woodland or building is occupied with agricultural land or pasture and the occupation is ancillary to that of the agricultural land or pasture; and also includes such cottages, farm buildings and farm houses, together with the land occupied with them, as are of a character appropriate to the property.'

It seems likely that this definition would be available to be cited in an income tax or other context.

Further help may be obtained for those cases in which the expression 'husbandry' is defined, as to which see section **5.2:5**.

Yet another source of authority is cases under the Rating and Valuation Acts, most recently *Assessor for Lothian Region v Rolawn Ltd* 1990 SLT 433. In this case it was held that growing and selling high quality turf was an agricultural operation and that the lands were entitled to be derated. The judgments in this case include numerous rating authority cases, in which the rateability of various marginal activities was debated.

Whilst the position for arable, dairy and livestock is reasonably straightforward, that is not so for fruit and vegetables. The definition cited above for 'farm land' is expressed to exclude 'market garden land', which means:

'Land in the United Kingdom occupied as a nursery or garden for the sale of produce (other than land used for the growth of hops) and "market gardening" shall be construed accordingly.' (TA 1988 s 832(1).)

The effect of this separate definition needs to be studied. One consequence has been to raise the question of whether a domestic house with a garden attached, whose owner is accustomed to sell surplus produce, is a 'market garden'.

This question has been considered in a series of precedent cases, and the answer seems to be that the definition of a market garden is applicable only where commercial purposes are the predominant purposes. Where home consumption or pleasure or pride in ownership is the dominant purpose then the garden is not a 'market garden'. This is so even if there are occasional sales, from the 'garden gate'. Whilst this might be important where no other farming activity is carried on, it will not have much significance where the sales of vegetables or fruit are merely part of a larger activity. Thus a farm shop, located on the farm premises and selling partly farm produced goods, and partly goods bought for resale is unlikely to be treated as a separate trade.

Since farming is to be treated as a trade (TA 1988 s 53), it is charged to tax under Schedule D Case I in the ordinary way, provided the land is in the UK. If the land is situated abroad, different problems arise, and these are considered in section **17.6:3**. That also applies to market gardening. The ordinary rules for calculating profits under Schedule D Case I apply, subject, however, to one major exception.

All the farming carried on by one person, or partnership or body of persons is treated as one trade (TA 1988 s 53). This rule, which does not apply to market gardening, can have major effects on the computation of farming profits and losses. It applies so as to aggregate profits and losses (including capital allowances) of more than one farm into a single taxable source of income, when more than one farm is operating at the same point of time but in different parts of the country.

That one farm may be situated in the North of Scotland and the other in Worcestershire is immaterial. Nor is it relevant that the two farms are managed as separate economic units, nor that separate sets of financial accounts are prepared. The principle was argued in *Bispham v Eardiston Farming Co (1919) Ltd* (1962) 40 TC 322, where it was held that the company carried on only one trade, so that losses on the Worcester farm could be aggregated with profits of the farm in Scotland. But the rule does not apply to farming on land overseas. The expenses incurred by a UK farmer in visiting Australia with a view to buying a farm were held not to be deductible (*Sargent v Eayrs* [1973] STC 50).

Similarly, there is no cessation of trade, nor any new trade commenced, where a farmer ceases farming at one farm, sells up, buys a new farm and starts afresh there. The rules for cessations and commencements substituting different basis periods do not normally come into operation. However, if there has been a significant interval of time between the giving up of one farm and starting off at another, the Revenue will take the view that a trade has ceased and a new one commenced. What is a significant period varies with all the facts of the case, but periods in excess of a year are capable of being regarded in this way.

The point is not an academic one. The farm being disposed of may have been uneconomic, producing trading losses capable of being applied to relieve the profits realised on the new farm. Those losses will be available for bringing forward in that way if the two sets of farming operations amount to a single continuing trade. If one trade wholly ceased, then the accumulated tax losses at the date of cessation cease to have value (TA 1988 s 385).

This rule applies to farming carried on by one person, partnership or body of persons. It does not apply where there is a change in the personnel farming a particular farm. A farmer may take his son into partnership and continue farming the family farm without any practical change in the way the business is conducted. Despite that, the trade formerly carried on is considered for tax purposes to have ceased, and a new trade has commenced. However, it is possible to avoid the fiscal effects, that is, the change in the basis of assessment to actual year basis, by making the appropriate election for the continuation basis (TA 1988 s 113(2)).

The rules so far described for determining what is a trade of farming are supplemented by further definitions and explanations. For example, the agricultural land and buildings allowance described in section **5.2:5** is capable of being claimed by the owner or tenant of any 'agricultural or forestry land'. Such reliefs are given primarily against agricultural and forestry income. The meaning of these expressions is considered in section **5.2:9**.

Again, for the purposes of restricting certain loss reliefs which would otherwise be available to persons carrying on a trade of farming or market gardening, those expressions are to be interpreted as above, but with the difference that activities outside the UK are not to be excluded (see section **17.6:3**). Therefore, the word 'farming' does not have one precise meaning for income tax purposes. There is one principal meaning, and some supplementaries, and it is always necessary to know for what purpose the word is being construed.

If a particular activity does not, as a matter of fact, fall within the definitions given above, it may still be taxable as representing the carrying on of some other trade within Schedule D Case I. Alternatively, the activity may represent casual or occasional profits chargeable under Schedule D Case VI (TA 1988 s 18(3)). Case VI applies to commissions, profits from certain speculative activities, various payments for services rendered, and income from furnished lettings (see section **5.6**). The borderline between Case I and Case VI is by no means clear.

Case VI is applied where the item is of an income or profit nature but the activity is not substantial or continuous enough to amount to a full-scale trade.

Fees receivable for the services of a stallion have been repeatedly held to be chargeable under Case VI (*Malcolm v Lockhart* (1917) 7 TC 99), and so have moneys received from the sale of nominations to a stallion in respect of shares held in a thoroughbred ownership syndicate (*Benson v Counsell* (1942) 24 TC 178). However, the breeding of horses where the serving has been limited to animals on the farm, has been held to be farming under Case I (*Lord Glanely v Wightman* (1933) 17 TC 634).

The effect of liability under Case VI as opposed to Case I is generally disadvantageous. Deductions under Case VI are more restricted than under Case I, and the profit is treated as investment not earned income. Farmers should, wherever practical, include all receipts in a single set of accounts to arrive at a result showing the activities of their farming trade as a whole. Items omitted and shown separately in a return form may fall to be classified as apt for Case VI.

Finally, capital receipts arising, for example, from the sale of land are not subject to income tax under Case VI, but may be subject to capital gains taxation (see also section **5.7**). Gratuitous receipts are not subject to income tax, but may become the subject of liability to inheritance taxation.

2.3   DEDUCTIONS IN COMPUTING PROFITS

2.3:1   Introduction

One of the purposes of classifying income according to the nature of the source is to prescribe different tests for the deduction of expenditure against different classes so as to arrive at 'taxable' income. Since farming is classifiable under Schedule D Case I, as a trade carried on in the UK, farmers are entitled to whatever deductions are permitted under Schedule D Case I, as well as those generally applied in the whole system of income tax. The combined effect may be summarised in **2.3:2–5**.

2.3:2   Income and capital

Income tax is a tax upon receipts of income, not receipts of capital, and as a corollary, expenditure of a capital nature is not deductible for income tax purposes, although such expenditure may be otherwise deductible, for example for capital gains tax purposes. Moreover, special tax reliefs have been created for relieving certain capital expenditure, for example on agricultural buildings. Allowances for buildings and plant are given after taxable profits have been calculated, and therefore do not breach the rule stated above (see section **5.2**).

But what is capital expenditure? Unfortunately, there is no comprehensive and infallible test. A number of different tests have emerged from precedent case law and together they amount to a helpful code of practice. Even so, disputes are still capable of occurring, where the facts of particular expenditure fall on the borderline, and it is notorious that Inspectors of Taxes are not always consistent in their approach. Much may depend on the sum of money involved, the rate of income tax for a given year and other extraneous considerations, which may colour the issue, so making the question of whether a given item is 'capital' or not into a critical one. These surrounding irrelevant factors need to be stripped away in addressing the central problem.

First, capital expenditure has a once-and-for-all-time quality about it, whereas income expenditure tends regularly to recur. A supplementary test laid down by the courts stipulates that the question is whether the expenditure has been made 'not only once and for all, but with a view to bringing into existence an asset or advantage for the enduring benefit of the trade'. So a substantial contribution to an employees' pension fund ranked as capital expenditure and was not deductible, because it brought into being, so the court held, the advantage of a contented work force, whereas the pensions themselves would have been of a revenue nature and therefore annually deductible (*Atherton v British Insulated and Helsby Cables Ltd* (1925) 10 TC 155).

A similar test is made to examine whether the expenditure has been laid out on the creation, acquisition, improvement or modification of a fixed asset, for example, land, farm building or machinery. Because fixed assets are of an enduring nature, that expenditure will be 'capital'. On the other hand, expenditure on the maintenance or repair of such an asset may be said to bring nothing new or enduring into existence, so that the expenditure is 'revenue' and therefore deductible. In practice, this is an item which often gives rise to dispute. Suppose that the slate roof of a farm building is unsound, and a farmer replaces it with a tile roof. On one view this is merely a repair to the whole premises. On another, there will be an element of improvement, which is capital expenditure, and in respect of which the Inspector will seek some disallowance. What part of the total sum spent should be so treated? That is often a contentious question, for it depends upon assumptions that events occurred other than the actual events. It may be that it would have cost more to replace the old roof with a slate one than it did a tile one. In the end, these issues depend not upon interpretation of the law, but upon careful negotiation with the Inspector, and the conduct and success of those negotiations will depend on a knowledge of the practice.

Payments in connection with trading stock, which is *circulating* not *fixed* capital, tend to be deductible as on revenue account. By nature, large lump sum payments are more likely to produce long-term capital benefits than comparatively small regular ones. But care is needed, since appearances can be deceptive. It is possible to pay a capital sum of £10,000 by ten annual instalments of £1,000 per annum for ten years. The fact that payment is deferred in this way does not change the quality of the payment from capital to income. Labelling a payment as of a 'revenue' nature will not help, as the Inspector is always entitled to look not at the designation given, but at the true nature of what has occurred.

2.3:3   The true commercial profit

Expenditure will be disallowed if it is not deductible in arriving at the true commercial profit on business or accounting principles. Into this category falls income tax itself, deemed not an expense of earning profits, but an application of them. The bookkeeping treatment of any item is therefore relevant, but not conclusive, since this rule is subject to particular prohibitions and what have been judicially called 'invasions' by the income tax Acts.

2.3:4   Exceptions from prohibitions

The income tax Acts do not expressly enumerate allowable deductions in calculating taxable profits. What they do is to expressly prohibit certain items, which might otherwise have been thought to qualify as deductions, and then to give exemptions from these prohibitions. An example will help make clear this rather complex process, for example:

'Section 74 General rules as to deductions not allowable

Subject to the provisions of the Tax Acts . . . no sum shall be deducted in respect of:
. . . (c) the rent of any dwelling house or domestic offices or any part thereof, except such part as is used for the purposes of the trade . . . and the sum so deducted shall not . . . exceed two-thirds of the rent paid . . .'

In the past, the application of this rule led to deductions more generous than perhaps might otherwise have been anticipated. The two-thirds of domestic premises rule was usually applied to farmhouses. It was used as a reasonable apportionment between deductible and non-deductible expenditure including ordinary annual outgoings such as rent, water, electricity, etc and also repairs, renewals and maintenance expenditure (see section **4.4:1**).

Recently however, the Revenue has changed its approach. The view is that a 'mechanistic rule of thumb' applied without reference to the facts of the particular case has ceased to be appropriate. The business proportion of running expenditure on a farmhouse is to be determined by reference to the particular facts of the case concerned. In the past, it is said there were more farm workers employed on the land and those workers would eat in the farm kitchen and live in the farmhouse. Nowadays, however, farmhouses are used for business purposes only to a limited extent and the bulk of the expenses relate to the domestic circumstances of the farmer and his household. These are the arguments which the inspector is likely to put forward when seeking to restrict the fraction applicable.

2.3:5 For the purposes of the trade . . .

Finally, there is a wide ranging, general prohibition against the deduction of expenditure 'not being money wholly and exclusively laid out or expended for the purposes of the trade . . .' (TA 1988 s 74(a)). This rule is frequently invoked in a whole variety of contexts, has been many times interpreted by the courts, yet is still capable of re-interpretation.

The effect of it is to prescribe that money must be spent as a matter of commercial expediency. Money may be spent in the course of the business; the expenditure may be connected with the business; business cash may be used; the item may be entered in the business books; none of these is sufficient. Nor is it relevant whether the money be paid under legal obligation or not. Instead, attention needs to be directed towards the underlying purpose, as to whether the expenditure is made to promote the business and earn profits from it. Neither the moral intent, nor the sense of duty prompting payment is relevant; the test is always *commercial* advantage.

How remote may be the objective? Clearly some degree of remoteness is permitted, but at a certain point the balance tips. Suppose a farmer makes an advance of money to a supplier in the expectation this will secure helpful relationships. The supplier's business fails and the farmer loses his debt. This represents a borderline example capable of being variously decided. The more remote the purpose, the less likely is the expenditure to be deductible. The more readily and earlier earnings can be shown to flow from the expenditure, the easier it will be to secure deductibility. The various prescriptions summarised above are not alternatives; *all* must be satisfied. An item may be challenged by the Inspector under more than one head, and even if ample justification can be demonstrated under one head, deductibility may be lost under another.

2.4 COMPENSATION

Government interventionism in agriculture has taken a variety of forms: *commodity price fixing*; *taxation*; and *grants and subsidies* to name but three. One of the least precise and systematic areas for consideration is the interaction of government grants and subsidies with government taxation. No clear statement of principle seems to have emerged; it is necessary to analyse the purpose and function of any government grant in order to form a view as to how it is likely to be treated for tax purposes.

If a grant is receivable for loss or sterilisation of a *capital* asset, land, buildings or plant, then prima facie, it will not be liable to income tax, but will be liable to capital gains tax. If what has been received is in substitution for *earnings or profits*, or represents a government subsidy of earnings or profits, then it will probably fall to be included in the profit computation for income tax.

There is a third possibility: certain grants are receivable as an incentive towards capital expenditure on plant or buildings. Expenditure out of the farmer's pocket may qualify for tax relief in the form of capital allowances. But he will not be able to claim on that part of the expenditure which has been met from a government source.

These principles are not always strictly observed. In some cases, treatment is governed by precedent or concession, and some precedents were set at a time when the alternatives of income tax and capital gains tax were not both on the statute book.

In the attached list, a number of out of date precedents have been deliberately included, in that they may serve as a basis for argument by analogy.

2.4:1 Table of compensation receipts

Nature of Compensation	Statutory Authority	Taxation Treatment
Coastal flooding acreage payments for rehabilitation	Coastal Flooding (Emergency Powers) Act 1953; see *Watson v Samson Bros* (1959) 38 TC 346	Not liable to tax as made to restore productivity of capital asset
Ploughing grants made as contribution towards expenditure of ploughing	Agricultural Development Act 1939; see *Higgs v Wrightson* (1944) 26 TC 73	Taxable as income
Reimbursement of development programme expenditure by growers	Agriculture and Horticulture Act 1964 s 2; Small Horticultural Production Business Scheme 1964 (SI 1964/963)	Deducted from allowable expenditure and therefore effectively taxable
Grants for investment in capital assets	EEC Farm and Horticultural Development Scheme 1974	Deductible from capital expenditure before capital allowances

Nature of Compensation	Statutory Authority	Taxation Treatment
Grants for: livestock purchases; keeping records; preparation of development plan; guidance premium	EEC Farm and Horticulture Development Scheme 1974	Taxable as income
Compensation to outgoing farm tenant following notice to quit	Agricultural Holdings Act 1948 s 34; see *Davis v Powell* [1977] 1 All ER 471, [1977] STC 32	Not liable to income tax, nor liable to CGT
Compensation for reorganisation	Agriculture (MP) Act 1968 s 9	There is a restriction on the amount which escapes income tax to four times the rent
Compensation for compulsory acquisition	Agriculture (MP) Act 1968 s 12	As above
Grant under the Dairy Herd (Alternative Enterprise) Scheme	See *White v G & M Davis* [1979] STC 415 and *IRC v W Andrew Biggar (a firm)* [1982] STC 677 (restrictions of dairy herd production)	Treated as income and liable to income tax
Grant towards farm capital expenditure	Agriculture Act 1967 ss 31, 32, 33; EEC Farm and Horticulture Development Schemes 1974 and 1980	Capital expenditure is treated as reduced by grant for capital allowances purposes
Cereal deficiency payments: lime subsidies		Taxable as income of accounting year in which payment is notified
Grant for giving up uncommercial unit	Agriculture Act 1967 s 27 (as amended); TCGA 1992 s 249	Not liable to income tax or CGT
Compensation on acquisition by local authority	FA 1969 Sch 19	Liable to CGT
Compensation for compulsory slaughter of animals	TA 1988 Sch 5(6)	Taxable as income, but late election for herd basis may be made (TA 1988 Sch 5 para (6))

Nature of Compensation	Statutory Authority	Taxation Treatment
	Agriculture and Horticulture Grant Scheme 1980; Agriculture and Horticulture Grant (Variation) Scheme 1981 (replaced Farm Capital Grant Scheme and Horticulture Capital Grant Scheme)	Deductible from farm expenditure capital expenditure or expenditure is reduced by grant for capital allowances purposes
Grant towards farm expenditure	Agriculture and Horticulture Development Scheme (replaced Farm and Horticulture Development Scheme)	Deductible from allowable expenditure or capital expenditure is reduced by grant for capital allowances purposes
Grant towards farm expenditure	Agriculture and Horticulture Development Regulations 1980; Agriculture and Horticulture Development (Amendment) Regulations 1981 (implements EEC Directive 72/159 and EEC Directive 72/268)	Deductible from allowable expenditure or capital expenditure is reduced by grant for capital allowances purposes
Capital sum or annuity payable on giving up or changing use of non-economic land	The Farm Structure (Payments to Outgoers) (Variation) Scheme 1981 (extended 1976 Scheme)	Capital sum to individuals aged under 55 is non-taxable, annuity payable to individuals 65 years or over is taxable as income
Grants to encourage livestock enterprises	Hill Livestock Compensatory Allowance; Sheep Annual Premium Scheme; Suckler Cow Premium Scheme	Taxable as income
Compensation on slaughter (trading stock basis)	Brucellosis Eradication Scheme	Taxable as income, 33% is added to profit for each of three years following year of slaughter

Nature of Compensation	Statutory Authority	Taxation Treatment
Grants towards planting/restocking	Forestry Grant Scheme (from 1 October 1981)	Schedule B basis – not taxable. Schedule D basis taxable as income
Grant towards capital projects to improve marketing/processing	EEC Regulation 335/7 – Marketing and Processing	Capital expenditure is reduced by grant for capital allowances purposes
Grant aid for new producer organisations in early years of operation	EEC Regulation 1035–72 Producer Organisation	Not taxable as organisation not carrying on taxable trade
Grant towards employer's costs incurred in employee training	Agricultural Training Board Grants	Deductible from allowable expenditure
Contribution to eligible costs for modernisation and renovation of properties	Local Authority Housing Grants	Deductible from expenditure ranking for ABA
Capital grants towards cost of constructing country parks, picnic areas, farm trails, etc	Countryside Commission Grants	Expenditure unlikely to be tax deductible – to extent that it is, the grant is offsettable
Compensation for surrender of milk quota	Milk Supplementary Levy (Outgoers) Scheme 1984	Treated as capital and liable to capital gains tax
Compensation for milk quota loss of profits	Milk Supplementary Levy (Outgoers) Scheme 1984	Treated as income and liable to income tax

The various forms of compensation described above all have some relationship with farming business activities. They are not to be confused with compensation paid for loss of, or on retirement or removal from, office or employment, often described as a redundancy payment or a 'golden handshake'. This class of compensation is subject to its own separate income tax regime. Briefly, if an employee receives such compensation as a term or condition of his employment, the compensation is taxable as income in the ordinary way. In contrast, where compensation is given ex gratia, on termination of employment, the first £25,000 is not liable to tax, and any excess over £25,000 is taxable at half the recipient's marginal rate (TA 1988 s 188 and Sch 11).

2.4:2   Milk quota

Milk quota is a European Community phenomenon, and its legal nature is not easy to define in terms of the law of property in England. It is the result of surplus milk supply. These surpluses were regulated by EEC Council regulations 856 and 857 dated 31 March 1984, which came into force on 2 April 1984. Under these regulations each community country was allocated a share of community milk production: and this share is divided amongst producers. Thus a *milk quota* is the specific quantity of dairy product which a producer can produce without creating liability to pay a levy for over production.

Milk quota is not an interest in land and cannot be transferred separately from the land. The analogy has been made with a licence to sell liquor. It is certainly a licence which can be sold with freehold land, with certain tenancies, and which can be leased. Its ownership can change involuntarily on the termination of a tenancy and on other grants, assignments and transfers of interest in land. All these different transactions can give rise to taxation consequences.

DISPOSALS

Normally milk quota is treated as a chargeable asset, separate and distinct from the land to which it relates. Disposal of milk quota is normally liable to capital gains tax, computed separately from any land which is being sold or being transferred at the same time. 'Disposal' has a special meaning for capital gains tax (see section **7.1:1**).

It has been suggested that the different view taken in *Faulks v Faulks* [1992] 1 EGLR 9 should affect the treatment of milk quota for capital gains tax purposes. That case concerned the interpretation of a partnership deed, and the application of the Partnership Act 1890. It was not, of course, a tax case, but that in itself is not conclusive. In the course of a judgment about whether milk quota should be included amongst the assets of a partnership, the judge decided it should not be so included. It was available (he held) to a deceased partner in his capacity as tenant of land not as a partner in a partnership. Moreover he regarded quota not as an asset but as the elimination of a liability. In the Revenue view, that decision is irrelevant, but opinions may differ.

As regards the basis of computation, the Revenue take the view that when quota was acquired by allotment in 1984, that would have been a non-arm's length transaction, with no corresponding disposal. The market value would have been nil and hence the allowable acquisition cost also nil. In other cases, the normal acquisition cost rules apply. In neither case is there an allowable deduction relating to the cost of land to which quota is 'attached'. Nor is a disposal of quota to be treated as a part-disposal of any land (Inland Revenue Tax Bulletin No 6 February 1993). Again, there have been alternative views put forward, in particular, that quota is an asset 'derived from land', or from an interest in land, so that a part disposal formula is capable of being applied (TCGA 1992 s 43). The advantage of the part disposal formula is that where milk quota acquired by allocation in 1984 is being disposed of, a proportionate part of the cost base (or market value as the case may be) of the land can be set against the milk quota sale proceeds. This part cost with indexation added (see section **7.2:2**) can substantially reduce the gain on disposal of quota, or even in exceptional cases transform a gain into a deductible loss.

Where the land and the milk quota are being disposed of in a single trans-action, there will be (in the Revenue view), two separate transactions for the purposes of capital gains tax. If the two transactions form part of a single bargain, the acquisition cost or the disposal proceeds as the case may be will need to be apportioned on a basis which is just and reasonable (TCGA 1992 s 52(4)).

Roll-over relief was not at first conceded for milk quota on the grounds that it was not an acquisition or disposal of a qualifying asset, but this relief was conceded by the Finance Act 1988 s 112. The relief was made available for disposals of assets or acquisition of a replacement asset after 29 October 1987. For roll-over relief, it is sufficient if the new assets be acquired within a period three years after the date of disposal of the asset on which the gain arises (see section **7.4:2**). Thus the possibility of a roll-over relief claim involving pre FA 1988 disposals of milk quotas continued effectively until 29 October 1990.

Retirement relief is also available on milk quota (see section **7.6**).

COMPENSATION

Compensation to tenants for milk quota on the termination of a tenancy is also now regarded as within the scope of capital gains tax. The Agriculture Act 1986 Sch 1 paras 1–4 imposes liability on landlords to pay compensation to tenants for milk quota on the termination of tenancy. Certain short tenancies are excluded from this rule. Again, where an incoming tenant pays a premium under a lease to a landlord, and part of that premium is referable to milk quota, that part will be within the cost base for capital gains tax purposes.

PARTNERSHIP

Where a farming business is being carried on in partnership (see section **6.1**) milk quota may be registered in the name of the partnership firm, and regarded as a capital asset of the business. In such cases, the part of the gain or disposal apportioned to quota will be allocated amongst partners as gains arising on other partnership capital assets are allocated, that is by reference to the partnership shares of capital and the individual capital accounts of partners. If quota has been registered in the names of individual partners allocation of the gain will be by reference to the destination of the quota disposal proceeds. (See TCGA 1992 s 52(4) and Statement of Practice 17 January 1975 para 2.)

INHERITANCE TAX

For inheritance tax (see section **8.1** below) the value of milk quota can be regarded as included in the value of the land transferred. This treatment is advantageous for owners of tenanted land who accordingly qualify for agricultu-ral property relief (see section **8.5**) on the value of the milk quota, assuming the land itself qualifies for agricultural property relief.

Although milk quota can be regarded as included in the value of land transfer-red by an owner-occupier, this is obviously inapplicable where, for example, a tenant's share of milk quota is disposed of to a landlord on termination of a tenancy. In these circumstances, the milk quota will be regarded as a separate asset, and should fall to be treated as included in the value of the farming business. Thus business property relief (see section **8.3**) will be available at the rate of 100%, since F(2)A 1992.

MILK QUOTA AND VALUE ADDED TAX

When land is sold together with milk quota, the transaction may be treated as a single supply of land, and the milk quota is therefore exempt. This, however, is subject to the option to tax having been exercised (see section **9.4**). However, when identifiable separate amounts are paid for land and milk quota, this will be treated as a separate supply of land exempt subject to the option to tax, and a separate supply of milk quota which would be standard rated.

2.4:3   Potato quota

Potato quotas are effectively licences to produce, transferable at a price, to other producers.

The potato quota is treated as a separate fixed asset and disposal is liable to capital gains tax, separately computed from any land which may be sold or transferred at the same time. Where land and potato quota are disposed of in a single transaction, the disposal needs to be apportioned between the land and the milk quota on a just and reasonable basis.

Roll-over relief for capital gains tax on quota disposals has been conceded with effect from 29 October 1987 (see section **7.4**).

Income from leasing potato quota is liable to income tax in the ordinary way.

2.4:4   Other quotas

The new European Community agricultural quota for the premium given to producers of ewes and suckler cows has been added to the list of assets which qualify for capital gains tax roll-over relief. In the Inland Revenue Budget Press Release 1993, it was anticipated that more similar quotas will be introduced in the future. A general power to add, by Treasury Order, to the list of assets which qualify for roll-over relief was taken. (FA 1993 s 86).

2.5   PROFIT AVERAGING

2.5:1   Introduction

On 26 October 1977, the then Chancellor of the Exchequer announced a package of new measures designed to relieve the exceptional incidence of high income taxation created by two special factors: first, that the weather can produce substantial fluctuations in income between one year and another, which under a graduated rate system pushes liability into higher rate brackets in one year, without necessarily providing adequate compensation for that in another year.

Secondly, this effect is particularly damaging because farming is a highly capital intensive industry, requiring substantial investment. High taxes discourage investment, and the industry as a whole was suffering.

The system enacted was based upon the simple arithmetic concept of adding together the profits of two successive years and dividing by two. Baldly stated, that may sound attractive, but in practice a variety of limitations are imposed.

2.5:2   Meaning of 'profit'

For the purpose of averaging relief, profits are taken before any allowance is made for:

(a) trading losses sustained in the year of assessment, or those carried forward or sideways so as to be applied to profits for the period (see section **2.6**);

(b) any deduction or addition for capital allowances or balancing charges (see section **5.2**).

Thus if there is an adjusted loss for one year, that is treated as 'nil' and the average over the two years becomes one half of the profit for the other year.

2.5:3   Tests for relief

It is a precondition for relief that the profit of one of the two consecutive years does not exceed 70% of the profit of the other (TA 1988 s 96(2)). This difference equal to at least 30% of the higher figure is assumed to be needed to justify the relief. However, there is a marginal relief, where the profits of one year exceed 70% but do not exceed 75% of the other year (TA 1988 s 96(3)). Profits are deducted from the amount chargeable for the higher year and added to the lower year. The amount so transferred is ascertained by an arithmetical formula. The difference between the two years' profits is multiplied by three, and 75% of the higher year profits is deducted from that amount.

Example 1 Averaging relief

	£
Profits 1991–92	14,000
1992–93	6,000
	20,000 ÷ 2 = 10,000
Averaged Profits 1991–92	10,000
1992–93	10,000

Example 2 Marginal averaging relief

Profits 1991–92	16,000
1992–93	11,800 = 73.75%
Then difference =	4,200 × 3 = 12,600
75% of 16,000:	= 12,000
Transfer:	= 600
Marginally averaged profits:	
1991–92	15,400
1992–93	12,400

Example 3 Loss for one year

Profits 1991–92	9,000
Loss 1992–93	(2,000) = nil
	9,000 ÷ 2 = 4,500
Averaged Profits 1991–92	4,500
1992–93	4,500

2.5:4   Other conditions: making claims

Averaging is an optional facility, and needs to be claimed within two years from the end of the second year included in any averaging computation (TA 1988 s 96(8)). In practice this should give adequate time to ascertain whether a claim is worthwhile. However, claims need not necessarily be made for all years, because the actual figures for any year are always taken into account in any averaging claim for the following year. In effect, every year's results may fall to be included in two claims, one in which those results form the first of the two years, and one in which they form the second.

Further flexibility is created by the rule that if the profits of either or both years are adjusted for any reason, the averaging on the unadjusted profit basis becomes invalid. A further claim can, however, be made to average the newly adjusted profits. Notwithstanding that the normal time limit for an averaging claim may already have expired, a fresh claim can be made at any time before the end of the year of assessment following that in which the adjustment was made.

A claim cannot be made for a year which precedes a year in respect of which a claim has already been made, nor can claims be made for years of commencement or discontinuance, including years for which those rules apply on a change in a partnership (TA 1988 s 96(4)). Otherwise averaging applies to partnerships in much the same way as it does to individuals. The claim is applied to the partnership profits as a whole, not to individual shares. The claim must be made by all individual partners. Companies have no right to claim averaging relief (TA 1988 s 96(11)).

Once profits have been adjusted by an averaging claim, the adjusted profits are applied for all taxation purposes in place of the unadjusted profits with one exception; averaged profits are ignored by the Inspector in determining whether the assessments for penultimate and ante-penultimate years fall to be increased on a cessation of trading.

2.6   FARMING LOSSES

2.6:1   Introduction

The UK tax system recognises the business taxpayer's right to offset losses sustained in his trade or profession against what would otherwise be his taxable income, so as to extinguish or reduce the tax due on that income. (Losses arising out of the ownership of land are not dealt with in this section (see section **4.3**)). The result of the aggregation of trading losses with income may be to 'discharge' (ie cancel) assessments made on that income; or to create repayment of tax already paid. Thus, loss relief can be an alleviation of farming risk, since up to 40% of the cash invested and lost may be recoverable in the overpaid tax.

The value of a tax loss may be measured: it depends on the rate of tax otherwise payable on the income relieved. The higher the rate, the greater the value of the loss.

Where the risk of loss for a particular period or a particular transaction is substantial, attention should be given to the possibility of tax relief at an early stage, since failure to qualify for relief at the right time, and in the hands of the right individual can effectively aggravate the effect of the loss. A tax loss in the hands of one person, for example a company, will not usually qualify for relief against the income of another person, for example a shareholder. The possibility of loss may thus determine the form which a transaction takes. For example, a farmer who buys a new and speculative non-farming business may decide he wishes its potential liabilities to be kept separate from the assets of the family farm. To achieve this, he may arrange for the new business to be owned not by the farming partners but by a new limited company incorporated for the purpose. Commercially this would be a prudent step, but the effect might be to make the initial trading losses of the new business not relievable against farming profit, even though those profits were being used to subvent the new venture. To some extent this danger has been alleviated by legislation (TA 1988 s 574).

The loss relief system is complex, and there are detailed rules for the marrying up of losses for particular periods with profits of corresponding periods. For a complete survey see *Simon's Taxes* E.1.6. What follows is a brief summary of the system, with particular reference to the reliefs and relief restrictions applicable to farming. This summary incorporates three stages in the process:

Stage I   Establishing the quantum of the loss.

Stage II   Selecting the destination of the loss: how it is to be applied.

Stage III Establishing the validity of the loss, so as to ensure relief is not restricted.

2.6:2 Establishing the amount of the loss

Tax losses can be usefully regarded as tax profits through the looking glass. An allowable loss is computed according to the same principles as a taxable profit, by commencing with the balance shown by the profit and loss account and making all the necessary additions and subtractions which together are known as the computation of adjusted profits (or losses). Hence there may be an adjusted loss even though the farm be producing a commercial profit for the same period and vice versa.

Example

Net loss per profit and loss account	(1,000)
Add Private proportion of heat and light	450
Loss on sale of motor car	300
Capital expenditure amongst repairs	250
General reserve	100
Adjusted profit for tax purposes	£100

In the above example, the conversion occurs by reason of non-deductible items being included in the Profit and Loss Account. Conversion from profit to loss may occur by reason of properly deductible items having been excluded from the Profit and Loss Account, and debited to drawings or to reserve accounts.

The question also arises as to what accounting period is to be taken to establish the amount of loss. The following table sets out the various rules for the different classes of loss relief:

Section	Class of relief (Individuals)	Period to be taken
TA 1988 s 380	Set off against total income of tax year	The accounting year ending in the tax year of claim, *except*: (i) the first three years of a new trade; (ii) the fourth year where s 62 applies: that is where a claim has been made for the second and third years of assessment to be based on the actual profits of both those years; (iii) any year immediately following a year in which a loss has been computed to 5 April; (iv) where the claimant so requires; (v) a year of cessation: in all these cases, losses are to be computed for the tax year by time apportionment
TA 1988 s 385	Carry forward against subsequent profits of the same trade	Accounting period showing a loss

Section	Class of relief (Individuals)	Period to be taken
TA 1988 s 388	Terminal loss relief, on cessation applied against earlier profits	Loss in the year of assessment in which the trade is permanently discontinued *plus* loss in that part of the preceding year beginning 12 months before the date of discontinuance
TA 1988 s 381	Relief for losses in early years of trade carried back	Loss in year of assessment in which the trade was first carried on *plus* loss of the next three years of assessment
TA 1988 s 401	Relief for pre-trading expenditure	Expenditure incurred not more than one year before a trade commenced
TA 1988 s 574	Relief for losses on unquoted shares in trading companies	Capital losses sustained on disposal of shares in any year of assessment

For certain classes of loss the amount can be increased by including certain qualifying capital allowances. The augmentation of different losses by capital allowances is described below.

Section	Class of relief	Capital allowances to be included
TA 1988 s 383	Set off against total income of tax year Carry forward against subsequent profits	Capital allowances for the year of assessment for which the year of loss is the basis year Capital allowances exceeding balancing charges and taxable profits for the relevant year, but allowances brought forward can be applied first against profits and charges
TA 1988 s 388	Terminal loss relief against earlier profits	Capital allowances for year in which the trade is permanently discontinued plus the appropriate proportion for the preceding year
TA 1988 s 381	Relief for losses in early years of trade carried back	Capital allowances for the year of loss so far as not effective for that year

2.6:3   Selecting the destination of the loss

It is convenient to summarise in tabular form various possible alternative applications of any tax loss as follows:

Income against which loss is applicable	Section
(a) total income of the year of loss; or	TA 1988 s 380
(b) total income of the year succeeding the year of loss; or	TA 1988 s 380
(c) profits of a business in which the loss was sustained assessed in future years (indefinitely); or	TA 1988 s 385
(d) profits of a ceasing business in which the loss was suffered, for the three years of assessment last preceding the year of loss; or	TA 1988 s 388
(e) total income of the three years of assessment last preceding that in which the loss was suffered, taking income for an earlier before income for a later year; or	TA 1988 s 381
(f) directors' remuneration (primarily) or dividends from a company to which a business in which the loss was sustained has been transferred wholly or mainly for shares; or	TA 1988 s 386
(g) total income for year in which there occurs a disposal of unquoted shares in a trading company; or	TA 1988 s 574
(h) income of year of assessment in which a trade is newly set up (pre-trading expenditure)	TA 1988 s 401
(i) capital gains of companies	TA 1988 s 345(1)
(j) capital gains of business	FA 1991 s 72 (see section **2.6:4**)

For companies, the rules are different. Trading losses may always be carried backwards in time and applied against the corporation tax profit of the last preceding accounting period (TA 1988 s 393) (see section **6.2**). As for accounting periods ending on or after 1 April 1991, the period has been expanded to three years 'so as to give companies greater flexibility in the use of trading losses' (FA 1991 s 73). Capital allowances are a deduction in computing the profit or loss for corporation tax, so that in effect, excess allowances become a corporation tax loss, which may be carried forwards or backwards in time; or applied against other classes of income for the same period; or against the taxable profits of other companies in a group, under a claim for group relief.

Excess first year allowances for plant and machinery may be carried backwards in time for three years, rather than for one accounting period (as for losses), provided the trade in which the machinery or plant was used was carried on in earlier years.

Care should be taken in deciding whether and how to claim loss relief, and whether any claim should be augmented by the relevant capital allowances. If the taxable profits of an individual for a year are reduced to nil by the incidence of personal reliefs, there will be no advantage in a claim, and losses will be consumed, instead of being carried forward to other years. On the other hand, it is advantageous to apply losses to reduce taxes as soon as permissible. Carryback losses are particularly valuable, when they create a repayment of tax paid for earlier years, so assisting cash flow at a time when assistance may be badly needed.

The order of priorities amongst different loss reliefs is not entirely clear. For example, there is some doubt whether loss relief must be claimed against total income of the year of loss before it can be claimed against total income of the year succeeding the year of loss. The Revenue view is that loss is to be applied according to the order in which loss relief claims have been made. Where loss relief claims are made at the same time, the Revenue will accept the order of priorities specified by the claimant (Inland Revenue Tax Bulletin May 1992).

Since independent taxation (see section **19.2:1**) loss relief may not be applied against the taxable income of a spouse.

2.6:4 Farm losses and capital gains tax

Until the Finance Act 1991, farming losses were not offsettable against capital gains tax liability. This rule seriously affected the ability of farmers to sell surplus assets so as to raise cash to reduce their bank borrowings. New relief was enacted in the Finance Act 1991, when the stated purpose was to bring unincorporated businesses into line with companies, which could already set trading losses against both income and their capital gains.

It is only the trading losses of the year of sale or the year preceding the year of sale which are available to offset the gain. Any trading loss which is not set against income or gains of the current or succeeding year are available to be carried forward and set against future trading profits.

Relief against gains is given in priority to relief for capital gains tax losses brought forward from earlier years, and in priority to annual exemption, which is thus lost.

So called 'hobby farming' losses (see section **2.6:5** below) do not qualify for relief against capital gains tax.

2.6:5   Establishing the validity of the loss

In 1960, rules (TA 1988 s 384) were introduced to counter so-called 'hobby-farming'. The practices attacked involved the acquisition of agricultural land and buildings capable of development and capital appreciation. After incurring improvement and renewals expenditure deductible for income tax (so creating tax losses relievable against other income), the land could be sold to produce a gain not then subject to any capital gains tax.

The Chancellor explained his intention to restrict loss relief in respect of farming losses in particular to activities conducted on reasonably *commercial* lines. He explained that the new clause was not designed to debar relief for stud farming, in which there is a view to the overall realisation of profit in the long term; or for any undertaking run as a serious business, such as 'genuine' farming operations on marginal land; but was intended to deny relief in 'extreme cases' where the trading activities bore no relationship to commercial criteria.

This test was incorporated into the wording, which as enacted, prohibits relief for any year unless it is shown that for the year of assessment in which the loss was sustained, the trade was being carried on on a commercial basis and with a view to realisation of profits in the trade. If a trade is being carried on with a reasonable expectation of profit, that fact shall be conclusive evidence that there was an intention to make profits. This was to meet the case where, exceptionally, a farmer might point to activities which could reasonably be expected to produce a profit, even if the main test was not satisfied.

This section applies only to losses under TA 1988 s 380 (set-off against total income) and the capital allowances which could be used to augment that class of loss. It is extended to partnerships, and changes in partnerships, and meets the possible situation of a change in the nature of trade during the period over which the loss was sustained.

However, it will be apparent that the test is a subjective one (ie as to what was in the mind of the farmer). In practice, this apparently proved unsatisfactory and a further test was enacted (TA 1988 s 397). This is, by comparison, based on the objective phenomenon of a loss having been sustained for the previous five successive years. When that occurs, it is an inference (but not made explicit by the section) that the farm is not being run on a commercial basis and loss relief is denied.

Where there is a change in a partnership, (see section **6.1:5**) continuing partners from the old partnership continue to have old losses attributed to them. If no continuation election has been made (see section **6.1:5**), incoming partners start with a clean slate.

This is subject to a let-out in which the onus of displacing the restriction falls upon the farmer. The section is not to apply if the claimant can show that the whole of the activities in the year following the prior five years were of such a nature, and carried on in such a way, as would have justified a reasonable expectation of future profits if those activities had been carried on by a competent farmer or market gardener, but that if that farmer or market gardener had undertaken those activities at the beginning of the prior period of loss, he could not reasonably have expected those activities to become profitable until after the end of the year following the prior period of loss.

It is often difficult to convince the Inspector that the let-out should apply. Any argument put forward will be more persuasive if supported by a Farm Plan or budgets analysing the financial projections and results.

For this purpose a 'loss' means a loss as computed for income tax purposes without deduction for capital allowances, not a commercial loss as disclosed by the Profit and Loss Account.

It will be apparent that if a loss be shown for four successive years, but then a profit emerges in the fifth year, the section has no application. To state the rule cynically, a profit once every five years is sufficient to avoid the effect of the section.

This can sometimes be secured by correct apportionment of expenditure amongst the years in question. It may be prudent to defer certain Revenue expenditure on, for example, repairs and renewals until a succeeding year; alternatively sales may need to be brought forward, into an earlier year.

Finally, where the section does apply, the owner-occupier of a farm may nevertheless claim such relief for the cost of maintenance, repairs and insurance as he would have been able to claim as a landlord (see section **4.3:3**). This relief was given by Extra-Statutory Concession (B5) which was amended on 18 February 1993. The purpose of the amendment was to make clear that in applying the concession, the conventional apportionment of one-third: two-thirds will not be invariably applied. Instead, Inspectors of Taxes will have regard, it is stated, to the particular facts of each case (see section **2.3:4**).

Chapter 3

Farm stocks

3.1 FARM ANIMALS

3.1:1 Introduction

In *The Wealth of Nations*, Adam Smith described *fixed* capital as that which an owner turns to profit by keeping it in his possession, and *circulating* capital as that from which he makes a profit, by parting with it, and letting it change masters. It is in that sense that circulating capital is said to 'circulate' (*John Smith & Son v Moore* (1921) 12 TC 266 at 282).

A farmer's land, buildings and plant clearly represent his fixed capital, permanently retained. His produce, whether it consists of crops, wool, fruit or milk equally clearly represents circulating capital, because they are produced to be sold at a profit. Farm animals can fall into either category: they may be 'retained' in the form of a pedigree herd (or flock) to produce milk, wool or offspring; or they may be reared and sold, in which case, they may be said to 'circulate'.

The income tax rules offer a choice of two different treatments corresponding to the underlying distinction. The general rule is that animals are treated as trading stock. This is, those items unsold at the beginning of the period and those unsold at the end of the relevant period must be taken into the reckoning for the purpose of arriving at the true profit of the period.

Alternatively farmers may elect for a quite different treatment: the *herd basis* (TA 1988 Sch 5). The effect is that valuations of production herd animals are excluded from the computation of trading profits: the cost of the original herd, and additions to it, are not deductible in computing profits. Nor are the proceeds of sale included, so that a profit is not taxed, nor a loss relieved. The herd basis is explained in greater detail below (see section **3.2**).

3.1:2 Trading stock basis

It is convenient to summarise the effect of the trading stock basis as follows:

Item	Treatment
Stock at beginning of year	Deduction in computing profit
Cost of animals bought	Deduction in computing profit
Price of animals sold	Addition in computing profit
Stock at end of year	Addition in computing profit

Inspectors of Taxes sometimes require a numerical reconciliation of animals at the beginning and end of the period, as a test of the accuracy of the accounts. Births and deaths naturally fall to be shown, and these often account for what may seem discrepancies in the eyes of the Inspector.

Identifying what is stock-in-trade is not usually difficult: the major problem is determining what is its correct value for tax purposes. Stock valuation is a professional skill, but the tax code dictates its own method, which is to ascertain, by physical identification, the historic cost price and the current market price of each item, and then to select the smaller figure of the two. In many kinds of businesses, problems have arisen as to the precise meaning of 'cost' and 'market' values. In particular, in manufacturing businesses, there are often problems of the attribution of expenditure to arrive at 'cost' (see section **3.1:3**). The purpose of permitting valuation at market price is to allow a deduction for an anticipated loss on ultimate sale. It is not permitted to envisage a forced or break up sale of a farm; the market to be contemplated is either that in which the stock was bought, or that in which it will ultimately be sold.

In arriving at market value, it is permissible to deduct identifiable items of expenditure, directly connected with the sale of the stock. That might include an auctioneer's commission, but an Inspector may take a restrictive view of this class of items (see section **3.1:5**).

It is the practice of the Revenue to require a consistent basis of stock valuation from one year to another. Subject to this, the Revenue practice is to accept any method recognised by the accountancy profession which does not violate the taxing statutes as interpreted by the courts.

When a farm business ceases, the general rule is that stock is valued at market value (TA 1988 s 100(1)(*b*)). But this is not necessarily so, if the business is ceasing because the farmer has died (TA 1988 s 102(2)).

3.1:3 Livestock bred on the farm

The Revenue have explained in detail in an Economic Note (BEN 19) the basis on which in their view farm stock should be valued. This statement is the result of consultation with the Central Association of Agricultural Valuers, the Institute of Chartered Accountants, the Institute of Taxation, the Royal Institution of Chartered Surveyors, the Country Landowners Association and the NFU. It supersedes a previous agreement with the NFU. Clearly, the basis explained by the Revenue would not affect individual rights of appeal, nor will it be invariably applied, particularly if the facts of the case require a different approach.

In general, it is stated that farm stock valuations at cost should include the costs directly attributable to producing or rearing the stock in question. It is preferable also to include, except in certain cases, a reasonable proportion of the costs which are indirectly attributable to the production of stock to the extent that those costs relate to the period of production as this will result in a more accurate matching of costs with resulting sales income. Either method, if applied consistently, is acceptable.

As regards livestock, 'direct' costs include purchase costs or insemination costs, plus additional maternal feed costs in excess of maintenance. They also include the costs of rearing to the valuation date or maturity, if earlier, including:

(a) feed costs including forage;
(b) vets' fees including drugs;
(c) drenches and other medicines;
(d) ringing, cutting and dehorning; and
(e) supervisory employee or contract labour costs.

Indirect costs include depreciation and maintenance of farm buildings; rent and rates; general employee or contract labour and machinery costs.

Strictly, livestock should be valued on an animal by animal basis, but it is acceptable to value animals of a similar type and quality together on a global and average basis classified according to age.

3.1:4 Valuation of livestock: 'deemed' cost

'Deemed' cost should not be adopted where it is possible to ascertain actual costs from the records. Deemed cost should not be used for purchased animals if less than the original purchase price plus, if the animal were immature when purchased, the cost of rearing from the date of purchase to the valuation date or, if earlier, to maturity.

Deemed cost means a reasonable estimate of cost arrived at by taking a specific percentage of open market value. Open market value, for this purpose, should be based on the assumption of a willing buyer and a willing seller of the animal as a production animal free from, for example, movement restrictions. It is not acceptable to treat cull value as the open market value of production animals as this does not recognise the value of the future income stream from produce and/or progeny.

The percentages to be applied to open market value are as follows:

Cattle   – 60% of open market value
Sheep and pigs – 75% of open market value

It is emphasised that deemed cost valuations are only valid for home bred or home reared stock or stock acquired some time before maturity and matured on the farm. Valuation of immature and unweaned animals, according to the deemed cost method, based upon the value of animals of a similar age and type, is acceptable with one exception. If it is appropriate to value mother and progeny together, because that is the market unit, that should be done.

The exception is where the mother is on the herd basis and there is no market, or a very limited market, in unweaned progeny (for example unweaned lambs at foot). Failure to recognise the young stock at all in the valuation is not acceptable. Costs of producing the progeny should be carried forward to be set against the eventual sale price.

3.1:5   Market value

Market value is considered to mean the net realisable value of stock, in particular the sale proceeds it is anticipated will be received from the eventual disposal of the stock in the condition in which the farmer intended, at the balance sheet date, to subsequently market it. It is not acceptable to value stock on the basis that it would have been sold in the forced sale in a possibly immature state. Net realisable value includes any grants and subsidies intended to augment the sale price of stocks and for breeding/production animals, the ancillary stream of income from the sale of their progeny and produce.

Capital gains tax
It should be noted that farm animals are exempt from capital gains tax. This is so, whether treated as trading stock or on the herd basis. They are regarded as wasting assets which are 'tangible movable property . . .' (TCGA 1992 ss 44, 45).

3.1:6   Horses

Horses working on a farm may be treated either as trading stock or as fixed assets, providing the treatment is consistent. (As regard stud-farming see section **2.2**.)

3.2   THE HERD BASIS

3.2:1   Introduction

In the section dealing with farm animals (see section **3.1**), the distinction between *fixed* capital and *circulating* capital was discussed. In this section, the rules for treating animals as fixed capital are explained in detail (see TA 1988 Sch 5). The questions to be considered are: How to secure this apparently attractive basis? What are the effects whilst the basis is in operation? What is the effect at the end of the day, when the herd comes to be sold, or when the farm itself is disposed of, or when the owner of the herd finally retires?

3.2:2 Nature of herd

Farm animals have the characteristics of machines in that they convert grass into milk or wool. So the herd basis treats animals kept for production (or reproduction) in the same way as plant or machinery. The basis can be applied to dairy herds or ewe flocks, or to pigs or poultry or thoroughbred horses kept for breeding (TA 1988 Sch 5 para 8). It cannot apply to working horses or working dogs; or to animals kept for public exhibition or racing or other competitive purposes. It cannot apply to 'flying flocks', that is, sheep or cattle held for resale, even though these beasts may produce milk, wool, etc during the time they are held. All such animals are to be treated as trading stock.

Moreover a production herd means a herd of animals of the same species (irrespective of breed) kept for the sake of their products, the products being obtainable from the living animal. That means the young of the animal; or other product, not being a product obtainable by slaughtering the animal, ie meat (TA 1988 Sch 5 para 8).

The effect of this last requirement is that a farmer can be on the herd basis for his Jersey herd, and on the trading stock basis for his pedigree ewes. However, if he has a Jersey herd and a Guernsey herd, either both or neither must be on the herd basis, since both herds are of the same species.

Generally, a herd comprises mature animals, but there is an exception to this rule; where (as is the case with acclimatised hill sheep) the land on which the herd is kept is of such a kind that replacements cannot be made save from animals bred and reared on that same land. In that case animals so bred, replacing old animals, are treated as part of the herd (TA 1988 Sch 5 para 8(2)).

Cows, ewes and other female creatures are treated as 'mature', when they give birth to their first young, and laying birds are 'mature' when they first lay.

A single animal or bird, which otherwise qualifies, can be treated as a 'herd'. By concession (12 November 1990), the herd basis may be applied to a farmer who has a part share in a herd of animals, or a share of one animal, eg a pedigree bull.

3.2:3 The election

The herd basis is not automatic: a farmer must elect for it (TA 1988 Sch 5 para 2), within a stipulated period after he begins to keep the herd in question. The period is two years from the end of the first tax year of assessment which will be affected by his having set up the herd. There is only one other occasion on which he secures a fresh right to elect: it is when a substantial part of his stock has been compulsorily slaughtered, eg because of disease, and the farmer becomes entitled to compensation (TA 1988 Sch 5 para 6). Then within two years measured from the end of the year of assessment when the liability is first affected by the receipt of compensation, an election can be made. That is to assist a farmer who through unexpected circumstances would have had to include the compensation in his trading profits, so eroding its value by a substantial tax liability, and preventing the purchase of replacement beasts.

For this purpose, at least 20% of the total number of mature animals in the herd is regarded as 'substantial' so bringing this quite valuable relief into operation.

Election is made in writing specifying the class of animals to which it relates (TA 1988 Sch 5 para 2(2)). Once made, election is irrevocable. But if a farmer ceases to keep a production herd of that same class for a period of at least five years, he is permitted to start afresh. That is, he will thereafter have a new right to make an election, if he subsequently acquires a new production herd.

3.2:4   **Effect of the herd basis** (TA 1988 Sch 5 para 3)

(A) INITIAL COST

The initial cost of the herd is *not* deductible in arriving at the computation of taxable profits. Additions are not deductible and the value is not brought to account (TA 1988 Sch 5 para 3(2)).

(B) ADDITIONS

When an animal is added by transfer from trading stock, there is included, as a trading receipt, the cost of acquisition and rearing, or breeding and rearing. This latter may be on a conventional basis, eg 75% market value (TA 1988 Sch 5 para 3(3)). The object of this adjustment is to compensate for whatever past deductions have been allowed in respect of that particular animal.

(C) REPLACEMENTS

When a herd animal dies or ceases to form part of the herd, and is replaced by another animal, the proceeds of sale of the old animal are included as a trading receipt; and the cost of the animal which replaces it is deductible as a trading expense. However, if the cost of the replacement has already been deducted, because it is home bred, etc no further deduction is due. If the replacement beast is of better quality than that replaced, the additional cost reflecting the element of improvement is not deductible (TA 1988 Sch 5 para 3(4)).

(D) REPLACEMENT OF WHOLE HERD

If the whole herd is sold and replaced, the rules in (c) above apply as though there had been sold the number of animals in the old herd, or in the replacement herd, whichever is the less. The object is the same as for (c) above (TA 1988 Sch 5 para 3(5)).

(E) SALE OF WHOLE HERD

If the whole herd or a substantial part is sold, within a period of 12 months, any profit or loss arising is not included in the computation of taxable profits (TA 1988 Sch 5 para 3(6)). This is the corollary of the fact that the cost was not deducted at the outset when the herd was acquired. However, if, within five years of sale, the seller begins to acquire a new production herd of the same class, then the new animals are treated as replacing the old, and (c) and (d) above apply. However, the sale proceeds of the old animals will be brought into the computation of taxable profits for the period in which the new animals were acquired, although possibly received much earlier. If the sale of the old herd, or part of it, was due to factors beyond the farmer's control, eg notice to quit and inability to find a new farm, and the new animals are of worse quality than the old, the amount included as a receipt will not exceed the amount deducted for the cost of the replacement.

(F) OTHER SALES

If none of the above circumstances applies, and a herd animal is sold, then the profit or loss is included in the computation in the ordinary way (TA 1988 Sch 5 para 3(7)). Profit or loss is computed by comparing with the proceeds of sale the cost of home breeding and rearing; or acquisition cost.

(G) SHARE FARMING

See section **17.4:4**.

3.2:5 Deciding whether to elect

The decision whether to elect for the herd basis may not be an easy one, for there will usually be a range of factors:

(a) The greater the difference between the cost of animals in the herd and their ultimate market value, the greater the advantage of the herd basis. The difference will be greatest for pedigree beasts. There will usually be a useful difference in the case of a home bred, good quality herd. If, on the other hand, high quality beasts are bought in at full market prices, the difference between cost and market value is likely to be smaller, and the advantage of the herd basis correspondingly reduced.

(b) The larger the herd, the more important the question of the election may be.

(c) The stage of career of the individual farmer, and his plans for the future will be relevant. If prospects include retirement, or giving up, say, dairy farming within the foreseeable future, the possibility of a tax-free realisation then can be very attractive.

(d) In a period of inflation, the herd basis is additionally valuable in keeping unrealised profit out of the tax computation.

(e) On the herd basis, more detailed records need to be kept, and the Inspector will tend to become involved in livestock numbers and values.

(f) The herd basis offers potential for tax free profits but carries risks. For example a farmer forced to retire because of a slump in the livestock market might find losses in this department unrelieved against other farming profits.

(g) Problems arise when there are changes in the persons carrying on a farming business, or when the business is transferred to a company.

Where a sole trader changes to a partnership (or vice versa) or where the constitution of a partnership is changed, the Revenue requires a fresh election to be made, if the herd basis is to be retained. This is so, irrespective of whether or not there is an election to apply the continuing basis to the partnership assessments (see TA 1988 s 113(2)). If the new partners decide not to make a fresh herd basis election, the trading stock basis will be applied.

Where a cessation occurs, and a new business is commenced, there are anti-avoidance provisions, which in certain circumstances give the Revenue the power to substitute, if necessary, market price as the transfer price from the ceasing business to the newly commencing one. The circumstances are either that:

(i) transferor and transferee control each other or are under common control. 'Control' means that one party can conduct the affairs of the other in accordance with his own wishes; or

(ii) the sole or main benefit expected to arise would result from the operation of the herd basis rules.

(h) Problems arise when share farmers seek to elect for the herd basis (see section **17.4:4**).

Example: The herd basis

Replacement of whole herd

Mr Black sells for £90,000 a herd of 50 pedigree cows (£1,800 per head), which originally cost £1,000 per head. He buys a new herd of 45 cows at £1,500 per head of same quality at a total cost of £67,500.
Then:

Proceeds of sale of 45 cows of old herd	£81,000
Cost of 45 cows of new herd	£67,500
Add in computing profit	£13,500

Profit on sale

5 cows: not replaced: 5 × £1,800	£ 9,000
Less cost: 5 cows at £1,000	£ 5,000
Add in computing profit	£ 4,000

Total addition £13,500 + £4,000 = £17,500.

3.3   GROWING CROPS

3.3:1   Growing crops

The nature of a farmer's stock has already been discussed in its application to farm animals, ie livestock, (see section **3.1**). The same principles may be applied to growing and harvested crops, which may be regarded as the equivalent of the 'work in progress' of a manufacturing business, and which therefore must be brought into the computation of taxable profits.

The general rule is that growing and harvested crops should be valued at their cost, or if lower, their net realisable value. Costs which are directly attributable to buying, producing and growing the crops should be included. Such costs will consist not only of the expenses of acquiring the 'raw materials', eg the seeds, but also the following items:

(a) fertilisers;
(b) beneficial sprays, which includes preventative sprays and any sprays which are not applied to remedy a particular infestation or crop deficiency;
(c) seasonal licensed payments (for example shorter term hire of land to grow a particular crop) but not normal farm rents;
(d) drying;

(e) storage;

(f) employee (including director) or contract labour and direct machinery costs, eg fuel, servicing, rental, spares and the reduction in value due to wear and tear caused by actual usage for the activity concerned incurred on cultivations; and

(g) crop working and harvesting.

As regards indirect costs, examples are:

(a) depreciation and maintenance of farm buildings;

(b) rent and rates; and

(c) general employee, contract labour and machinery costs.

3.3:2 Deemed cost

Valuation should only be based on deemed cost where it is not possible to ascertain actual costs from records. Dead stock, ie harvested crops, may subject to this rule be valued on a deemed cost basis and the percentage of open market value acceptable is 75% (85% for valuations as at dates before 31 March 1993).

Reference should be made to the Revenue Statement of Practice describing valid and non-valid bases of valuation (SP 3/90) and also to the Business Economic Note (BEN 19) published in March 1993. Formerly, there was an influential agreement between the Inland Revenue and the National Farmers Union to the effect that where the normal value of tillages, unexhausted manures and growing crops did not exceed £7,000, and a detailed valuation had not been completed, a certificate that the value at the beginning of the relevant period did not materially differ from that at the end was accepted in lieu of that detailed valuation. Even where the value exceeded £7,000, a detailed valuation was not always required.

Where a valuation was required, eg on a cessation, the correct basis was a 'full waygoing basis', ie the same basis as a valuer would have used for the purpose of computing compensation due to a tenant from his landlord had he been giving up the tenancy on the valuation date and seeking commercial compensation accordingly. This basis seems no longer to be required.

3.4 COOPERATIVES

Where stock is marketed through a farm cooperative acting as agent for the farmer it must be included in the valuation. Where it has been pooled and cannot be identified as belonging to any particular farmer, the unsold proportion must be included. This may be computed by adopting the fraction $a \times \dfrac{b}{c}$ where:

'a' is the amount in the pool which came from the particular farmer;

'b' is the amount in the pool not sold at the valuation date;

'c' is the amount in the pool not sold at the valuation date plus the amount sold from it up to that date.

Where the cooperative does not act as agent, then stock held by it will obviously not be included in the valuation.

3.5   GRANTS AND SUBSIDIES

Grants and subsidies which are directed towards specific expenses should be regarded as reducing those expenses in the farm accounts. If those expenses are in turn included in the cost, for stock valuation purposes, then the amount included should be the net cost after deducting the related grants or subsidies.

Generally, grants and subsidies intended to augment the sale prices of stocks should be taken into account in calculating the net realisable values of those stocks.

Chapter 4

Agricultural rents

4.1 HISTORY OF SCHEDULES A AND B

In 1963, the taxation of income derived from land was thoroughly revised and the present relatively straightforward basis of Schedule A was enacted (FA 1963 s 15). To understand the current system, it is necessary to refer back to its predecessor, remnants of which still survive in fossilised form.

Under pre-1963 law, income from land was taxed under Schedules A and B. The scope of Schedule A was limited to income derived from ownership of land, capable of occupation. The chargeable person was the occupier. If he paid a rent as tenant, he was permitted to deduct income tax from the rent payable, so giving himself relief and transferring the burden of tax to the owner. If he was an owner occupier, he was left to bear the burden of tax himself, so creating liability on notional income – the value of occupation.

The measure of this liability was an arbitrary one, determined by valuation. First was ascertained the gross annual value, the theoretical amount at which the property was worth to be let for a year, landlord paying for all repairs, and tenant paying rates and other occupier's outgoings. From the gross, a fixed statutory repairs allowance was deducted, so as to arrive at the net annual value, the amount being charged to tax at the appropriate rates.

There were many additional rules. Leases for 50 years or more were excluded and treated differently. From 1940 tax was chargeable under the Schedule D excess rent rules, on the excess of actual rent receivable over the theoretical Schedule A assessment, so making the latter only one stage of a two-stage tax. Maintenance claims could be made to increase the statutory repairs allowance to the actual amounts spent, on a five-year averaging basis. The net annual values of business property, for example farms, were deductible in the Schedule D computations.

The scope of Schedule B was limited to the occupation of land, other than residential and business property. Originally, farming and market gardening had been within Schedule B, and liability was confined to a notional net annual value. In 1941, farmers occupying land exceeding £300 in annual value were brought within Schedule D and in the following year, this threshold was lowered to £100. Those within Schedule B were taxed on the notional basis of three times annual value. All farming and market gardening was brought within Schedule D in 1948 and Schedule B applied only to amenity lands.

Until 6 April 1988, Schedule B also applied to woodlands, but on that date it was finally abolished (see section **13**).

FA 1963 repealed the concept of an owner-occupier's enjoyment of notional income, and all related rules. Under the new classification Schedule A was abolished, and Schedule D Case VIII became the land charging Schedule. Case VIII was renamed Schedule A in FA 1969. The collection rules were much simplified, but the principle of collecting from payer, instead of recipient, has not been entirely abandoned. However, this principle is now limited to those cases where the owner fails to pay the due tax. Then the collector may demand the tax from any derivative lessee (a tenant) who becomes entitled to deduct any tax so paid from payments of rent to his landlord. The tax demanded from the tenant must not exceed the relevant rent, and there are rules permitting repayment of any excess (TA 1988 s 23). This also applies where a landlord is non-resident: TA 1970 ss 53, 89 (TA 1988 s 43).

4.2   CURRENT SCOPE OF SCHEDULE A

4.2:1   Introduction

The fundamental difference of treatment between farmers and landowners derives from the fact that the Taxes Acts impose a different basis of charge depending upon whether tax is chargeable under Schedule A or Schedule D. Schedule A covers all income from land in the UK, not necessarily agricultural land. The wording of the Act (TA 1988 s 15) is important for it produces an ambit of charge both detailed and wide in scope, in which almost every word can be interpreted as adding some special significance.

4.2:2   The charge

Tax under this Schedule shall be charged on the annual profits or gains arising in respect of any such rents or receipts as follows, that is to say:

(a) rents under leases of land in the UK;
(b) rent charges, ground annuals and feu duties, and any other annual payments, reserved in respect of or charged on, or issuing out of such land; and
(c) other receipts arising to a person from, or by virtue of, his ownership of an estate or interest in or right over such land or any incorporeal hereditament or incorporeal heritage subject in the UK.

Tax under this Schedule shall be charged by reference to the rents or receipts to which a person becomes entitled in the chargeable period (TA 1988 s 15).

So many words of technical meaning are included here that a special glossary is needed:

Glossary

annual	profits arising in a particular year, and not necessarily implying any recurrence or repetition.
entitled	liability is imposed whether or not the amount has been actually received, but when it has become due and payable; that is when it 'arises'. The question when a lessor becomes entitled to his rent was considered in *Strick v Longsdon* (1953) 34 TC 528. The Crown contended a lessor was entitled as soon as a lease was executed, even though it was not payable until later.
UK	England, Wales, Scotland and Northern Ireland (but not the Channel Islands or the Isle of Man).
land	includes ('unless the contrary intention appears') messuages, tenements and hereditaments, houses and buildings of any tenure.
rent charge	a chief rent.
ground annual	Scottish equivalent of chief rent.
feu duty	Scottish equivalent of leasehold ground rent.
incorporeal hereditament	a right over land, eg an easement.

incorporeal	
heritable	
subject	Scottish equivalent of above.
rent	the word is not generally defined, but is probably confined to its technical meaning, ie payments reserved by a lessor on a demise of land.
lease	includes an agreement for a lease, and any tenancy but does not include a mortgage or heritable security.

Theoretically, it may be important to distinguish between a rent under a lease and 'other receipts . . . from land'. That is because there are different sets of rules for permissible deductions depending upon whether or not the assessment falls on rent under a lease. Fees or rents for sporting rights (a right to go onto land to take game) would be 'sums other than rents under a lease' falling into this category.

4.2:3   Exceptions to Schedule A

So inclusive appears to be the rule, that it is necessary to identify exclusions. The charging rules do not apply to:

(a) any yearly interest; or
(b) profits or gains charged under Schedule D from mines, quarries and other concerns, eg gravel pits and canals;
(c) rents or royalties in respect of certain mining operations;
(d) rent under a lease including use of furniture (unless the landlord elects for Schedule A);
(e) profits from woodlands managed on a commercial basis (TA 1988 s 67(1)(*aa*)).

All these classes of income are chargeable under Schedule D.

Further sets of exemptions from Schedule A emerge from other parts of the Taxes Acts. For example, use of the phrase 'annual profits or gains' implies receipts of an income nature, so excluding capital receipts, which may, however, be liable to capital gains tax. Premiums under leases are separately charged (see section **4.2:5**). What is important is that where no tenancy is created, the receipts are not within the third head of charge (see section **4.2:2**(c)). This applies to the receipts of hotels, boarding houses, etc and can apply to grazing rents (but see section **5.1:2**).

Further exceptions arise in practice, although there may be little or no statutory basis for the treatment adopted. A trader under Schedule D who lets part of his business premises, is often allowed to treat the rent received as a source within his Schedule D Case I computation. This applies to farm cottages occupied by farm workers. Where this concession is given the amounts in issue are usually trivial.

4.2:4   Basis of assessment

The basis of assessment under Schedule A is the current year basis, ie the rents arising in the relevant tax year (TA 1988 s 22). One disadvantage of this system is that tax is payable on 1 January in any year, and since the amount of rents for the year cannot be finally known until after 5 April – some three months later – the assessment has in the first place to be based upon a provisional figure (TMA 1970 s 29(1)(c)). To surmount this difficulty, the assumption is made that all the amounts relevant in computing the assessment are the same as in the previous year. Tax is chargeable on this basis, subject to an adjustment either way, when after the year's end the final figures are known (TA 1988 s 22). When a property has been sold, or otherwise ceased to be owned, after the beginning of a year (6 April) but before the following 1 January, the taxpayer can give notice to the Inspector, so that the rents from this property are excluded from the provisional assessment. If the amounts of rent are substantial, then clearly such notification is helpful in avoiding overpayment of tax at provisional assessment time. Such a notification must compare the likely rent-roll for the year with that for the preceding year, so as to show the reduction and to demonstrate that the reduction derives from the sale, etc of a particular source (TA 1988 s 22(2)).

The Inspector does have power to obtain information about rents from a number of sources, eg tenants, occupiers, former tenants and agents. There are elaborate penalty provisions for failure to comply with a notice requiring information.

4.2:5   Premiums

The scope of Schedule A is further extended by special provisions (TA 1988 s 34) under which premiums receivable on granting short-term leases and other comparable capital sums are treated as rent and taxed as if income. In the normal course, agricultural landowners are not much concerned with premiums. Two aspects call for special attention.

First, transactions which contrive to convert rent into capital sums receivable at the time of grant of a tenancy, or in connection with it are not likely to be successful in avoiding tax. On the contrary, they can positively increase the burden of liability. A premium can be subject to capital gains tax, but that part chargeable to income tax is not also chargeable to CGT (TCGA 1992 Sch 8 para 3). Secondly, care is needed throughout a tenancy, for a sum paid by a tenant in consideration of waiver or variation of a tenancy may fall into the 'premium' class (TA 1988 s 34(4)).

The relevant law was enacted when the taxation of rents was revised in FA 1963. The objective was to counter widespread avoidance secured by granting leases at a premium plus a lower rent. But for the special provisions applying to premiums, they would escape income tax as not being 'annual profits or gains'. It will be remembered that no substantial capital gains taxes had been enacted in 1963, although there was, at that time, a short-term gains tax on the statute book.

(A)   MEANING OF 'PREMIUM'

Premium is defined to include any 'like' sum (TA 1988 s 24), whether payable to the immediate or superior landlord, or to a person connected with either of them. Any sum paid at the time of granting a tenancy is presumed to be a premium unless some other sufficient consideration can be demonstrated.

A notional premium can arise where a landlord requires the tenant to carry out work on the leased premises. Then the value of the premium is deemed to be the value of the lease, less what its value would have been if the obligation had not been imposed (TA 1988 s 34(2)). If the cost of the work had been deductible in computing the landlord's Schedule A liability, then no charge arises. That would be where the work was in the nature of ordinary repairs, maintenance or management, rather than a building, an improvement or other capital items.

Similar liability can arise later during the duration of the lease, where a capital sum becomes payable in lieu of rents; where a sum is payable as consideration for surrender of the tenancy, or variation or waiver of the lease terms (TA 1988 s 34(5)). Premiums payable by instalments remain premiums, but there are instalment provisions under which payment of the tax can be deferred over eight years ending not later than when the last of the instalments is payable (TA 1988 s 34(8)).

(B) CALCULATION OF LIABILITY

A system of discounting is provided, so that the longer the lease (up to the Schedule A maximum of 50 years), the less the charge to tax on the premium received. There are special rules for ascertaining the duration of leases (TA 1988 s 38). The discounting has the effect of reducing the chargeable premium by one-fiftieth of the premium for each complete year of the lease other than the first.

Example

Giles grants a tenancy of land and buildings at a rent of £1,000 per annum plus a premium of £10,000 for a term of 21 years. Then the Schedule A liability is computed as follows:

Premium 10,000 less 4,000 (20/50 × 10,000) = £6,000	
Rent	£1,000 pa
Schedule A liability	£7,000

(C) CAPITAL GAINS TAX

In general, premiums receivable on leases are subject to capital gains tax (see section **7.7:2**), but that part subject to income tax is not also chargeable to capital gains tax. Thus in the example above, £4,000 would be chargeable to capital gains taxation.

(D) TOP-SLICING RELIEF (TA 1988 SCH 2)

The effect of charging premiums under Schedule A is to aggregate into one tax year, 'income' which commercially relates to the years of the lease, and which, if spread over the tax years of the lease, might be chargeable at lower rates of tax. To compensate, a special relief is given, equal in value to the difference between the tax chargeable on the assumption the whole premium is included as income for one tax year; and that which would have been chargeable, if the rate were what it would have been if only one year's proportion of the premium had been so included.

To ascertain one year's proportion, the whole premium sum is divided by the number of years of the lease. In the example, ante, £6,000 would clearly be chargeable at higher rates of tax than £6,000 ÷ 21 = £285. It is always assumed that the amount chargeable represents the top-slice of the taxpayer's income at his highest rate or rates. In the above example, and assuming taxable income including the premium for 1980–81 was £22,250, the tax on £6,000 would have been calculated as to £5,500 at 65% plus £500 at 60%. The tax on £285 would have been chargeable at 45%, so that the effect of the relief would be to reduce the applicable rate to 45%.

4.2:6   Similar receipts

Other kinds of receipts taxable in the same way as premiums are as follows:

(a) An increase in the value of a reversion to a lease, attributable to a tenant's obligation to improve the premises, or carry out building operations (TA 1988 s 34(2)).

(b) Receipts in commutation of rent, or for the right to surrender a lease made under the terms subject to which the lease was granted (TA 1988 s 34(4)).

(c) A capital receipt for the variation or waiver of the terms of a lease (TA 1988 s 34(5)).

(d) Receipts for the assignment of a lease originally granted by a landlord at an undervalue (TA 1988 s 35).

(e) Where property is sold subject to a condition that it shall be sold back to the vendor (or a person connected with him) at a lower price. The taxable amount is the excess of sale price over resale price, less 2% for each complete year after the first between the date of sale and date of resale (TA 1988 s 36).

Where the recipient is a landlord, liability is under Schedule A. Where he is not, as under (e), liability falls under Schedule D Case VI (see section **2.2**) but such transactions cannot give rise to loss relief (TA 1988 s 392). Agricultural land is rarely the subject of such transactions, and usually, there will be little or no advantage to be secured by adopting these forms.

4.3 SCHEDULE A DEDUCTIONS

4.3:1 Introduction

The importance of securing full permitted deductions from taxable income cannot be over-emphasised. Where deductions are generous taxation liability may be determined in amounts which can be readily met out of net inwards cash flow. Where deductions are circumscribed, the effect may be to produce inadequate net cash receivable to pay taxes. Similarly, the effect may be to produce a very small after-tax yield on capital invested, leaving nothing to fund ultimate taxes on capital.

Under Schedule D (see section **2.3**), the general position is that all items and classes of expenditure are prima facie deductible subject to certain critical tests. Under Schedule A, the position is the reverse: only those particular deductions enumerated in the Taxes Acts are allowable in computing taxable income. The effect is to make rents more heavily taxed than farm profits, even when the two classes of income are enjoyed by the same individual, and when the rate of charge expressed as a percentage is the same. This is one of the numerous distinctions between the two classes, which makes it important to determine into which class a given item falls.

The deductions from rent enumerated in the Act are as follows (TA 1988 s 25):

(a) maintenance, repairs, insurance and management;

(b) services, other than maintenance and repairs, which the owner is obliged to provide, but for which he receives no separate consideration;

(c) rates, or other charges on the occupier which he is obliged to pay;

(d) rents, rent charges etc, reserved, charged on, or issuing out of the land.

Deduction is not due until the amount has been actually paid, although rent becomes taxable as soon as the landlord becomes 'entitled'. Moreover, the payments must be made by the landlord. No deduction is due if and in so far as the payment is balanced by the receipt of insurance moneys, or is recovered from some other person, unless that person is himself taxed (TA 1988 s 31(5)). No expense can be deducted more than once, and no expense can be deducted if it has been otherwise allowed in computing the income of any other person. Finally, an item of expense must, if possible, be deducted in the year in which payment is actually made. If such a deduction is not possible, then it must be deducted in the earliest available year (TA 1988 s 31(3)). The effect of that is that the taxpayer has no choice in the matter and cannot allocate expenses to a year for which, for example, his rate of charge was higher. The overall effect of these provisions is to create a narrow and rigid regime.

4.3:2   Sporting rights

Income from sporting rights is taxable under Schedule A in accordance with the principles described above but subject to a special relief, designed to meet the possibility that a landowner may be accustomed to let sporting rights over his land, but fails to do so for a particular year or years (TA 1988 s 29). In that event, the expenditure he incurred on maintaining or managing the game would fail to qualify for any tax deduction. That would be because income from sporting rights is not 'rent payable under a lease', and the maintenance etc expenses would not be 'an expense of the transaction' as is technically required.

To remedy this, a special relief permits expenses which would have been deductible against income from sporting rights to be set off against rents receivable from other properties let at a full rent and not on a tenant's repairing lease. The set-off may be made against rents for the year the sporting rights are not let, or may be carried forward and set against rents of future years.

Where sporting rights are enjoyed by a farmer or landowner, and are not let out, so as to produce income, expenses of maintaining a shoot may be disallowed in computing the profits of the farming trade. The wages of a gamekeeper, cost of stocking with game, cartridges, etc, will not be regarded as having been incurred wholly and exclusively for the purposes of earning the profits of a farming business.

Similarly, if a farm business is carried on by a company, expenses of the company incurred in providing sporting rights for the benefit of directors or employees will be treated as benefits-in-kind in their hands and liable under Schedule E, as if additional emoluments.

Sporting rights means rights of fowling, shooting or fishing, or of taking or killing game, deer or rabbits (TA 1988 s 29(5)). 'Game' is defined as deer, partridges, grouse and black game (Agricultural Holdings Act 1948 s 14(4)). Ground game is defined as hares and rabbits (Ground Game Act 1880 s 3).

4.3:3   Excess expenditure and allowances

One of the consequences of the Schedular principle (see section **2.1:4**) is that expenditure deductible from one class of income is not automatically deductible against other classes taxable under other Schedules. However, agricultural land enjoys a special privilege, in that where a landowner's expenditure on maintenance, repairs, insurance and management is too big to be wholly relieved in the computation of his Schedule A assessment, the excess can be relieved against income from other sources, for the chargeable period in which the expenditure is incurred; or the next following period (against income from other sources); or any subsequent period against income from particular sources, that is, income from farming, or ownership of agricultural land (TA 1988 s 33).

The effect is to make excess expenditure of the qualifying class into a form of loss relief (see section **2.6**) transferable against income from all other sources, including investment income, for example dividends and interest. Moreover, this treatment is extended to capital allowances for machinery and plant (see section **5.2:2**) provided for use or used on the estate.

The calculation proceeds by stages. First, the amount of excess maintenance etc expenditure is calculated, and this may be augmented by capital allowances. Next, that excess is subject to a limitation: it is not to exceed the amount it would have been if the estate had not included parts used wholly or partly for purposes other than husbandry.

Finally, the amount, plus any amount brought forward from the previous year's claim, may be made the subject of an election to be set off against any other income of the year. In so far as not used in such an election, the amount is carried forward and is made available to offset rental income of a future year or years, without limit of time.

The advantage of an election is that relief and probably repayment of tax are secured earlier, so benefiting cash flow, and the possibility of an election should not be overlooked. There is a time limit: two years from the end of the year for which it is made. Separate elections are needed for each year for which the relief is to be claimed.

It is worth noting that similar treatment is accorded to capital allowances on agricultural or forestry buildings and works (CAA 1990 s 132) (see section **5.2:5**), so that the combined amount available to relieve other income may be comprised of expenditure of six different categories:

  (a) excess maintenance etc, expenditure of the current year;
  (b) excess machinery and plant allowances;
  (c) excess agricultural buildings allowances;

plus respective amounts for the previous year.

This relief accords recognition to the fact that an agricultural estate is often substantially subvented or endowed by income from non-agricultural sources.

4.4 THE RESIDENTIAL EXPENDITURE OF LANDOWNERS

4.4:1 Introduction

The upkeep cost of country houses has risen steeply in recent years. Inflation, the age of historic houses, and the shortage of craftsmen have all contributed. Owners have sought to preserve buildings for historic or architectural reasons, or because they are deeply attached to them, when economic considerations would have simply required demolition. Many owners and advisers have therefore pondered whether part of annual maintenance and repair costs can become deductible against income taxation. This section addresses itself to that question, and to alternative methods by which offsetting of property expenses can be secured.

There are major statutory hurdles to be surmounted. For farmers, the general rules as to expenses not allowable for the purpose of computing trading profits specifically mention that rent of domestic offices or dwelling houses 'except such part thereof as is used for the purposes of the trade or profession . . . and where such part is so used' shall not generally, unless special circumstances arise, exceed two-thirds of the rent paid (TA 1988 s 74(*c*)).

Similarly, disbursements or expenses on maintaining a taxpayer, his family, or his establishment, or sums expended for domestic or private purposes are all disallowable (TA 1988 s 74(*b*)). In practice, the apportionment principle is applied to rent, rates, light, heat, repairs, maintenance, telephone and other outgoings of those who live on their business premises, including farmers who live in their farmhouses. The two-thirds maximum rule is interpreted variously, and sometimes physical comparisons of the respective floor spaces or numbers of rooms are required.

The normal allowance for a farmhouse is one-third, which recognises that the building is primarily part of the farm, and that the farmer lives there in order to farm his land. The proportion deductible may therefore be contended to be more generous than a strict physical apportionment of floor space would produce. However, Inspectors have become more insistent that lower fractions are appropriate.

Whatever proportion be ascertained, it is usual to apply it to all items, for example, maintenance, insurance and repairs, unless it emerges that part of the total of these was clearly confined either to the private or the business part of the premises. In those circumstances, the Inspector may seek to depart from the ordinary arithmetic apportionment.

For landowners, the position is more complex. Where a landed estate is comprised of a home farm and one or more tenanted farms, the question may arise as to whether the mansion house is a farmhouse for the purposes of securing appropriate deductions in the Case I home farm profit computations. The proportion not allowable in that computation will not ordinarily be allowable against the rentals receivable from the tenanted farms save in the special circumstances when a 'one estate election' can be made. Ability to make such an election is clearly of value, and the question should be examined at the time of acquisition of a landed estate.

4.4:2   One estate election

The nature and purpose of the 'one estate election' (TA 1988 s 26) cannot be understood without again turning back to 1963, when taxation of owner-occupied property was abolished (see section **4.1**).

Under the former system, the 'net annual value' of an owner-occupier's property was liable to income tax under Schedule A. This annual value was determined by estimating how much the property would have been worth to be let for the year, and deducting from that amount (the 'gross annual value') a statutory repairs allowance on a fixed percentage scale.

This statutory repairs allowance was capable of being increased to the amount actually expended on the repair and maintenance of a property, for the relevant period. A claim to substitute actual expenditure was designated a maintenance claim. One further relief claim was possible: where the expenditure on repairs and maintenance exceeded the whole taxable net annual value of a particular property, the excess was capable of being transferred and applied to relieve tax arising on rents from other properties forming part of the one estate.

When the present system was introduced in 1963, the special form of relief was preserved for future years, but only for taxpayers and their successors in title, who at the time made a claim.

Thus, a one estate election can only be made where an estate was 'managed as one estate' at the end of the tax year 1962–63 (ie 5 April 1963), and the then owner so elected within the stipulated time limit, which was 12 months after the end of the first chargeable period for which he became entitled to make it (TA 1988 s 26(3)). The latest date for election would therefore have been 5 April 1965.

'One estate elections' should therefore be regarded as a form of transitional relief, and the question of making an election arises only when a qualifying estate is first acquired and the previous owner or owners had all so elected back to 1963. Once made, a valid election applies throughout a period of ownership and cannot be revoked.

The effect of election is similar to the pre-1963 effect: it is to transfer surplus reliefs from one property to others, in particular from an owner-occupied mansion house, so as to be applied to reduce Schedule A tax on rentals receivable from tenanted farms. That can be of great value where the upkeep of the mansion house is costly, and but for a one estate election, where the cost would need to be met out of fully taxed income. There are, however, a series of restrictions.

First, an estate, for the purposes of a claim, means land in one ownership managed as a single entity, and properties which are geographically remote from one another may not qualify. Next, there has to be added in to the computation of relief an amount equal to the annual value of the owner-occupied properties, as representing a notional rent at which they could be let (TA 1988 s 26(1)(*b*)). In the case of property let at less than a full rent, an amount must be added to increase the actual rent to the full annual value.

No such addition is required for an estate office, or tied cottages occupied rent–free. In the past, this exclusion has included cottages of forestry workers occupied for the purposes of the trade where the woodlands have been managed as part of a whole estate. After 5 April 1993, when transitional arrangements for woodlands comes to an end, it appears that the annual value of such cottages representing a notional rent will need to be included in the computation.

In the one estate computation, the actual rents and the notional rents are added together, and the repair and maintenance expenditure on the properties deducted. The resulting profit is chargeable to Schedule A, but may be offset by losses on other properties not forming part of the estate. Similarly, if the result of the one estate election computation be a loss, that loss is available to offset other Schedule A income. But losses may not be used to offset rents receivable on leases where the tenant is liable for all repairs, or substantially all the repairs to the property comprised in the lease.

If a one estate election is in force, its value can be augmented by bringing into the computation additional properties (TA 1988 s 26(3)). These may be properties newly acquired, or those already owned to which unified management is being applied. If the property newly bought in is let at a full rent, no problems arise. If it is not, then the expenses of it can be deducted only if:

(a) the additional property was managed as part of the estate; and
(b) the owner was at the end of 1962–63 entitled to some equitable interest under a will or settlement, such that he might become in the future owner of the additional properties.

When an election is in force, its value may serve as a deterrent to breaking up the estate. If mansion houses and tenanted farms devolve differently under a will, the benefit of the relief will be lost, and the owner of a mansion house will be obliged to meet upkeep costs without this form of tax relief.

Those who have lost the benefit of a one estate election, and those who have never enjoyed the benefit will wish to ponder the question of how, alternatively, similar relief may be secured. They may consider opening to the public (see section **14.5**), so that the showing of the house and its contents becomes a trade or business within Schedule D Case I.

Then all the house running expenses, including maintenance and repairs, will become deductible in computing the profit or loss, less some agreed proportion to reflect the domestic occupation of the house, if any. The practice shows considerable variations. Where all the premises are shown, including the residential quarters, the restriction can be a modest one, perhaps as low as 15%. Where part of the premises are retained as private, the practice is to count the number of rooms involved and restrict in the proportion that 'residential' rooms bear to rooms opened to the public.

Chapter 5

Farming and landownership

5.1 FARMING AND LANDOWNERSHIP

5.1:1 The two activities distinguished

This section explains why the two activities farming and landownership are distinguished for tax purposes under their respective Schedules A and D, and what are the important consequences of the distinction.

The rule that any item of income can be taxed only once under its appropriate Schedule has already been mentioned, and this is the starting point of a chain of argument.

The principle derives from judgments in early precedent cases, particularly *Salisbury House Estate Ltd v Fry* (1929) 15 TC 266 in which it was decided that rents were taxable under Schedule A, and that was the only permissible Schedule of assessment which exhausted all possible tax liability. At the time, Schedule A tax was chargeable upon an artificial amount (the 'net annual value'). The Revenue sought also to tax under Schedule D the excess of the actual rent receivable over the artificial amount assessed.

The court rejected this approach. Since the *Salisbury House* case, the old basis of charge under Schedule A has been changed, but the principle established by the case remains valid: landowners liable on rents under Schedule A cannot also be taxable under Schedule D, on those rents.

To recapitulate, Schedule A charges profits arising in respect of leases of land, and other receipts arising from or by virtue of an *ownership* of an estate or interest in or right over land. Schedule D, on the other hand, charges profits arising from the *occupation* of land. For the purposes of this book, taxpayers in the former category are described as 'landowners' and those in the latter as 'farmers'. In the latter category a trade or business is carried on; in the former it is not. One individual may concurrently operate in both capacities in respect of different land. He may at the same time be a tenant of other land.

Differences of treatment flow from this classification: farming profits are by definition 'earned' income. The rental income of landowners is not earned, and was therefore liable to investment income surcharge at the rate of 15% (FA 1971 s 32; FA 1980 s 18(1)(b)). Investment income surcharge was abolished from 1984/85, so eliminating one critical distinction, and changing the relationship between the two categories.

Other differences of treatment are equally dependent upon the particular Schedule of charge. Some historic differences have been abolished as the law has changed, but old cases, those, for example, distinguishing between income under Schedule B (abolished: FA 1988) and Schedule D can still be relevant. One is that trading profits under Schedule D have a special basis of assessment, usually the profits arising in the preceding year (TA 1988 s 60). Schedule A income is assessed on a current year basis (TA 1988 s 22). The effect is to allow farmers a longer period of use of money before tax is payable.

Differences in the methods of calculating the taxable profit are examined in detail elsewhere (see section **4.3**). The rules as to what expenses are deductible are more generous under Schedule D than Schedule A. Because permitted deductions are larger, taxable income emerges smaller.

Again, losses sustained in carrying on a trade under Schedule D are capable of being relieved against a wider range of other income and profit than losses sustained under Schedule A. The scope of relief for the latter is confined to future Schedule A income, so if outgoings continue to exceed rents received, a landlord can never hope to secure relief.

5.1:2 The borderline situation

As a result of all these differences borderline situations in which the circum-stances are capable of being regarded by the courts as justifying charge under one or other Schedule assume considerable importance. The best practical applica-tion is the treatment of 'grazing rights', under a grazing agreement for a period of less than 12 months with no right of renewal. Such an agreement does not create a tenancy under the Agricultural Holdings Act 1948, tantamount to occupation. To secure Schedule D treatment, an owner needs to demonstrate that he is himself an occupier carrying on activities which amount to farming the land, for example fertilising and seeding it, repairing and maintaining fences etc. He will be able to put forward the contention that he is growing grass as a crop. There is no difficulty in perceiving that a person who grows grass, cuts it, makes hay, and sells the hay in the market is a farmer.

The argument is that a person is equally to be classified a farmer, if having grown the same crop, he permits livestock to graze it whilst growing; or lets another harvest it for hay or silage.

There have been several cases in the courts from which the principle described above may be adduced, but the decisions are not always reconcilable with each other. In *Gittos v Barclay* [1982] STC 390, the landowner undertook some man-agement functions. There were no tenancy agreements, the occupiers being mere licensees. However, it was held that the landowner's activities amounted only to normal management by an owner and there was a distinction to be drawn between these activities (mere exploitation of ownership) and the trading activi-ties of a trader. In *IRC v Forsyth Grant* (1943) 25 TC 369, the issue turned on who was the occupier of land, because farming is statutorily defined as 'the occupation of land for the purposes of husbandry'. The owner of certain grass parks let for grazing on a seasonal basis was held the occupier, and secured Schedule D treatment. In two Scottish cases (*Mitchell v IRC* (1943) 25 TC 380; *Drummond v IRC* (1951) 32 TC 263), the tenant was held to be the occupier having regard either to his unbroken beneficial occupation, year after year, or because the owner bore none of the expenses incidental to occupation, or had not visited or been 'on' the lands for '20 years'. The time factor emerges as an important ingredient in the judicial decision.

The most recent case on this topic, heard in 1969, is *Bennion v Roper* (1969) 46 TC 613, in which it was held that income arising from grazing rights fell squarely under Schedule A, not as the appellant had claimed, under Schedule D. The judgment was based upon the finding that there was 'a perfectly ordinary tenancy agreement of 210 acres for a period of a year and 11 months at a rent payable by half yearly instalments'. The existence of a tenancy emerges as undoubtedly fatal to a Schedule D claim.

Another borderline situation is illustrated by *Lowe v J W Ashmore Ltd* (1970) 46 TC 597. The company carried on the trade of farming but sold to building contractors the right to cut and take turf from the land. It was held that the profit was part of the farming trade because the fact 'that the grass is sold together with the earth in which it is rooted' did not prevent the transaction from falling under the head of farming. The court held that alternatively the profits were assessable under Schedule A. The taxpayer had contended that he was selling part of his ownership, that is a grant of fee simple of an area of 26½ acres, two inches thick. This argument was rejected on the grounds that what had been sold was a profit à prendre for a limited period. It is worth noting that this case was litigated before the introduction of capital gains taxation, and is of limited authority.

Lowe v J W Ashmore Ltd was carefully distinguished in *McClure v Petre* [1988] STC 749. In this case the taxpayer received from contractors £72,125 under two agreements licensing them to enter onto land to deposit sub-soil. There was a supplementary payment of £4,000 under a licence to use a disused railway cutting on similar restorative terms. These payments were held to be not liable under Schedule A, principally because the land once used for dumping could never again be used for that purpose. There was nothing in the dumping agreement to compensate the taxpayer for lack of the use of land or loss of income from the land. Indeed the tenant had continued to pay rent to the taxpayer throughout the agreement period. The principle was that where a transaction realised permanently the capital value of one of a number of valuable characteristics, the proceeds of that transaction could be in the nature of capital (*Haig's Trustees v IRC* (1939) 22 TC 725). It is arguable that the switch from income tax to capital gains tax liability represents a modest advantage, but that view fails to take account of the value of indexation and other reliefs.

Study of these cases will be helpful in indicating how grazing and similar agreements should be drafted, and what, on any proposed set of commercial terms, are the prospects of securing Schedule D treatment. A specimen form of agreement is included at Appendix I. This treatment may achieve immediate income tax reductions. Future inheritance tax and capital gains tax liabilities may also be reduced as income tax principles have been imported into the structure of capital taxation as tests for certain reliefs (see sections **7.5** and **8.3:1**).

Thus the issue as to whether given transactions fall under Schedule D or Schedule A may prove even more significant than at first appears. This aspect is considered in more detail in section **17.4**, under the heading 'contract farming'. That is a term given to arrangements under which a landowner, who would not otherwise be carrying on a business, puts himself into the position of doing so by virtue of a special agreement conferring rights and obligations, which he enters into with an individual who might otherwise have become his tenant. That is not the only objective of a contract farming agreement, but it is likely to be a major one.

Another expedient worth consideration by landowners is the incorporation of an estate management company, use of which can convert a proportion of rentals receivable into earned income (see section **17.5:5**).

The remainder of this section describes certain reliefs available to both farmers and landowners and the treatment of analogous sources of income which commonly arise to both farmers and landowners, other than the two respective principal sources: from profits and rents. A farmer is likely to be capable of maximising the value of his small subsidiary incomings by treating them as part of farm profits, ie by including them in his farm accounts in the expectation that a beneficial *de minimis* doctrine will apply. The relatively small amounts involved will not justify segregation and separate assessment on strictly correct lines. A landowner has no such scope for manoeuvre.

All these factors do not always operate together, but often those that do, encourage landowners to try to take land in hand, and not to relet when a farm falls vacant. It may be that these factors plus non-taxation factors will be so persuasive as to hasten the decline of the landlord-tenant system and replace it with other arrangements. Contract farming and limited companies both seem candidates to serve as replacements.

5.2 CAPITAL ALLOWANCES

5.2:1 Introduction

The return on capital for all types of farm in England and Wales has consistently been lower than the yield on securities of all classes during the past decade. Various taxation consequences follow: for example, farming is particularly vulnerable to capital based taxation. Similarly, tax allowances designed to provide for the depreciation of capital assets assume particular importance. This section deals with two such forms of allowance: for *machinery and plant*; and for *agricultural buildings*. Because the latter is peculiar to agriculture it is dealt with in greater detail than the former. Landowners are equally entitled to both classes of allowance. Since, however, machinery and plant is usually acquired for the purposes of a trade, landowners rarely have claims in respect of that class.

The UK tax system recognises the commercial practice of making reserves out of profits to provide for replacement of capital equipment, which by its nature wears out. If a tractor costs £10,000 and has a working life of ten years, it is a distortion to charge the cost of a new one all in one year – that in which the new one is bought. Instead, the tax system spreads tax relief on the cost over the lifetime of the tractor, on a stipulated basis. The same principle is applied to buildings and works. The depreciation charged in the farm accounts is disallowed in arriving at the adjusted profits for tax purposes, and capital allowances on the stipulated basis are given as a separate deduction.

The reliefs given annually during use may or may not fall to be tested for adequacy when the capital item is sold or scrapped. Sometimes, the rules provide that at that point in time, the history of past tax reliefs is examined to ascertain whether those reliefs were or were not adequate. If not – because the whole cost of the item has not been relieved – then a 'balancing allowance' may be made, to adjust the former arbitrary tax allowances to coincide with the facts of the matter. On the contrary, the item may be sold at a price which demonstrates that it did not depreciate as rapidly as tax reliefs had assumed. Then a 'balancing charge' may be made to recapture over-generous past reliefs. This balancing charge – which may be regarded as a negative tax relief – can never exceed the reliefs already given. It is not to be confused with a capital gain, liability on which arises only when the sale or disposal price exceeds historic cost.

Capital allowances – including balancing allowances – serve to reduce profits chargeable to tax, whilst balancing charges are added to taxable profits. If the farming business is being carried on by a partnership, capital allowances are first deducted from the firm's profit as a whole, and thereafter the net is divided amongst the individual partners (see section **6.1:4**). When claimed by a company, capital allowances are deducted in arriving at the profit chargeable to corporation tax.

Capital allowances – when applied to reduce profits – may have the effect of converting a profit into a loss or may increase an already existing loss. In that event, the allowances are available for relief in the same way as would be the loss so created or augmented (see section **2.6**).

Capital allowances of both classes: machinery and plant (CAA 1990 Pt II); and buildings and works (CAA 1990 Pt V) may be claimed by all types of person engaged in agriculture: owners of tenanted land; owner-occupiers and tenants. The test is whether the claimant has incurred the requisite expenditure, and a claim is not barred because, for example, the money is spent erecting a building on land owned or occupied by another person.

Similarly, machinery and plant may be purchased by one or more of the partners in a farming partnership without ever becoming partnership property. It will belong to the partners who bought it, even though the partnership as a whole may use it. If the owners receive a consideration for use, eg a lease rent, they will be able to claim capital allowances and deduct them from that rent before it is taxed. If they do not receive any such consideration, the partnership as a whole will be able to claim the capital allowances against its partnership farming profits. The same principle is applied to farm buildings.

This book deals with only those forms of capital allowances commonly applicable to agriculture. Relief is also available for capital expenditure on industrial buildings and structures (CAA 1990 Pt I); mines and oil wells (CAA 1990 Pt IV); dredging (CAA 1990 Pt VI); scientific research (CAA 1990 Pt VII); patent rights (TA 1988 s 520); acquisition of 'know-how' (TA 1988 s 530). The possibility of allowances under one of the classifications should not be overlooked.

Finally, it should be noted that the forms of capital allowances, the rates of allowances, manner of giving relief, and general procedures have been repeatedly changed over the years.

5.2:2   Meaning of 'machinery' and 'plant'

The system described here is that introduced for machinery or plant bought on or after 27 October 1970. The system operative before that date may still continue to apply to equipment owned by many farmers. Two sets of calculations will therefore be needed in such cases, the 'old' and 'new' system items being treated separately.

Over the years, there have been repeated disputes between the Revenue and taxpayers as to the meaning of the terms 'machinery' and 'plant'. There is no statutory definition, and therefore the words have their ordinary meaning. The former term is probably easier to construe than the latter: it has been held that *plant* is the apparatus used by a businessman to carry on business, the goods and chattels, fixed or movable, permanently kept. Plant does not include buildings, but there is often a problem in distinguishing one from the other. Grain silos are plant (*Schofield v R & H Hall Ltd* (1975) 49 TC 538). Prefabricated buildings are not (*St Johns School v Ward* [1974] STC 69).

Glass houses are not 'plant' but premises, in which a grower's trade is carried on. On that basis, they qualify for agricultural buildings allowances (see section **5.2:5**). In some circumstances, the Revenue will accept that a glass house unit and its machinery are inter-dependent, forming a single entity, functioning as apparatus within a grower's business and as such will qualify as plant.

In the Revenue view, these units will be 'of an extremely sophisticated design, including extensive computer controlled equipment, without which the structure cannot operate to achieve the optimum artificial growing environment for the particular crops involved. The equipment will have been permanently installed during the construction of the glass houses and will normally include a computer system which monitors and controls boiler and piped heating systems, temperature and humidity controls, automatic ventilation equipment and automatic thermal or shade screens.'

5.2:3   Structure of relief

The general structure of the relief is as follows. In the past, there were various first year allowances, all of which were abolished as from 1 April 1986. From that date, there was an annual allowance, the 'writing down' allowance of 25% of cost (CAA 1990 s 24). It is not given if the whole cost has already been relieved by a 100% writing down allowance.

As from 1 November 1992 and until 31 October 1993, a new first 40% first year allowance has been introduced. This is given in place of the writing down allowance of 25%, and the balance of expenditure continues to be written down for tax purposes in subsequent years at 25% pa on a reducing balance basis.

Allowances are not separately calculated for each item of plant or machinery, but instead all owned is treated as a 'pool' of expenditure, on which relief at 25% is calculated. Before calculation, additions and subtractions are made to represent items bought and sold during the period.

The amount subtracted is always the proceeds of sale of plant or machinery, or in the case of loss, the amount of insurance or compensation moneys. If the sale etc, price exceeds the balance on the pool account, a balancing charge restricted to the allowance given, is made on the excess.

Writing down allowances are optional and can be disclaimed. The effect of disclaimer is to increase the balance on the pool account and therefore the amount available for relief in future years.

There is a limitation applicable to motor cars costing more than a stipulated maximum price (currently £12,000) which reduces the writing down allowance to 25% of the stipulated maximum for any year (ie £3,000). The limit has been increased over the years to keep up with rising costs, and the Treasury has powers to make further increases in future (CAA 1990 s 34).

The machinery or plant on which the allowance is claimed must belong to the taxpayer. However, this rule does not impair the rights of agricultural tenants to claim allowances, because under tenancy law they will acquire legal rights over the fixtures etc, which they may install on their landlord's land or buildings.

There is another set of special rules (CAA 1990 s 60) where plant or machinery is bought under a hire purchase agreement. Each instalment paid is treated partly as a hire charge, which is wholly deductible, and partly as an instalment of the purchase price qualifying for capital allowances. A first year allowance could be claimed for the relevant year on the capital element in the instalment paid at the time the contract to acquire the asset is made, even though the plant or machinery might not have been brought into use on that date. The balance of capital expenditure is treated as having been paid when the item is brought into use on the farm, and writing down allowances are given then, as if no balance remained outstanding.

Yet another set of special rules operates where assets, usually motor cars, are used partly for business and partly for private purposes (CAA 1990 s 79). The full allowances otherwise due are abated as is thought to be 'just and reasonable having regard to all the circumstances', and the allowance and charges are calculated as if the expenditure formed a separate pool of its own. The question of the respective proportions of private and farm use can become a disputed one, and the Inspectors often ask for records to be kept.

5.2:4 Renewals basis

Under this treatment, no capital allowances as such are given, and the cost of depreciation is allowed only in the year in which an item of machinery or plant falls to be replaced. The effect is therefore to concentrate relief into a single year, which may be disadvantageous, unless that year is a particularly profitable one, producing adequate income to absorb the deduction.

Relief on the renewals basis is given as a deduction in computing the adjusted farming profit. It is based on the net cost of renewal, that is, the cost of the new machine less the sum received if any on disposal of the old one replaced. If the new machine represents an addition or improvement on the old one, the relief is restricted accordingly. That rule can lead to disagreement, since all new machinery tends to represent improvements on older models.

The renewals basis dates from years before full capital allowances were given. It is possible to change from renewals to the normal system at any time, but clearly allowances cannot be claimed on both bases for any given year of assessment.

5.2:5   Agricultural buildings and works

In FA 1985 and 1986, the structure of capital allowances for agricultural buildings and works was substantially changed, significantly to the disadvantage of farmers and landowners.

Under the old rules, enacted in 1968, agricultural buildings and allowances were particularly valuable because they were never recaptured by balancing charges. Although a building might ultimately be sold for an amount equal to full cost, the allowance was not withdrawn or recaptured. If a building were sold for more than its historic cost, there was liability to capital gains tax, but not the cancellation of income tax allowances previously given.

Under the 1985 and 1986 rules, allowances for agricultural buildings were closely aligned with those for industrial buildings. The allowance takes the form of a writing down allowance over 25 years, that is at the rate of 4% per annum (see section **5.2:10**).

Expenditure incurred before 1 April 1987 under a contract made before 14 March 1984 may be eligible for allowances under previous rules (see section **5.2:9**) which continue to be allowed in appropriate cases.

If an item of plant qualifies for both capital allowances and agricultural buildings allowances, either may be claimed (CAA 1990 s 25(7) and s 124(3)).

(A) AGRICULTURAL LAND

In this context, 'agricultural land' is statutorily defined (CAA 1990 s 133(1)) and means land, houses or other buildings in the UK occupied wholly or mainly for the purposes of husbandry. 'Husbandry' is not defined, so that the word has its ordinary meaning. In practice, it is regarded as including any method of intensive rearing of livestock on a commercial basis for the production of food for human consumption, but there has been a series of precedent cases fought over issues other than agricultural buildings allowances, which help to interpret the word in borderline cases.

In particular, it has been decided that poultry farming and fish rearing are within the term 'husbandry'. So is the use of land for the purpose of grazing sheep. On the other hand, a farmers' cooperative butter-making business was held not to be husbandry. Land used for market gardening is agricultural land, so it is not necessary to decide whether or not market gardening is husbandry.[1]

(B) FORESTRY LAND

This expression means woodlands in the UK (CAA 1990 s 133(1)), the profits of which are by election assessable under Schedule D, and any houses or other buildings occupied together with and wholly or mainly for the purposes of such woodlands. That would include forestry workers' cottages etc (see section **13.1:3**). Allowances for forestry land have been withdrawn for periods after 20 June 1989, save for transitional relief to 6 April 1993 (CAA 1990 s 131).

1 See *Reid v IRC* (1947) 28 TC 451; *IRC v Cavan Central Co-operative Agricultural and Dairy Society Ltd* (1917) 12 TC 1 at 10; *Lean and Dickson v Ball* (1925) 10 TC 341 at 345; *Jones v Nuttall* (1926) 10 TC 346; *Long v Belfield Poultry Products Ltd* (1937) 21 TC 221; *Thornber Bros Ltd v Macinnes* (1937) 21 TC 221; *Watson Bros v Hornby* (1942) 24 TC 506; *Keir v Gillespie* (1919) 7 TC 473.

5.2:6 Qualifying expenditure

The following conditions must all be satisfied:

(a) The expenditure must be capital expenditure (CAA 1990 s 122(1)) (see section **2.3:2**). Capital expenditure excludes items of maintenance or repairs, and any amount which the claimant is able to claim as a deduction in computing profits; or from which any person paying it is entitled to deduct tax at source.

(b) The money must be spent on the construction (CAA 1990 s 122(1)), reconstruction, alteration or improvement of farmhouses, farm or forestry buildings, cottages, fences or other works. 'Works' includes drainage and sewerage works, water and electricity installations, walls, shelter belts of trees, glasshouses on market garden land, and the reclamation of former agricultural land.

(c) It is important to note that where items are included amongst repairs and renewals, and are disallowed by the Inspector as representing 'improvements', the amount disallowed may then be made the subject of an agricultural buildings allowances claim. A similar situation arises where, shortly after the acquisition of the farm, expenditure is disallowed under the rule in *Law Shipping Co Ltd v IRC* (1923) 12 TC 621; that is, on the grounds that the farm was bought at a low price because it was in a dilapidated condition.

(d) The expenditure must be incurred for the purposes of husbandry or forestry on agricultural land or forestry land, of which the person incurring the expenditure is owner or tenant (CAA 1990 s 122(1)).

(e) If the expenditure is paid partly from a subsidy, grant or contribution from government, public or local authority, the allowance is limited to the net, after deduction of that subsidy (eg under the Farm Capital Grant Scheme or the Farm and Horticulture Development Scheme) (CAA 1990 s 153).

5.2:7 Who can claim

The allowance is normally made to the owner or tenant who has incurred the qualifying expenditure. Landlords may claim, where they have provided the building for use in the trade carried on by a tenant, or have made a contribution to the total cost. The tenant who has erected the building, or provided the remainder of the cost, is treated as having incurred expenditure of the net amount after deducting the landlord's contribution.

If the land on which the buildings stand is sold, or a tenancy comes to an end during the currency of the allowance, the allowance for the year of transfer is apportioned between old and new owners (or tenants) on a chargeable period basis. Allowances for the remaining complete years are given to the transferee (CAA 1990 s 122(3)–(6)).

Where a tenancy comes to an end, there is a special test to determine who shall enjoy the remainder of the allowances given to the former tenant. If the incoming tenant buys the buildings etc on which relief has been claimed, he becomes entitled to these allowances. If not, the buildings are treated as reverting to the immediate landlord, and the allowances are accordingly allotted to him.

Where only part of the land in question is transferred, only the allowances attributable to that part are accordingly transferred.

Special problems arise where land has been settled on trust. In *Sargaison v Roberts* (1969) 45 TC 612 a farmer settled his land on trust, and the trustees leased it back to him. He claimed that he had not parted with the whole of his interest in the land, and was therefore entitled to the remainder of the allowances for expenditure incurred before the settlement and lease back. It was held that he was so entitled. This precedent may be relevant, where family farming partnerships are created during the currency of existing allowances (see section **15.3**).

5.2:8   Farmhouses

Where the expenditure is incurred on a farmhouse, not more than one-third can qualify (CAA 1990 s 124(1)). The proportion may be reduced if the accommodation and amenities of the farmhouse are out of relation to the nature and extent of the farm. Similarly, if expenditure is incurred on an asset used partly for husbandry (or forestry) and partly for some other purpose, the expenditure is apportioned for the purpose of the allowance.

The question may therefore arise as to what is a farmhouse. In *Lindsay v IRC* (1953) 34 TC 289 the taxpayer lived abroad, and farmed through agents. The only house was occupied by an employee, the head shepherd. It was found as a fact that this was a farmhouse and the expenditure on it fell to be restricted to one-third. That was because it was occupied by the person 'running the farm'.

On the other hand, in *IRC v John M Whiteford & Son* (1962) 40 TC 379 a house built for a farmer's son (and partner in the business) was held to be an agricultural cottage, so that there was no restriction to one-third of the expenditure.

The general principle seems to be that on each farm there can be only one farmhouse, the building which is regarded as the central controlling point of the farm. Other houses occupied by individuals working on the farm may be 'cottages'.

Since the annual allowance under the new Agricultural Building Allowances rules is now only 4% per annum, it does not seem likely that the question of what is or is not a farmhouse will be disputed in this connection. However, it should be borne in mind that the issue may be more important for capital gains tax, inheritance tax or value added tax.

5.2:9   Nature of allowance (old rules)

The old rules continue to apply for expenditure incurred before 1 April 1986, or if under an existing contract before 1 April 1987 (CAA 1990 s 122).

An initial allowance of 20% could be claimed for the first year of assessment starting after the end of the basis period in which the expenditure is incurred. As from 1 April 1986, the initial allowance was cancelled. Expenditure was treated as having been 'incurred' when the sums become payable. A writing down allowance of 10% was available for that period, and the remainder of the expenditure was also relieved at the rate of 10% per annum over the next seven years (FA 1978 s 39; CAA 1990 s 132(1)). As from 1 April 1986, the rate of annual allowance was reduced to 4%.

The initial allowance was optional. It could be claimed in whole or part by notice in writing not later than two years after the end of the accounting period in which the expenditure was incurred.

It is important to recognise that agricultural buildings allowances are applied to relieve certain classes of income in special order. The classes are primarily: agricultural income for the year (CAA 1990 s 132(1)); that is, rentals under Schedule A (see section **4.2**); and farming profits etc, under Schedule D (see section **2.2**). Then, secondarily: if the allowance exceeds that income, there is a choice of alternative applications.

The unused balance may be carried forward and set against agricultural income in the next succeeding year, and so on for future years without limit of time. Alternatively, a claimant may apply to have the unused allowance set off against other kinds of income for the same year as that in which the relief fell due; or, so far as not allowed in that year, for the next following year, but not in later years. Such a claim must be made within two years of the end of the year concerned.

Where a farming business has been permanently discontinued, and unexhausted allowances remain, those for the last 12 months before cessation may be carried backwards in time and set off against profits for the last three years of assessment. The procedure follows that for terminal loss relief (see section **2.6:3**).

5.2:10 Nature of allowance (new rules)

Under the new rules (CAA 1990 s 123–s 130) the allowances are similar in structure to those for industrial buildings. The allowance is calculated on a straight line basis at the rate of 4% pa, so that the total cost is extinguished after 25 years.

As from 1 November 1992, there was introduced a new 20% initial allowance for expenditure incurred on agricultural buildings contracted for in the 12 months ending 31 October 1993, and which have been brought into use by 31 December 1994. For this purpose, qualifying expenditure includes expenditure on existing and part completed buildings which have not previously been used, and which are bought from a person whose trade is the construction of a building for sale. The balance of relief is given annually at the rate of 4% of the cost of the building, as from the year in which the building is brought into use.

If the building is sold, a purchaser takes over the right to the allowances for the residue of the original 25-year period. There then arises a 'balancing event' which depends upon the 'residue' of expenditure: that is, the original cost less the allowances already made. This residue is set against the disposal proceeds or, if appropriate, any insurance compensation moneys. If the residue exceeds the proceeds of disposal, the difference is the subject of a balancing allowance. If the sale proceeds exceed the residue, the difference is the subject of a balancing charge. This charge may not exceed the allowances actually made. A balancing event also arises when a building is demolished, destroyed or ceases to exist as such (CAA 1990 s 129(1)(*b*)). There is no specific requirement that the building must continue to be used for agricultural purposes.

A balancing event is secured by making an election not more than two years from the end of the period in which the sale occurred. Both vendor and purchaser must make the election.

The new rules provide for agricultural buildings allowances to be set primarily against agricultural income.

It should be remembered that allowance is given for qualifying expenditure on *new* buildings. If land is bought with an existing building etc erected, no allowance is due, other than the remainder of the allowances already current.

Forms of claim (No 461) are obtainable from the Inspector. It is helpful to keep a record of allowances due for the years ahead, since these represent a valuable asset in the event of a sale of whole or part of the farm. How much value is attributable to allowances depends to some extent upon the marginal rate of a farmer's liability for any year. The higher the rate, the more valuable the allowances.

Example: Capital allowances – agricultural buildings (new rules)

In the year to 31 March 1994, Mr White erects a new cowshed which costs £40,000, with additional costs for drainage £4,000 and electricity £6,000.

His landlord contributes £10,000 to the total cost:

Allowances		
1993–94	Cost	£40,000
	Drainage	£ 4,000
	Electricity	£ 6,000
		£50,000
	Landlord	£10,000
		£40,000
IA 20%		£ 8,000
AA 4%		£ 1,600
	WDV cf	£30,400

Example: Capital allowances – agricultural buildings (old rules)

In the year to 31 March 1985, Mr Black erects a new cowshed which costs £40,000, with additional costs for drainage £4,000 and electricity £6,000.

His landlord contributes £10,000 to the total cost:

Allowances		
1985–86	Cost	£40,000
	Drainage	£ 4,000
	Electricity	£ 6,000
		£50,000
	Landlord	£10,000
		£40,000
IA	20% × 40,000 =	£ 8,000
WDA	10% × 40,000 =	£ 4,000
	WDV cf	£28,000

5.3 MINERALS

5.3:1 Introduction

Agricultural landowners often have the opportunity to exploit valuable natural deposits in their land, and by doing so raise additional cash for investment in their farming businesses or estates etc. Care is needed before commencing exploitation, since the taxation consequences are exceptional in various respects, and contain pitfalls.

By way of preliminary, the owner of agricultural land may or may not be the owner of minerals and other deposits under the surface. He will not be the owner where land has been sold or transferred in a conveyance where minerals are specifically excepted, or where there is a severance of interests created by statute. For example, gold, silver and precious metals are statutorily vested in the Crown, and coal and associated minerals in British Coal.

Tenants of farm land may also have rights, unless the landlord has reserved minerals out of the lease. Since damage may be done to the surface or subsurface of land, which may need to be remedied or restored, tenants may become involved as parties in transactions with prospectors or developers.

A farmer may himself become a mineral prospector or operator. The business will be taxed under Schedule D Case I separate and distinct from his business as a farmer. Mines, quarries, gravel pits, sandpits, brickfields, salt springs or works, waterworks, and other concerns of like nature are chargeable under Schedule D Case I, without the ordinary rules determining whether a trade is being carried on being applied (TA 1988 s 55). For individuals, liability is to income tax; for companies, corporation tax.

5.3:2 Sales of minerals

If a landowner sells outright his mineral bearing land; or sells the minerals themselves, he will have made a part disposal for capital gains tax (see section **7.1**). Roll-over relief or retirement relief may be due (see sections **7.4** and **7.6**). If he sells his land to a mineral operator, with an option to repurchase when the working ceases, the price difference between sale and ultimate repurchase may fall to be treated as a premium chargeable under Schedule A (TA 1988 s 36; see section **4.2**). A better course is to sell the minerals separately so producing liability for capital gains tax as a part disposal. He may then separately grant a lease to the mineral operator, so as to give him access to the working site, at a modest or nominal rent taxable under Schedule A.

Alternatively, the owner may stipulate for a royalty based on the tonnage of minerals worked, or as a percentage of the open market sale price of the mineral. Much depends on the nature of the mineral concerned. Such royalties are subject to deduction of income tax at source by the payer (TA 1988 s 119). Where the payment is made 'out of profits or gains brought into charge to tax', ie out of taxable income, the payer retains the tax deducted so effectively giving himself relief for the payment made. Where there is no such taxable income for the year of payment, the payer hands over the tax deducted to the Revenue.

The position of the payer is not relevant in determining the liabilities of the recipient. His basis of liability is unique: half the sum received is treated as income and liable to income tax; or if the recipient is a company, to corporation tax. The second half is treated as capital, and the total received in a tax year is treated as a capital gain (TA 1988 s 122; see also Mineral Royalties (Tax) Regulations 1971, SI 1971/1035).

The half liable to income tax is treated as falling under Schedule D, and is subject to a claim to deduct expenses of management. The deduction is restricted to half the total, to correspond with half the total receipt, classified as income. The half liable to capital gains tax is not treated as a part disposal, but wholly as a gain. No expenses of management are deductible against this half, nor is roll-over relief available.

The whole of the royalty receivable will have been subject to deduction of income tax at source (TA 1988 s 348), but this is treated as a provisional deduction, and is credited first against the income taxable half of the royalty, and second against the half subject to capital gains tax. Any excess of tax deducted is then available for repayment (TA 1988 s 122; Mineral Royalties (Tax) Regulations 1971 SI 1971/1035).

When a mineral royalty ends, the landowner may be left with land worth less than it was worth before the minerals were worked. There is a form of terminal loss relief (FA 1970 Sch 6 paras 3–9) designed to give relief for this against capital gains tax, either in the year of final loss, or against gains taxed in the previous 15 years, more recent years' gains being extinguished in preference to earlier years' gains. This relief is not due if the owner's interest in the land terminates with the end of the mining lease. In order to avoid immediate payment of tax, possibly many years before relief and repayment occurs, it will be advantageous to grant leases of smaller separate areas at a time, so that relief becomes due as each operating area becomes successively exhausted, and the royalty in respect of it comes to an end.

5.4   WAYLEAVES

An owner of land has the right to license others to pass wires and lines over it, or pipes under it. The rights granted to others are known as wayleaves, or easements. The consideration receivable is subject to special tax treatment, depending upon its nature, in particular whether it has the characteristics of capital or income (see section **2.1:2**).

Once-and-for-all receipts for permanent easements will have the characteristics of capital and will not be liable to income tax, but to capital gains tax (see chapter 7). If the consideration receivable does not exceed £20,000 in any one year of assessment, the recipient may claim that the receipt should not be treated as giving rise to a charge, but should be deducted from his base cost, for the purpose of computing liability on a future disposal. This is on the assumption that the disposal is 'small in value' which will normally be so for the owner of even a modest farm or estate. For this purpose 20% or less by comparison with the value of the total holding is normally regarded as small.

However, if the once-and-for-all payment includes compensation for loss of growing crops or loss of profits on the erection, for example of electricity pylons, or the installation of pipes, or other works, that compensation will fall to be treated as a trading receipt liable to income tax, or as the case may be, corporation tax.

If the payments are periodic and therefore of an income nature, the rent receivable is liable to income tax, not as a trading receipt but either under Schedule D Case III, or under Schedule A.

Liability arises under Schedule D in respect of easements which include any right, privilege, or benefit in or over land in connection with electric, telegraphic or telephonic wires or cables. It extends to poles and pylons supporting wires, and to apparatus, including any transformer unit, used in connection with them (TA 1988 s 120). It does not include for example, gas, water or oil pipelines, the income from which is assessable under Schedule A (TA 1988 s 15).

A payer is under an obligation to deduct and withhold income tax at source from Schedule D classes of payments so that formal assessments on recipients are not usually required. If they are, the ordinary basis of assessment rules for Schedule D Case III will apply.

It is helpful to bear in mind the different taxation consequences when wayleave payments are being negotiated. The calculation of the payment will normally take into account the width of the strip affected, the value of the land, at 'so-much a yard' run of pipeline etc. Whilst a rental may seem appropriate at the outset, it may emerge as a modest sum wholly subject to income tax. A lump sum receipt exempt from such taxation may prove more valuable as a source of finance.

5.5 RESIDENCES OF EMPLOYEES

5.5:1 Accommodation as income

Before the present era of high income taxation, wages and salaries were normally payable in cash, with one or two exceptions traditional in particular industries. In recent years, the practice of paying employees in kind has become widespread largely because of the tax advantages to be secured: company cars; employee loans; goods and services have become familiar rewards to large industrial company employees. These are now subject to tax as *benefits in kind* with special rules for measuring liability.

In agriculture, the conventional facility offered by an employer is living accommodation. The question arises as to whether and when this becomes a taxable benefit in the hands of employees; and what circumstances will provide exemption. 'Job-related accommodation' has become the source of a series of further reliefs, designed to give employees concerned parity of treatment with those not living in such accommodation. The justification is that job-related accommodation lasts only as long as the job, and after retirement an employee should not be put into the position of having forfeited tax relief he would have enjoyed had he been an owner-occupier throughout his working life.

In principle, an employee provided with accommodation is treated as receiving emoluments equal to the value of the accommodation (TA 1988 s 145). The value is the rent which would have been payable had the premises been let from year to year, the tenant bearing the usual tenant's rates and taxes, and the landlord bearing the cost of maintaining the property in a state to command that rent (TA 1988 s 145(2)). In practice, the gross annual value for rating purposes was generally taken as the value of the benefit. Whilst that was so, a favourable low benefit was usually produced since rating valuations were rarely up-to-date.

Since the introduction of the community charge, domestic rating lists have been no longer maintained. For newly built properties, and those where there has been a material change of circumstances, the benefit is to be based on what would have been the gross annual value had the domestic rate system continued. The District Valuer provides this notional figure to the Inspector.

However, if the employer himself pays rent for the premises at a rate higher than the annual value as ascertained above, the amount of rent actually payable falls to be substituted as a taxable benefit. Whichever basis be adopted, there are to be deducted any amounts repaid to the employer, that is the rent etc paid to him by his employee (TA 1988 s 145(1)).

With effect from the year 1984–85, there is a supplementary charge for employees occupying more expensive accommodation, (TA 1988 s 146). Where the property plus improvements costs more than £75,000, the employee is treated as having received additional emoluments, the amount of which is determined by applying the 'official rate of interest' to the amount by which the cost or, in certain circumstances, market value exceeds £75,000.

The 'official rate' of interest is fixed by the Treasury on the basis of interest rates, and is 7.75% with effect from 6 March 1993, in line with typical mortgage rates.

Market value is to be substituted for historic cost only where historic cost was £75,000 or more. If historic cost plus improvements were less than £75,000, the accommodation is not subject to this additional charge.

Example

Cost of farm manager's house	£85,000
Less: statutory limit	£75,000
Excess	£10,000

Schedule E liability (additional) £10,000 at 7.75% = £775 pa.

Where an employee is exceptionally provided with more than one property, the £75,000 threshold is applied separately to each.

This charge applies irrespective of the total emoluments of the employee and is not confined, as are some classes of taxable benefits, to directors of companies and higher paid employees. Four classes of employees are, however, exempted:

(a) where it is necessary for the proper performance of an employee's duties that he should live in that particular accommodation;

(b) where the employment is one where it is customary for employers to provide accommodation for their employees;

(c) where the residence is connected with the employer's security arrangements (TA 1988 s 145(4));

(d) where there is an extra statutory concession applying to the provision of free board and lodging to lower paid agricultural workers. The provision of board and lodging is recognised as traditional in farming whether the lodging be on or off the farm. The value of the board and lodging is not taxed, despite any entitlement to take a higher cash wage in lieu of board and lodging, which may be provided to the employee by the Agricultural Wages Acts.

The following conditions must be satisfied:

(i) the worker be not a director nor in higher paid employment (TA 1988 s 167);

(ii) the wages contract with a farmer must provide for a net cash wage plus free board and lodging;

(iii) where the board and lodging is not in the farmhouse itself, the farmer must have a contract with the third party for the provision of board and lodging, and payments under this contract must be made direct to the third party.

Where the worker receives a gross cash wage, he is taxable on this amount.

The most clearly established and relevant class of the four is (a), where the employee becomes a *representative* occupier, as opposed to a *beneficial* one. Until FA 1977, the status was established by case law. In a series of cases, a bank manager (*Tennant v Smith* (1892) 3 TC 158); Church ministers (*Reed v Cattermole* (1936) 21 TC 35; *IRC v Leckie* (1940) 23 TC 471); a colliery manager (*Gray v Holmes* (1949) 30 TC 467) and a police officer (*Langley v Appleby* [1976] STC 368) sought exemption from taxation on the benefit, because it was part of their duties to reside at the particular premises in question, the better to carry out their various duties. The word 'representative' implies representation of the employer. There is no doubt that farm managers or workers living in a farmhouse or farm cottage rent free should qualify as representative occupiers. Their duties will be of a nature which will require their presence on the farm at all times of day or night.

More difficulty may arise in practice where the accommodation is located some distance from the farm, so that the argument as to requiring presence is less persuasive. In that case, reliance on exemption (b) is possible. In practice, there may be difficulty in establishing that a resident agent's occupation is representative, and this will depend upon the nature of his duties. Further difficulties arise if the accommodation is provided by a corporate employer for a director. Exemptions in (a) and (b) above do not apply (TA 1988 s 145(5)), unless the director has no material interest in the company (less than 5% of the ordinary shares); and works full-time for the company.

On the other hand, it may be possible to escape liability as a beneficial occupier, not because of the 'representative' occupier exemption, but because the accommodation is not provided 'by reason of the employment'. That may be acceptable where the employer is an individual farmer, and he makes provision in the normal course of domestic, family or personal relationships. That might apply where the employee in question is a son, with a substantial share interest, or one who failed to qualify under the representative tests. That argument would be weakened if the cottage had previously been occupied by another employee.

5.5:2 Capital gains tax (representative occupiers)

Special privileges are accorded to representative occupiers. An individual who lives in job-related accommodation may find on leaving his job that another residence which he has owned has lost the capital gains tax exemption for principal private residences (see section **7.3:3**). That would be because he has failed to occupy it continuously.

To meet this situation, the occupation of the job-related accommodation, for example the farmhouse (after 30 July 1978), is treated as if it were occupation of the employee's own house, providing he intends in due course to go and occupy it (TCGA 1992 s 222). Whether he does so intend is a question of fact. If he has occupied it before the relevant sale, that would clearly represent persuasive evidence. If the sale occurs before occupation, the intention can still be demonstrated, particularly if the proceeds are applied to buy another home.

For the purposes of capital gains tax, the definition of the four classes of job-related accommodation is the same as above; and there is a similar denial of relief where the accommodation is provided by a company for a director unless he has no material interest *and* works full-time, unless the company is non-profit making or a charity.

5.5:3 Interest payable

Special reliefs are accorded to representative occupiers, designed to compensate them for their inability to occupy their own property (TA 1988 s 356).

Interest payable is not generally deductible for income tax, save where the money has been borrowed for a qualifying purpose, one of which is the purchase or improvement of a house, land, caravan or house-boat (see section **16.2**). If the house is for the borrower's own occupation, it must be his main residence, or that of a dependent relative, or former or separated spouse. Temporary absences of up to one year may be ignored in deciding whether a residence is used as a *main* residence. There are also reliefs which provide that periods of up to four years may be ignored, where an individual has been required to move because of his employment, and also where overseas tours of duty are involved (TA 1988 s 356).

However, none of these reliefs is apt for a representative occupier, who may fail to occupy his own property throughout his working career as say, a farm manager living in job-related accommodation. He will be able to obtain relief for interest paid on or after 6 April 1977, provided that at the time the interest is paid, the property is used by the borrower as a residence or is intended to be so used during the first 12 months of a new loan (TA 1988 s 356).

The borrower must intend to use the property, in due course, as his only or main residence. (As to evidence of such an intention see section **5.5:2**.) 'Job-related accommodation' is defined according to the rules set out above (TA 1988 s 356(3)), and the denial of relief for certain directors also applies (see section **5.5:2**; TA 1988 s 356(4)).

Certain other restrictions upon relief derive from the general rules as to the deductibility of interest. In particular, a loan, the interest on which is eligible for relief in accordance with the above principle, falls to be taken into account in arriving at the maximum loan of £30,000, the limit for interest relief (TA 1988 s 357). Interest on a loan exceeding this amount will be proportionately ineligible for relief. If the amount of existing loans already exceeds £30,000, interest on an additional loan is ineligible.

Again, if interest is deductible because the property acquired has been let, the interest is eligible for relief only against the letting income for the current year, or may be carried forward to future years' income from rents (TA 1988 s 355(4)). The limitation of loans to £30,000 as a test for eligibility of interest relief is not applicable if interest is deductible against letting income.

Despite the various restrictions of relief the position of those occupying agricultural workers' accommodation has been much improved. There is now no reason for an employer to seek a rent *solely* for tax reasons, and the provision of rent-free accommodation is distinctly advantageous, since the employee enjoys it, without it increasing his tax bill. The exemption does not extend to a cash allowance paid for the purpose of compensating an employee for his having to rent a residence from a third party, and that arrangement should be avoided. If accommodation is not available to an employer, it will be beneficial for *him* to become the tenant, so that his employee can become a representative occupier.

Further reliefs extending to non-employees were enacted in FA 1984 s 25 (TA 1988 s 25). The effect is to give the reliefs described above to self-employed persons, eg tenant farmers, buying a home of their own, but who are under a contractual obligation to live in accommodation provided for them as part of the terms of their trade, profession or vocation. If the accommodation is provided by a company in which the borrower has a material interest, or by a partner, relief is not given.

5.5:4   Loans provided by employers

Loans to employees by employers are liable to income tax as benefits in kind. There are special rules for measuring liability. Only directors and employees earning £8,500 pa or more (including gross expenses payments and the value of benefits in kind) are taxable. The amount chargeable to tax as a benefit is based upon the difference between the interest paid by the employee, if any, and the interest which would have been payable on the loan at an 'official rate' of interest. As from 6 March 1993, the official rate is set at 7.75%, but the rate varies in line with interest and mortgage rates. This 'official rate of interest' is also used to measure the value of living accommodation (see section **5.5:1**. above).

5.6   FURNISHED LETTINGS

5.6:1   Introduction

Many farmers let accommodation to holiday visitors, so creating tax liabilities on their rental incomes. That accommodation may include part of the farmhouse itself; cottages; or caravans, situated on farmland. In principle, rents from this class of lettings are assessable under Schedule D Case VI, a residual class designed to catch in the tax net all forms of annual profits not specifically classified under other Cases or Schedules (TA 1988 s 18(3)).

In the computation of profits for tax purposes, no attempt need be made to apportion between the amount receivable for use of the property and the amount for use of furniture. A single Case VI assessment is made on the profits arising for the year of assessment. These are calculated by deducting from the rent receivable the following classes of items: rates and similar outgoings, if paid by the owner; salaries and wages; costs of cleaning, heating, lighting and insurance where paid by the owner; maintenance, repairs and renewals; wear and tear of furniture fixtures and fittings.

As an alternative to renewals, an allowance of 10% of rents receivable may be given in lieu (if the landlord pays rates, rents for this purpose are net).

5.6:2   Schedule A treatment

An owner has a right to elect for the income attributable to the property and the income attributable to the use of furniture to be taxed separately, so that the property rent falls under Schedule A (TA 1988 s 15). This may be a valuable election, if the owner has other property falling within Schedule A, and an excess of expenditure on one property is capable of being offset against rent from another property. The benefit of this offset would be lost if the whole of the income from furnished lettings fell within Schedule D Case VI.

In the ordinary course, furnished lettings will be properties classifiable as having been let at full rents, and not on tenants' repairing leases. Thus, the Schedule A offset will be made against other properties within this category, as opposed to any properties let on tenants' repairing leases, or let at less than full rent. This aggregation of rents receivable and expenditure incurred, applying either for the year in which the excess arose, or for a future year, should produce the result of less tax being payable overall.

5.6:3   Furnished lettings as a trade

The question of whether profits from furnished lettings could amount to income from the carrying on of a trade assessable under Schedule D Case I remained uncertain until recent years. The practice seemed to be that where a letting included an element of service, it could amount to the carrying on of a trade, and in practice this treatment was sometimes accorded to 'Farmhouse Bed-and-Breakfast' lettings traditionally carried on by farmers' wives. If the income from such a source were small, it was by convention often included in farm accounts, although the danger of this treatment was that the Inspector divided the profits in accordance with the division of farm profits, so making the furnished letting profits not wholly attributable to the wife.

However, two judgments have led to the conclusion that holiday lettings cannot constitute a trading activity under Schedule D Case I. In *Gittos v Barclay* [1982] STC 390, it was held that the letting of two holiday villas in Cornwall were correctly assessed under Schedule D Case VI as income from furnished lettings. This was so despite the element of trading apparently involved, for example managing the properties under a registered business name, advertising the properties, cleaning them etc. Again in *Griffiths v Jackson* [1983] STC 184 income from lettings of some 20 residential properties divided into flats or bedsitting rooms and let, furnished and equipped, to students on a short-term basis, was finally held not to amount to a trade, but again to be within Schedule D Case VI.

It is still difficult to predict what will be the practice as a result of these two cases and as a result of the legislation in FA 1984 (see below). When income from furnished lettings was subject to the investment income surcharge, the distinction between Case I and Case VI was more important, and it may be that cases which have been settled on an informal basis will not be disturbed. It may be easier to secure Schedule D Case I treatment if separate accounts for the furnished letting activity are prepared and submitted, as is usual for substantial activities, camp or caravan sites, where the owner supplies site maintenance and other services, or where capital costs have been incurred.

Where Case I treatment is accorded and a balance sheet is supplied, capital allowances will be available on all plant and machinery. Since the abolition of investment income surcharge, the main advantage of Case I treatment will be the availability of loss relief on Case I principles. Under Case VI, losses can be applied only against other sources of income within Case VI, either for the current or succeeding years. Thus, the advantages of securing Case I treatment may remain substantial.

5.6:4   Furnished holiday lettings

As self-catering accommodation became more popular, a more generous regime became necessary and this was grudgingly introduced in 1984.

In order to qualify for preferential treatment:

(a) a letting must be commercial, with a view to profit;
(b) it must be furnished accommodation;
(c) the accommodation must be available for commercial letting to the public generally, for periods totalling in aggregate not less than 140 days;
(d) it must actually have been let for periods totalling 70 days;
(e) for a period comprising seven months, not necessarily continuous, it must not have been in the same occupation for a continuous period exceeding 31 days.

These tests need to be satisfied with reference to the tax year, for persons other than companies, and with reference to a 12 month accounting period for companies. If they are satisfied, then for all practicable purposes the furnished letting is to be treated as if it were a trade with all the relevant deductions and loss reliefs for income tax purposes including capital allowances, and retirement annuity relief; and qualifying for important roll-over, hold-over and retirement reliefs for capital gains tax (see sections **7.4** to **7.6**). However, for inheritance tax, business property relief has not been conceded. (See section **8.3**.)

5.6:5 Furnished holiday lettings roll-over relief

Roll-over relief will be due on the disposal of property which has been let commercially as furnished holiday accommodation providing the conditions set out in **5.6:4** above are satisfied.

In addition the Inland Revenue have indicated that roll-over relief will be due when properties are let out during the main holiday period on a short-term basis, but during the quieter part of the year are let on a long-term basis. Some of these longer lettings may be to the same person for more than 31 days. The Revenue view is that providing the letting during the main holiday period satisfies the above tests, the longer lettings in any other part of the same year of assessment will not preclude relief (ICTA 1988 ss 503, 504 and TCGA 1992 s 152).

5.6:6 'Rent-a-room' relief

This new relief was introduced as from 6 April 1992 to encourage those with spare rooms in their houses to let them out (F(2)A 1992 Sch 10). Residences in which the rooms are let must be the individuals' only or main residence.

'Residence' means a building (or part of a building) occupied or intended to be occupied as a separate residence. It includes a caravan or a house-boat. A residence qualifies if it is an individual's only or main residence at any time in the basis period. The test is based on the income tax rules for mortgage interest relief, and not the capital gains tax personal private residence exemption (see section **16.2:2**). Generally the relief is given on a Schedule D Case 1 basis, so that the basis period is normally the proceeding year. Commencement and cessation year adjustments apply.

It appears that the relief can be claimed by both owner-occupiers and tenants. Relief is given in terms of the gross rent accruing for a particular period up to an amount of £3,250 for 1992–93, but it is possible that this figure will be varied by Treasury order in future years. If the gross amount accruing (not allowing any deductions) exceeds £3,250, the recipient may elect:

(a) to pay tax on the amount by which the rent exceeds £3,250 without any relief or deductible expenses; or
(b) to calculate the profit from the letting by deducting expenses incurred from the gross rent, and paying tax on the net profit in the ordinary way.

The choice of alternative (b) is effectively an election not to claim the relief which will be the more advantageous course if, for example, deductible expenses produce a net allowable loss. Alternative (a), on the other hand, is likely to be advantageous where the gross rents marginally exceed the threshold of £3,250.

There are no stipulations concerning the length of the tenancy, so that the exemption is applicable to bed-and-breakfast accommodation offered to holiday makers in a farmhouse. Relevant sums for the purposes of the exemption include those receivable for goods or services, including meals, cleaning and laundry. However, relief will not be available on cottages let to holiday makers, which will not qualify as an 'only or main residence', unless such a cottage had been separately occupied by a member of the farming family.

If a farmhouse is in multiple occupation, and each occupier takes in paying guests, the exempt amount of £3,250 is divided amongst the occupiers. Participation in the rent-a-room 'scheme' will not destroy personal private residence exemption from capital gains tax (see section **7.3**).

5.7   TRANSACTIONS IN LAND

5.7:1   Introduction

So far, farmland and buildings have been described as *fixed* capital, that which an owner turns to profit by keeping it in his possession, and using it to yield produce, eg crops, wool, fruit or milk. The comparison has been made (see section **2.3:2**) with *circulating* capital, that from which an owner makes a profit by parting with it. Farm animals may fall into either category: fixed capital, when they are taxed on the herd basis (see section **3.2**); circulating capital when dealt with as stock-in-trade.

The same principle applies to farm land. In the course of a lifetime's ownership of a farm, some land is inevitably bought and sold. A farmer may change farms; he may expand or contract his acreage; he may sell to raise cash, or for other commercial or personal reasons. In particular, a sitting tenant may have an opportunity to buy his landlord's freehold, and may then resell it, and use the proceeds to pay off liabilities or to buy a farm elsewhere. It is important to recognise that, first: when a sale occurs, the Revenue will consider whether and in what form liability arises on the profit or gain. Secondly: there is the question of possible tax relief for any loss or deficiency arising on a sale; and thirdly: there is the question of the taxation treatment of purchase costs, as to whether tax relief is available either immediately or in the future. Because of high land values, even relatively small disposals can trigger off substantial tax liabilities, which justify close attention before a sale occurs, and not afterwards.

It may be objected that a farmer or landowner, who, finding his property increasing in value over the years, sells part, and uses the proceeds to develop the remainder, does not appear to have transformed his land from fixed capital to stock-in-trade. On the face of it, he has merely realised part of his fixed capital, and reinvested the proceeds. In practice, however, the boundary line between the two forms of activity is by no means clear, and much depends upon the precise facts of the case.

The Revenue can be zealous in pursuing the contention that the individual has been carrying on a trade or a business of *dealing in land*, with the surplus taxable under Schedule D Case I (see section **2.1:3**). This contention may be advanced where the land is owned by an individual who is not already carrying on a trade, eg a landowner or even an employee, or where it is owned by an individual who is already trading, for example as a farmer. Moreover, an individual, may be concurrently both an investor in land and a dealer in land, and the burden of proof may be on him to show which land is held as investment and which as stock-in-trade.

Again, it should be noted that, contrary to popular belief, a single transaction is sufficient to create a prima facie case. Finally, the Inspector's initial inquiries are often justifiable on the grounds of other possible forms of tax liability arising on the profit on sale. That profit may be liable to capital gains tax; it may be liable under the anti-avoidance provisions relating to 'artificial transactions' in land (TA 1988 s 776). The inspector's initial inquiries may be directed towards ascertaining which form he should pursue.

5.7:2 Badges of trading

Suppose a farmer knows that he is about to undertake certain transactions in farm land. Will the Revenue contend that he is carrying on a trade or business of buying and selling land? According to what criteria will the Inspector decide a trade has been carried on?

One answer is that whether or not a trade has been carried on is primarily a question of fact. That means that the Commissioners (and therefore the Inspector) are entitled to examine the facts of the matter – all the events which have occurred – to ascertain whether those events amount to carrying on of a trade. There is however a subordinate question of law: whether on the evidence, the conclusion drawn from the facts was justified, but that is not an element over which the farmer has any control (see section **19.2:5**).

Since the facts are so important, the way in which the transactions occur, and in which they are reported to the Inspector, may determine the class of tax liability arising. The precedent cases give guidance as to what facts lead to liability under Schedule D Case I as a 'trader' and what facts do not. Circumstances which give rise to such liability have become known as the 'badges' of trading, and are now readily identifiable, as follows:

(A) MOTIVE

Probably the biggest single factor is that of motive or intention. The question of when the intention to sell was formulated may be central. Purchase of land with a view to early resale may not be absolutely conclusive but it can be a significant admission. It should always be borne in mind that motive can be inferred from the surrounding circumstances, in the absence of the farmer's statement of his intentions, and even in the face of his own statement as to what his intentions were.

In *Cooksey and Bibbey v Rednall* (1949) 30 TC 514 a solicitor and a farmer jointly bought a farm with the aid of mortgage finance. Each had participated in other property ventures which had been admitted to be dealing. Indeed, they had in partnership developed five housing estates. After purchase, the farm was let as an investment, but after some 15 years of ownership it was sold at a substantial profit, which the Inspector and the Commissioners held was a profit from an adventure in the nature of trade.

On appeal to the High Court, the appellants contended they bought the farm for their own occupation and finding they could not work it, let it as an investment. The court held that the General Commissioners' decision was not supported by evidence and the assessment was discharged.

Different features of this case will be referred to later, but the existence of the retention/owner occupier motive should be noted.

(B) CIRCUMSTANCES OF ACQUISITION

Where an asset is acquired involuntarily, ie by gift or inheritance, it is easier to demonstrate that a subsequent sale is not by way of trade. This is bound up with the question of motive since in an involuntary acquisition, the urge to resell cannot then have been formed.

(C) NATURE OF THE ASSET

There are precedent cases involving large quantities of commodities, so large as to establish that the purchaser must have bought with resale in mind. Alternatively, some articles by their nature imply personal enjoyment rather than resale, for example precious chattels. Generally, however, land does not carry any such inescapable inference, since it is susceptible to treatment as an investment, for own occupation, and for profitable resale.

(D) MODIFICATION

What happens to an asset during the period of ownership is relevant. Erection of buildings, or division of land into smaller units, may serve as evidence that an attempt is being made to put the asset into a more marketable condition.

(E) TIME

The interval of time between acquisition and resale may be relevant. Holding for many years is prima facie evidence of investment, whereas immediate resale may be said to preclude the argument that investment was the original intention. However, this factor is not conclusive. It will be noted that in *Cooksey's* case a 15-year period of ownership did not deter the Inspector from claiming liability.

(F) METHOD OF SALE

Organised activity designed to promote a sale is prima facie evidence of trading. Sale to a sitting tenant on the other hand would supply a contrary indication. The circumstances of sale, for example the need to raise cash without delay, may justify a premature sale.

(G) NUMBER OF TRANSACTIONS

A number of separate transactions may suggest a habitual and continuous activity, a general pattern which as a whole constitutes a trade. On the other hand, there is no doubt that the Revenue will contend that a single transaction is capable of constituting a trade if other factors point in that direction.

(H) TRADING INTERESTS IN THE SAME FIELD

This was a big factor in *Cooksey*'s case. Had the appellants not had substantial other property dealing activities, the Revenue might not have raised the issue.

(I) FINANCE

The purchaser may have borrowed money on terms which imply that an immediate resale to repay the loan is an essential element. In *Turner v Last* (1965) 42 TC 517 a tenant farmer purchased 13¾ acres comprising two fields of which he had formerly been tenant, borrowing for the purpose. The inference at this stage might have been that he intended to go on farming the land himself. However, his financial circumstances were such as to imply that he could not own the land indefinitely. In the year of purchase he sold 10¾ acres having obtained planning permission, for a profit of £11,277. He was held to be carrying on a trade and to be taxable accordingly.

It should be noted that an application for planning consent may be regarded as falling under the heading 'Modification' above.

(j) DESTINATION OF PROCEEDS

What is done with the proceeds of sale may be relevant, not so much as a factor in itself, but because it throws light on the original sale motives.

(k) COMPANIES

The profit-seeking motive is more readily capable of being assigned to a limited company, or for that matter a partnership, than to one single individual, since profit-seeking is the *raison d'etre* of corporate existence. The leading case is *St Aubyn Estates Ltd v Strick* (1932) 17 TC 412 in which a limited company was specially formed to take over a landed estate and develop it. Reference was made to the company's memorandum and articles to ascertain what it had power to do, as well as to what it in fact did. It was held that this was not a case of mere realisation of assets but that a trade of property dealing had been carried on.

It must be recognised that none of these factors ((A)–(K) above) is conclusive in itself. On the other hand, the existence of the profit-seeking motive does appear to carry much weight, and some of the other factors fall to be included merely because they help disclose what motives might have been. This may be relevant in a case where it is advantageous to secure liability under Schedule D Case I rather than under capital gains tax. That might be because, for example, trading losses were available to extinguish Schedule D Case I liability; or because Schedule D liability could be attributed to a partnership, so reducing total tax at stake.

'Badges of trading' were enumerated and analysed in detail by the court in the case of *Marson v Morton* [1986] STC 463, to which reference should be made.

In this case, the sale of a parcel of land with planning permission by a potato merchant company was held not to be a trading transaction. This case is also important because of the General Commissioners' finding that it is not open to the court to interfere with the Commissioners' decision, if they had not misdirected themselves in law.

The Revenue will not usually permit a profit or loss on land sales to be included in a computation of farming profits, unless the amounts involved are trivial. The view is that the one is a trade separate and distinct from the other. Nor is a profit on land sales capable of being assessed within Schedule D Case VI as 'other profits or gains' and any attempt to do so should be resisted (see section **5.7:3**).

To some extent, the taxation of capital gains has reduced the Revenue tendency to argue that the trade of dealing in land is being carried on. Before 1965, if the trade could not be established, the gain escaped all taxation, so that the issues were often keenly fought.

However, the difference of treatment as between Schedule D liability and capital gains tax liability may be material. The following factors might be relevant:

(a) the rate of charge;
(b) the year for which liability arises;
(c) ability to offset losses of either class;
(d) basis of computation for capital gains tax, ie indexation, and rebasing as at 1982 value;

(e)   part disposal computation for capital gains tax;
(f)   date of payment of relevant tax under alternative liabilities;
(g)   creation of precedent for future transactions.

5.7:3   Artificial transactions in land

Two different classes of land transactions have so far been mentioned. When a farmer or landowner changes farms, contracts his acreage, or sells to raise cash to buy other land, then, prima facie, he is disposing of a capital asset, so as to become liable to capital gains tax (see chapter 7). Alternatively, if a farmer or landowner embarks on the separate trade or adventure in the nature of trade of buying and selling land, he will become liable to income tax under Schedule D Case I. However, there is a third class of liability, representing a dangerous trap into which it is possible to fall, whilst escaping the two more familiar areas of liability. In TA 1988, the relevant section (TA 1988 s 776) carries the title 'artificial transactions in land', because the law was enacted to counter the avoidance of taxation under Schedule D Case I by artificially varying the form adopted for the transaction. However, the title is misleading, because s 776 may catch transactions where there is little or no element of artificiality, and is wide enough to embrace those where the avoidance element is not present. This was confirmed by the case of *Page v Lowther* [1983] STC 61, in which it was held that the side heading of s 776 'artificial transactions in land', did not restrict the scope of the section.

The section applies in three different sets of circumstances:

(a)   where land or property deriving its value from land is acquired with the sole or main object of realising a gain from disposing of the land;
(b)   where land is held as trading stock;
(c)   where land is developed with the sole or main object of realising a gain from disposing of the developed land (TA 1988 s 776(2)).

It is not easy to summarise these circumstances in a sentence. The best that can be done is to say that the profits caught are the product of speculative buys; land held as stock; and development schemes. Each circumstance needs to be considered in turn and this is done under heads (a)–(c) below.

(A)   LAND OR PROPERTY DERIVING ITS VALUE FROM LAND, ACQUIRED WITH THE SOLE OR MAIN OBJECT OF REALISING A GAIN FROM DISPOSAL

The sole or main object of realising a gain should be the object at the time of acquisition (*Sugarwhite v Budd* [1988] STC 533 CA).

In this category 'land' includes 'buildings'. 'Property' deriving its value from land includes shares in a company owning land, interests in partnerships or under trusts. So a typical transaction caught under this sub-category might be the purchase of shares in say, a farming company, followed by a sale by the company of its land to realise a gain which, prima facie, was of a capital nature. The ambit of TA 1988 s 776 is repeatedly widened to bring in possible alternative contrivances, for example the use of equitable interests in land; benefits of options; rights of control; routing transactions through third parties etc. A series of separate transactions may be looked at together for the purposes of construing s 776.

There is one exception from the definition of land; the sole or main residence of the taxpayer which would be exempt from capital gains tax (TA 1988 s 776(9)).

(B) TRADING STOCK

By definition, the sale of land held as trading stock would be subject to income tax (or corporation tax) as part of the profits of a trade, so it is difficult to see why this sub-category should be needed. However, it would apply to deal with any exceptional circumstances where the profits from the sale of land would not be chargeable because, for example, the relevant trade had ceased.

(C) DEVELOPMENT WITH SOLE OR MAIN OBJECT OF REALISING A GAIN FROM DISPOSING OF DEVELOPED LAND

It is important to recognise the distinction between this sub-category and the first badge of trading described in section **5.7:2**. For trading to be established, the Inspector must be able to show that the prospect of resale at a profit was in mind at the time of acquisition of the land. That is not a prerequisite under s 776, and all that is needed to establish liability is the prospect of gain at the time development was undertaken. From the standpoint of the farmer or landowner, a development, for example conversion of a building from one use to another, is safe only if the new use is in connection with the trade of farming or the activity of landownership. If a building be converted for use as a workshop etc, there might be liability under this head. That is particularly relevant at the time of writing, when there is an official programme urging the conversion of disused farm buildings to establish rural crafts and industries.

In all the three categories described, there are provisions designed to take account of the use of indirect methods (TA 1988 s 776(4), (12)), to transfer or transmit rights in property, and to enhance or diminish its value. Gifts and transfers for nominal consideration, the use of trusts, and the introduction of unconnected third parties to act as conduits are also envisaged. For example, a taxpayer, who was able to ensure that an opportunity to make a gain was transferred to two companies was held to be liable in substitution for the companies (*Yuill v Wilson* [1980] STC 460).

Where a gain is taxable under s 776, it is treated as income falling under Schedule D Case VI (TA 1988 s 776(3)). This is a classification likely to create a higher tax bill than either capital gains tax, or as a trading profit, since liability will be at income tax rates. The statute gives little guidance as to how the gain is to be computed. The method is to be 'just and reasonable' under the circumstances, allowing expenses attributable to the land disposed of. Where a freehold is acquired and a reversion retained on disposal of a lease, account may be taken of the way in which trading profits would be calculated in such circumstances. There is no reference to losses under the section being deductible, but it is reasonable to suppose that if two or more transactions occurred, and one was profitable and one was not, the Revenue would claim tax only on the net amount. On the other hand, there is little prospect of 'losses' calculated under the rules of the section being deductible against any other classes of income.

Where the prospective liability falls under (a) or (c) above, the taxpayer under threat of liability may make application to the Revenue for a clearance certificate, inviting the Inspector to notify him as to whether or not liability arises (in the Inspector's view) under the section (TA 1988 s 776(11)). Such an application may be made before or after the relevant transaction, but there is little point – and there may be some disadvantages – in making one after irreversible events have occurred. Providing full and accurate details of the proposed transaction are given, the Inspector's decision binds the Revenue, and the Inspector cannot change his mind and claim liability. On the other hand, the Inspector's ruling is not conclusive, and it is open to the taxpayer to challenge an assessment, if necessary on appeal to the Commissioners.

It must be frankly recognised that there are tactical disadvantages in making a clearance application under this section. The need for a 'full and accurate disclosure of facts and considerations relating thereto which are material . . .' is bound to draw the attention of the Revenue to the transaction, and the response is likely to be to refuse a clearance, and to look again at the problem when the accounts and relevant tax returns are submitted. When that is the outcome, the net effect will have been to create a contentious issue, perhaps quite gratuitously.

Clearly, those who embark on the complex transactions envisaged in s 776, should be capable of recognising the danger it represents. The more vulnerable class of farmer or landowner is he who sells a piece of land, confident his liability will be confined to capital gains tax and/or extinguished by roll-over relief. The unexpected claim under s 776 can destroy the whole economic purpose of such a sale, if only some 60% of the proceeds are left intact for reinvestment.

Chapter 6

Partnerships and companies

6.1 FARMING PARTNERSHIPS

6.1:1 What is a farm partnership?

The Northfield Report (Report of the Committee of Inquiry into the Acquisition or Occupancy of Agricultural Land (Cmnd 7599) paras 120–126) included useful analysis of different types of farming partnerships; the circumstances in which partnerships are commonly used; and a prediction that use of them would increase in future. The classification adopted in the Report is open to challenge but will serve as an introduction to more technical aspects. Three of four identifiable types are catalogued:

Type A A farmer and sole trader is joined in the business enterprise by his son, who, as he grows up, plays an increasing management role. He becomes a partner to reflect this, and ultimately takes over the business at the end of his father's career.

Type A.1 A spouse may become a working partner during her husband's lifetime, because she is involved in the day-to-day running of the business – often on the book-keeping or correspondence side. Alternatively, she may become a partner after her husband's death, with her son(s) or other beneficiaries. That would be because of her experience of running the farm and/or to protect her inheritance under her late husband's will.

Clearly, there are infinite variations on these two family themes.

Type B In this type of situation, the owner of land who does not wish to farm it himself, enters into partnership with an individual, who may be described as a working farmer, and who supplies working capital (other than land and buildings) and labour. Both parties receive a share of profits, but the latter may also receive a salary or management fees.

The arrangement is common where the parties might have entered into a landlord/tenant relationship but one or both did not wish to do so. The disinclination may have been due to taxation considerations, or to a desire to avoid constraints imposed by landlord and tenant laws, or to other reasons. It is often adopted where land is owned by a financial institution, for example, an insurance company, which may wish to avoid the diminution of value which would occur if its lands owned with vacant possession became subject to a tenancy.

Type C Alternatively, there is a 'management' partnership. This implies that the landowner-partner provides the seed, fertilisers and sprays, that is items relating to his land; and the other partner supplies machinery and labour. Profits are divided in accordance with a pre-arranged formula. It appears that this is a common formula in arable farming but is probably more specialised than Types A and B.

The popularity of partnerships is obvious, but more recently has been declining, and is being replaced by contractual arrangements, as described in Chapter 14.

Northfield estimated that over half of all farming income was enjoyed by partnerships in 1975–76, and that only a 'small proportion' of holdings were farmed by companies. Taxation factors have been the biggest single influence, will probably continue as such on the general assumption that a partnership enables a farmer to spread income around members of his family, so that more personal reliefs will be available than if the same profit remained receivable by one taxpayer.

It is wrong to consider tax factors in isolation. There are economic advantages to be derived from two or more individuals combining capital and labour skills, and in turn these advantages are matched by certain risks. There are also general legal considerations and some understanding of what rights and obligations are created by partnerships is needed, so that the tax factors can be seen in perspective.

The Partnership Act 1890 provides the classic definition of partnership: the relationship which subsists between persons carrying on a business in common with a view to profit (PA 1890 s 1(1)). Companies are not partnerships and the mere joint ownership of land or other property is not in itself sufficient to create the partnership relationship. In England, a partnership is not a legal person separate and distinct from the individual members of it, although this is so in Scotland (*Re Sawers, ex p Blain* (1879) 12 ChD 522).

The maximum number of individual partners allowed is 20 with exception for professional firms. Anyone can be a partner, including a minor (*Lovell and Christmas v Beauchamp* [1894] AC 607), a person of unsound mind (*Imperial Loan Co Ltd v Stone* [1892] 1 QB 599), and a limited company. A partnership is possible between two or more limited companies to farm together the land owned by them.

Partnership law provides that each partner is an agent of the partnership ('the firm') and of each of the other partners. The act of each partner can therefore bind the firm and the other partners (PA 1890 s 5). This rule is excluded only where the person acting does so without authority in the particular matter *and* the person with whom he is dealing either knows he has no authority, or does not know or believe him to be a partner. This is an exceptional combination of circumstances.

A firm is not bound where a partner pledges its credit for his own private purposes, unless he has been specially authorised to do so. Also a partnership may agree to restrict the power of a partner to bind the firm, but to be effective, notice of such a restriction of power must have been received by the person with whom the partner is dealing in a contravention of the restriction.

In consequence, partners in a firm have a collective responsibility for the contracts (PA 1890 s 9) and torts (PA 1890 s 10) (civil wrongs) of the other partners. Each partner is jointly liable for partnership debts incurred whilst a partner. A creditor can therefore proceed against a substantial partner rather than a man of straw, and he can sue two or more partners jointly in a single action, and enforce judgment against the one of substance. The partner who is obliged to meet debts can seek contribution from the others, but his chances of recovery will depend on the ability of the others to pay. To some extent this risk is capable of being covered by insurance, but it should be borne in mind, particularly when establishing a partnership with a minor or inexperienced partner, at whose mercy the other partners may ultimately find themselves.

In such circumstances, consideration should be given to a limited partnership (Limited Partnerships Act 1907; Limited Partnerships Rules 1907). Briefly, a limited partnership can include a limited partner whose liability is limited to the capital he has contributed, and who does not take part in the management of the partnership business. If he does, he is treated as a general partner, whose position is similar to that of a partner in an ordinary partnership.

It is worth noting that one taxation disadvantage of a limited partnership is that the limited partner's share of profit is not treated as earned income. This disadvantage and the rigid rules of limited partnerships can be avoided by using a limited company as the partner, to replace the limited partner. Although there will be no limit to the company's liability as a partner, each shareholder of the company will become liable only to the extent of his issued share capital.

6.1:2   The partnership agreement

Partnerships are regulated by an agreement entered into by the partners. This should take the form of a deed drafted by a solicitor. Deeds normally specify the name of the firm; state the partnership capital; regulate the shares of profits and losses; provide for keeping accounts; describe the duties of the respective partners; envisage the events of retirement, death, dissolution, arbitration, expulsion etc. The Inspector of Taxes may ask for sight of the partnership deed as confirmation of existence of the partnership, but a deed is not essential. A partnership depends upon the intention of the parties, and a deed will be ineffective if not acted upon. On the other hand, individuals may be held to be trading in partnership, even though no formal agreement exists, and although they never consciously intended the partnership relationship. Written notes or correspondence may provide evidence one way or another.

A partnership agreement takes effect for tax purposes as from the date of execution, and cannot be used to secure a 'back-dating' (*Waddington v O'Callaghan* (1931) 16 TC 187). On the other hand, a partnership may have existed before execution of a deed, in which case the deed will operate to confirm existence of the partnership. Since the selection of operative dates is a factor in tax planning, this rule can be relevant.

Whether a partnership does or does not exist is a question involving both fact and law. The intentions of the partners will be a question of fact, determinable in accordance with evidence. But the Partnership Act 1890 does contain rules for determining whether a partnership exists. Similarly, whether a partnership has ceased to exist is probably also a mixed question. If partners cease to conduct themselves as such, for example completely vacate a farm, sell off the stock etc, they will be treated as ceasing to trade in partnership. The element of trading is essential, and a partnership which simply owns assets, or manages investments, is not conceivable.

It is possible for individuals to farm together without constituting themselves as partners. They would contract together on, for example, an annual basis, so as to determine respective responsibilities. Each individual in a joint venture would remain a sole trader, and what follows would not apply (*G Hall & Son v Platt* (1954) 35 TC 440). But where a partnership is constituted, there are special taxation considerations originally devised for income tax, but also affecting all capital taxes. The possible effects of these rules need to be carefully studied before adopting the partnership structure.

6.1:3   Partnership accounts

The accounts of a farming business owned by a partnership will be prepared on similar lines to those of the accounts of a sole trader, but will include additional features designed to reflect the separate interests of the partners, and the terms of the agreement amongst them as enshrined in the partnership deed. In particular:

(a) Separate capital and drawing accounts will be maintained for each partner.
(b) At the end of each accounting period, the trading profit or loss will be divided in accordance with the partnership agreement, and the respective share of each partner credited (or debited in the event of a loss) to his capital account.
(c) If a partner is entitled to salary, the Profit and Loss Account will be debited and capital (or drawings) account credited.
(d) If interest is payable on partners' capital, the Profit and Loss Account will be debited and capital account credited. Conversely, interest may be chargeable on overdrawn capital when the entries will be reversed.
(e) The partners may jointly own land and buildings, in which case the land will appear amongst assets in the Balance Sheet.
(f) Alternatively, the land may be owned by one, more than one, or all the partners and let to the partnership on a tenancy. It would not then become a partnership asset and would not appear on the face of the accounts.

Each of these different sets of arrangements has different taxation consequences.

6.1:4 Partnership income tax

Although a partnership is not a separate legal person, it is partly treated as one for taxation purposes. The rule is that where a trade is carried on jointly by two or more persons tax on the profits of the trade must be computed jointly, and a joint assessment made in the partnership name (TA 1988 s 111). The calculation of the total tax will therefore depend on:

(a) the total profits for the accounting period; and
(b) the terms of allocation of the profits for the year of assessment of which the profits constitute statutory income; and
(c) the personal reliefs and rates of charge for the year of assessment of each of the partners as applied to his allocated profit share for that year.

Example

Suppose that the farming profit at Blackacre Farm was £21,000 for the year to 5 April 1993. During that period, Mr Black was entitled to two-thirds of the profit and his son Jet to one-third. However, on 6 April 1993, Mr Black handed over more responsibility to Jet, and it was agreed they would henceforth share the profits equally.

Then the liability of the year of assessment 1993–94 on the preceding year basis will be £21,000 allocatable £10,500 to Mr Black and £10,500 to Jet, because that was the sharing arrangement for that year. The accounts, on the other hand, will show an allocation of £14,000 and £7,000, because that will have been the allocation for the period to 5 April 1993. This discrepancy between accounts and tax assessment can be a source of confusion.

Losses are apportioned in the same way as profits. A 'salary' or partners' interest on capital is not for tax purposes treated in accordance with the nomenclature but as part of the overall profit-sharing arrangement. Subject to the terms of the partnership deed, these items will enter into the allocation of profits amongst the partners.

Example

Assuming the Blackacre Farm profit of £21,000 as above, then in the year 1993–94, Mr Black is entitled to interest on capital of £2,000, and Jet to a salary of £5,000 before the residue of profits are shared. Then the calculation will be as follows:

	Firm	Black	Jet
	£	£	£
Total	21,000		
Less interest	2,000	2,000	
	19,000		
Less salary	5,000		5,000
	14,000		
Less equal shares	14,000	7,000	7,000
Total allocation	£21,000	£9,000	£12,000

It is the obligation of the precedent acting partner to make and deliver a return of income on behalf of all the partners (TMA 1970 s 9). The precedent acting partner is the first named in any agreement, or in the usual name of the firm. Individual tax returns showing the partnership profit share are also required from the partners. Partnership income tax is a debt of the firm, that is all the partners at the time the debt was incurred. Sleeping partners (those inactive in the business) nevertheless remain jointly liable for all the partnership tax.

A salaried partner, if truly a partner under the agreement and not a mere employee, is in a similar position. Whether an individual is or is not a partner is a question of fact. The Inspector will seek to ascertain whether that individual exercises the rights and performs the obligations of a partner; whether he has right of access to the firm's books and power to operate the firm's bank accounts; whether he has authority to buy and sell (at the market) in the firm's name, and generally to pledge the firm's credit. Above all, it is evidence of partnership that an individual is holding himself out to creditors and customers that he is a partner.

It is not uncommon for the Inspector to remain sceptical as to the existence of a partnership, particularly where a wife or children are involved. It is therefore important to ensure that the appropriate changes in the bank account etc are made at the right time to be effective.

6.1:5   Change of partners

Where there is a change in the persons carrying on a trade, that trade is treated for income tax purposes as having been permanently discontinued and a new trade set up (TA 1988 s 113). This will apply when a farmer sets up a partnership in the first place; when a new partner is taken in or an old partner retires; or when a partner dies, irrespective of whether he is replaced.

Example

Mr Black, Mrs Black and their son Jet are trading under the style of 'Blackacre Farm', and Mr Black dies on 1 January 1988. Mrs Black and Jet continue to farm at Blackacre. Then the business will be treated as having ceased during 1987–88, which will be the last year of trading of the old business, and the profits will be based on the current period 6 April 1987 to 31 December 1987. The first assessment for the new business for the year 1987–88 will be based on the period 1 January 1988 to 5 April 1988.

The effect of discontinuance may be to switch the basis period for the final, penultimate and ante-penultimate years of assessment to the current year basis, which in combination with the current year basis for the first years of the commencing business may create more liability than if the preceding year basis had applied throughout. This result can be avoided by an election under TA 1988 s 113. All the persons engaged before and after the change may by notice in writing elect that discontinuance treatment shall not apply. The notice must be signed by all including the personal representatives of a deceased partner, and must be sent to the Inspector within two years of the date of change. This time limit is strictly observed but in November 1992 the Financial Secretary to the Treasury indicated certain circumstances in which the Inland Revenue would accept late elections. These were:

(a) where there has been some relevant and uncorrected error on the part of the Inland Revenue which has had the effect of misleading the partners or their agent about whether the requirements of the law had been met; or
(b) at the crucial time one of the required signatories or the agent was not available for unforeseeable reasons, eg illness; or
(c) there was some other difficulty about obtaining all the required signatures and the Revenue had been notified before the time limit expired that each of the signatories had individually decided to make an election and had been given reasons why the election could not be made within the time limit.

Oversight or negligence by a partner or agent or a deliberate decision to delay the election because its effect on tax liabilities was not clear by the expiration of the time limit were not, it was stated, reasons for admitting late elections.

Careful examination of the results for the relevant periods and the forecast results for periods still to come is essential before making an election for continuance. An election should be advantageous in times of rising profits, and disadvantageous when profits are falling. It is also important to weigh the effects on partners joining or leaving against those on partners who are continuing throughout.

Where notice is given early, it can be revoked before the expiry of the two-year period. This is by concession.

Where there is a change, there are special rules providing for apportionment of the tax between the partners respectively carrying on the business before and after the change. There are also rules to meet the situation of a second change, to which the cessation rules apply within two years of a first change. Then the effect of the cessation is to override the election for continuation, if appropriate.

A change in the profit-sharing basis, or a change of trustees, does not in itself constitute a cessation. Nor does the admission or retirement of a corporate partner. Changes were made in the Finance Act 1985 to counter the advantages of what were considered to be artificial discontinuances of partnerships. These rules apply to changes of partnership after 19 March 1985. The treatment of the old partnership remains the same. However, in the new partnership the preceding year basis does not apply for the first three years of assessment. After that, the preceding year basis begins to operate, but the partnership may elect for the current year basis for another two years.

It is important to remember that this rule applies only where a continuation election could have been made and has not been made. It has no application where there is no capacity to make a continuation election, because no one person has been engaged in the trade both before and after the change. That is to say, there is no one individual who was a member of the old partnership and is a member of the new one.

This book does not examine in detail the taxation of company partnerships (see TA 1988 s 114), since this is not an ownership framework which has been used by farmers or landowners. Since to date there is little use of companies, it seems unlikely that company partnerships (a more sophisticated mechanism) will become popular; nor do there seem to be any particular advantages to be derived from them. However, where a member of a partnership is a company, the company is liable to corporation tax, calculated as if its profit share was derived from carrying on a separate business. Similarly, the share allocable to the individual partner or partners becomes liable to income tax as if that were a separate trade. Joining or leaving a partnership is not in itself an event which brings to an end a company's accounting period.

6.1:6   Partnership losses

The general rules as to the calculation and application of losses as described in section **2.6** apply to farm partnerships. The adjusted loss is divided amongst the partners according to the loss sharing basis (if any) set out in the partnership agreement. However, salaries and interest on capital are both taken into account. If the effect of doing so is to produce a profit for one partner and a loss for others, the profit is eliminated by scaling down the losses.

Example

Suppose an adjusted loss be £20,000, allocable as follows:

		Black	Mrs Black	Jet	Total
	£	£	£	£	£
Salaries		15,000	10,000	5,000	30,000
Interest		10,000	15,000	25,000	50,000
Loss	(20,000)				
Add: Salaries	(30,000)				
Interest	(50,000)				
Total	(100,000)	(20,000)	(30,000)	(50,000)	(100,000)
		5,000	(5,000)	(20,000)	(20,000)
Scaled down			5/25	20/25	
Share of loss		nil	(4,000)	(16,000)	

The share of loss created is personal to a partner, and can be used as if it were the loss created by sole trading, and cannot be transferred to other partners. This can be disadvantageous if losses are allocated to a partner without other income, instead of to a partner with investment income, which would have otherwise been relieved by application of farming losses. Where losses have arisen, additional care is needed in deciding whether to make an election for the continuing basis of assessment as described in section **6.1:5**. The combination of the two sets of calculations: the partnership loss allocation; and the different bases of assessment, can produce a whole range of alternative results.

In particular, where a change is treated as a permanent discontinuance, unrelieved losses (and capital allowances applied to augment losses) can still be carried forward to the new partnership by a continuing partner.

6.2 FAMILY FARMING COMPANIES

Family companies are, by comparison with partnerships, relatively unpopular as farming occupation media despite some commercial advantages. The Inland Revenue estimated the number of farming companies to be 14,000 in 1982, compared with 220,000 self-employed individuals and partnerships. These and other relevant statistics are to be found in House of Lords Select Committee to the European Community; State Aids to Agriculture (Session 1981/82, 7th Report) (HMSO). There are several trends which suggest that company farming may increase: first, the increasing need for capital from outside sources to supplement the traditional self-financing base. Secondly, there has been some easing of corporate tax rules and rates, which have proved a deterrent; and finally, because of the law securing family succession to tenancies, landlord and tenant relationships may be replaced by corporate structures in which the parties who would formerly have been landlord and tenant strike a different bargain and become co-shareholders and co-directors. There is little evidence of change to date.

Companies are classifiable into public and private; limited and unlimited (Companies Act 1985 s 1). This section examines the tax regime applicable to private limited companies, which are legal persons separate and distinct from the owners ('shareholders'), who are liable for the company's debts only to the extent of their shareholding. The shareholder owns shares in the company; the company owns the business, and income and capital taxes are chargeable accordingly. One company can own shares in another, so creating an ownership chain, which can be long and intricate.

Limitation of liability reduces the risk of speculative ventures. At least two shareholders are needed, but share capital can vary widely in amount and in the rights and obligations attaching.

The objects of the company and the rights and obligations of the various parties are set out in two formal documents, which together constitute the birth certificate of a company: the Memorandum (Companies Act 1985 s 2) and the Articles of Association (Companies Act 1985 s 7). Strictly, the birth certificate is the Certificate of Incorporation issued by the Registrar of Companies at whose offices, company Memoranda, Articles of Association, and Annual Accounts are available for public inspection. Each company must have its own registered office, not necessarily at the farm, for it is common practice to use an accountant's or solicitor's office address.

Management of the farm will be carried on by the directors of the company, who will be paid salary or fees for their services, in place of the profit share they would have enjoyed as partners. An individual may be both a shareholder and a director, or one without the other. If all the company's profit is paid out to directors as remuneration, the company will have no tax liabilities. Companies are liable to corporation tax, and the individual directors to income tax, and two sets of liabilities are computed separately.

A company can become a tenant of a farm, although the tenancy may be granted to it by individual owners who are also its shareholders. As a company may continue indefinitely, the tenancy will continue also, so that owners will be reluctant to grant farm tenancies to companies owned by strangers. Companies are brought to an end by a formal process of liquidation or winding up, which may be voluntary on the part of the shareholders; or compulsory, that is imposed on them by creditors. After payment of debts, any surplus is returned to the shareholders, and tax liabilities follow this event.

Whether or not incorporation is a practicable step depends upon the facts of a case, but generally, the larger the farm, the more helpful it is likely to be. It is possible to summarise non-fiscal advantages and disadvantages as follows:

ADVANTAGES

(a) Limitation of liability; but in practice this is often eroded, in that bankers can ask for shareholders'/directors' personal guarantees of a company overdraft.

(b) The ability to raise additional finance because of the capacity to give a floating charge over company assets. Neither an individual nor a partnership has this capacity. The effect is to pledge company assets in support of borrowings, even though those assets may be changing in the course of farming operations, eg livestock.

(c) The separation of one farm from another, and segregation of a farming business and its assets from other assets, for example a portfolio of personal investments, or a newly acquired business in another more speculative industry.

(d) The ability to bring in individuals (eg tenants, children or employees) as small co-shareholders, where their participation in a partnership would be impracticable.

(e) The ability to create more beneficial pension schemes for directors. The contribution made by the company can be wholly deductible for corporation tax.

DISADVANTAGES

(a) Loss of flexibility, due to the need to maintain statutory records of meetings and decisions, and comply with regulations often designed to protect investors in public companies, and sometimes irrelevant to family companies.

(b) Loss of privacy, in that accounts and returns must be filed with the Company Registrar, where they may be inspected by customers, creditors and competitors.

(c) Certain additional legal and accounting costs, including capital duty payable on formation and certain subsequent increases in share capital.

(d) Prohibition of loans to directors, capable of making access to the company's funds difficult.

(e) The cessation of business on creation of a company causes technical redundancy of employees, but this can be overcome by giving notice and offering terms identical to those of the existing employment.

The above lists of advantages and disadvantages are clearly not exhaustive. The respective taxation factors are examined at section **15.6**.

6.3 CORPORATION TAX: SUMMARY OF SYSTEM

Since 1965, companies have been taxed under a separate regime: corporation tax,[1] the salient features of which are as follows:

(a) Companies pay corporation tax at a flat rate on all profits whether or not distributed to shareholders. The rates have been and are to be as follows:

Year ending 1 April	89	90	91	92	93	94
'Financial Year' commencing 1 April	88	89	90	91	92	93

Corporation Tax Rate	35%	35%	34%	33%	33%	33%
Small Companies' Rate	25%	25%	25%	25%	25%	25%
Small Companies' Relief Fraction	1/40	1/40	1/40	1/40	1/50	1/50

(b) The small companies' rate is applicable to companies with profits not exceeding £250,000. Where a company's profits exceed £250,000 but do not exceed £1,250,000, the corporation tax chargeable on its income is reduced by the fraction (shown above) of the difference between the company's profits and £1,250,000. The effect is to produce a rate scale tapering from 25% to the corporation tax rate.

(c) Apart from certain special rules, profits are calculated in accordance with the principles used for income tax.

(d) When a company makes distributions (pays dividends) to its shareholders, it becomes liable to advance corporation tax on the dividend. Advance corporation tax is calculated as a fraction of the dividend, and that fraction is currently 1/3rd so that part of the corporation tax paid by the company is imputed to the shareholders (see Introduction for the changes enacted in FA 1993). Shareholders in companies paying at the small company rate secure full imputation of corporation tax to their dividends.

(e) Advance corporation tax for an accounting period can be offset against a company's corporation tax on its profits ('mainstream corporation tax') for that period. Excesses of advance corporation tax over mainstream corporation tax are capable of being carried backwards to former periods, or carried forwards in time to future periods, subject to detailed rules.

(f) Shareholders receiving dividends are entitled to a credit for advance corporation tax, which can be offset against their personal tax liabilities. In FA 1993, the value of the tax credit was reduced from 25% to 20%. However, basic rate taxpayers have no additional tax to pay. Higher rate taxpayers pay 5% more for 1993–94, and those entitled to repayment will be repaid 5% less.

(g) Corporation tax is due and payable nine months after the end of the relevant accounting period. For example, if the accounting years ends 31 March, tax on the profits of that period is payable on the following 1 January (see *Simon's Taxes* D2. 111).

(h) Directors' salaries and fees are deductible in computing the paying companies' corporation tax. Thus directors who are also shareholders have a choice as to whether to pay salaries to themselves, so that tax is chargeable at their personal rates; or not to pay salaries, so that the corresponding fraction of profit remains chargeable to corporation tax. Employers' National Insurance Contribution is, of course, payable on salaries.

(i)   Companies are chargeable to corporation tax on capital gains at the corporate rate appropriate to the company. With effect from 17 March 1987, the lower rate for corporate gains has been cancelled. Capital gains are henceforth treated as corporate income, and ACT can accordingly be offset against corporate gains.

(j)   Companies are entitled to relief for trading losses, which may be allowed against profits or capital gains of current periods, or carried forward or backwards in time for three years. However, companies' losses are not capable of being relieved against shareholders' or directors' incomes, save in special cases.

(k)   A company is close when it is controlled by its directors or five or fewer shareholders. 'Control' is exercised by the voting power of a shareholder's shares.

(l)   At one time, close companies were obliged to distribute fixed proportions of profit as dividends, unless business requirements made distribution prejudicial. This process was known as income apportionment or shortfall, and was abolished in FA 1979. Close investment holding companies do not qualify for the 'small companies' corporation tax rate, and there are powers to restrict credit for advance corporation tax where dividends have been paid disproportionately to secure reliefs (TA 1988 ss 231(3A) and 231(3B)).

(m)   Loans to shareholders in close companies are subject to tax upon the amount of the loan grossed up for advance corporation tax. When the loan is wholly or partly repaid, the company may claim a corresponding tax repayment.

(n)   There are detailed rules which make taxable value passing out of a company into the hands of shareholders. Such deemed distributions include company assets transferred to shareholders at less than their full market value; interest or other consideration for the use of money; payments for restrictive covenants.

(o)   When a company is liquidated, the distributions by the liquidator to shareholders are liable to capital gains taxation. Other aspects of company taxation are discussed in section **15.6**.

---

1 For a detailed survey, see *Simon's Taxes*, Division D2.

Chapter 7

Capital gains and losses

7.1 GENERAL SCOPE OF CAPITAL GAINS TAX

7.1:1 Introduction

The current version of capital gains tax was first enacted in 1965, and represents a second attempt to tax profits escaping the income tax net. Tax is charged upon capital gains arising upon the 'disposal' of an asset (TCGA 1992 s 1). A gain is calculated by comparing the historic cost or value of the asset on acquisition plus capital expenditure during the period of ownership as reflected in the asset sold, with the money or money's worth receivable upon disposal. This general rule has been modified by rebasing: the substitution of market value on a specific date for historic cost.

If disposal proceeds exceed historic cost or the rebased value as applicable, there is a taxable gain.

Capital expenditure includes amounts spent in improving or augmenting the asset after it has been acquired, but not items deductible for income tax (TCGA 1992 s 39). 'Disposal' has a wider meaning than sale, because it includes part disposals, and capital sums received on loss or destruction of an asset, for example insurance or other forms of compensation receivable when property has been destroyed (TCGA 1992 s 22). If cost, or the rebased value as applicable, exceeds the disposal proceeds that creates a loss relievable against other gains (TCGA 1992 s 16).

Capital gains tax presents problems to farmers and landowners for a variety of reasons. Agricultural land tends to be held for long periods of time, during the whole of the farming career, throughout life, and across the generations. Continually rising prices under inflation (see section **7.2:2**) make the historic cost basis seem trivial in relation to current values, so creating accrued capital gains tax liabilities which are a real deterrent to realisation. When current value is say, £2,000 per acre, and historic cost say, £20 per acre, which is not unusual, the contingent capital gains tax can be a third of the realisation proceeds. Natural reluctance to see values so eroded creates a lock-in effect, even when realisations are needed to repay or reduce financing obligations.

Another problem of special application to farmers and landowners arises because disposals by way of gifts, or otherwise than at 'arm's length' bargains, are treated as sales at market value as at the date of the gift (TCGA 1992 s 17). This general rule is subject to two qualifications: first, substitution of market value for acquisition cost cannot operate to increase the donee's acquisition cost above the consideration paid, unless there is a corresponding increase included in computing the chargeable gain or allowable loss of the donor, that is the person making the disposal. This is an anti-avoidance provision (FA 1981 s 86). Secondly, the harshness of the market value rule, which produced a tax bill without any cash coming in to pay it, has been modified by hold-over relief for gifts. Until the Finance Act 1989, this relief was generous in scope, but since has become limited, causing renewed planning problems (see section **7.5**).

7.1:2 Special structure

Capital gains tax has a special structure which is unlike that of any other tax. It is a tax separate from income tax, although it utilises all the machinery of income tax as regards returns of income; assessments; appeals; and collection. Originally capital gains tax was chargeable at a flat 30% rate, but from 1988–89 onwards capital gains are taxed at income tax rates that is, at present, either 25% or 40%. With effect from 1992–93, the lower rate of income tax, 25%, is applied to net chargeable gains to the extent that taxable income is inadequate to absorb the lower rate band. Net chargeable gains of any tax payer are treated as the top slice of his income in computing the capital gains tax liability. Despite all this, the tax remains a separate one with its own exemptions. There is an annual exemption for individuals of £5,500 for 1991–92 index linked. The corresponding amount for trustees is £2,500.

Capital gains tax is not chargeable on death, and the beneficiary under a deceased person's estate acquires inherited assets at their market values as at the date of death. Certain special classes of gains are statutorily exempt; eg those on private motor vehicles (TCGA 1992 s 263), savings certificates (TCGA 1992 s 121), growing timber (TCGA 1992 ss 37, 250), life policies (TCGA 1992 s 204), principal private residences (TCGA 1992 s 222), assets given for public benefit (TCGA 1992 ss 256–258), business assets when replaced in appropriate circumstances (TCGA 1992 ss 152–158), and transfers of business assets on retirement (TCGA 1992 s 163). No liability arises on gifts between spouses (TCGA 1992 s 58). A full list of reliefs and exemptions is given in section **7.2**.

7.1:3   Part disposal

For capital gains tax, the part disposal of an asset (where part is disposed of and part retained) is itself a chargeable event. There is a series of special rules for calculating gains on part disposals, based upon the principle of deducting from the sale proceeds the proportion of costs which the value of the part sold bears, at the time of disposal, to the value of the whole asset.

Thus the original whole cost falls to be apportioned and the deductible proportion is calculated as follows:

$$\frac{\text{Proceeds of part disposal}}{\text{Proceeds of part disposal} + \text{market value of part retained}} \times \text{cost}$$

Example

Suppose Blackacre, a farm of 300 acres originally cost £300,000.
In 1987 Mr Black sells 60 acres for £120,000, and at that date the value of the remaining 240 acres is £480,000. Then the chargeable capital gain is calculated as follows:

Sale proceeds	£120,000
To calculate deductible proportion:	
$\dfrac{120,000}{120,000 + 480,000} = \dfrac{120,000 \times 300,000}{600,000} =$	£ 60,000
Capital gain	£ 60,000

The residue of unallowed cost remains available for deduction against future sales.

This main rule is varied in particular cases. A special provision is applicable where there is a small part disposal of land.

The part disposal rule described above is not used, and instead the disposal proceeds are simply deducted from the historic base cost of the whole asset, so reducing the amount available to be deducted on future sales. This is an attractive alternative, since the effect is to delay liability, and it should therefore be borne in mind when arranging relatively small sales.

In order to secure this treatment two tests need to be satisfied:

(a) the land sold must not exceed 20% of the market value of the total holding (TCGA 1992 s 242); and
(b) the consideration receivable must not exceed £20,000 in a tax year (TCGA 1992 s 242).

It is sometimes practicable to spread a small sale over more than one year to satisfy these limits.

7.1:4 Farming transactions

Some familiar transactions can be free of capital gains tax provided care is taken. The grant of a tenancy over land at an annual rental without a premium should not normally give rise to capital gains tax liability. The creation of a business partnership involving the transfer of part of the net asset value of a farming business need not create any substantial capital gains tax liability since trading stocks effectively transferred will not be subject to capital gains tax. Nor should there be liability on business plant and machinery, the value of which would normally have fallen below the original cost. Nor does a farm sale price normally include an amount for goodwill, an asset on which capital gains tax would be chargeable.

As regards milk and other quotas see section **2.4** which explains the treatment for capital gains tax.

This section assumes familiarity with the general outline of capital gains taxation and concentrates upon the incidence of the tax and the reliefs from it relevant to farmers and landowners (for a general survey, see *Simon's Taxes*, Division C2).

7.2 RELIEFS AND EXEMPTIONS

Farmers and landowners should bear in mind the very wide range of capital gains tax exemptions and reliefs accorded to taxpayers generally. A checklist of these follows, showing in each case a reference to the statute where the law can be found, and references to the standard works, wherein further research can be pursued.

Capital gains tax reliefs and exemptions are varied in scope and purpose. In this section, three different classes have been distinguished: reliefs available to farmers in their capacity as owners of business assets; other reliefs and exemptions based upon the nature of the persons engaged in the transaction; and general reliefs. This classification should help those who have performed or who are contemplating a transaction to identify relevant features of it, which might justify relief.

7.2:1   Checklist of reliefs and exemptions

Section	Relief	*Textual reference*
Reliefs available to farmers as owners of business property etc		
TCGA 1992 s 163 and TCGA 1992 s 275 Sch 11 para 18	Disposal of family business on retirement	7.6
ss 152–158	Replacement of business assets	7.4
s 165	Gifts of business assets	7.5
s 242	Small part disposals of land	7.1
s 249	Grants on giving up agricultural land	2.4
s 250	Woodlands	7.5:5
TCGA 1992 ss 247, 248	Relief on compulsory purchase	7.4:2
General reliefs		
TCGA 1992 s 35 & Sch 4	Calculation of indexation allowance	7.2
TCGA 1992 s 62	Betting wins	—
s 62	Death	18.2:7
Reliefs based upon the nature of the asset disposed of		
TCGA 1992 s 222	Principal private residence	7.3:3
s 226	Residence occupied by dependent relative	7.3:5
s 262	Chattels worth £3,000 or less	—
s 45	Chattels with predictable life 50 years or less	—
s 204	Life policies on maturity or surrender	16.4
s 121	Savings certificates, premium bonds, British Savings bonds and SAYE deposits	7.1
s 263	Private motor vehicles	7.1
s 258	Works of art etc	14.6
s 269	Currency for private use	—
s 268	Decorations for valour	—
s 76	Interests under trusts	15.7:3
s 251	Debts	—
s 23	Compensation for personal injuries	—
Reliefs based upon the parties involved in the transaction		
TCGA 1992 s 257	Gifts to charities, national heritage bodies or for public benefit	14.6
s 58	Gifts between spouses living together	7.1
s 10	Gains by non-residents of the UK (unless trading here through branch or agency)	17.5:4

7.2:2 Inflation allowances

Because farmland is held for long periods of time by comparison with, for example, quoted shares, farmland sales are more vulnerable to capital gains tax based upon apparent appreciation of value, than shares which fluctuate in a daily market. The increase in land prices is often 'apparent' because it bears no relationship to income, but is derived from inflation. Thus inflation allowances for capital gains tax have a particular relevance for farmers and landowners.

The rules have been repeatedly changed since capital gains tax was first enacted, and the following Table of changes outlining the history of inflation relief may be helpful:

Historic table of inflation relief

	Period	*Statute*	*Scope*
I	*Pre 1965*		No tax on long-term capital gains.
II	*1965–1982*	FA 1965	Capital gains tax with no relief for inflation.
III	*1982–1985*	FA 1982 s 86 & Sch 13	Relief was given only for inflation between 1982 and 1985, calculated in accordance with the retail price index applied to historic base cost; and known as an 'indexation allowance'. The disposal must have been made more than 12 months after the date of acquisition of the asset concerned. No application to losses.
IV	*1985–1988*	FA 1985 s 68 & Sch 19	Relief for inflation occurring between 1982 and 1988 with right of election to be computed in accordance with RPI, but applied to the open market value of the asset as at 31 March 1982. The 12-month rule was abolished and the relief was extended to losses.
V	*1988 onwards*	TCGA 1992 s 35 & Sch 4	Value rebasing as at 31 March 1982 (see section **7.2:3**) indexation allowance computed by reference to retail price index applied to: a) market value as at 31 March 1982 or; b) historic cost; whichever the less. Indexation on post 31 March 1982 additions or enhancements is computed separately.

7.2:3 Capital gains tax: the rebasing formula

'Rebasing' means substitution of asset market value on a specific date in place of the historic cost base for the purpose of computing a capital gain. Assets held on 31 March 1982 are treated as having been disposed of and immediately re-acquired on that date at the 'market value'. 'Market value' means the price the asset might reasonably be expected to fetch in a sale on the open market (TCGA 1992 s 272). No reduction is to be made because the whole of the asset(s) is hypothetically placed on the market at one time.

The net sale proceeds, after deducting expenses of sale, are to be compared with market value as at 31 March 1982 adjusted for the increase in the RPI since March 1982, and the resulting gain or loss is chargeable to capital gains tax at marginal rates of income tax (that is 25% or 40% as the case may be).

For companies, the charge is to corporation tax (25% or 33% as the case may be).

For trustees of life interest trusts, the rate 25%; accumulation and discretionary trusts 35%.

There, is no option to adopt a time-apportioned basis as was the position when, originally, the base date of 1965 (being the date of introduction of capital gains tax) was used.

There is an overall limit to rebasing at 31 March 1982, in that it can only reduce gains or losses by comparison with the result under previous rules. Thus if rebasing produces a bigger gain or a bigger loss, the former rules continue to apply. Where the new rules produce a gain, but the old rules produce a loss, or vice versa, the disposal is treated as having produced neither gain nor loss.

There is right of election (TCGA 1992 s 35(5)) to secure that the restrictions by reference to the former rules shall not apply. This election, which is irrevocable, applies to all disposals including those made before the date of election, to which rebasing applies. It must be made within two years from the end of the year of assessment, in which the first disposal to which it applies has occurred. The Revenue's practice is to disregard certain exempt disposals for this purpose (SP 4/92). Also, the Revenue may allow a longer period.

Election is an all or nothing step, and does not permit a farmer to select only those transactions where it would be advantageous and discard those where it is disadvantageous. (See section **7.2:5** below.)

7.2:4   Rebasing: effects

When capital gains tax was first enacted, it included rules designed to exclude gains which had accrued before, but had not been realised until after, it had come into force. The 'coming-into force' date was 6 April 1965, and there were alternative systems for excluding either time basis apportioned or real increases in value allocated to periods before that date.

In the Finance Act 1982, the rules were changed to take account of inflation as a distorting element to be excluded in calculating capital gains. There were further important revisions in the Finance Act 1985, but the most significant alleviation was enacted in FA 1988 which introduces the system known as 'rebasing'. (The substitution of a revised 'cost' base.)

To recapitulate: rebasing requires that for disposals taking place on or after 6 April 1988, assets held on 31 March 1982 be treated as having been disposed of and immediately re-acquired on that date at their then market value (TCGA 1992 s 35). There is a restriction of the result: it can only operate to *reduce* gains or losses by comparison with the corresponding result produced by applying the rules in force before FA 1988. If rebasing produces a *bigger* gain or a *bigger* loss, the old rules continue to apply.

The rule is easily stated, but the effects not so easily analysed. The overall effect may not be wholly advantageous to the taxpayer. It may either reduce gains, or diminish loss relief. Where the new rule produces a gain, and the old rule produces a loss (or vice versa), the result is a neutral one: neither a taxable gain nor an allowable loss.

The general rule set out above is often described as the 'kink test'. It is worth enumerating alternative applications of the test, in all four of which 'rebasing' is *not* secured.

(a)   Where rebasing would produce a gain, and the old system would produce a smaller gain or a loss.
(b)   Where rebasing produces a loss and the old system would have produced a smaller loss or a gain.

(c) Where under the old system the asset is deemed disposed of at neither a gain nor loss, in consequence of a previous application of an earlier kink test.

(d) Where the disposal is a no gain/no loss transaction, because of the special relationship between the parties (TCGA 1992 Sch 3 para 1).

There is an important right of election that gains and losses should be computed only on the rebased value, electing that the old rules shall not apply (TCGA 1992 s 35(5)). Any such election, which is irrevocable, must apply to all disposals, including any made prior to the date of election to which rebasing may apply. It applies to all assets owned by a person in the same capacity. Thus election is an all-or-nothing step.

The general *effects* of election can be expressed as follows:

(a) Losses can be reduced or augmented.

(b) Gains can be reduced or increased.

(c) Where pre-election neutrality had been achieved because one system produced a gain and the other a loss, the result can be either a gain or a loss, the new result produced under the rebasing system. Thus a gain can be converted into a loss and vice versa.

The consequences of an election need to be examined more closely.

Example I (the value 'kink')

The purchase price of Blackacre Farm on 1 January 1980 was £50,000, and its market value on 31 March 1982 was £20,000. Blackacre was sold on 1 June 1988 for £100,000.

Rebasing computation

	£
Sale proceeds	100,000
Less: 31 March 1982 value	20,000
Gain	80,000
Less: Indexation (say)	7,000
Taxable Gain	£73,000

Old rules computation

	£
Sale proceeds	100,000
Less: Cost	50,000
Gain	50,000
Less: Indexation (say)	31,000
Taxable Gain	£19,000

∴ Rebasing is NOT applied.

Example II ('no gain/no loss')

The purchase price of Whiteacre Farm on 1 January 1980 was £50,000. The market value on 31 March 1982 was £90,000 and the sale price on 1 June 1988 was £100,000.

Rebasing computation

	£
Sale proceeds	100,000
Less: 31 March 1982 value	90,000
Gain	10,000
Less: indexation (say)	31,000
Allowable loss	£(−21,000)

Old rules computation

	£
Sale proceeds	100,000
Less: Cost	50,000
Gain	50,000
Less: indexation (say)	35,000
Taxable gain	£15,000

∴ No gain/no loss result.

7.2:5   Capital gains tax: rebasing: election test

It has been contended that rebasing of capital gains tax to 1982, as applied to sales at current market values, will effectively eliminate farmland from capital gains tax. It is suggested that after substituting the 1982 market value; and deducting the indexation allowance, most disposals of farmland would, at the time of writing, produce a loss rather than a gain. If this be so, many disposal computations will disclose gains on historic pre 1982 cost, and losses based on 1982 market value. On this assumption (which needs to be tested), an election (TCGA 1992 s 35(5)) will be advantageous, since it will produce a capital loss offsettable in the future.

In order to test the value of a possible election at a time immediately before a disposal in prospect (as far as practicable), the following procedural steps in the alternative computations should be carefully attempted:

I   Compute the capital gain or loss according to the old rules.
II   If the result shows no gain/no loss, this result stands (TCGA 1992 s 35(3)(c)(d)).
III   Compute the capital gain or loss under the new rules adopting the rebasing formula.
IV   If result I shows a gain, and result III shows a bigger gain: result I applies. This is equally true for losses (TCGA 1992 s 35(3)(a)(b)).
V   If result I produces a gain and result III produces a smaller gain; result number III applies. This is equally so for losses.
VI   If result number I produces a gain, and result number III produces a loss, or vice versa, the result is: no gain no loss (TCGA 1992 s 35(4)).

Beneficial elections

An election will be *beneficial* in the following circumstances:–

1   If in step IV the result is a loss, election will produce a bigger loss rather than a smaller loss.

2 If in VI above, the old rules produce a gain and the new rules produce a loss, the result of an election will be to preserve that loss for future offset.

3 If in V above an election has been made the result can only be disadvantageous, in its application to losses.

Clearly, the time to contemplate an election and therefore to make the test above is before a transaction which is in prospect. However, it is important not to ignore the possible disadvantages when other assets held by a person in the same capacity are sold. In order to evaluate the net advantage/disadvantage, in future it will be necessary to contemplate the disposal of all farmland or other assets, the key question being whether values had risen or fallen during the period between acquisition and 31 March 1982.

It is useful to envisage possible circumstances in which a disadvantageous election may seem tempting.

Suppose the facts are that the sale (Number 1) of one field ('Barleycorn') produces a loss under the new rules, but a gain under the old rules. Then in order to secure the valuable offset of the loss, an election is required and is made.

Now suppose a subsequent sale (Number 2 'Barleyfarm') after either a general rise in land values; or the attribution of development potential to the land produces a bigger gain under the new rules than under the old rules. Alternatively, suppose such an event produces a gain under the new rules and a loss under the old rules. The effect of an incorrect election on the Barleycorn sale is to increase overall liability.

Example Sale Number 1 'Barleycorn'

Barleycorn field is sold for £18,000 in 1989. It was inherited at a low market value of £5,000 in 1975 and its market value on 31 March 1982 was £20,000.

Rebasing Computation – Sale Number 1

Sales proceeds	£18,000
less: market value at 31 3 1982	£20,000
Loss	£−2,000
less: indexation (say)	£−7,000
Adjusted loss	£−9,000

Old Rules Computation – Sale Number 1 'Barleycorn'

Sale proceeds	£18,000
less: market value on inheritance 1975	£ 5,000
Gain	£13,000
less: indexation (say)	£ 7,000
Indexed gain	£6,000

Thus on Sale Number 1 a rebasing election appears advantageous. However, Barleycorn farmland value rises because of a possible bypass using part of it. The farm is sold for £500,000. The value at 31 March 1982 was £200,000 and historic cost in 1981 £400,000.

Rebasing Computation – Sale Number 2 'Barleyfarm'

Sale proceeds	£500,000
less: market value at 31 3 1982	£200,000
Gain	£300,000
less: indexation (say)	£ 76,000
Indexed gain	£224,000

Old Rules Computation – Sale Number 2 'Barleyfarm'

Sale proceeds	£500,000
Cost	£400,000
Gain	£100,000
less: indexation (say)	£152,000
Loss	£52,000

Thus the net effect of the incorrect election has been to preserve loss relief of £9,000 on Sale Number 1 but to create liability of £224,000 on Sale Number 2.

7.2:6   Capital gains tax: rebasing: roll-over reliefs

There are special provisions to deal with the situation where rebasing interacts with different categories of roll-over relief, on disposal of a replacement asset. The treatment depends upon whether the roll-over occurred:

(a) Before 31 March 1982; or
(b) After 31 March 1982.

The effects are different before and after these dates. Where the roll-over occurred before this date, the treatment is simple: the held-over gain is ignored, which means it is not recaptured on disposal occurring after 5 April 1988. This applies to the following categories of roll-over relief:

(a) Replacement of business asset (see section **7.4**).
(b) Gift by individuals (hold-over relief) (see section **7.5**).
(c) Transfer of business to a company (see section **7.4:2**).
(d) Replacement of assets lost or destroyed.
(e) Compulsory acquisition of land.
(f) Reorganisation of share capitals, mergers and company reconstructions.

Where relief has been given for roll-over after 31 March 1982, but before 6 April 1988, the result is different. The taxpayer realising the ultimate gain will not have held the asset on the 31 March 1982 so that the question arises as to which asset to apply the rebasing formula. The rules are arbitrary and give similar relief in two alternative sets of circumstances:

(a) *Where the deferred gains have reduced allowable expenditure on an asset acquired*
This applies to the general roll-over relief for replacement of business assets (see section **7.4**); and the general hold-over relief for gifts (see section **7.5**). Where either of these reliefs have been allowed so as to defer a capital gain which was wholly or in part accruing during the period prior to 31 March 1982; and the application was to reduce the allowable cost or expenditure on an asset acquired post 31 March 1982, then relief is given by halving the amount of the reduction.

This is a rough-and-ready compromise, designed to avoid the need to compute how much of the gain arose respectively before and after 31 March 1982.

The relief might have been increased by deferring claim until a later rather than an earlier occasion, that is, on a second replacement of a business asset. This possibility has been excluded by a correction in TCGA 1992 Sch 4. The possibility of a double relief claim has also been extinguished.

(b) *Deferred gains held-over without deduction from allowable expenditure*
There are certain exceptional situations, mostly outside the scope of this book, but which include the compulsory acquisition of land where there is a depreciating asset acquired (TCGA 1992 s 248(3)). The rule is that the deferred gain is reduced by one half, which achieves the same result as above.

7.3 FARMHOUSES AND COTTAGES

7.3:1 Introduction

One most important exemption from capital gains tax applies to gains arising on the disposal of, or of an interest in, a 'principal private residence' (TCGA 1992 s 222). The exemption applies to a gain arising on disposal of the dwelling house itself, and also land which a taxpayer has for his own occupation and enjoyment with the residence, as its garden or grounds up to an area (inclusive of the site of the house) of half a hectare (amended for 1991–92 and previously one acre) (TCGA 1992 s 222(2)), or such larger area as the Commissioners concerned may determine, on being satisfied that, regard being had to the size and character of the dwelling house, a larger area is required for the reasonable enjoyment of it as a residence (TCGA 1992 s 222(3)).

The exemption rule can be readily stated, but in practice can lead to uncertainties and disputes. This is partly because over long periods of time, houses can be used in a variety of ways, of which private residence is only one. A house can be used partly for business or professional purposes, most obviously a farmhouse. Alternatively, an owner may be absent from his house for a period, and the use of it may be varied, in that part may become occupied by tenants or lodgers. The rule exempting land with a house is not precise, and reasonable enjoyment is a subjective concept. The problem may be acute where a house is sold with, say, a paddock, cottages, stabling and outbuildings, whereas a town house with front and rear garden is less likely to raise difficulties.

7.3:2 Meaning of 'dwelling-house'

The fact that part of the house is used in the farming business does not preclude all relief. If part is used exclusively for the purposes of the trade, the gain is apportioned, and only the proportion applying to the private part is exempt. Apportionment is made on the facts of use, that is having regard to the area or number of rooms involved. The test for capital gains tax purposes is not the same as the test applied in the disallowance of expenses for the purposes of computing the profit under Schedule D (see section **2.3**). Where a room has not been used exclusively for the purpose of the trade, eg a parlour which is also used as a farm office, full exemption for capital gains tax may be due, even though there has been some restriction of expenditure for income tax under Schedule D. On the other hand, it does not follow that a failure to claim deduction under Schedule D guarantees full exemption from capital gains tax.

The expression 'dwelling house' has its ordinary meaning (*Batey v Wakefield* [1980] STC 572), although in *Makins v Elson* [1977] STC 46 it was held to include a caravan, jacked up and resting on bricks. The fact that the wheels were not resting on the ground, and that electricity, water and telephone were all connected was taken into account in arriving at the decision. See also *Markey v Sanders* [1987] STC 256 and *Williams v Merrylees* [1987] STC 445 which refer to *Batey v Wakefield* and deal with the important point of whether a separate out-dwelling can be part of the dwelling house.

7.3:3   Principal or main residence

No taxpayer can claim exemption on more than one house. If he owns more than one, for example a farm and a town house, he can elect within two years of the date of purchase of the second house which of them is to be his main residence for capital gains tax purposes. If he fails to elect the Inspector is authorised to serve notice of determination on him, against which he has a right of appeal.

7.3:4   Period of occupation

The extent of exemption is proportionate to the extent to which the house has been occupied by an owner, during his period of ownership. If he has lived in the house throughout, all capital gains are exempt. If for half the period of ownership he lived elsewhere and let his house, then only half the gain would be exempt. There are a series of exceptions to this general rule designed to meet special circumstances:

(A) OVERLAPPING OWNERSHIP

Where an owner is selling a house and moving to another, it is recognised that a period of overlapping ownership may occur. Full exemption continues to be given even though an owner had moved to a new house and did not live in the old one for a period of 36 months for 1991–92 onwards (previously 24 months) up to the date of sale. Similarly, where there is a delay of up to 36 months in taking up occupation of a new house, because building or decoration is being carried out, or because steps are being taken to sell the old house, this period will be ignored in calculating the subsequent gain on the new house.

(B) BREAKS IN OCCUPATION

A single period of absence not exceeding three years, or shorter periods aggregating not more than three years, are disregarded, providing that both before and after the periods the house was the only or main residence, and throughout he had no other house available for exemption. Periods before 6 April 1965 are ignored.

(C) ABSENCE ABROAD

A period of absence is ignored if, during it, the individual were working in an employment all the duties of which were performed abroad. The length of the absence is immaterial.

(D) EMPLOYER'S REQUIREMENTS

A period or periods are ignored if the absence was due to the fact that an employer required the owner to live elsewhere to do his job more effectively. For this exemption the maximum period is four years, whether at one time or in aggregate. All the exceptions under headings (B), (C) and (D) are additional to each other.

(E) LAND BOUGHT AND HOUSE BUILT ON IT

A period during which land was owned, and whilst the house was being built, may be ignored up to a period of 12 months or longer if there are exceptional reasons for it.

(F) ALTERATIONS TO USE

Where the use of a building has changed during ownership, for example part of the farmhouse has been converted to a dairy or vice versa, the exemption may be adjusted as the Commissioners consider just and reasonable. In practice, this may mean agreeing some compromise solution with the Inspector based upon the proportions of the whole building and the periods of time involved.

(G) REPRESENTATIVE OCCUPATION

The capital gains tax position is discussed in section **5.5:2**.

7.3:5 Other parties involved

(A) TRUSTS AND SETTLEMENTS

Exemption is available to trustees if, during their ownership of a property, a beneficiary under the trust has been occupying it as his only or main residence (TCGA 1992 s 225). This applies whether he is entitled to occupy, or is occupying by permission of the trustees. A similar concession is available to personal representatives, who sell a property used as a main or only residence by beneficiaries under the will or intestacy, who are entitled to the whole or substantially the whole of the proceeds of sale. This concession has been extended to include a legatee (Extra-Statutory Concession DJ 1988).

(B) DEPENDENT RELATIVES

Relief was also available to an owner who provides a house rent-free and without consideration to a dependent relative (TCGA 1992 s 226). The house must have been the sole residence of the dependant and only one dependant was allowed per owner. For this purpose a dependent relative was:

(i) a relative of the owner or owner's spouse incapacitated by old age or infirmity from maintaining himself or herself; or
(ii) a mother of either spouse who is widowed, separated or divorced, even if not incapacitated.

No income tests were prescribed.

The relief was abolished for disposals after 6 April 1988 save where the property was the sole residence of a dependent relative on 5 April 1988 or at an earlier date (TCGA 1992 s 226).

(c) LODGERS OR PAYING GUESTS

Where a paying guest lives with the owner and family sharing accommodation
and meals, the exemption is not lost (SP D15).

(d) PART LETTINGS

Where the whole or part of any principal private residence has been let by the
owner as residential accommodation, some relief may still be due. In such
circumstances any gain which would be chargeable because of the letting is
chargeable only to the extent that it exceeds the smaller of:

(i) an amount equal to the existing exemption by reference to occupation by
the owner; and
(ii) £40,000 for 1991–92 onwards (previously £20,000).

Example

Manor Lodge is partly owner occupied and partly let. It is sold for
£100,000. The historic cost was £70,000 and two-thirds of the gain is
attributable to letting and is chargeable:

Capital gains tax liability

	£
Sale proceeds	100,000
Cost base	70,000
Capital gain:	30,000
Less exemption for owner occupation	10,000
Gain before additional relief	£20,000

Additional relief
Either £10,000 or £40,000 (limit)

	£
(whichever the less) =	10,000
Chargeable gain:	£10,000

The net effect is that if the gain on the let proportion does not exceed half of the
overall gain, the additional relief will extinguish liability, subject to the £40,000
limit.

(e) JOINT BUT UNRELATED OWNER-OCCUPIERS

Where there are joint owner-occupiers of a property who are not husband and
wife, they will be entitled to relief. Each is treated as having an undivided share in
all the property (*Tod v Mudd* [1987] STC 141). This is on the assumption that
each has unrestricted access to the whole property, even though some part may,
in practice, not be used by both the joint owners.

If the property in joint ownership is divided into two or more separate and
identifiable homes, each exclusively occupied, relief is not accorded in respect of
any gain on the part not occupied by any owner. However, each may exchange
his interest so as to acquire sole ownership of the part each occupies, so as to
secure relief (Extra-Statutory Concession D26 para 3).

7.3:6 Other factors

(A) INTENTION TO RESELL, ETC

Where a purchase is made with the intention to resell at a profit, the exemption is lost, even though all the other tests are satisfied (TCGA 1992 s 224(3)). An intention to resell may be inferred from the events which have occurred.

(B) LAND AS GARDEN OR GROUNDS

The wording of the rule which exempts land occupied with a dwelling house is not precise and is capable of being differently interpreted. One problem concerns sales including land in excess of a half hectare in extent. If such land is farmed, the exemption is lost. On the other hand, it would not be lost where the land was used, say, to pasture horses kept for riding or hunting. Similar arguments could be advanced for woodlands retained for shooting, or river banks used for fishing.

One valid argument in support of exemption of a larger area is that larger houses tend to require larger grounds. Another is that the land sold was in close proximity to the house and within sight of it. Protection of a house by a 'green belt' of land might be a relevant factor. Where contentions of this class are put forward they may need to be supported by plans and photographs. In one case before the General Commissioners, exemption of 24½ acres was secured.

(C) LAND AS GARDEN OR GROUNDS: 'REASONABLE ENJOYMENT'

The question of what is required for the reasonable enjoyment of a dwelling house is often the subject of discussion. The Revenue has been known to cite in argument various precedent cases concerned with the compulsory purchase of land by a local planning authority in the interests of proper planning.

In a recent case *(Sharkey v Secretary of State for the Environment and South Buckinghamshire District Council* (1990) 62 P&CR 126; affd [1992] RVR 29, CA), it was held that the word 'required' meant something more than merely 'desirable'. That is, acquisition would have to be needed for the accomplishment of the purposes set out in the legislation.

However, the meaning of the word necessarily depends upon the context in which it appears, and these cases should be treated as being of limited authority.

(D) BUILDINGS AS 'LAND'

Under the Interpretation Act 1889 s 3, 'land' includes buildings. It is therefore arguable that a cottage or other building included in grounds is capable of qualifying for exemption as part of the grounds. In practice, the Revenue has been known to contend that a building not physically part of the main building cannot so qualify.

In such circumstances, it may be better to contend that a cottage, even if not physically part of the main dwelling, is nevertheless part of it in the sense that it is occupied with it, for example by employees (see *Batey v Wakefield* [1980] STC 572). (See section **7.3:2**.)

(E) SALE IN PARTS

It is necessary for the land to be occupied with the specified dwelling house at the time of sale. In *Varty v Lynes* [1976] STC 508 the house was sold first and the garden separately afterwards. The house and garden together were less than one acre, but the exemption was lost, because once the house had been sold, the garden ceased to be occupied and enjoyed with the house (the Revenue will not normally take this point unless the garden has development value).

Further problems may arise where the garden in question is a larger area than half a hectare, and the contention has been made that this larger area was required for the reasonable enjoyment of the residence (TCGA 1992 s 222(3)). If the garden is sold in parts, that contention may be less sustainable.

7.3:7   Two or more buildings

The question arises as to whether a 'dwelling house' can consist of two or more separate buildings. In *Batey v Wakefield* [1981] STC 521, it was decided that a separate bungalow adjacent to, but within the curtilage of a dwelling house, was part of the dwelling house although the bungalow was separately occupied by a part-time caretaker.

However, it is not clear how far this principle can be extended. In *Lewis v Lady Rook* [1992] STC 171, it was held in the Court of Appeal that the dwelling house was an entity and that separate buildings could be included only so far as they were within the curtilage of, and appurtenant to, the main house.

In *Honour v Norris* [1992] STC 304, the dwelling house in question consisted of four separate flats in separate buildings in a London square. One of the flats was sold and exemption was claimed on the grounds that what had been disposed of was part of the principal private residence. It was held that the circumstances were similar to those of an owner of a country house, who purchased a guest house in an adjacent village.

Reference should also be made to *Markey v Sanders* [1987] STC 256, and *Williams v Merrylees* [1987] STC 445, both of which refer to *Batey v Wakefield*, and which are helpful in providing illustrative facts.

7.4   ROLL-OVER RELIEF

7.4:1   Nature of relief

If all reliefs and allowances in the income tax Acts were placed in order of importance for farmers, roll-over relief (TCGA 1992 s 152 (many of the provisions described are concessional)) would appear at the head of the list. The relief is designed to meet a particular business situation: the sale of one asset in order to provide funds to purchase another asset for use in the business, and in farming this is a common phenomenon. Land, buildings and machinery represent capital costs, which cannot always be financed from cash at bank, or from borrowings. It is natural to contemplate sale of uneconomic, inconvenient, relatively distant or other land, to produce part or all the cash to buy a tractor, combine harvester, or another farm. But for roll-over relief, only the net after-tax proceeds would be available, which would be discouraging to business replacement and expansion. The relief applies where certain classes of business assets are sold or otherwise disposed of, and the proceeds of sale invested in new business assets. The capital gain which would have been chargeable on the asset sold is deducted from the historic cost base of the new asset in the computation of the gain on that asset, when it is in turn sold. Thus, tax is not completely excused, merely deferred, and the new asset remains 'charged or burdened with' this postponed tax, so increasing the ultimate tax bill on its sale or other disposal (see section **7.4:5 Example 1**).

There are two circumstances whereby the deferral can be converted into a complete exemption. First, death of the owner extinguishes all accrued gains on assets owned at death. Secondly, an owner's emigration may have this effect, although it will not do so where assets are used in businesses carried on in the UK.

There is no limit to the number of times a gain can be rolled over in this way, as shown in section **7.4:5 Example 3**. Also, assets charged with postponed tax can be the subject of a claim to hold-over relief (see section **7.5**) effectively compounding the deferred liability. Before the sale of any asset, it is necessary to review its history to ascertain whether the sale will trigger tax deferred from an earlier rolled-over (or held over) gain.

There are strict rules governing the relationships between the nature of the asset sold and that acquired, although there have been relaxations since the system was invented in 1965. Most of the present day difficulties in calculating and negotiating the relief derive from other related circumstances, for example when only part of the sale proceeds have been applied to the new purchase, or where the asset is used only partly for the purposes of a particular business. Problems arise when land is partitioned; when land is compulsorily purchased; and where roll-over relief interacts with other reliefs, for example indexation relief.

7.4:2 Tests for relief

(A) NATURE OF TRADE

Before 11 April 1978, the rule was that a replacement asset must be used for the purposes of the same trade as the asset replaced. Since 11 April 1978, two or more trades are to be treated as a single trade (TCGA 1992 s 152(8)). In any event, where a roll-over occurred before 31 March 1982, the effect of rebasing is that the held over gain is ignored on disposal of the replacement asset after 5 April 1982 (see section **7.2:6**).

(B) OWNERSHIP OF ASSETS

Old and new assets and the farming business generally must still be in the same ownership. There is a small exception to this rule which is helpful. Where land is owned by a shareholder but is farmed by that shareholder's family company the rule is breached but relief is given. The shareholder does not need to be a working director (TCGA 1992 s 157). The meaning of the expression 'family company' is examined in section **6.2**. In the converse situation, where the land is owned by a company but farmed by, say, a shareholder, the rule is enforced and the relief is forfeited.

(C) PARTNERSHIPS

The treatment of partnerships needs careful examination: first, to secure relief an individual partner in a partnership needs to show he had an interest in both old assets and the new. Farmland may be excluded from the partnership ownership and Balance Sheet, and be retained in the ownership of one or more of the partners.

There are advantages to be derived from this configuration (see section **15.2**). Roll-over relief remains due, providing the landowners who sold the asset are those who buy the new one. As they will have available the cash proceeds, this will usually be so. Owners of let land cannot claim roll-over relief, since their land is not a qualifying business asset. However, owners who are also partners can claim, irrespective of whether the partnership pays a rack rent for the land, or allows the partnership to occupy at a low rent or rent-free. Any necessary restriction of the relief due is measured not by reference to an owner's share of partnership profits, but to the extent of his interest in the new assets. Thus, an individual who has virtually retired from a partnership, receives but a small share of profit, but still owns all the land, can secure full roll-over relief on a replacement.

If a partner retires from a partnership after the sale of the old asset, but before acquisition of the new asset, he fails to have an interest in both, and no relief is due. Where, between the two same events, a partner's share in a partnership is varied, relief will be restricted if the amount of proceeds of the old asset attributable to him exceeds the cost of the new asset similarly attributable. It follows that, during a roll-over period, it is best to avoid partnership retirements and changes.

(d) HUSBAND AND WIFE

For this relief, each spouse is treated as a separate chargeable person. If for example, a farm owned by the husband is sold, and the proceeds of sale reinvested in a farm owned by the wife (or vice versa) relief is not due. In such circumstances, entitlement to relief can be restored by first transferring the farm owned and farmed by the husband to the ownership and occupation of the wife for a nil consideration. That transaction will not in itself create capital gains tax liability, but the stamp duty and commercial aspects will obviously need detailed consideration.

(e) TRUSTS AND TRUSTEES

Where farmland is owned by a trust, the life tenant who is farming the land is denied relief even where he has a beneficial interest in the property as conferred by the Settled Land Act 1925 s 19. Where, exceptionally, the farm is owned and farmed by the trustees of a settlement where there is no interest in possession, no problems arise.

(f) COMPANIES

Where land is owned by a shareholder but farmed by his family company relief is due (TCGA 1992 s 157). Two other corporate situations require examination: first, all the separate trades carried on by members of a group of companies are treated as a single trade.

For this purpose a 'group' implies 75% or more common ownership.

(g) TRANSFER TO A COMPANY

A more common situation is where the transaction concerns the sale of a farming asset by an individual on his incorporating a private company to carry on the farming business (TCGA 1992 s 162). The advantages of such a company are discussed throughout the tax-planning sections, and for the present purpose it is sufficient to note that a special form of roll-over relief is available, designed to meet the circumstances of this transaction and no other. The framework of the relief is as follows:

Transferor
The disposal of the asset must take place as a transfer to a company by an individual or individuals, not another company (TCGA 1992 s 162(1)). If the shares of individuals in a partnership do not match the ultimate shareholdings in the company, liability will arise.

The business
It is not adequate that a single asset be transferred; a whole business must be transferred as a going concern (TCGA 1992 s 155). That means all business assets must be transferred with exception only of cash. Where liabilities are transferred, it is Revenue practice not to treat them as consideration, for the purposes of relief. That is, if liabilities are not taken over, relief is not lost.

What is meant by 'going concern' was considered in the recent case of *Gordon v IRC* [1991] STC 174. The Revenue contended that because a second sale was immediately in prospect, the farm business was not being transferred 'as a going concern'. It claimed no right of property in the farm was ever legally transferred to the company. These arguments were rejected. It was held that the correct test was whether the business was operative at the date of transfer. Moreover a farming business could change its place of operation without breaking continuity of operation.

The consideration
The transfer must be wholly or partly in consideration for shares newly allotted by the company to the transferor. It is these shares which are charged with the deferred capital gains tax on the sale of the farm business. When the shares are later disposed of, their historic cost and acquisition date will be those of the assets in consideration for which they were issued. If the consideration be partly shares and partly cash, the chargeable gains are apportioned rateably between shares and cash in the proportions of respective market values. The part attributed to the shares is not immediately chargeable but is deferred as described above. The part attributable to the cash is chargeable forthwith to capital gains tax in the normal way.

It is a commonly held view that relief on transfer to a company applies only to farmers and not to landowners. However, there is a strong case for claiming that the letting of agricultural land, in certain circumstances, is a business for the purposes only of this relief. 'Business' is what is required to be transferred according to the wording of the section, and there is no reference to trades or vocations as elsewhere in the Taxes Acts.

(H) THE ASSETS SOLD

Returning now to the principal form of roll-over relief, the classes of assets which qualify are as follows (TCGA 1992 s 155):

  (i) buildings or parts of buildings occupied (as well as used) for the purposes of the trade;
  (ii) land occupied (as well as used) for the purposes of the trade;
  (iii) fixed plant and machinery not forming part of a building.

There are three further classes, ships, aircraft and goodwill, of lesser relevance.

It is immaterial that the asset sold and that acquired fall into different classes. In practice, capital expenditure on land, for example drainage, qualifies for relief. On the other hand, there is a requirement that the plant be 'fixed' and mobile plant, eg tractors, does not qualify.

In certain circumstances, a landlord may be required to dispose of a lease to a sitting tenant (Leasehold Reform Act 1967). Until October 1990, the Revenue took the view that in these circumstances no claim to roll-over relief arose, but by a statement of practice (SP 7/90) the Revenue has conceded that roll-over relief is available (TCGA 1992 s 247).

There are special rules for 'wasting' assets, as specially defined. Wasting assets means those with a predictable life not exceeding 50 years, and in relation to tangible movable property, for example tractors, means useful life having regard to the purposes for which bought. Plant and machinery is always regarded as having a predictable life of less than 50 years.

Where a wasting asset is acquired, the gain on the disposal of the old asset is held in suspense, until either the new asset is disposed of or ceases to be used for the purposes of the trade; or until ten years have elapsed since the date it was acquired, whichever occurs earlier. If, however, another non-wasting asset of the same class be acquired within the time limit stipulated above, the deferred gain may be carried forward and deducted from the historic cost of this third asset (TCGA 1992 s 154).

(i) THE ASSET ACQUIRED

Where the asset sold is subsequently repurchased for purely commercial reasons, that asset is regarded as a 'new asset' (Extra-Statutory Concession D16).

Where the new asset is simply capital expenditure to enhance the value of existing assets, that expenditure is also treated as a new asset provided:

(a) the assets improved are used only for the purposes of the trade, or
(b) the assets after completion of the work are taken into use only for the purposes of the trade (Extra-Statutory Concession D22).

Another set of problems arise where the new assets are not *immediately* taken into use for the purposes of the business. In these circumstances roll-over relief is available, provided that the delay is due to work needed on the asset; and that work begins as soon as possible after acquisition; and on completion of the work the asset is used for the purposes of the trade. If the asset is used for any non-business purpose during the intervening period, roll-over relief is lost (Extra-Statutory Concession D24). For example, a company acquired land for use in its business but, because of the existence of a lease, was unable to obtain immediate possession of it. A claim for roll-over relief failed (*Campbell Connelly & Co Ltd v Barnett* [1992] STC 316).

The Revenue has indicated in what circumstances it will allow roll-over relief in practice. If an asset is ready to use when acquired, it must be brought into use without delay if it is to qualify. If it is not ready for use, then relief will not be refused on the grounds it was not brought into use as soon as required, provided all reasonable steps are taken to make it ready for use as soon as practicable after acquisition, and it was then brought into use without unnecessary delay.

Another situation envisaged is where the new asset is not a separate identifiable asset, but is a further interest in an asset which is already in use in the trade, for example, a freehold reversion in farm land, in which case the further interest is treated as a 'new asset' (Extra-Statutory Concession D25).

Where what is received is a capital sum in compensation for buildings destroyed, and that compensation is invested in constructing or acquiring a replacement building, the construction or replacement cost is similarly treated as a 'new asset', separate and distinct from the land on which the buildings stand (Extra-Statutory Concession D19).

(J) PART USE; PART SALE PROCEEDS REINVESTED; PART CHARGEABLE GAIN (TCGA 1992 SS 152(6), 153)

An infinite variety of circumstances may arise, but the three described are commonly found in practice.

Part use
Buildings and structures (but not other assets) which have been partly used for business purposes and partly for private purposes qualify, but an apportionment needs to be made. This would apply for example to a farmhouse. An apportionment may also be required if the assets sold had not been used for the purposes of the trade throughout the period of ownership. Letting land does not count as using it 'for the purposes of a trade', so that a landlord who takes land in hand, farms it, then subsequently sells it, and replaces it with other land will have problems. He will be permitted to roll over only that proportion of his gain corresponding to the period of ownership during which he was an owner-occupier. That may be but a short period, if the object of getting the land in hand was to reorganise a whole estate.

This is another circumstance in which a wife can come to the aid of the tax planner. As a first step, the land is transferred to her, she farms it, then sells it and claims roll-over relief on the whole gain. That is because she will have farmed it for the *whole* period of *her* ownership so that no apportionment to reflect a period of use other than for the purposes of a trade will be required.

As the wife will take the land from her husband on a no loss/no gain basis, the transfer to her will not prevent the whole of the gain up to the date of sale from being successfully rolled-over.

Where assets have not been used for the purposes of the trade throughout the whole period of ownership, the relief is restricted in the proportion the period of trade use bears to the whole period of ownership. However, where the restriction might apply, the Revenue's concessional practice is to count the period only from 6 April 1965, where the asset was owned before that date. This is beneficial where, for example, land has been taken in hand since that date.

Where land is let as grazings (see section **5.1:2**), it is worth considering whether a Schedule D basis rather than a Schedule A basis of liability could have been claimed, so as to secure unrestricted roll-over relief at the time of disposal.

Part sale proceeds reinvested
The cost of a new asset may be less than the sale price of that sold. Then the amount equal to excess cash not reinvested is liable to immediate capital gains tax (see section **7.4:5 Example 3**).

The question arises as to what if any relief is due when an asset is the subject of a gift or is sold at less than market value, and market value is substituted, so giving rise to a chargeable gain. Then, concessionally, roll-over relief will be allowed, if an amount equal to the notional proceeds of sale is invested in qualifying business assets, and all other tests are satisfied.

Part chargeable gain
Where some proportion of the gain is not chargeable, for example by operation of the time apportionment rules, an adjustment needs to be made. The net proportion is rolled over, so that the reduction of the base cost of the new asset is correspondingly lower.

(K) PARTITION OF JOINTLY OWNED AGRICULTURAL LAND

Agricultural land is sometimes purchased or inherited by members of a family jointly. A farmer may bequeath his land jointly to his sons which is appropriate, so long as the farm is owned and managed by them as one unit. However, changing family or farming circumstances may make it desirable for different parts of the farm to be owned or managed as separate units. Thus, the land may need to be partitioned between the joint owners, so that each of them becomes the sole owner of the land which he will separately manage or farm.

Until 19 December 1984, the tax position was unsatisfactory and uncertain. However, the Revenue published an Extra-Statutory Concession on that date entitled 'Relief for Exchange of Joint Interests in Land.' Under this concession, the roll-over relief follows conventional form, save that the usage of the land up to partition and afterwards is irrelevant so that tenanted land qualifies. 'Land' includes buildings, except to the extent that the 'new land' acquired is or becomes a dwelling house which is a principal private residence. Restriction on the new land 'becoming' a principal private residence applies for the six years from the date of partition. Thus the restriction apparently applies to the construction of a dwelling house on the new land, and to the commencement of occupation of an existing house as a principal private residence. That is when, for example, a house let to or occupied by a farm employee ceases to be so let or occupied, and becomes occupied as the principal private residence of a farmer.

However, the relief is given on the partition of dwelling houses which are occupied by joint beneficial owners as their principal private residences. Each joint beneficial owner is treated as having acquired the interest of the other joint beneficial owner in the house which he occupies at the historic base cost, and on the original date on which the joint interest was acquired.

An earlier concession, granting roll-over relief on the partition of land on the dissolution of a farming partnership, seems no longer applicable as the more general concession seems to cover all cases which might arise in practice.

This concession (D26) has been extended to apply to changes to milk and potato quota occurring after 29 October 1987 – the day of the announcement of the extension of roll-over relief to milk and potato quota. (TCGA 1992 s 155).

Relief is only given where joint interests in milk or potato quota are exchanged together with joint interests in land. After the exchange, each joint owner must become the sole owner of the part of the quota relating to the land he now owns.

(L) COMPULSORY PURCHASE

Agricultural land is often acquired under statutory compulsory purchase powers, for example for use as a motorway or other public works construction. The disposal and acquisition are treated as taking place on the date when compensation for the acquisition has been agreed or otherwise determined, or if earlier the time when the public authority enters on the land in pursuance of their powers (TCGA 1992 ss 245, 246). After 5 April 1982, the capital gain realised on the disposal can be the subject of a claim to roll-over relief, so that it becomes deductible from the acquisition cost of replacement land. The ordinary roll-over relief rules apply, except that the relief is cancelled if at any time within the following six years the new land qualifies for personal private residence exemption from capital gains tax (TCGA 1992 ss 245–247).

The proceeds of a compulsory purchase of a tenanted farm may be reinvested in a vacant possession farm, and vice versa, without loss of roll-over relief.

Interest receivable on compulsory purchase compensation is of course subject to income tax, not capital gains tax, and the effect of this can be disadvantageous since interest tends to be treated as if it accrued wholly in the year of payment (TA 1988 ss 349(2) and 835(6)).

(M) TIME LIMITS

The new business assets must be acquired within a period of 12 months before and three years after the date of disposal of the asset on which the gain arises. It is the contract date, not the conveyance date which is taken for this purpose. The Board of Inland Revenue has a discretion to extend this limit, where for some reason acquisition of the new asset within the time limit was not practicable. The Revenue has stated that the length of the time extension sought is one factor to take into account, but not necessarily the most important factor. Where it is shown that tax payers had a firm intention to acquire the new asset within the time limit and were prevented from doing so by circumstances outside their control, the claim will be admitted provided 'the new assets are acquired as soon as reasonably possible' (Inland Revenue Tax Bulletin Issue No 1, November 1991.)

Collection of tax will not be held up pending the acquisition of a new asset, but must be paid and will become the subject of a repayment claim.

7.4:3 Shares in companies

Until FA 1993, gains from the sale of shares in companies were unrelieved by any form of roll-over relief, but FA 1993 Sch 7 Pt II rectified this omission. Generally, the machinery of the relief is the same as for all other roll-over reliefs. The capital gain which would have been chargeable upon the disposal of the shares, is deducted from the historic cost base of the qualifying new investment. Thus the new investment remains charged with the postponed tax, so increasing the ultimate tax liability on its future disposal.

In order to qualify for the relief 'the reinvestor' (as he is called) must make a material disposal of shares, and must acquire a qualifying investment within the period called 'the qualifying period'. This is the same as under other forms of roll-over relief.

Relief is available on disposals by individuals and in certain circumstances by trustees. Relief is not available on disposals by companies.

The terms 'material disposal' and 'qualifying investment' are carefully defined as follows:

(1) MATERIAL DISPOSAL (TCGA 1992 s 164A(3), (4))

The conditions to be satisfied throughout a period of one year ending with the date of disposal are:

(a) The company must be a trading company.
(b) It must be unquoted.
(c) It must be the reinvestor's personal company.
(d) The reinvestor must be a full-time director or employee.

A personal company is one in which the reinvestor holds 5% of voting rights.

(2) QUALIFYING INVESTMENT (TCGA 1992 s 164A(8), (9))

The conditions for a 'qualifying investment' are as follows:

(a) The shares must be ordinary shares.
(b) They must be shares in a qualifying unquoted company.
(c) The reinvestor must hold at least 5% immediately on the acquisition or within three years.
(d) It must not be the same company as the one whose shares were disposed of.
(e) It must be a company or group carrying on a qualifying trade, from which various financial and property dealing activities are excluded. More importantly, farming is also excluded. Thus this relief does not permit a farmer to dispose of shares in one farming company free of immediate capital gains tax, and acquire shares in another. Nor does it permit a disposal of shares to be followed by acquisition of an unincorporated business. However it enables a farmer to diversify out of farming into a different corporate activity.

Similarly, a company is not a qualifying company if it holds interests in land worth over half the company's chargeable assets. Generally, debts chargeable on the land and unsecured debts may be deducted in determining whether the land amounts to 50% of the company's chargeable assets.

There are supplementary rules, providing that the deferral is lost, if the company in question ceases to be a qualifying company.

7.4:4   Conclusion

Roll-over relief is usually claimed by persons carrying on the trade of farming, but it is available to those occupying woodlands, which are managed on a commercial basis (see section **13.1**). Public authorities, and persons carrying on professions, vocations, offices and employments may also claim. Landowners assessed under Schedule A are inevitably excluded as not carrying on a qualifying trade.

7.4:5   Examples. Capital gains tax: roll-over relief

Example 1 (whole gain relieved)

Bacon sells his farm at Blackacre for £100,000. The original cost of Blackacre was £60,000. He buys a farm at Whiteacre for £120,000, and claims roll-over relief:

	£
Sale price: Blackacre	100,000
Cost of Blackacre	60,000
Capital gain	40,000
Cost of Whiteacre	120,000
Less: capital gain on Blackacre	40,000
Cost base of Whiteacre on any future sale	£80,000

Example 2

The facts are as above. Later, Bacon sells Whiteacre for £200,000 and gives up farming.

	£
Cost base of Whiteacre as above	80,000
Sale price	200,000
Chargeable capital gain	£120,000

Note: This represents a gain of £40,000 on Blackacre, and £80,000 on Whiteacre.

Example 3 (part reinvested)

The facts are as in **Example 1** above, save that Whiteacre cost only £70,000, so that part of the proceeds of sale of Blackacre were not reinvested. Then the calculation would be as follows:

	£
Sale price: Blackacre	100,000
Cost of Blackacre	60,000
Capital gain	40,000
Amount reinvested	70,000
Less: cost of Blackacre	60,000
Amount of gain reinvested	10,000
Cost price of Whiteacre	70,000
Less: part gain reinvested	10,000
Cost base of Whiteacre in future sale	60,000
Capital gain as above	40,000
Less: part reinvested	10,000
Chargeable capital gain	£30,000

Example 4 (part gain relieved)

Bacon bought Blackacre, a tenanted farm, in 1974 for £60,000. It came in hand in 1976, when he started farming it. He sold it in 1984 for £100,000 and claims roll-over relief:

	tenanted	in hand
Cost of Blackacre apportioned as to four-fifths and one-fifth	12,000	48,000
Sale Price correspondingly apportioned	20,000	80,000
Capital gain		£32,000
Roll-over relief can never exceed the proportion of the sale price apportioned to the in hand period		£80,000

7.5   HOLD-OVER RELIEF

7.5:1   Introduction

Some countries have a separate tax specifically designed to impose a charge on gifts, but this country has always adapted other taxes to perform that function. Capital gains tax is used for this purpose, by adopting the fiction that the asset gifted is being sold at its current market value as at the date of the gift (see section **7.1:1**). In addition, some lifetime gifts have been chargeable to inheritance tax and its two predecessors: capital transfer tax and estate duty.

However, at different times reliefs have been accorded for different reasons, partly to reduce the burden of capital gains tax and partly to reduce the unfair element of double taxation. When a gift is made there is, of course, no cash realisation out of which to pay tax. A donor makes no real gain: in economic terms, he sustains a loss.

During the period between 1965 and 1974, gifts were chargeable only to capital gains tax on the basis of the open market value of the asset disposed of at the date of the gift. However, after capital transfer tax was enacted in 1974, and until 6 April 1980, gifts were subject to double taxation: to capital gains tax and capital transfer tax, with some partial relief.

In the Budget Speech 1980, the then Chancellor of the Exchequer conceded that this had been a source of grievance and that representations had been received from a large number of double tax payers. The double charge was then cancelled by creating a general form of hold-over relief, the scope of which was progressively extended until 1989.

In the Finance Act 1989 that welcome trend was suddenly reversed, and hold-over relief became limited to specialised transactions, principally those in which some inheritance tax became payable. The new argument was that it was wrong for relief from both taxes to be simultaneously available.

However, agricultural and business property (see sections **8.3** and **8.5**) has been accorded more generous treatment since 1975, as the table below shows.

The past hold-over history of an asset is obviously an indispensable piece of information needed at the time of its sale, since the effect of past hold-over relief may be to trigger deferred capital gains tax liability from an earlier gift. (See table opposite.)

7.5:2   Form of relief

The mechanics of hold-over relief have always been as follows:

By joint written election, any chargeable gain arising to a donor is to be subtracted from a donee's acquisition value (see TCGA 1992 s 165). Thus, if and when in turn, the donee sells, he will pay capital gains tax on the gain accruing during the donor's period of ownership, as well as during his own. The chargeable disposal may never occur; the donee may, in turn, claim similar relief so that no gain is ever taxed.

The relief is applicable to a gift or other gratuitous transfer, including, where applicable, the difference between a price paid and the deemed disposal price substituted because the price paid is below current market value. To the extent the donee pays any price, hold-over relief is lost. The effect is to make gifts rather than sales desirable when rearranging ownership of assets within a farming family.

HOLD-OVER RELIEF FOR LIFETIME GIFTS

Periods of Time	*Business/Agricultural Property*	*Other Property*
1965–1974	No relief	No relief
1975–1979	Relief for Agricultural Property (F(2)A 1975 s 55)	No relief
1978–1979	Relief for Agricultural and Business Property (FA 1978 s 82)	No relief
1980	Relief for Agricultural and Business Property (TCGA 1992 s 165)	Relief for gifts between individuals (FA 1980 s 79)
1981	Relief for Agricultural and Business Property (TCGA 1992 s 165)	As above plus relief for gifts to Trustees (FA 1981 s 78)
1982–1989	Relief for Agricultural and Business Property (TCGA 1992 s 165)	As above plus relief for gifts between Trustees (FA 1982 s 82)
1989 ff	Relief for Agricultural and Business Property (TCGA 1992 s 165)	Relief only where transfer is chargeable to:– a) IHT (and not a PET); or b) exempt by Trustees of A&M settlement; or c) specified exempt IHT transfer (eg for public benefit)

7.5:3 Scope of relief

Since 1989, the previous general hold-over relief on gifts has been withdrawn. This makes the special relief on gifts of business assets a particularly valuable one, and the scope of the relief needs to be carefully considered. In order to qualify for the relief an individual must make a disposal of:

(a) an asset or an interest in an asset used in his trade, profession, or vocation; (see section **2.2**)

(b) an asset or an interest in an asset used in a family company's trade, profession or vocation; (see section **7.6:7**) or

(c) unquoted shares or securities in a trading company which qualifies as a family company (TCGA 1992 s 165(1)). The expression 'family company' means one in which the donor exercises at least 25% of the voting power, or in which his family, as defined in the legislation, can exercise at least 51% of the voting power and he himself can exercise at least 5% (TCGA 1992 s 165(8));

(d) an asset or an interest in an asset qualifying for agricultural property relief at 50%. This includes gifts of land occupied by family farming partnerships where transitional relief is still due (see section **8.4**);

(e) commercially managed woodlands (see section **13**);

(f) assets used in furnished holiday lettings (see section **5.6:4**). Agricultural property qualifying for relief at 30% is not included;

(g) Agricultural land with 'hope' or 'development' value. Relief is given on the whole of the gain, not merely the part reflecting the agricultural value of the property gifted.

The relief applies to partners as to other individuals carrying on a farming business permitting them to hold over gains on transfers of business assets amongst members of the partnership. Farmland owned by a partner but let to the partnership is included for this purpose.

Where only part of an asset has been used for business purposes or business use has not continued throughout the whole period of ownership, time or other apportionments are to be made so that only a part of the gain will qualify. Similarly, where the disposal is of shares in a family company (see section **7.6:7**) the proportion of gain relieved is that which the chargeable business assets bear to all the chargeable assets of the company. These rules are all directed to restricting relief to the business elements.

7.5:4   Effect of past hold-over relief

Where a gift was received before 1 April 1982 and hold-over relief had been claimed by election, the re-basing to 31 March 1982 (see section **7.2:3**) will effectively extinguish taxation of the held over gain. Thus the hold-over relief granted to the donor will never be recaptured in the hands of the donee.

A held over gain made after 31 March 1982 but before 6 April 1988 is not, of course, affected by re-basing, even though the donor may have owned the asset in question on that date. In these circumstances, special relief is given on a subsequent disposal on or after 6 April 1988 in an amount equal to one half of the reduction in the donee's acquisition cost. The effect of this compromise approach is to recapture half of the hold-over relief awarded and to allow half of it to be lost forever.

This form of relief applies to gifts of busines assets (TCGA 1992 s 165); and to gifts generally under the legislation in force up to 1989 (FA 1980 s 79, now repealed). Thus the general gifts relief, although repealed, has been fossilised in the legislation and continues to have an effect.

7.5:5   Woodlands, etc

Woodlands qualify for hold-over relief providing they are managed on a commercial basis with a view to realisation of profit. This excludes amenity or shelter woodlands, where trees are not felled for timber. The relief will apply to the gift of the solum, that is the land on which the trees stand, since gains on the sale or gift of trees themselves are exempt from capital gains tax (see section **13**).

Furnished holiday lettings also qualify (TCGA 1992 s 241).

7.5:6   Gifts to trustees

Gifts of assets to discretionary and life interest trustees qualify for hold-over relief irrespective of whether the asset is or is not a business or agricultural asset. That may be because the gift is not a potentially exempt transfer for inheritance tax, and the general objective is to avoid a double charge. Gifts of farm business assets by individuals to trustees may also qualify for hold-over relief under the provision for business assets (see section **7.5:3**).

Where the assets are gifted by trustees or where there is a deemed disposal of assets, for example on the termination of a trust (see section **15.7**), hold-over relief can be claimed provided the business is carried on either by the trustees themselves; or by the relevant beneficiary under the trust; or by a company in which the trustees hold at least 25% of the voting rights (TCGA 1992 Sch 7 para 2). For this purpose the relevant beneficiary is the beneficiary who had an interest in possession under the trust immediately before it came to an end.

7.5:7   Valuation

In the past, it has been necessary for the market value of assets, which are the subject of hold-over relief to be agreed with the Revenue. However, on 26 October 1992, the Revenue issued a Statement of Practice (SP 8/92) under which Inspectors will accept hold-over relief claims without any need to value the assets. The new concession is voluntary and applies only when both parties make a signed application, giving details of when and at what cost the asset was acquired, and any expenditure since then. They also must indicate they have satisfied themselves that the market value of the asset is in excess of the cost plus indexation to that date. If this request is not made, held-over gains are calculated in the ordinary way.

7.6   RETIREMENT RELIEF

7.6:1   Introduction

Farmers often treat the capital invested in their farms as the equivalent of a pension fund. Hence, on retirement, the taxation of farm assets is of considerable importance. Good husbandry, inflation, and rises in land values have tended to produce substantial gains on all asset disposals occurring at the end of a farming career.

To some extent these gains are capable of being alleviated by hold-over relief (see section **7.5** above), which defers payment of the tax. However, there is another exemption: retirement relief – available to those aged 55 years or over, which is advantageous in that it cancels, instead of deferring, tax.

During the years 1965 to 1985, retirement relief depended substantially on extra-statutory concessions, but the rules are now more precise. The relief is a valuable one. For disposals after 19 March 1991, chargeable gains of up to £600,000 secure relief. The first £150,000 of gain is wholly exempt, and of the excess £450,000, up to one half is exempt. The limits are subject to abatement in proportion to the 'qualifying period' (see Section **7.6:5**). As husband and wife are treated as separate persons, this exemption can be effectively doubled. The maximum relief available is reduced to the extent that relief has already been given on earlier disposals.

Although the tests for relief are stringent, it should be borne in mind as a possible aid to transactions both independently and in combination with other reliefs.

Although the heading to the section of the Act (TCGA 1992 s 163) uses the term 'retirement' this is misleading, since the claimant need not be giving up farming in order to secure the relief. It is sufficient that he sells or gives part of the business, and is over 55 years of age at the date of disposal (TCGA 1992 s 163). There is no distinction made in the application of the relief between a sale, or a gift, when the open market value of the asset is substituted and the gain calculated accordingly. However, since by definition no cash is available to pay taxes on the occasion of a gift, in that circumstance the retirement relief is perhaps more apt, and certainly more valuable.

7.6:2   Subject of relief

Relief is accorded to an individual who makes a 'material disposal' of chargeable business assets (TCGA 1992 s 163), used for the purposes of a trade, profession or vocation, or an employment carried on by an individual. The definition of business assets includes:

(a) the whole or part of a business; or
(b) one or more assets which, at the time the business was carried on, were in use in the business.

If the business ceases, relief is not lost, provided assets are disposed of within 12 months from the date of cessation. However, this period can be extended.

Business assets would include, for example, a farm cottage occupied by a farm worker, whilst a cottage let to an individual outside the farm would be treated as a non-qualifying investment. Stocks and shares held as investments similarly fail to qualify for relief even if they be included in the farm Balance Sheet.

It is not sufficient that the disposal consists simply of an asset, or a number of assets. Such assets must together amount to a farming business or part of a business. Whether they do so or not is a question of fact and degree, depending upon all the surrounding circumstances of a particular case. In *McGregor v Adcock* [1977] STC 206 the taxpayer owned 35 acres on which he had carried on a mixed farming business for more than ten years. In 1973, when 68 years of age, he secured planning consent to develop 4.8 acres, which he sold, realising a chargeable gain of £64,481, continuing to carry on farming on the remainder of the land. The General Commissioners found in favour of the taxpayer, but this was reversed in the High Court. The ratio of the decision was that the nature and extent of the farming business was so unchanged after the sale, it could not be said that part of the business had been sold.

The *McGregor* case was decided upon its own specialised facts, and should not be regarded as barring a claim to relief where the asset sold is an identifiable unit, for example the dairy part of a mixed arable and dairy farm. The sale in *McGregor* was of a relatively small proportion of the total land, and this appears to have been one determining factor. The judge said: '. . . if a man is farming 200 acres and sells off 190 of those acres, it may very well be that the nature and extent of the man's activities after the sale would be so wholly different from what they were before the sale that the inevitable conclusion would be that there had been a disposal of part or even the whole of the farming business . . .'

Whether a disposal amounted to part of a business was considered again in two cases adjudicated together: *Mannion v Johnston* and *Atkinson v Dancer* [1988] STC 758.

In the first case, the taxpayer made two sales of 17 acres and shortly afterwards 18 acres, out of his total 78 acres on which he grew corn and potatoes and reared bought-in stock for fattening and resale.

In the second case the taxpayer sold nine acres out of 22 acres of freehold land, plus 67 acres of leasehold land on which he carried on mixed farming. The Commissioner's determination that part of the business had been sold was held to be unreasonable and the Revenue arguments were accepted.

In the judgments, the point was made that the sale of a chargeable business asset will not in itself represent the sale of the business or any part of it 'this notwithstanding that it will be virtually inevitable that the sale of the land on which the business has been conducted will reduce the activity of the farmer and probably his profits'.

In practice, the Revenue acceptance that the disposal of 50% of a farm holding qualifies for relief, seems to be based upon the proposition that a disposal on this scale will reduce the activities to such an extent as to amount to the disposal of part of a business. Where less than 50% is disposed of, the judgment in *Atkinson v Dancer* seems to represent the authority for refusing to grant relief.

A further point arises in practice. Where the land sold is replaced by new land, the Revenue has been known to take the view that the implication of a replacement is that the activities and profits have not been reduced to such an extent as to amount to a sale of part of the business. The argument is that the purchase of new land represents a course of conduct which is inconsistent with 'retirement' using the word in its ordinary business sense.

7.6:3   The claimant

The taxpayer must be aged 55 years or over, or be retiring on the grounds of ill health. The former tapering relief for disposals occurring within five years before retirement age has been cancelled.

In the Revenue view, it must be the claimant's own ill health which has caused the retirement. For example, the claim that the ill health of a partner has forced another partner to retire is not grounds for relief in the Revenue view.

A husband and wife who qualify are each entitled to their own separate exemptions. No specific claim is required. This is not always helpful, as it may cause the relief to be exhausted against gifts of assets which also qualify for hold-over relief, with the result that sales of assets which fail to qualify for hold-over relief go unrelieved.

Retirement under the age of 55 on grounds of ill health must be specifically claimed by the farmer, within two years of the end of the tax year in which his disposal took place. His claim must be supported by such medical evidence as the Revenue may reasonably require. It is worth noting that the Revenue has taken powers to challenge a claim. The test is whether an individual has ceased to be engaged in farming by reason of ill health and is incapable of engaging in work of the kind which he previously undertook in connection with farming; and that he is likely to remain permanently incapable of engaging in this class of work. In so far as farming may involve heavy manual work, the test should not be difficult to satisfy, even where a farmer continues to enjoy reasonable health. For example, he may be employing a member of his family to accept management responsibilities or to perform the manual work.

Where the farmer carries on his farming business as a company (see section **6.2**), and has been a full-time working director of it, he may similarly retire on ill health grounds, the test being that he has ceased to work for the company and is incapable of working for it in a managerial or technical capacity. Retirement on grounds of ill health must be total. That is, the incapacity must seem to be permanent.

7.6:4   The retirement

The term 'retirement' is misleading, since the claimant need not be giving up farming in order to secure relief. It is sufficient that he sells or gives part of his business, and is over 55 years at the date of disposal. There is no distinction made in the application of the relief between a sale, or a gift, when the open market value of the asset is substituted, and the gain calculated accordingly.

However, there has to be some clear connection between a disposal and retirement. Difficulties may arise if a retirement takes place in stages, with progressive realisation of assets over a period of time. This may provoke the contention that there has been no single disposal of the farm business as a whole.

Example

Giles retires as an owner-occupier in 1987, and lets his land to Bill who farms it until 1992. In that year, Bill gives up and Giles sells the land. His disposal and his retirement were separate events, and it appears no relief will be due.

7.6:5   Retirement relief: qualifying period

The total exemption of £150,000 of gains depends upon a qualifying period during which the qualifying conditions have been satisfied. The period is ten years, and the maximum relief is reduced pro rata to the length of the qualifying period. Thus the minimum relief for one year is £15,000 total exemption, plus one half of the next £45,000. The qualifying period refers to ownership of the business, not ownership of a particular asset.

There are a number of alleviations to what seems a strict rule. Suppose a farmer starts as a sole farmer, then brings members of his family into partnership, and then, perhaps, transfers his business to a limited company, during the ten-year qualifying period. He should retain the reliefs, provided the detailed tests as regards his company director status are satisfied.

Again, it may be that his business was not carried on continuously through the ten-year period up to the date of retirement. A gap of up to two years is permitted, without loss of the period earlier in time. The period of gap does not necessarily itself count towards the ten years. It is not necessary that the business carried on before the gap should be the same business as that carried on after the gap.

Again, periods may be counted, during which the farming business in question was owned by the retiring tax payer's spouse; or the spouse's family company of which the spouse was a full-time working director. It is a pre-condition that the farm was transferred at some time to the retiring farmer.

Whilst it is possible to make up the ten years with periods of ownership of an earlier business, no credit can be similarly given in satisfying the requirement that the relevant business must have been owned for a period of one year before the relevant disposal.

7.6:6   Partnerships

A business carried on in partnership is treated as if owned by each partner. Thus a disposal of an interest in the partnership assets, is treated as a disposal of the whole or part of the partnership business. This secures relief, in so far as gains are realised on partnership balance sheet assets.

Additional problems arise, where an asset is owned by an individual but used by a partnership of which he is a member. This structure is common in the farming industry and is repeatedly referred to in this book, in particular in the tax-planning sections. The disposal of this asset must be 'associated with', the owner's 'withdrawal' from the partnership business. 'Withdrawal' includes partial withdrawal, and the business may continue.

Where, however, rent has been payable for the asset, usually land, to a landowning partner the land is treated as a non-qualifying investment, save for the proportion representing the individual's own share of the rent paid. A larger fraction may qualify if the rent were less than market rent. If a full market rent has been payable to avoid a grant of tenancy, thus creating an adverse inheritance tax position, retirement relief may be forfeited.

7.6:7 Companies

Retirement relief is available where there is a disposal of shares in a qualifying company. The company must be a family company, of which the retiring individual must be a full-time working director. That is, he must be required to devote substantially the whole of his time to the service of the company in a managerial or technical capacity. The function of agriculture undoubtedly satisfies this test.

'Family company' is a technical term, and meant one in which the retiring individual holds at least 25% of the voting rights. Alternatively, one in which he holds 5% or more and the combined holdings of himself, his spouse, or the ancestor, collateral or lineal descendant of himself or his spouse, amount to at least 51%. FA 1993 has amended these requirements, and it is now provided that the shareholding condition is limited to a single individual 5% test. Employees as well as directors qualify, so long as all the other conditions are satisfied.

In practice, most farming companies will be found to satisfy this test. It should be noted that all these conditions need to be satisfied at least for the minimum period of ten years to secure the maximum relief. However, it appears that if 25% has been owned for ten years, and the residue 75% owned, for say, one year, full relief will be due on 100%.

Relief is given only to trading companies, so that if the company holds assets other than trading assets, the relief is restricted in proportion to the value which total assets bear to trading assets. If the company has no non-trading assets, the relief is not restricted. Let land is, of course, not a trading asset.

A similar restriction is made where there is a disposal of shares in the family holding company of a trading group of companies. Again, only trading assets are eligible for relief and a disposal of shares is examined to determine the 'appropriate proportion' of aggregated gains. The appropriate proportion is calculated by dividing the value of the group's business assets by its total assets. To avoid double counting, a holding of shares in a subsidiary company by one member of the group is not counted as a chargeable asset. If a subsidiary company is not wholly owned, the value of both business assets is reduced by multiplying those values by a fraction which excludes minority or other interests.

The full-time working director test is made slightly less stringent where there is a group of companies or where companies are carrying on complementary businesses, so as to form a composite whole. This might apply where different companies have been set up to farm separate farms. Where the retiring individual works for more than one company, he may be treated as a full-time working director of any of the companies which qualifies as a family company.

Another situation contemplated is where the assets disposed of are owned personally by a director of a company and used in the trade of that company. Usually, that will be farmland. Relief is granted where the following conditions are satisfied:

(a) the individual owner is a full-time working director;
(b) the asset, which is usually land, has throughout the period of ownership been occupied rent free for the purposes of the company's trade;
(c) the disposal is associated with the disposal of shares within the company.

Where the conditions in (a) and (b) above are satisfied at the time of disposal but were not satisfied at some earlier date, only a proportion of relief will be due. Similarly if the rent were less than market rent, a corresponding proportion of the gain will remain eligible for relief. These rental requirements need to be borne in mind when setting up family farming partnerships and companies (see sections **15.3:3** and **15.6:10**).

Relief is also due if the disposal of the shares is in course of a liquidation of the company. Such a disposal takes place when a liquidator distributes to shareholders, and that must be within one year (or longer permitted period) of the date when the farming business ceased.

7.6:8   Trustees

Relief may be claimed by the trustees of a settlement on the disposal of:

(a) shares or securities in a company (see section **6.2**). The beneficiary under the trust must be a full-time working director of the company; and the other corporate tests must be satisfied. It is the beneficiary who must qualify as having reached the age of 55 years or retired through ill health; or

(b) where the farming business has been carried on by a life tenant beneficiary under the trust, (the 'qualifying beneficiary'). He must have had an interest in possession in the assets which are the subject of relief. Joint life tenancies and partnership businesses do not debar relief.

7.6:9   Ancillary businesses

FURNISHED LETTINGS

Retirement relief is available for those carrying on the business of furnished holiday lettings (TCGA 1992 s 241). It is not accorded to woodlands, even if carried on for income tax purposes under Schedule D. Retirement relief is not accorded to the letting of land in general under Schedule A.

MILK QUOTA

Milk quota is treated as a chargeable business asset for the purposes of retirement relief (see section **2.4:2**). Thus, a sale of quota at the time of and together with a sale of farmland may amount to part of a business. On the other hand, if the land is sold on one date to one buyer, and milk quota is sold separately on another date to a different buyer, a claim for retirement relief may fail.

There is more chance of success where the sale of a quota is connected with the disposal of the dairy herd, milking parlour and other equipment. This will enable the claimant to indicate that the quota was part of a particular activity or enterprise, so that the sale did cause a change in the nature of the activities carried on, to such an extent that it could not be said that the 'nature and extent of the farming business was unchanged'. In particular, the Revenue may ask for proof that the sale of milk quota interfered with farming business as demonstrated by earnings before the quota sale and earnings after the quota sale. In one case, where the milk quota was sold together with a dairy herd and milking equipment but a suckling herd was retained, there was shown to be a profits reduction in excess of 50%, and retirement relief was conceded to be due (see section **7.6:2**).

7.6:10 Interaction of retirement and hold-over reliefs

When a farmer makes gifts of business assets, he may have entitlement both to retirement relief and to hold-over relief (see section **7.5**). The order of priorities is that retirement relief (an exemption) is given first. If the whole gain is relieved, then no recourse to hold-over relief will be required. If the whole gain is not relieved, hold-over can be claimed for the unrelieved excess (TCGA 1992 Sch 7 para 8).

ORDER OF PRIORITY OF LOSSES

Gains and losses on assets forming a business or part of a business are aggregated, and retirement relief is then applied to any net gain remaining. Gains and losses on non-business assets are separately aggregated, and remain unaffected by retirement relief.

7.7 TRANSACTIONS IN LEASES, TENANCIES AND REVERSIONS

7.7:1 Introduction

English law regulating transactions in land is complex, and every general principle, once having been stated requires qualification. What follows is a necessarily brief, selective outline of landlord and tenant law offered as a preliminary to the taxation treatment.

The basis of a leasehold tenancy is a grant by a landlord to a tenant of exclusive possession of the property which is the subject of the lease, plus the intention to create the landlord and tenant relationship. Such leases may exist for any fixed period of time, or operate 'periodically', that is from year to year. At the end of the period of the lease, a tenant hands back the land to his landlord, together, theoretically, with all the buildings on it. The tenant may also be liable for dilapidations, that is, depreciation of the land occurring during his period of tenancy. The respective obligations of landlord and tenant may be governed by common law; by statute, for example, the Agricultural Holdings Acts; or by the terms of the lease, which will stipulate the rent payable and responsibilities for other outgoings. Landlord and tenant do not have total freedom to contract, and a tenancy may be subject to statutory rules, overriding the terms agreed by the parties.

In agriculture, the influence of the Agricultural Holdings Act 1948 has been considerable. The Act recognised that farming is a long-term activity, and one objective was to give tenants security of tenure, virtually for life. This principle was reinforced and extended by the Agriculture (Miscellaneous Provisions) Act 1976, which introduced a scheme of rights of succession to farm tenancies by members of a tenant's family (see chapter 1).

The Agricultural Holdings Act provides three-year rent reviews for farm tenancies in England. In combination, the various provisions designed to protect tenants have made landlords reluctant to let, have created a shortage of new tenancies, and have tended to result in a tenancy having considerable value attributed to it. The amount of that value and the taxation treatment of transactions in tenancies are both open to dispute, bearing in mind that agricultural tenancies are usually, under the terms of a tenancy, unassignable. It may be that only one 'buyer' is in the market – the landlord, who is anxious to extinguish the tenancy, to secure vacant possession and farm himself. The taxation advantages of doing so may be a factor in mind, but he may want the farm to add to the home farm, or to extend his existing farming operations more profitably, or for occupation by a son or other member of the family.

7.7:2   The landlord's liabilities

If the landlord makes a payment to the tenant, he will be doing so to secure vacant possession by way of surrender of the lease, so enhancing the value of his reversion. The payment will therefore augment the landlord's cost base for capital gains tax purposes, and relief will be secured if and when the freehold is sold for an ultimate capital gain.

If the landlord pays nothing, no tax considerations arise. Where exceptionally, the tenant makes a payment to the landlord, to induce him to accept surrender, that sum will be liable to capital gains tax in the hands of the landlord. The relevant cost base would normally be nil. (See, however, section **4.2** for liability to income tax under Schedule A.)

Where vacant possession is acquired, and there is a disposal of the whole interest, liability may arise under Schedule D Case I as an adventure in the nature of trade, but the Revenue has indicated that it would not mount an attack under TA 1988 s 476 (see section **5.7:3**).

7.7:3   The tenant's liabilities

If as is usual, the landlord makes a capital payment to the tenant, the latter will be liable to capital gains tax. In computing the tax, deductions will be due for expenditure by the tenant on improving etc the land and any buildings surrendered with the tenancy.

If the landlord pays nothing for the surrender, the whole of the tenant's asset will have been lost or destroyed in the act of surrender, and it may be that a loss will arise for capital gains tax purposes, on the principles described. On the other hand, if the landlord and tenant are connected persons, it may be the Revenue will seek to infer or substitute an 'arm's length' price as consideration for the surrender with consequential effects on the capital gains tax computation (TCGA 1992 s 17 but hold-over relief may be claimed). If, exceptionally, the tenant pays the landlord, the payment will fall to be treated as expenditure incurred in the disposal of the asset, so, presumably, producing a loss.

The tenant's position will differ if what he receives is not a payment for the surrender of his tenancy, but compensation in respect of disturbance under the Agricultural Holdings Act 1948 s 34. Such payments are intended to reimburse the tenant for the loss or expense suffered in having to quit. Up to one year's rent can be claimed with proof of loss and up to two years' rent if particular proof can be provided. These receipts are not derived from an asset, and therefore no liability arises. Similar treatment is accorded to comparable payments of up to four years' rent made under the Agriculture (Miscellaneous Provisions) Act 1968, as compensation for surrendering the tenancy on a notice to quit from the landlord or on a notice of entry served by the local authority. Payments of this class are made where land is required for private or public development or for other non-agricultural purposes, and the tenant would be entitled to compensation under the Agricultural Holdings Act 1948 s 34. This receipt is wholly exempt from income taxation and capital gains tax (*Davis v Powell* [1977] STC 32).

Any element of compensation which includes specific payments for loss of profits, growing crops, manurial values etc, will be treated as part of trading profits and liable to income tax. Lump sums may fall to be apportioned between taxable elements of this class, and non-taxable elements relating to the tenancy.

Where capital gains tax arises, there may well be mitigation of the liability via one or more of the reliefs described in sections **7.3–7.6**. A tenant farmer receiving compensation may be retiring from farming and therefore entitled to retirement relief. Alternatively, part of the compensation may relate to the farmhouse and garden, which is exempt from capital gains tax as the principal private residence. Thirdly, if the outgoing tenant intends to continue farming either as a tenant of another farm, or as an owner occupier, and invests the proceeds of sale in qualifying assets, he may become entitled to roll-over relief. All these reliefs which mitigate the burden of taxation on the tenant may become factors in the negotiation of the price between the parties, and should be borne in mind by advisers when values are being determined.

Finally, one attractive view is that security of tenure is not a chargeable asset for capital gains tax purposes, so that if a tenant had no lease or other tenancy, and were merely a tenant at will, in pursuance of statutory right or 'non-proprietary rights', no liability would arise on surrender of vacant possession. This view is not normally accepted by the Inland Revenue, save as applicable to disturbance compensation payments already described.

7.7:4 Extension of leases

In so far as the extension of a lease involves the surrender of an old lease and the grant of a new lease, liability to capital gains tax may arise, (see section **7.7:2**). Under an Extra-Statutory Concession however, the surrender of a lease at its expiry date and the grant of a new lease for a longer period would not be regarded as a disposal or part disposal of the existing lease for capital gains tax purposes, provided all the following conditions are complied with:

(a) The transaction is between unconnected parties at arm's length. It will not therefore be available for tenancies between a landowner and a family farming partnership of which he is a member.

(b) The transaction is not part of, or connected with a larger scheme or series of transactions.

(c) A capital sum is not receivable by the lessee for his surrender.

(d) The property which was the subject of the old lease and which is the subject of the new lease are similar in extent.

(e) The terms of the new lease other than its duration and rent payable do not differ from those of the old lease.

It will be apparent from the above that the value of this concession is extremely limited.

7.7:5 Sales and leaseback

During periods when borrowing costs are high, the sale of a freehold to a financial institution and a lease-back from that institution may seem an economic method of raising cash. The object may be to buy additional land, or to provide working capital, or funds for capital transfer tax mitigation. The rent payable represents the equivalent of interest on borrowed money, but is generally at a lower rate. On the other hand, the landowner will have parted with the reversion, which he would have retained had the land been mortgaged or charged.

In the ordinary course, the sale of the freehold would be at full (tenanted) value, and the lease rent would be similarly a market one. The line of attack mounted by the Revenue is that the sale and leaseback amount only to a part disposal by the original owner-occupier, and that a substantial value (related to the 'vacant possession premium') should be attributed to the tenancy. The effect can be to reduce significantly the base cost to be set against the disposal proceeds, and to increase correspondingly the realised capital gain. The problem can arise in other contexts, for example where land is disposed of subject to reservation of sporting rights over it.

The nature of a sale and leaseback lends itself to compensating adjustments, for example, the inflation of the sale price, with matching inflation of the rent payable. One device has been for an owner to grant a long lease (over 50 years) at a nominal rent (ground rent) at a substantial premium. The grantee – an institution – then grants a short leaseback to the former owner at a high rent during the early years of the lease, effectively repaying the premium, diminishing to a lower rent in the later years of the lease. The object was to create a large deductible rent payable, and a large relatively untaxed premium receivable. Anti-avoidance legislation has been enacted to counter this abuse (TA 1988 s 779).

The effect of that legislation is to restrict the rent payable to the commercial rent, that which could be obtained on an open market letting of the property at a uniform rate. However, the recipient remains taxable on the full rent receivable. There is little evidence that this practice has been adopted for agricultural land. Mostly sales and leases back are on ordinary terms, and may be adopted where a farm is being acquired by a farmer from a third party, and the institution intervenes to provide the finance for the purchase. In these circumstances, there can be no doubt that the terms will be at arm's length. If the farmer buys from the third party at one price, and then resells to the institution at another, that may be justified by the fact that the first transaction applies to land with vacant possession, and the second to tenanted land. However, there is in such circumstances a danger that the anti-avoidance legislation may apply.

There is a further set of anti-avoidance provisions (TA 1988 s 780), applicable where the sale is made by a lessee under a short lease (less than 50 years), and where the leaseback is for a term not exceeding 15 years. Then the capital sum receivable by the assignor is partly treated as an income receipt. The proportion to be so treated is calculated by applying the formula:

$$£x = \text{capital sum received} \times \frac{16 - \text{term of years of new lease}}{15} \text{ (TA 1988 s 780(3))}.$$

Where the rent payable under the leaseback is deductible in computing farming profits, the taxable proportion of the capital sum is treated as a receipt of the farming business. If the rent is not so deductible liability is under Schedule D Case VI.

Sales and leaseback transactions may also be attacked under TA 1988 s 776 (see section **5.7:3**).

7.7:6 Purchase and sale of reversion

Another transaction familiar to practitioners is where the tenant purchases the freehold reversion, releases his tenancy, and sells the land with vacant possession. In these circumstances, the question arises as to when the intention to sell was formulated. If before the purchase, there would be prima facie liability under Schedule D Case I as an adventure in the nature of trade (see section **5.7**). If after the purchase, liability should be to capital gains tax on the authority of *Taylor v Good* [1974] STC 148, where it was held that a person who buys property without the intention of resale is not trading, merely because he takes steps to enhance the value of his property before selling it. But the application of TA 1988 s 776, artificial transactions in land (see section **5.7:3**), should be borne in mind.

7.7:7 Mergers of leases and reversions

Special problems arise in calculating indexation allowances due on a disposal, where a lease has been merged with a superior lease or with the freehold reversion. That would have occurred when a tenant farmer acquired the freehold, and his agricultural tenancy ceased to exist.

Under Extra-Statutory Concession (D42) taking effect 29 June 1992, the acquisition costs of a lease are to be determined by reference to the original date of acquisition, even though that lease may have ceased to exist at the time of disposal of the property, because it has merged with a superior interest, for example the freehold reversion. Indexation, therefore, falls to be calculated having regard to historical cost or, where rebasing applies, on the value as at 31 March 1982. Unless, exceptionally, a capital sum was paid for acquisition of the agricultural tenancy, the market value on the rebasing date is likely to be of more substantial value.

7.7:8 Valuation of agricultural tenancies

At the time of writing, the Revenue view seems to be that the value of a tenancy becomes relevant for capital taxation purposes:

(a) On a sale and leaseback (see section **7.7:5**); and
(b) also where the tenancy has been granted to a company, and the shares of the company are to be valued on an assets basis for capital taxation purposes, either on a sale not at arm's length (capital gains tax) or on a gift (inheritance tax).

The reasoning in (b) is that a tenancy in favour of a company confers a perpetual right, since no death can occur to bring the tenancy to an end.
(c) Where a tenancy has been granted to a partnership by one of the partners.
(d) For capital gains tax, the attribution of value to a tenancy is often a contested issue because the tenancy has no historic cost base to be set against the proceeds of disposal. The situation has been improved by the introduction of rebasing as at 31 March 1982 (see section **7.2:3**). For tenants whose tenancy was in being at that date a rebasing election (TCGA 1992 s 35(5)) may have the effect of creating an offsettable loss for capital gains tax purposes. On this reasoning, it would be necessary to value the tenancy as at 31 March 1982, recognising that the higher the value at that date the larger the aggregable loss on ultimate disposal.

At one time, the Revenue did not appear to contend that on the death of a tenant, and the succession to his tenancy, a value for the tenancy fell to be included in his estate for capital transfer tax purposes. The current position under inheritance tax is not quite clear.

The former view was that the successor acquired under succession law, not a right to the tenancy itself, but a right to apply successfully for a new corresponding tenancy. Thus it was argued, the existing asset was never transferred, but was extinguished and a new asset had come into being.

The change from capital transfer tax to inheritance tax does not of course affect these arguments, it is merely that the Revenue is less willing to accept the reasoning set out above.

In general the argument has turned on the question of whether non-assign-ability is a major factor in determining the market value. The basis of the Revenue position for capital gains tax purposes has been the principle in *IRC v Crossman* [1937] AC 26. The principle may be stated as follows: when property is subject to a restriction on assignment, the valuation should proceed on the assumption that one assignment to a hypothetical purchaser would be made. It would be assumed in making this valuation that the hypothetical purchaser would be taking the tenancy subject to the same rights and obligations as had been enjoyed by the vendor. Thus if the tenancy were not assignable, its resale capacity would be limited, and its value would be correspondingly reduced.

It is not certain that the *Crossman* principle applies to inheritance tax as it applied to estate duty. It has been argued that inheritance tax provides its own rule for the treatment of property which cannot be freely assigned (Inheritance Tax Act 1984 s 163). This provides that an exclusion or restriction should be taken into account only to the extent that consideration in money or money's worth was given for it.

The argument was advanced, but not resolved, in *Baird's Executors v IRC*, a Scottish land tribunal case heard on the 14 June 1990 (1991 SLT (Lands Tr) 9). The facts were that a father with his landlord's consent transferred to his daughter-in-law and grandson an otherwise non-transferable tenancy. The tax payers contended that as the tenancy interest transferred was unmarketable at the time of transfer due to the prohibition against assignment, the value of the transferor's estate was not diminished and so the value of the transfer must have been nil.

It was submitted that the decision in *Crossman* and other cases should be disregarded because they applied to shares in private companies. The Land Tribunal was not persuaded. It held, on the basis of *Crossman*, that the restriction on assignment should be disregarded for the purposes of the hypothetical open market sale; although the property had thereafter to be valued in the hands of the hypothetical purchaser as subject to the same restriction. It appeared that the tenancy in question had itself been so transferred on several occasions with the landlord's consent.

There was also relevant evidence of value to be drawn from examples:

(a) payments by landlords to tenants to give up tenancies;
(b) sales and leaseback, where a tenancy was acquired;
(c) compensation for compulsory acquisition.

So the reality of the situation was that a tenancy might be regarded as readily transferable and that a fair test generally to apply was 25% of vacant possession value plus improvements.

Currently, the debate concerning the valuation of tenancies has moved from the question as to whether a tenancy is capable of valuation to the question of what should be the correct basis of valuation. The Revenue view emerged clearly from a meeting between Revenue representatives and the Law Societies on 3 February 1992 arranged to discuss the valuation of agricultural tenancies. It seems to have been agreed that the principles of the *Crossman* case applied in general, where an asset is subject to restrictions on disposal. It also appears to have been agreed that there were various special factors to be considered:

(a) The benefits attaching to the tenancy, eg residential accommodation, rights of compensation for disturbance, waygoing (Scotland), dilapidation claims, improvements, manurial rights, and the fact that the rent might currently be less than the market rent.
(b) The principle that there should be no automatic presumption that the value of a tenancy could be arrived at by a method based upon a standard percentage of the vacant possession premium or value.
(c) Consideration of who might be in the hypothetical market for the tenancy.
(d) The weight to attach to the various factors relevant in valuing the tenancy, which would be a matter of fact and for negotiation in each case.

The area of disagreement, apparently, was whether the Revenue had been correct to use as a valuation starting point a percentage of the vacant possession value of the land or the vacant possession premium. It was also agreed it was open to the taxpayer to adduce evidence at an early stage if the character of the landlord was to be a factor in determining the value, namely that there was evidence that he was likely to make a bid for vacant possession of the land, or not, as the case might be. If the issue had arisen, for example, on the death of a tenant farmer within seven years of transferring his tenancy, such evidence could be submitted at the same time as the accounts for the estate were sent in. The Revenue would then be on notice from the outset that the question of a bid by the landlord was a matter that the taxpayer believed was not a factor to take into account.

It was agreed that if taxpayers were given an opportunity to adduce such evidence that would resolve many difficulties. Evidence of landlord's intention was, the Revenue agreed, admissible in existing open cases without any guarantee being given that the Revenue would accordingly modify its approach to valuation (see Law Society's Gazette, 18 March 1992 p 15).

It is worth adding that from the practical stand-point, negotiating or establishing a low value for a tenancy may no longer be as valuable as hitherto.

For inheritance tax, agricultural property relief at 100% may extinguish the valuation problem. For capital gains tax, the general fall in values since 1982 may produce a similar effect, assuming, of course, that a corresponding valuation basis be applicable on both dates – at Budget Day 1982, and the date on which the disposal or deemed disposal occurs.

Where a tenancy falls to be valued for capital taxation purposes, the basis of valuation will normally be the total comprised of the tenant's improvements, tenant right, and the capitalised value of the difference between the rent payable and an open-market rent, as determined by the Lands Tribunal. This value would then be reduced or discounted to take into account non-assignability as appropriate.

7.7:9 Jurisdiction

In the past, problems have arisen as to the determination of liability to inheritance tax, when a question of agricultural land valuation is involved. The procedure has been for the taxpayer to appeal to the Special Commissioners (see section **19.2:5**) against the Revenue Notice of Determination. However, if the issue was solely one as to the value of the land, the appeal fell to be heard by the Land Tribunal rather than by the Special Commissioners. Thus, if the Special Commissioners declined jurisdiction, or there was a dispute as to which body had the relevant power, a complex position was reached and many outstanding appeals were held up.

This administrative difficulty has been resolved in FA 1993 by giving the Special Commissioners power to refer to the Land Tribunal questions as to the value of land in inheritance tax appeals. This extends to inheritance tax appeals a facility which already exists for other taxes (TMA 1970 s 47).

7.8   CAPITAL GAINS TAX: OPTIONS

Options widely used in land transactions, have special consequences for capital gains tax, and careful planning is needed. An option is a conditional contract, in which one party pays the other to obtain a period of time within which to consider whether or not to buy or sell.

The first step, when the right to buy or to sell at a later date is created, is called the 'grant' of the option. The second step, when the purchase or sale, in accordance with the option, is completed is called the 'exercise' of the option. If the contract binds the grantor to sell, it is a 'put' option. Conversely, if the contract binds the grantor to buy, it will be a 'call' option. This preliminary explanation is necessary, because the capital gains tax consequences vary depending upon whether or not the first step only takes place, or whether both steps are ultimately completed.

For capital gains tax purposes, it would be logical when an option over land is granted for a consideration, that this were a part disposal of the land. However, logic is ignored and the option is treated as a separate asset so that the grant of it is a disposal (TCGA 1992 s 144(1)). It is therefore necessary to distinguish two situations; first, where the option is exercised; and secondly, where the option is abandoned.

(A) EXERCISE OF OPTION

If the option is subsequently exercised, the original grant and the subsequent exercise are treated as a single transaction (TCGA 1992 s 144(2)).

The treatment of the consideration paid for the option is as follows:

> The grantor of the option adds the consideration for a 'put' option to the sale proceeds; alternatively he deducts the consideration for a 'call' option from the acquisition cost. The cost to the grantee of an exercised option is part of the total cost of the land.

As regards the timing, a disposal is treated as having taken place at the date of exercise. Thus a sale cannot be carried out in two stages by introducing an option as a separate step, so as, for example, to take advantage of a vendor's two successive years' annual exemptions. However, for the purposes of determining the starting date of indexation allowance, the cost of an option is treated as an item of expenditure separate and distinct from the price paid for the option. Thus it can be said that the tax rules are not even-handed in their application as between the two parties.

(B) ABANDONMENT OF OPTION

If the option is abandoned, that is the rights granted by it are never exercised, the treatment is similarly unfair. The grant of the option stands as a separate disposal, and any amounts received by the grantor will be subject to capital gains tax (TCGA 1992 s 144(1)). Normally, the only costs deductible will be legal or professional expenses. As regards the grantee the abandonment of his rights under the option does not qualify as a disposal for capital gains tax purposes so that no deductible capital gains tax loss arises. There is an exception to this rule if the option was to acquire business assets or traded options on a recognised Stock Exchange (TCGA 1992 s 144(4) & F(2)A 1987 s 81(5)).

Although a simple abandonment of an option is not deemed to be a disposal, where a payment is made as consideration for abandonment, that amount can create a disposal so giving rise to a loss or a gain for capital gains tax purposes.

One factor which makes these rules important is that where deposits are paid in contemplation of a land transaction, and that deposit is not subsequently returned, but is forfeit, the transaction falls to be treated as the grant and the abandonment of an option to purchase. The recipient of the deposit becomes liable to capital gains tax, but the payer of the deposit is not treated as having sustained a deductible loss. Thus the price of entering into land transactions where a deposit is irrecoverable can be higher than at first may appear.

Example

Giles agreed to purchase Black Acre Farm from Black and paid him £10,000 as a deposit. He decided, on reflection, not to proceed, and under the terms of the agreement was unable to recover the deposit he had paid. The treatment of the parties for capital gains tax is as follows:

Giles

Although he has lost the £10,000 he cannot claim loss relief because he has made no disposal (see above).

Black

He has disposed of the option and has received £10,000 which is liable to capital gains tax less deductible legal expenses etc.

Consideration receivable as option money can be the subject of a claim to roll-over relief (see section **7.8:2**).

7.8:1 Options as wasting assets

An additional complication is that because options are 'wasting' assets, acquisition costs are progressively written off. A wasting asset is one with a predictable life of fifty years or less. On disposal, the historic cost and any acquisition expenditure are reduced in accordance with a 'wasting' formula on a straight line basis over the lifetime of the asset remaining at the date on which the cost or expenditure was incurred. The effect is to reduce the amount of a deductible loss.

Options to acquire business assets and financial options are not, however, treated as wasting assets (TCGA 1992 s 45(2)). Leases of land are wasting assets, in respect of which expenditure is reduced, not on a straight line basis, but in accordance with statutory percentage tables (TCGA 1992 Sch 8 para 1(3)).

Wasting assets which are *tangible moveable* property are exempt from capital gains tax, unless capital allowances can be claimed. Thus options to buy or sell land are the principal category of asset to which the straight line write-off applies.

7.8:2   Roll-over relief

If roll-over relief would be due on a disposal of the land which is the subject of the option, it may also be claimed in respect of a gain arising on the grant of an option. That is to say, the consideration receivable as option money can be the subject of a claim to roll-over relief. Generally, roll-over relief will only be available where the land is occupied and used for the purposes of a trade (see section **7.4**).

Chapter 8

Inheritance tax

8.1 GENERAL SCOPE OF INHERITANCE TAX

8.1:1 Sources of inheritance tax

This section summarises the principal features of inheritance tax as an essential preliminary to consideration of more specialised and advanced material (for more detailed treatment see *Capital Taxes Encyclopaedia* Vol I, Butterworths).

Inheritance tax, introduced in the Finance Act 1986, replaced capital transfer tax which, in turn, replaced estate duty by a series of phased stages. Capital transfer tax operated from 26 March 1974 (lifetime gifts) and 13 March 1975 (transfers on death) until 18 March 1986.

It is impossible to understand the nature of inheritance tax without some preliminary understanding of the two taxes which preceded it, because it draws elements from both. Estate duty was a tax payable on all property passing on death, but was extended to property which had been given away during the five years preceding the date of death. The obvious purpose of this extension was to counter tax avoidance based on 'deathbed' donation, and gifts made in the declining years of the deceased's life.

Capital transfer tax varied this principle. It was a lifetime gift and death tax charged at the time of the gift at increasing rates having regard to the cumulative total of lifetime gifts, with a final cumulation of the property passing on death. There were two rate scales, one for lifetime gifts and one for transfers on death. Originally, the two scales merged, but in the Finance Act 1981 and again in the Finance Act 1984, major changes were made: the maximum rate applicable on death was reduced from 75% to 60% with a lifetime scale of half the rate on death. Since 15 March 1988, there has been a flat rate of 40% on death, and 20% for lifetime transfers.

In 1981, the principle of lifetime cumulation (requiring that *all* past transfers be taken into account in determining what rate on a progressive scale should be applied to the next transfer) was abandoned. Cumulation was limited to ten years, so that in fixing the rate on any transfer, reference needed to be made to past transfers within a period of ten years immediately before the transfer in contemplation. The period is now limited to seven years (IHTA 1984 s 703).

A special relief for agricultural property was introduced in FA 1975 Sch 8, at the time when capital transfer tax was first enacted, but this regime was substantially amended in FA 1981 Sch 14 (see sections **8.4** and **8.5**). A separate special relief for business property was first introduced in FA 1976 Sch 10 (see section **8.3**).

The value and importance of both these sets of reliefs was substantially increased when the rates of relief, previously 30% and 50% were increased to 50% and 100% respectively in F(2)A 1992. Generally, the higher rate of relief applies to land with vacant possession and the lower rate of relief to tenanted land. Relief at the rate of 100% is, of course, equivalent to total exemption from inheritance tax and the introduction of this unprecedented rate of relief has significantly reduced the burden of tax for owner-occupiers and, to a lesser extent, for owners of tenanted land.

In its Budget Press Release 1992 the Inland Revenue stated that the changes would take some 400 estates out of inheritance tax for deaths in 1992–93 and that a further 1,600 estates would benefit from the increase in reliefs.

8.1:2 Inheritance tax: outline

This feature – cumulation – has been significantly varied under inheritance tax. Some gifts (but not all gifts) made during the deceased's lifetime, more than seven years before the date of death, are totally exempt from inheritance tax. These, principally, are gifts made by one individual to another; or by an individual to the trustees of a life interest or a maintenance and accumulation trust (see section **15.7:7**); or to the trustees of a trust for a disabled person. These gifts are named 'potentially exempt transfers' ('PETs'). A potentially exempt transfer is one whose tax consequences are uncertain until death. No tax is payable at the time of making the gift. If the donor dies more than seven years after making the transfer, that transfer will be exempt from tax both at the time of making the gift and at death. If death occurs within seven years of making the gift, there is no liability on making the gift, but the gift will be included in the taxable estate then, subject to progressive percentage rate reduction after three years: death in year four: 20%; year five: 40%; year six: 60%; year seven: 80%.

It will be apparent that the scope of charge of inheritance tax is similar to that of estate duty: it is chargeable on property passing at death, and its application to lifetime gifts is retrospective and designed for anti-avoidance purposes. On the other hand, the structure of the tax adopts that of the capital transfer tax legislation. It is payable on a 'transfer of value'. Transfer of value is any disposition by which the value of a transferor's estate is reduced immediately after the transfer (IHTA 1984 s 3(1)). The value transferred is equal to the amount of the reduction, which is not necessarily the same as the amount of the increase of the donee's estate.

This important principle can be illustrated by consideration of a 51% controlling shareholder in a company, making a gift of 2% of his shareholding. This 2% will represent a negligible value addition in the hands of the donee, but loss of control of the company by the donor can represent a substantial diminution of his estate for inheritance tax purposes.

Another important criterion borrowed from capital transfer tax is that of *intention*. A disposition is not a transfer of value if it were not intended to confer benefit and either:

(a) it was at arm's length between unconnected persons; or
(b) was such as might have been expected to have been made in such a transaction (IHTA 1984 s 10(1)).

Thus a poor bargain as such will not attract liability. By 'poor bargain' is meant, for example, the sale of land for £900,000 which could have been said to have been worth £1m. But for this provision liability would have arisen on £100,000.

In *IRC v Spencer-Nairn* ([1991] STC 60), the Revenue contended that the mere fact that a sale had taken place at an undervalue was itself evidence that the condition in (b) above was not satisfied. This was rejected by the Court. The undervalue was attributable to a specific error as regards the respective obligations of the parties in the sale, not to any intention to confer gratuitous benefit.

The importance of agricultural property relief and business property relief has already been mentioned. Since F(2)A 1992, the rates of relief of 100% and 50% for vacant possession land and tenanted land respectively have made these reliefs more important than hitherto. However, the reliefs are given only against specific qualifying assets, and in accordance with very detailed provisions. Thus 100% relief does not necessarily imply total exoneration from inheritance tax for the whole of a farmer's or landowner's estate.

8.1:3   Transfer of value

A transfer of value (see section **8.1:2** above) is not necessarily taxable. All such transfers are classifiable as follows.

(A) EXEMPT TRANSFERS

This means that a transfer has occurred, but in circumstances or as between parties in which there is some special exemption, for example a gift between husband and wife (IHTA 1984 s 18).

(B) POTENTIALLY EXEMPT TRANSFERS

This is an important inheritance tax concept. A potentially exempt transfer is a transfer made by an individual on or after 18 March 1986. It must be either a gift to another individual or to the trustees of a maintenance and accumulation, or life interest trust (see section **15.7:4**); or to a trust for disabled persons (IHTA 1984 s 89). During the period between the date of gift and the date of death, the transfer is treated as exempt. No tax is payable, and the cumulative total of chargeable transfers remains unchanged. At death, the seven years prior to death are reviewed to disclose what potentially exempt transfers have lost their exemption potential. All PETs made within that period become retrospectively taxed as if chargeable when made, save that the rate(s) applicable are those in force at the date of death. A sale at undervalue can give rise to a PET.

(C) TRANSFERS OF EXCLUDED PROPERTY

In this class, the exemption depends upon the nature of the property itself, for example, foreign property in the ownership of a non-domiciled individual; settled property, settled by non-domiciled settlor; and reversionary interests (IHTA 1984 ss 6(1) and 48(1)).

(D) CHARGEABLE TRANSFERS

All others (as regards gifts with reservation see section **8.1:5**).

TABLE OF RATES OF TAX
(From 6 April 1993)

£ Cumulative chargeable transfers	Rate	£ Lifetime cumulative chargeable transfers	Rate
0–150,000	0%	0–150,000	0%
over 150,000	40%	over 150,000	20%

8.1:4   Calculation of inheritance tax

Calculation of inheritance tax depends upon a series of rules which in combination make the calculation extremely complex.

The application of the cumulative principle has already been explained (see section **8.1:1** above). The effect of cumulation is to make the scale of charge steeper than it first appears.

The same is true of a second principle, that of 'grossing up'. It is the donor who is primarily accountable for inheritance tax. Grossing up arises on lifetime transfers which are chargeable as distinct from potentially exempt transfers. However, there are some exceptional situations where grossing up occurs on death. For lifetime transfers, the theory is that the donor should calculate the addition for tax deducted from any gift he makes, and hand it over to the Revenue. That is practically possible when the gift is cash, but not otherwise. If the donor gives, say, land, he is treated as having made a net gift of the value of the land, and by a grossing up process is deemed to have given that amount plus the amount of the inheritance tax thereon.

This awkward concept derives from the consequential loss formula: that the measure of liability is the loss to the donor's estate. That estate will have been diminished by the amount of the gift plus the amount of tax on the gift.

Another complication in the calculation of tax is 'aggregation'. Where more than one item of property is the subject of one chargeable transfer, the tax chargeable on the aggregate values transferred is attributed to the properties in the proportion which they bear to the aggregate. However, transfers which are exempt from liability are also exempt from the aggregation rule.

The inheritance tax code contains major anti-avoidance rules. In particular, the Revenue has taken power to look at a number of transactions together so as to counter an attempt to avoid tax by fragmentation of value or effect. A transaction may be comprised of a series of transactions, or may be achieved by what are called 'associated operations' (IHTA 1984 s 268). This is a concept which operated under estate duty. There is a very wide definition of what may constitute associated operations, and an operation includes an omission to act.

There are important rules stipulating how property must be valued (IHTA 1984 s 160ff). The value of any property is the price it might reasonably be expected to fetch, if sold in the open market at the time (IHTA 1984 s 160). There are special reliefs as to falls in value before and after death (see section **19.5**); and special provisions as to related property, that is, property held by both husband and wife (IHTA 1984 s 161).

8.1:5 Retained benefits

The concept of gifts with reservation is one revived from estate duty (see section **8.1:1** above). The object is to counter an avoidance device which might otherwise be attractive: that donors could give property away, so reducing their taxable estates, but continue to enjoy the use of it or the income from it, so that its lifetime value would be unimpaired.

The general principle of reservation of benefit is easily stated, and it is not difficult to exemplify. The example usually cited is that of a donor who gives a house to his son, but continues to live in it rent free. It is immaterial whether he lives in it for a whole year or only part of a year; or whether he has a legal right to live in it; or whether his occupation of it is by virtue of a contract. It can be said that his gift has 'strings' attached, and to that extent, his gift is treated as having failed.

The difficulty arises in identifying the limits of the rule and in precisely defining what is a gift with reservation.

The definition adopted is borrowed from estate duty. Reservation is deemed to apply where:

(a) possession and enjoyment of the property is not bona fide assumed by the donee at or before the beginning of the relevant period; or

(b) at any time in the relevant period, the property is not enjoyed to the entire exclusion, or virtually the entire exclusion, of the donor and of any benefit to him by contract or otherwise.

The relevant period is the seven-year period ending with the death of the donor. Thus, the rule envisages that a gift may be subject to a reservation which may automatically cease at some later date.

Arrangements where the occupation of property is divided amongst a family, not necessarily at full market price, are familiar in the farming industry. Family farming partnerships (see section **15.3:3**) and family farming tenancies (see section **15.2:5**) may both involve transactions which fall within the reservation of benefit rule. At the time of writing, considerable uncertainty exists as to the ambit of the rule, but attempt must be made to see which sets of transactions fall within its scope.

The Inland Revenue has indicated that the gift with reservation treatment does not apply to a gift of an undivided share in land merely because the land is occupied by all the joint owners including the donor.

It also seems to be clear that the rule does not apply to a partnership, provided that the profits and losses of the partnership are shared amongst the partners according to their respective interests in the partnership assets.

If a first slice of profits or partnership salary is payable to a donor, the test for reservation of benefit is whether the arrangement is one which might reasonably be expected under arm's length arrangements between unconnected parties. This is a general test applied by the Capital Taxes Office in a variety of circumstances involving changes in the ownership of land farmed by family farming partnerships, failure to review rents, assumption of donor's liabilities, and other similar events.

8.1:6   Retention of benefit: reliefs under IHTA

Under estate duty, the concept of reservation of benefit proved a source of major litigation. The first question for consideration is to what extent the estate duty case law defining reservation of benefit is applicable for inheritance tax purposes. There are strong arguments against the outright adoption of estate duty principles. If a precedent is needed, it was held in another context that estate duty cases were not influential in deciding the meaning of the phrase 'interest in possession' for capital transfer tax (*Pearson v IRC* [1980] STC 318).

Another new element is the influence exerted by the 'associated operations' rule (IHTA 1984 Sch 20 para 6(1)(c), see section **8.1:4**). Many of the cases determining the meaning of retention of benefit antedate the associated operations rule, and it is arguable that if that rule had then been in existence, the application of retention of benefit would have been held to have been much narrower.

Thirdly, under inheritance tax, the retention of benefit rule does not apply where the donor obtains his benefit by reason of hardship, but the relief is limited only to the situations where:

(a) the benefit is occupation of a house or land;
(b) the occupation results from an unforeseen change in the circumstances of the donor since the date of the gift;
(c) the donor has become unable to maintain himself due to age or infirmity;
(d) permitting the donor to occupy the property is reasonable provision by the donee;

(e) the donee is a relative of the donor or of the donor's spouse (IHTA 1984 Sch 20 para 6(1)(b)).

Fourthly, the inheritance tax retention of benefit contains a *de minimis* qualification which was not included in the estate duty rule. It requires the entire or 'virtually' the entire exclusion of the donor. The precise significance of 'virtually' is not clear, but the word must be intended to include such possibilities as occasional visits to a property by a donor so that his exclusion from it is not absolute (IHTA 1984 s 102(1)(b)).

Finally, occupation of the land, or the right over land, or the possession of a chattel is to be disregarded, if it is for full consideration in money or money's worth (IHTA 1984 Sch 20 para 6(1)(a)). So where a donor gives his house to his son, but continues to live in it, there will be no retention of benefit providing he pays a full market rent under a lease. Again, where a father gives the whole of his farm to his son, but continues to receive a share of profits, there will be no retention of benefit if he gives full consideration by continuing to contribute his services at a level, or on a scale, which justifies the share of profits which he receives.

Retention of benefit does not apply to exempt transfers, for example those between spouses (IHTA 1984 s 102(1)).

8.1:7 Retention of benefit: the precedent cases

In the light of the qualifications set out above (see section **8.1:6**), study of the estate duty cases may seem only of academic interest. This is not correct, and the cases are helpful in determining the shape of any tax plan.

In *Munro v Stamp Duty Comrs of New South Wales* [1934] AC 61 the donor, together with his six children in partnership, farmed his land. As a first step, he gave the land to his children, but continued as a partner in the farming business until his death. It was held that the property gifted was not the land, but the interest in the land, subject to the rights of the partnership. Thus, the land had no complete right of occupation attached at the time when it was the subject of the gift. So there was no reservation of benefit.

This decision falls to be compared with the reasoning in another leading estate duty case: *Chick v Stamp Duty Comrs of New South Wales* [1958] AC 435, [1958] 2 All ER 623. In this case, the gift of grazing land preceded the establishment of the partnership. The partnership between son and father was an arm's length arrangement, but despite that, it was held that the son had not retained possession and enjoyment of the farmland to the entire exclusion of the donor. So that when the donor died some 80 years after the original gift of the land, the land fell to be included in his estate for estate duty purposes.

The reasoning here was that the creation of the partnership amounted to a reservation of benefit out of the preceding gift.

Clearly, this difference in timing is capable of occurring in a wide range of transactions involving partnerships, tenancies, and in the corporate contexts, gifts of shares, employments etc. It is necessary to examine every family transaction to see whether retention of benefit can be said to be an element in it. If it is, the gift and the attempt to reduce the taxable estate will fail.

It should be noted that the retention of benefit concept can never apply to gifts between spouses. However, it does arise as regards gifts to trustees, and transactions involving trusts (see sections **15.7:3** and **15.7:5**).

8.2   INHERITANCE TAX: CHECKLIST OF RELIEFS AND EXEMPTIONS

Reliefs available to farmers on transfers of their property

IHTA 1984

Part V Ch I; FA 1987 s 58 and Sch 8	Business property relief
FA 1975 Sch 8	Full-time working farmer relief
Part V Ch III	Woodlands
Part V Ch II	Relief for agricultural property

GENERAL RELIEFS

s 18	Transfers between spouses
FA 1975 s 22(4)	Surviving spouse exemption (deaths before 13 Nov 1974)
s 19	Gifts not exceeding £3,000 pa
s 20	Outright lifetime gifts maximum £250 per donee per annum
s 13	Dispositions allowable in computing income tax or corporation tax
s 154	Transfers after death on active service
s 21	Normal expenditure out of income

RELIEFS BASED ON THE NATURE OF ASSETS DISPOSED OF

s 30	Gifts of heritage assets
s 27	Creation of maintenance funds associated with heritage assets
s 47/48	Transfers of reversionary interests
s 12	Provision of retirement reliefs
s 15	Waivers of company dividends
s 191	Falls in value of assets after death
s 227/229	Payment of tax by instalments
s 234	Interest-free instalments of tax

RELIEFS BASED ON PARTIES INVOLVED IN THE TRANSACTION

s 18	Transfers between spouses
s 22	Gifts in consideration of marriage made by parents, grandparents etc
s 11	Lifetime gifts for maintenance of children and relatives
s 23	Gifts to charities
s 24	Gifts to political parties
s 25 and s 26	Gifts for public and national purposes
s 86	Trusts for benefit of employees
s 142	Deeds of family arrangement

8.3   BUSINESS PROPERTY RELIEF

8.3:1   Introduction: nature of property relieved

During the years 1978–1981 business property relief (IHTA 1984 ss 103–114) effectively displaced full-time working farmer relief as a principal reduction of tax to be secured or maximised in any tax-planning exercise. It is broad in scope, available against both lifetime transfers and on death, and when qualifying property becomes chargeable under the rules for trust property. Since 1981, agricultural property relief applies to land, and business property relief applies only to tenants' capital in the farm business as opposed to land and buildings.

The scope of business property relief was extended in 1978 and again in F(2)A 1992 ss 72, 73 and Sch 14. There is now a range of categories of assets to which the relief applies, determining the rate at which relief is given (IHTA 1984 ss 104, 105 as amended by F(2)A 1992 Sch 14.)

Category of assets		*Value relieved*
CLASS I	Business or interest in a business.	100%
CLASS II	Controlling shares or securities in an unquoted company.	100%
CLASS III	Controlling shares or securities in a company quoted on the unlisted securities market.	100%
CLASS IV	Shares or securities in an unquoted company conferring more than 25% control.	100%
CLASS V	Shares or securities in a company listed on the unlisted securities market conferring more than 25% control.	100%
CLASS VI	Shares or securities in an unquoted company not so conferring 25% control.	50%
CLASS VII	Shares or securities in a company listed on the Unlisted Securities Market not so conferring 25% control.	50%
CLASS VIII	Shares or securities conferring control in a fully quoted company.	50%
CLASS IX	Land, buildings and machinery used in a business carried on by a partnership in which the transferor is a partner; or by a company in which he is a controlling shareholder (quoted or unquoted).	50%
CLASS X	Land, buildings and machinery used in a business in which the transferor had a life interest.	50%

For this purpose, 'business' includes a profession, but it does not include ownership of tenanted land, which is excluded as representing the holding of investments (IHTA 1984 s 105). Nor possibly does it include a business carried on otherwise than for profit, that is, where farming loss relief has been denied for income tax under the 'hobby' farming rules (IHTA 1984 s 103).[1]

For the purpose of business property relief, the distinction between the business itself and the assets used in the business is made in the same way as for capital gains tax retirement relief (*McGregor v Adcock* [1977] STC 206; *Finch v IRC* [1983] STC 157). This problem is particularly acute for trust assets used by a tenant for life, the subject matter of the *Finch* case. A specific relief at the rate of 30% is available for certain assets held in trust and used by a tenant for life (IHTA 1984 s 103(3)).

Another danger area arises because relief is excluded for a business which, by itself, might appear to qualify but is considered to be merely part of a larger, non-qualifying business (IHTA 1984 s 105(3)). This problem may occur with woodlands on an agricultural estate, which may be held to be part only of the larger non-qualifying business of letting land. Steps should be taken to establish that the woodlands amount to a separate business in their own right, for example by establishing and maintaining Forestry Commission dedication schemes and by maintaining separate sets of financial accounts.

A holding of shares is treated as conferring 'control', if as a result of holding it, the holder can control the majority of the voting powers on all questions affecting the company as a whole (IHTA 1984 s 269). Shares which are 'related property' fall to be taken into account (IHTA 1984 s 161). Shares held by the trustees of a settlement are deemed to be held by a tenant for life (IHTA 1984 s 269). A new category of substantial minority shareholdings was introduced by the Finance Act 1987. This meant shareholdings of more than 25%, but not more than 50% (Sch 8).

The rates of relief shown are applied before any other reliefs or exemptions applicable, for example annual exemptions:

Example

Value of business asset given	£100,000
Business property relief at 50%	£ 50,000
	£ 50,000
Annual exemption	£ 3,000
Chargeable transfer	£ 47,000

The effect of this order of priorities is to maximise the value of the relief (IHTA 1984 s 114).

1 Opinions differ. See A L Chapman *Capital Transfer Tax*, 3rd edn p 227.

8.3:2   Individuals and partnerships compared

The application of business property relief to individual farmers and farming partnership interests is not entirely clear, but the following summary of the position may be helpful:

Asset ownership by	Qualifying asset transferred	Rate of relief Pre-FA 1992	FA 1992
(a) Individual	Business or interest in business	50%	100%
(b) Individual	Identified asset	NIL	NIL
(c) Partnership	Whole partnership share	50%	100%
(d) Partnership	Part partnership share	50%	100%
(e) Partner	Whole or part partnership share	30%	50%
(f) Partner	Identified asset used by partnership (not live or dead stock)	30%	50%
(g) Trustee	Identified asset of business carried on by life tenant (not live or dead stock)	30%	50%

A gift of assets effected by transfer from one partner's capital account to another partner's account represents a transfer of an interest in a partnership in whole or part, as the case may be, qualifying for business property relief. It will be observed that in situation (f) above, relief at 30% is available, whereas in situation (b) above no relief is available. The logic of this is elusive.

8.3:3   Tests for relief

The only test is whether the transferor owned the property transferred for a minimum of two years immediately before the transfer (IHTA 1984 ss 106, 107). Alternatively, relief is due if the property 'replaced' other business property, and one or other property had been held for a combined period of two years out of the five years immediately preceding the transfer.

There are various further alleviations of the two-year test designed to meet special circumstances.

(a) Where the transferor acquired the property transferred on the death of his or her spouse, the spouse's period of ownership is added to the transferor's own, to make up the two qualifying years.

(b) If the transferor (or the spouse) acquired the property as a result of an earlier transfer eligible for relief, and one or both such transfers took place on death, the two-year period is waived. The successor must be carrying on the relevant business.

(c) If the transferor can satisfy the two-year test by amalgamating:
  (i) a period during which the property was used in a business carried on personally by him; with
  (ii) a period when it was retained, but used by a company of which he had control, and to which the business had been transferred.

In these special circumstances, the CTO has indicated that it would concessionally grant relief.

These alleviations make it worthwhile studying the history of any property before abandoning claim to relief.

There are no stipulations as to the amount of time an owner commits to the business, nor as to his income from it. Nor are there any quantitative limits for relief as for full-time working farmer relief. Hence farming units with more than 1,000 acres or £250,000 value can secure relief at full rate, which would have been denied to them before FA 1976. For transfers between 1976 and 1978, the position was that the first 1,000 acres would have been relieved at 50%, but the excess of land and all working capital was relieved at 30%. The question arises as to whether full-time working farmer relief needs to be considered or whether it has become wholly redundant (see section **8.5:6**).

8.3:4   Business property relief and potentially exempt transfers

The application of business property relief to property which is the subject of a potentially exempt transfer produces a complex position.

As a preliminary, it is worth noting that if a potentially exempt transfer is duly converted into an exempt transfer because the transferor has survived for more than the stipulated seven years after the date of the gift, there is no problem. The difficulties arise only if the transferor fails to survive the seven year period, in which case there may be a clawback of business property relief if certain conditions are not satisfied.

The complexities derive from the time limits which begin to run at the date of transfer; but also because the new rates of relief for agricultural property introduced by F(2)A 1992 apply to deaths on or after 10 March 1992 in respect of a potentially exempt transfer of value made before that date. The concept of potentially exempt transfers was introduced under the inheritance tax regime enacted by FA 1986, which took effect from 18 March 1986. Thus, inheritance tax on gifts made during a period of nearly six years before F(2)A 1992 may be retrospectively affected by that Act. In such circumstances, gifts during that period may attract agricultural property relief at 1992 rates and thus it is possible that, if 100% relief be due, there will be complete exemption from inheritance tax although that would not have been known at the time the gift was made.

The 100% relief attaches an increased importance to the conditions to be satisfied, so that, it may be worth reviewing past events in detail to ascertain whether relief is secured (see section **8.3:5** below).

8.3:5   Conditions to be satisfied

If death occurs within seven years of a potentially exempt transfer, inheritance tax is due on the death and the application of business property relief will depend upon all the following conditions being satisfied.

Similarly, where the transfer was a chargeable (and not a potentially exempt) transfer, and the death occurs within the seven year period, the same tests for business property relief are applicable. In these circumstances, the tax on the original life time transfer remains unaffected, and the tests for business property relief are relevant only so far as additional tax is due because the transfer will be taxed at death rate instead of lifetime rate.

The conditions are that:

(a)   The property which has been the subject of the transfer must have been retained in the ownership of the transferee throughout the period commencing with the date of the transfer and ending with the date of death of the transferor or the date of death of the transferee, whichever is the earlier (IHTA 1984 s 113A(3)(a), (4). It appears that even a gift by the transferee to his spouse will destroy entitlement to relief.

(b)   If the transferor predeceases the transferee, there is deemed to have been a notional transfer of value of the property immediately before his death, and the tests for relief are applied as at that date.

(c)   If, however, the transferee predeceases the transferor, the test is applied to the property in relation to the transfer of value made by the transferee immediately before he died (IHTA 1984 s 113A(3)(b)).

(d)   Quoted shares, and controlling shares in an unquoted company are not subject to the test in (b) or (c) above. The conditions as at the original transfer remains the only condition applicable (IHTA 1984 s 113A(3A)).

(e)   The property must be in the ownership of the individual at the relevant date and it must not be, at that date, subject to a binding contract for sale (IHTA 1984 s 113).

8.3:6   Replacement property and potentially exempt transfers

There are important and complex provisions permitting the replacement of the original property by new property after a potentially exempt transfer (IHTA 1984 s 113B). If the transferee has disposed of all or part of the original property before the date of his own death, or the transferor's, whichever be the earlier, and he has invested the proceeds in new and relevant business property, that property will be treated as qualifying for business property relief subject to detailed stipulations as follows:

(a) The whole of the proceeds of sale of the original property must be rein-vested in replacement business property. If only part of the proceeds of sale is applied in acquiring replacement property, the relief will be lost (IHTA 1984 s 113B(1)).

(b) The replacement property must be acquired within twelve months after the date of disposal of the original property. It is worth noting that the replacement must not have been acquired *before* the disposal (IHTA 1984 s 113B(2)(a)).

(c) The disposal of the original property and the acquisition of the replacement property must be made on arm's length terms (IHTA 1984 s 113B(2)(b)).

(d) The fact that one category of business property replaces another category does not destroy the relief, but the rate of relief is not to exceed that which would have applied had the replacement not been made. Thus if property eligible for 50% relief be replaced by property eligible for 100%, relief will be available at 50% on the new property until the new property itself qualifies by being held for two years.

(e) These replacement rules do not apparently apply to shares in unquoted companies which do not confer control. But some continuity is secured by invoking the capital gains tax share reorganisation and share exchange provisions, under which the ownership period of an earlier shareholding is deemed to be part of the ownership period of a new shareholding (see IHTA 1984 s 113A(b) and TCGA 1992 ss 126–136). Thus, for example, where a business is transferred to a company in consideration of an allotment of shares in that company and the transferor secures control of the company, the replacement rules are satisfied and business property relief will not be lost.

(f) Where the transferee predeceases the transferor, the two year ownership requirement is not imposed at the time of the notional transfer on death as regards replacement property. If it were, relief would be cancelled where a transferee died within two years of the transfer to him.

(g) Where there is more than one replacement of a property there is nothing to suggest the relief will be lost, provided in all other respects, the rules are satisfied.

(h) A situation which requires careful consideration is where the conditions above are satisfied only as regards a part of the original property. In such circumstances, it may be that part of the value which was the subject of the potentially exempt transfer will continue to qualify for business property relief; and part of the value will be chargeable without that relief (IHTA 1984 s 113A(5)).

The provisions permitting replacement of one business property with another are similar to those applicable to agricultural property relief (see section **8.5**). However, the detail differs from those according roll-over relief for capital gains tax (see section **7.4**), and from those governing replacement of business property by other property during the ownership period *before* the date of transfer. Great care is needed to avoid applying the wrong set of rules.

8.4   FULL-TIME WORKING FARMER RELIEF

8.4:1   Introduction

Full-time working farmer relief was repealed with effect from 10 March 1981 so the inclusion of the detailed rules for this relief requires explanation. In the first place, that explanation is to be found in the transitional provisions enacted in FA 1981 (see section **8.5:7** below). Under these provisions, full-time working farmer relief was fossilised in the law, in the sense that relief may still be applied to gifts of tenanted land after 10 March 1981 provided:

(a) tests for the relief were satisfied on 10 March 1981; and
(b) certain tests have been satisfied throughout the period between 10 March 1981 and the date of the gift.

The tenancy will have been granted to a family farming partnership (see section **15.2:1**).

The effective life of this relief was further extended in F(2)A 1992, which increased the rate of relief from 50% to 100% of value of agricultural property. Thus the benefit of the relief now is to secure 100% exoneration from inheritance tax, whereas before F(2)A 1992 the benefit was to secure 50% relief against tenanted (not vacant possession) value, the 'double discount'. Thus where there is a transfer of land tenanted by a family farming partnership, it is worthwhile contemplating a notional transfer as at 10 March 1981, and applying to it the tests set out below. Insofar as these tests are satisfied, relief will be at the rate of 100%, ie exemption from inheritance tax.

8.4:2   Nature of property relieved

This relief was first enacted in 1975 (FA 1975 Sch 8), at the time when capital transfer tax reliefs were narrow and meagre in scope and it ceased to have effect for transfers made on or after 10 March 1981 (FA 1981 s 92(3)). A number of different tests needed to be satisfied before entitlement to relief was conceded. These tests went to the nature of the property transferred; the identification of the occupier of the property; the capacity of the transferor as evidenced either by his activities or his income; and finally there were stipulated limits of scale. Relief applied to agricultural land or pasture; to woodlands only if occupied with agricultural land, and if the occupation was ancillary to agricultural land; cottages, farm buildings and farmhouses; and to land occupied with such buildings of an appropriate character.

8.4:3   Tests for relief

(A) IDENTIFICATION OF THE OCCUPIER

The property transferred must be occupied by the transferor or a company controlled by him for the purposes of husbandry at the time of the transfer, and must have been so occupied by him throughout the immediately preceding two years (FA 1975 Sch 8 para 3(1)(b)). This rule excluded owners of tenanted property from relief. The period of two years' occupation did not need to have been completed at the particular property which was the subject of the transfer. Periods at a previous property could count, provided agricultural property had been occupied for at least two out of the preceding five years. The relief extended to a transfer after retirement provided that the conditions for relief had been satisfied at that time, and the land had been occupied for the purposes of agriculture from that time to the date of transfer by a member of the transferor's family.

(b) CAPACITY OF THE TRANSFEROR

There was a further series of tests ensuring that the transferor was wholly committed to farming, not a person who regarded it as one activity or source of income amongst many. In not less than five of the seven years ending 5 April immediately preceding the transfer he needed to have been wholly or mainly engaged in the UK in any of the following activities: farming either alone or in partnership with others; farming as an employee; a director of a UK farming company, that is one carrying on its trading in the UK as its main activity; or a person undergoing full-time education, not necessarily agricultural education (FA 1975 Sch 8 para 3(2)).

(c) RELEVANT INCOME

All these several conditions were taken to be automatically satisfied, if the transferor's income had a particular source, or sources. He needed to show that not less than 75% of his 'relevant' income had been derived from his engagement in agriculture. 'Relevant' income for this purpose meant the aggregate of his earned income in any five of the last seven years of assessment (for income tax purposes) immediately preceding the transfer; excluding: all investment income (that is, interest, rents or dividends); all pensions, superannuation, or compensation for loss of office; and all wife's income, earned or otherwise (FA 1975 Sch 8 para 3(3)). If the transferor could satisfy this test in terms of figures, the 'wholly or mainly' problem did not need to be tackled. On the other hand, if all his activities had been unprofitable, yielding nil income for income tax purposes, then 'relevant' income would be nil and 75% of nil would still be nil. On this result, the 'wholly or mainly engaged' test might still be capable of satisfaction. In this connection, it was the relevant facts at the time of transfer which were to be examined. The comparative amount of *time* spent on agricultural activities was one criterion, but the Capital Taxes Office had regard to the income derived from different activities and the importance of the farming activity in the context of his life as a whole.

(d) BASIS OF CALCULATION OF RELIEF

After 6 April 1976, the relief was given as a discount of 50% of agricultural value (100% since FA 1992).

(e) LIMITS

The part of land eligible for relief (see FA 1975 Sch 8 para 5) when added to parts eligible under all previous chargeable transfers must not have exceeded £250,000 in value, or 1,000 acres in area (rough grazing land was counted as one-sixth of its actual area (FA 1976 s 74(6))), whichever basis be more favourable to the taxpayer. For this purpose, all chargeable transfers made on the same day were to be treated as one. Where the relief which could otherwise be given exceeded these limits, the excess was to be attributed to the agricultural properties concerned in proportion to their respective values or areas as the case might be.

8.4:4   Companies as occupiers

It was sufficient that the occupier of the property which was the subject of the transfer be not the owner himself, but a company 'controlled'[1] by him. This relaxation applied satisfactorily where the owner had incorporated his farming business, but had not transferred to his farming company the ownership of the land. In those circumstances the company would have occupied under a tenancy, and paid a rent to the owner.

The legislation also envisaged an alternative situation – where an owner had taken further steps of transferring his land to his company, and had died possessed of shares or debentures in that company, held in place of the relevant land. Then full-time working farmer relief was available against those shares or debentures, providing (a) the agricultural property formed part of the company's assets; and (b) the company's main activity was – and had been for two preceding years – agricultural. There was a further proviso – (c) that the shares or debentures must have given the transferor control, immediately before the transfer. In those circumstances, the capacity and income tests were still applied to the shareholder. In so far as the transferor's interest in the company was represented not by shares or debentures but by a simple balance on loan or current account, the relief was lost.

1 For the meaning of control, see FA 1975 Sch 4 para 13(7).

8.4:5   The two reliefs

The interaction of the two reliefs, *business property relief* and *full-time working farmer relief*, needs examination. The former was more accessible than the latter, being subject neither to tests nor limitations of scale. However full-time working farmer relief remained applicable in the following sets of circumstances:

(a) Where the transferor had retired, and farming was being carried on by a member of his family, or by a family partnership of which he was not a member, no business property relief would have been due, but full-time working farmer relief was due, providing all the relevant tests were satisfied.

(b) Where land was let by the transferor to a partnership, in which he was a partner, business property relief was due at 30%, but full-time working farmer relief might have been due at 50%, subject to the quantitative limits and other conditions.

(c) The same is true, where land was let to a company in which the transferor was controlling shareholder.

(d) Business property relief requires ownership for two years immediately preceding the transfer, whereas full-time working farmer relief requires mere occupation, capable of being comprised partly of a period during which the transferor was a tenant.

(e) A life tenant in possession is treated as a beneficial owner for full-time working farmer relief, but business property relief on land, buildings, machinery or plant was not available until allowed by FA 1981 s 100(3).

The interaction of full-time working farmer relief and agricultural property relief is examined at section **8.5:8**. See also sections **15.2:1** to **15.2:4**.

8.5   AGRICULTURAL PROPERTY RELIEF

8.5:1   Introduction

The measure exempting agricultural property from inheritance tax was described in the course of the 1992 Budget debate as an important and historic decision. Agricultural property relief at its new rates represents another attempt to accommodate the special economic problems of business and land owners whose enterprises are vulnerable to death duties. It supplements business property relief (see section **8.3**) and replaces full-time working farmer relief (see section **8.4**). It is applicable (at its current rates of 100% and 50%) to transfers of value made on or after 10 March 1992 and charges or further charges arising on a death on or after 10 March 1992, in respect of a transfer of value made before that date. In the past a number of reasons had been given for the relief, eg that capital transfer tax had been holding back the supply of land for new entrants to the farming industry, and that it was important to maintain a proper balance between owner-occupied and tenanted land, allowing for their different values.

The extension of relief has changed the general tax planning considerations applicable to agricultural property, in particular as to the relative importance of inheritance tax (see section **15.2:6**). Relief applies to:

(a)   agricultural land or pasture;

(b)   buildings used in connection with intensive rearing of livestock or fish if occupied with agricultural land, and the occupation of the building is ancillary to it;

(c)   woodlands occupied with agricultural land if occupation is ancillary to it;

(d)   cottages, farm buildings and farmhouses (together with the land occupied with them) as are of a character appropriate to the property (IHTA 1984 s 115(2));

(e)   shares in farming or landowning companies (see section **8.5:2**);

(f)   stud farms engaged in the breeding and rearing of horses, and for grazing associated with that activity (FA 1984 s 107);

(g)   sporting rights (see section **8.5:11**).

The limitation of relief to farmhouses which are 'of a character appropriate to the property' can cause difficulty. The Revenue view is that in interpreting this section, 'agricultural property' includes agricultural land or pasture, and farm buildings and farm houses if (and only if) they satisfy the stated condition. If they do not satisfy the stated condition, they do not qualify for relief. Thus a large and expensive 'farmhouse' standing in a relatively small acreage might be disqualified as 'inappropriate'. Further problems may arise because, in the Revenue view, the 'property' qualifying is limited to property being transferred by the transfer of value in question, and excludes property which, for example, was farmed by the deceased farmer but which was not comprised in that transfer of value because it has been in the ownership of another member of the deceased's family. Opinions differ. One alternative view is that farm houses are, by definition, 'agricultural land', and immediately qualify as such. That construction seems to make the proviso concerning 'character appropriate to the property' a redundant one, and it is difficult to see how it could succeed. This difference of interpretation has become more important since agricultural property relief was increased to 100% in F(2)A 1992. Moreover, the value of a farm house may be substantial by comparison with a small acreage of agricultural land.

Where at the time of transfer, the property is subject to a binding contract of sale, no relief is due, but this restriction is not applicable where the contract of sale is to a controlled company in consideration of shares, or in course of a company reconstruction or amalgamation (FA 1981 Sch 12 para 13). Family farming partnership agreements sometimes contain standard clauses stipulating terms of sale of partnership interests or property on future dissolution of the partnership; such clauses can result in relief being denied under this provision, and are to be avoided.

Relief is limited to agricultural property situated in the UK, the Channel Islands or the Isle of Man (IHTA 1984 s 115(4)). Unlike full-time working farmer relief (see section **8.4**) it is given automatically and need not be specially claimed. Nor are there any limits of scale corresponding to £250,000 or 1,000 acres. The relief is available on qualifying property owned by trustees of discretionary trusts, or where there is a vested life interest in trust property.

The definition of 'property' effectively limits agricultural property relief to 'landlord's capital', so that 'tenant's capital', that is, the value of plant and machinery, stocks on hand, tenant right and trade debtors still falls to be relieved (if at all) by business property relief provisions (see section **8.3**).

8.5:2   Categories of relief

The different categories of relief for agricultural property are as follows:

Category of asset		*Value relieved*
Class I	Interest in agricultural property conferring right to vacant possession within 12 months.	100%
Class II	Agricultural property qualifying for relief under FA 1975 Sch 8 on 10 March 1981; which has been owned since that date but which does not confer a right to vacant possession (limited to the lower of £250,000 or 1,000 acres).	100%
Class III	Interest in other agricultural property (ie tenanted land).	50%

8.5:3   Tests for relief

There is no requirement that the transferor be wholly committed to farming, or that he derive some stipulated proportion of his income from it. Separate tests are provided for farmers and landowners:

FARMERS

Farmers must have occupied the property transferred, for the purposes of agriculture, throughout the period of two years ending with the date of transfer (IHTA 1984 s 115(3)).

LANDOWNERS

Landowners must have owned the property transferred throughout the period of seven years ending on the date of transfer, and the property must have been occupied for the purposes of agriculture by the transferor or another throughout that period (IHTA 1984 s 115(3)).

COMPANIES

There are corresponding tests where farming or landownership is carried on through the medium of a company controlled by the transferor (IHTA 1984 s 122). The agricultural property which is the subject of the transfer must form part of the company's assets, and part of the value of the shares or securities of the company must be attributed to it. The transferor must have control of the company immediately before the relevant transfer.

There are three possible sets of circumstances foreseen by the legislation.

(1) CONFIGURATION A: COMPANY OWNS LAND AND FARMS IT

It is necessary to establish what proportion of shares held by a controlling shareholder can be attributed to the value of the land which forms part of the company's assets. The process of attribution can involve complex arithmetic. (As to the meaning of control see IHTA 1984 s 269.) So long as control exists before the gift, then gifts of minority holdings may qualify for relief.

A transfer of qualifying shares will attract relief at 100% of vacant possession value, provided the shareholder has owned the shares and the company and the land for at least two years. This rule is modified where the shares owned on the date of the transfer had not been owned for the two-year period, but replaced other qualifying property, eg shares or other property attributable to the underlying property owned by the company. This would apply where there had been a company reconstruction or an exchange of business for shares. Where other eligible property can be established, the period of ownership of it and the period of ownership of the shares transferred must amount to two out of five years ending on the date of transfer. Business property relief would produce the same result. Shareholders with less than 25% control secure only 50% business property relief. 'Substantial' minority shareholders secure 100% (see section **8.3**).

(2) CONFIGURATION B: COMPANY OWNS LAND AND LETS IT

The result is as above, save that the relief is limited to the rate of 50%. The controlling shares and the land must have both been respectively owned for seven years.

Where eligible property is involved, the combined ownership period must amount to seven years out of ten years ending on the date of transfer. Minority shareholders get no relief.

(3) CONFIGURATION C: SHAREHOLDER OWNS LAND; COMPANY FARMS IT

In this situation the controlling shareholders are treated as personally occupying the land, and thus secure 100% relief against vacant possession value. Two years' qualifying period is required. Minority shareholders are not treated as occupiers, but merely as owning tenanted land, and are entitled to 50% business property relief on their shareholdings. In determining what proportion of the value of shares is attributable to land, the Revenue will treat the company's tenancy as a valuable asset.

There is no stipulation that the company's main activity should have been agriculture (see section **8.4:3**).

8.5:4 Replacements of property

Replacements of one property by another are permitted in making up the requisite two or seven years of occupation or ownership. For occupation by farmers, the two-year minimum qualifying period of occupation may include occupation of the property transferred and other agricultural property replaced by the property transferred, providing the combined period of occupation amounted to at least two out of the five years ending on the date of transfer.

For ownership by landowners, the corresponding qualifying period is seven out of ten years and the tests to be satisfied are ownership by the transferor and occupation by him or another person for the purpose of agriculture. Relief is not to exceed what it would have been had any replacement not been made. However for this purpose changes resulting from formation, alteration or dissolution of partnerships are ignored. These provisions have been adapted from the business property relief rules.

As regards replacements of property following a lifetime transfer, see section **8.5:9**.

8.5:5   Substitute and replacement owner-occupiers

Occupation of the property by a company controlled by the transferor is treated as the transferor's occupation. By analogy, the same rule is applied to Scottish partnerships, which are separate legal persons under Scottish law (IHTA 1984 s 119). Where a transferor became entitled to the property on the death of another person, he is deemed to have owned it from the date of death. If he subsequently occupies the property, he is similarly deemed to have occupied it from the date of death. If he inherited the property on death from his spouse, his periods of both occupation and ownership are deemed to include the spouse's corresponding periods (IHTA 1984 s 120).

The two-year occupation/seven-year ownership rule is also extended in the following combination of historical circumstances:

(a) where there was an earlier transfer of property (whole or part) which was or would have been eligible for relief (ignoring the two-year/seven-year rule); and

(b) either that transfer or the subsequent transfer occurred on death; and

(c) as a result of the earlier transfer, the transferor of the subsequent transfer (or his spouse) became the owner of the property; and

(d) the transferor in the subsequent transfer, or the personal representative of the earlier transferor is the occupier of the property at the time of the subsequent transfer (IHTA 1984 s 120).

If all these tests are satisfied, the two-year/seven-year rule is waived, but relief is limited to what it would have been had any replacement not been made. For this purpose, partnership changes are ignored. Where only part of the value transferred was attributable to a property previously transferred, a corresponding reduction in value is to be made in the subsequent transfer.

It is worth noting that relief does not extend to a transfer made after retirement and FA 1975 Sch 8 para 3(4), granting relief where occupation is by a member of the same family, has not been reproduced. In particular relief does not extend to situations, where owner-occupation has ceased on retirement and then the farm is let. If a transfer on death then occurs before the completion of the seven-year ownership period, no relief is due, even though occupation had continued for two years before retirement.

8.5:6   Nature of relief

Relief is limited to the agricultural value of property transferred by a transfer of value (IHTA 1984 s 116). The agricultural value is the value of property if subject to a perpetual covenant prohibiting its use otherwise than as agricultural property. The effect is to exclude any element of development or hope value from relief. As regards the rates of relief see section **8.5:2**.

The categorisation into two classes is achieved by stipulating that the appropriate percentage reduction is 100%, if the interest of the transferor in the property immediately before the transfer carries the right to vacant possession or the right to obtain it in the next 12 months. This would meet the situation where a landlord had given his tenant notice to quit at the end of the statutory period (Agricultural Holdings Act 1948 s 1), providing no counternotice has been served. It would not apply where a letting is for a period between one year and two years, or for a fixed term granted with consent of the Ministry of Agriculture. In these cases, no security of tenure is acquired (Agricultural Holdings Act 1948 s 2). If in such a case, the valuer took account of the certainty of recovering possession at the end of the period, so as to value the land at vacant possession value less a modest discount, the result would be disadvantageous.

If the 100% test is not satisfied, relief at 50% is due. If the interest in the property transferred is held by joint tenants, tenants in common, or their Scottish equivalents, the rights of all may be attributed to any one of two or more.

8.5:7   Transitional provisions

Under the so-called double discount rules, full-time working farmer relief could be secured on transfers of let land. The relevant details of tax planning arrangements are fully described in section **15.2**. As a transitional measure, where such arrangements had been in force before 10 March 1981, the old relief will continue to be allowed on the first transfer of property after 10 March 1981. This is achieved by providing that the appropriate percentage of relief is 50% (100% since FA 1992) if:

(a)   on a pre-10 March 1981 transfer, full-time working farmer relief would have been due, up to the relevant limits of scale (restriction to £250,000 or 1,000 acres, whichever is the greater, all transfers to be taken into account); and

(b)   at no time between 10 March 1981 and the date of the relevant transfer was there a right to vacant possession; and

(c)   such a right had not been eliminated by any act or deliberate omission by the transferor during that period (IHTA 1984 s 116(3)).

Thus the benefit of the double discount with the full 100% relief against *tenanted* value is enjoyed only if the land were subject to a binding tenancy before 10 March 1981. If the tenancy were first created after 27 March 1975, when CTT was introduced, it must be shown that the grant was made for full consideration in money's worth if the reduction in the value of the land, occasioned by the grant of the tenancy, is not to be taxed as a transfer of value.

In order to ascertain whether transitional relief is due, it is therefore necessary to contemplate a notional transfer occurring before 10 March 1981, and apply to it the full-time working farmer relief rules. The tests for full-time working farmer relief include time limits, amount of time engaged in farming, relevant income etc (see section **8.4**), and failure to satisfy any such test will extinguish transitional relief. Where limits of scale in (a) above are exceeded the excess attracts relief at 30%. Where property passes on death from one spouse to another, the succeeding spouse's estate is entitled to transitional death-time relief.

The new relief has been drafted so as to ensure that the tax planning arrangements described in section **15.2** will not create the double discount in respect of transfers after 10 March 1981, save only where the 100% relief is due under the transitional provisions.

It may be possible to justify a basis of valuation which includes some discount from full vacant possession value.

In these circumstances, the interest in the property immediately before transfer would be such as to qualify for the 100% relief. On the other hand, if, on the date of transfer, the right to recover possession of the property will not be obtained for, say, a year and a day but is certain on that date, relief may be limited to 50% of the vacant possession value, so producing an unattractive result.

8.5:8   The three reliefs

In section **8.4:5** the interaction of business property relief and full-time working farmer relief was considered. Various sets of circumstances were envisaged, where full-time working farmer relief was due, although business property relief was not. In most of these circumstances, those of a retired farmer; land let to a partnership of which the transferor is a member; land let to a company by controlling shareholders; and a mixed ownership and tenancy history over two years, the position is now that agricultural property relief will be due at the lower rate of 50% equal to the 50% due under the transitional relief provisions described above. Full-time working famer relief was allowed on application being made for the relief by the transferor. Business property relief and agricultural property relief, however, are given without application.

Where agricultural property relief is due, business property relief is automatically excluded (IHTA 1984 s 114). This is favourable to the transferor in certain specialised circumstances: for example, where the farming business is carried on by a partnership and the land is owned by a member of the partnership and let to it. Agricultural property relief carries with it the benefit of tax payable by interest free instalments, whereas business property relief does not.

Again, where the farming business is carried on by a partnership, and the land is owned by one of the partners and occupied by the partnership without a formal tenancy agreement, agricultural property relief should be claimed at the rate of 100%. This is because the landowner would be able to secure vacant possession so satisfying the 100% rate test.

For business property relief, however, an identified asset used by a partnership attracts relief at the rate of only 50% (see section **8.3:2** above).

8.5:9   Agricultural property relief and lifetime transfers

The interaction of agricultural property relief and the system of lifetime transfers has required the creation of a separate series of retention rules applicable to the period after the date of transfer. The problems and the tests involved are similar to those applicable for business property relief (see section **8.3:4**).

It is necessary to distinguish, firstly, between potentially exempt transfers and chargeable transfers. If a potentially exempt transfer is converted, because a donor has survived for more than seven years after the gift, there is no problem. The test is relevant only where the donor fails to survive the seven-year period, in which case agricultural property relief is lost unless:

(a) The donee has retained the original property transferred throughout the period from the date of the transfer to the date of the donor's death; or the death of the donee if earlier. There is the usual requirement that the property must not, at the latter date, be subject to a binding contract of sale.

Where the donee is a trustee and there is no interest in possession, the trustee is to be treated as the donee (IHTA 1984 s 124A(8)). Where the trust confers a beneficial interest in possession, that beneficiary is the transferee.

(b) The original property must have been agricultural property immediately before the death of the donor, and must have been occupied by the donee for the purposes of agriculture throughout the relevant period. Where the original property consisted of shares in a company, the property must have been owned by the company and similarly occupied for the purposes of agriculture throughout the period (IHTA 1984 s 124A(3)(c)). The possibility of share capital reorganisations or exchanges of property for shares are both foreseen.

(c) There is a relaxation of these rules permitting the replacement of the original property by other property. The consideration received for the sale must have been reinvested in farm land retained by the donee at the date of the donor's death. The disposal of the original property and the purchase of the replacement property must have been made in arm's length bargains within a time limit of 12 months. There are detailed rules applying to identify the replacement property with the original property, and to ensure occupation for agricultural purposes throughout.

These replacement rules are comparable to, but not identical with, roll-over relief provisions for capital gains tax (see section **7.4**); and with agricultural property relief provisions governing permitted replacement of property during the ownership period *before* the date of a gift (see section **8.5:2**).

It seems that a partial replacement of land by other land is not permitted. There is a requirement that the whole of the proceeds of sale must have been reinvested.

Where, after a potentially exempt transfer, agricultural property relief is retrospectively lost, because these conditions have not been satisfied, the tax due will not take agricultural property relief into account, nor will the cumulative total be reduced by that relief.

Where the first transfer was a chargeable one, and the conditions are not satisfied, agricultural property relief is similarly cancelled for the calculation of additional tax at the death time rate. However, the cumulative total brought forward is not changed, so tax chargeable on the subsequent transfers is unaffected by loss of relief.

The following example illustrates the danger of acquiring replacement property before disposal (see section **8.3:5(e)**).

Example

Giles gives Blackacre Farm to his son Sam on the 1 January 1993, his retirement date. 100% agricultural property relief is available on this gift. Sam farms Blackacre for two years. On 1 January 1995, he puts Blackacre into the market because he is, on that date, buying the adjacent farm, Whiteacre. Six months later, having at last found a buyer for Blackacre, he sells it. For capital gains tax purposes, roll-over relief is due.

On 1 January 1996, Sam's father Giles dies. There will be a withdrawal of the 100% agricultural property relief given on Giles's lifetime gift to Sam.

8.5:10   Agricultural property relief: trusts

Full-time working farmer relief (see section **8.4**) was not accorded to trustees of discretionary settlements, so that there could never be an entitlement to transitional relief by trustees (see section **8.5:6**).

On the other hand, agricultural property relief can be claimed by the trustees of the discretionary settlement provided that they can satisfy all the tests (IHTA 1984 s 115(1)(*b*)). Where there is an interest in possession in trust property, the life tenant is treated as the beneficial owner of the trust land. He becomes entitled to the agricultural property relief subject to his satisfying the conditions as if the land were held in his free estate.

8.5:11   Sporting rights

The income tax treatment of sporting rights is described in section **4.3:2**.

The treatment of sporting rights for agricultural property relief purposes is best regarded as a question of valuation. One of the tests for agricultural property relief is that the land should be 'occupied for the purposes of agriculture.' Hence, if land is not farmed, there can be no relief. On the other hand, it does not follow that, for valuation purposes, the particular pattern of farming adopted by the transferor should continue for all time. It is arguable that the valuation may take account of the possibility that a hypothetical purchaser may adopt a different type of farming. If the land is not farmed intensively, to allow for the enjoyment of sporting rights, it may be that the agricultural value would be higher if the valuation were made without having regard to any sporting rights. Another line of argument is to ensure that the correct course is to value the land as if it were used only for agriculture. On this basis the value is likely to be higher than if the agricultural value were determined after having deducted the value of the sporting rights.

It is understood that the value of fishing rights cannot in any circumstances form part of the agricultural value of agricultural land.

In *Earl of Normanton v Giles* [1980] 1 All ER 106 it was held that a cottage occupied by a gamekeeper was not occupied by an employee working in agriculture for the purposes of the Rent (Agriculture) Act 1976. This case is sometimes cited as authority for the proposition that the value of sporting rights should be excluded in determining the agricultural value of land. This is probably not correct. That statute contained its own definition of agriculture, and in any event the treatment of sporting rights should be considered along the lines above, before the authority of this case is accepted.

Chapter 9

Value added tax

9.1 GENERAL SCOPE OF VALUE ADDED TAX

9.1:1 Introduction

Value added tax, unlike all the other forms of taxation described in this book, is not a home grown product, but an import from the countries of the EEC where widespread evasion of taxes based on income and profits had lead to introduction of taxes based on turnover or gross earnings of businesses, a base not so readily concealed or misstated. On 11 April 1967, the EEC by a First Council Directive, directed member states to harmonise their various turnover taxes by a system of value added tax, and to do so as soon as possible. The directive defined value added tax as involving the application to goods and services of a general tax on consumption, exactly proportional to the price of the goods and services, whatever the number of transactions which take place in the production and distribution process before the stage at which tax is charged. On each transaction, value added tax is to be chargeable ... after deduction of the value added tax borne directly by the cost of components ... up to and including the retail trade stage.

These principles are enshrined in the United Kingdom version of value added tax, a multi-stage indirect tax charged on the supply of goods and services in the United Kingdom where the supply is a taxable supply made by a taxable person in the course of a business (VATA 1983 s 2). The 'supply of goods and services' is a phrase which requires explanation. The word 'supply' is used in its ordinary sense and apparently means to furnish or to serve. Thus in any supply there must be two parties: the party which 'furnishes or serves' the goods or services; and the person who receives those goods or services. A person cannot supply himself (but see section **9.3:2**).

The word 'supply' is not defined in the legislation other than the statement that 'supply' includes all forms of supply (VATA 1983 s 3(2)(*a*)). Clearly, the word has a wide meaning, and 'anything ... done for a consideration' amounts to a supply, including the grant, assignment or surrender of any right and performing what is to be done under a contract irrespective of whether this requires positive activity. (VATA 1983 s 3(2)(*b*)). If a supply is not made for a consideration, it is outside the scope of value added tax (VATA 1983 s 3(2)(*a*)). Consideration may be in cash or kind, but where a 'gift' is made in accordance with a contract of employment, the goods or services given represent a supply, and the services of the employee represent the necessary consideration. (*Customs and Excise Comrs v Oliver* [1980] STC 73). There is an exception to the rule that supply requires consideration (see **9.3:2** below).

The value added tax base is turnover, not income. When a trader sells goods or services, he adds value added tax to his price. That is called 'output' tax. When the trader buys materials, goods for resale or services, he is obliged to pay his suppliers value added tax on the price. That is called 'input' tax. He deducts the input tax from the output tax, and the difference, representing tax on his own 'value added', he pays to HM Customs and Excise.

If, on the other hand, his input tax exceeds output tax, he is entitled to repayment of the excess or some later set off.

Example

	Price	VAT at 17½%
Trader A makes components and sells to B for	10	1.75
Trader B assembles and sells to C for	14	2.45
Trader C sells wholesale for	20	3.50
Trader D sells to consumer for	26	4.55

Then the value added and value added tax at each stage will be as follows:

			value added	VAT at 17½%
Trader A			10	1.75
Trader B	output	14		
	input	10	4	0.70
Trader C	output	20		
	input	14	6	1.05
Trader D	output	26		
	input	20	6	1.05
Totals of value added and VAT			26	4.55

A 'supply' may be a supply of goods or a supply of services. Where goods are sold outright that is a 'supply of goods'; if goods are hired or leased, that is a 'supply of services' (VATA 1983 Sch 2 para 1). In this connection, the sale, assignment, or grant of an interest in land for a term exceeding 21 years is treated as a supply of goods (VATA 1983 Sch 2 para 4).

Goods or services supplied in the United Kingdom are so chargeable, and the importation of goods is chargeable as at the time of importation (VATA 1983 s 2). The export of goods is zero-rated (see section **9.2:3**).

9.1:2   Effects of changes in FA 1989

Before the Finance Act 1989 value added tax was, for farmers and landowners, a relatively straightforward tax, the impact of which was limited. Food and sales of live animals for human consumption were (and still are) zero-rated (VATA 1983 Sch 5 Group 1). Sales of farmland and grants and assignments of tenancies were exempt (VATA 1983 Sch 6 Group 1). The main problems concerned the apportionment of input tax; and the treatment of VAT on specialised transactions, for example the grants of rights to take game, and shooting and fishing rights generally.

However, the Finance Act 1989 introduced major changes designed to harmonise UK VAT with value added tax in other European countries and to comply with a decision by the European Court of Justice on 21 June 1988. This determined that zero-rating of industrial and commercial building, and construction of civil engineering and community works was in breach of the European Community Sixth Directive, and that UK law must be amended. The UK had resisted these changes for some time. When the European Court gave its decision, it upheld the UK view that zero-rating was acceptable for new residential housing, seeds, animal foodstuffs and live animals yielding food for human consumption (see para **9.2:3**). The required changes to the UK VAT system were introduced in the first Budget and Finance Act after the European Court decision (see FA 1989 ss 18–26 and Sch 3).

9.1:3 Principal changes in FA 1989

The following check-list of principal changes taking effect from 1 April 1989 may be helpful:

(1) NEW NON-RESIDENTIAL BUILDINGS

Sales of new or partly completed non-residential buildings, previously exempt became standard rated (VATA 1983 Sch 6 Group 1). New buildings are those sold within three years of completion. It is possible for a 'new' building to be sold more than once during this three-year period and to be standard rated on each sale. Farmhouses and cottages are outside the scope of this provision, but farm buildings, farm roads and other works are caught.

(2) ASSIGNMENTS AND SURRENDERS OF TENANCIES

Grants of tenancies in land remain exempt. Surrenders and assignments of tenancies to landlords are no longer exempt from VAT and become standard rated. The need to pay VAT on surrender of a tenancy represents a new cost factor in the management of tenanted land, where a landlord has not elected that his letting activity shall be treated as taxable (see para **9.4** below).

(3) OPTIONS FOR LANDOWNERS

An option is introduced so that an agricultural landowner can make an election to waive VAT exemption. He can opt to tax rents so recovering input tax on repairs and improvements. Options once made are irrevocable. Outright sales of land in respect of which an option has been made become themselves liable to VAT (see section **9.4** below).

(4) SPORTING RIGHTS

The former treatment of sporting rights is reversed. When land is sold with sporting rights, the rights are to be valued so that standard rate VAT is chargeable on that proportion of the total (see section **9.2:2** below).

(5) BUSINESS ASSETS

Where business assets are disposed of, even by gift, this can be a taxable supply, although no consideration is receivable (VATA 1983 Sch 2 para 5). Where the option to tax agricultural land has been exercised (VATA 1983 Sch 6A 3(4)), gifts of farmland may attract VAT at the standard rate (see section **9.4**).

9.2 RATES OF CHARGE

9.2:1 Alternative rates

Although value added tax is a comprehensive tax, not all goods and services are equally taxed, and three different treatments need to be distinguished: standard rate; zero-rate; and exemption. The standard rate is currently 17½%. Zero-rate and exemption represent different forms of relief, and since the former applies to farming and the latter to rents, these expressions require fuller explanation.

9.2:2   Standard rate

Value added tax was increased from 15% to 17½% with effect from 1 April 1991. The VAT fraction to be used when calculating the tax element of a VAT inclusive price is $\frac{7}{47}$ rather than, as previously, $\frac{3}{23}$.

9.2:3   Zero-rate

The greater part of the produce sold by farmers is zero-rated (VATA 1983 Sch 5 Group 1). There are four categories:

- (a) food of a kind used for human consumption;
- (b) animal feeding stuffs;
- (c) seeds or other means of propagation of plants comprised in (a) and (b);
- (d) live animals of a kind generally used as or yielding or producing food for human consumption.

There are a number of specialised exceptions from the above four categories. Supplies in the course of catering, which includes the supply for consumption on the premises on which it is supplied and any supply of hot food for consumption off those premises is standard rated. So are certain accepted foodstuffs, for example, ice cream; chocolate and sweets; certain drinks; potato crisps and other 'snack' items; pet foods, and so on.

Services in the disposal or treatment of sewage; emptying of cesspools and similar tanks are zero-rated. Work on protected buildings is zero-rated. 'Protected building' means a building which is listed within the meaning of the Town and Country Planning Acts; a scheduled monument within the meaning of the Ancient Monument and Archaeological Areas Act 1979 or the Historic Monuments Act (Northern Ireland) 1971 (see para **9.6:6**).

Services provided in connection with the keeping of animals are standard rated, but the grant of grazing rights may be zero-rated as a supply of (b), animal foodstuffs (see section **9.6:4**).

Wool is not zero-rated. 'Animals' do not include horses or dogs not normally kept for food, but live rabbits are included.

The effect of zero-rating is that output is technically taxable at a nil rate, so that the farmer is entitled to reclaim the total input tax which he has paid. Farmers may make monthly or quarterly VAT returns so as to obtain regular repayments of VAT on their inputs. A monthly return is advantageous from the cashflow standpoint, whereas a quarterly return imposes less of a burden.

The general outcome is that a farmer is substantially excluded from the value added tax system, so that, theoretically, the economics of farming are unscathed by the tax.

When claiming repayment of input tax, the following categories of expenditure should be reviewed:

contract work;
fertilisers and lime;
haulage and transport;
medical products;
motor fuel and repairs and servicing to vehicles and equipment;

capital equipment and commercial vehicles;
repairs and maintenance of farmhouses and farm buildings;
animal feed;
seeds and livestock;
fuel and power.

This is not intended to be an inclusive list.

9.2:4 Exemption

Exemption, on the other hand, sounds attractive, but the word is misleading. A person making exempt supplies cannot charge tax on the goods and services he sells. Nor can he recover the input tax which he paid on the goods and services which he has bought, so that he is left to suffer this tax himself. The grant, assignment or surrender of any lease of land is an exempt supply, and the effect is to prevent tax being charged on any rent or premium under a lease or tenancy, or grant of mineral rights whether by lease or licence. 'Land' includes buildings, walls, trees, plants and other structures attached to the land. Exemption does not apply to the following:

(a) Sale of the freehold in a new or partly completed building, other than a building designed as a dwelling house or intended for residential or charitable use.
(b) Provision of accommodation in an hotel, inn, boarding house or similar establishment; of sleeping accommodation or accommodation in rooms provided in conjunction with sleeping accommodation; or for the provision of a supply of catering.
(c) The provision of holiday accommodation in a house, flat, caravan or tent.
(d) Provision of seasonal pitches for caravans and facilities at caravan parks.
(e) Parking facilities for vehicles.
(f) Tent pitching or camping facilities.
(g) Rights to fell and remove standing timber irrespective of whether taxed under different income tax schedules.
(h) Gallop fees, that is fees charged by a land owner for allowing horses to gallop over his land.
(i) Grant of facilities for sports or physical recreation.
(j) Entertainment seating facilities.

On all these transactions value added tax is chargeable at the standard rate.

Admission fees to historic houses are not within the definition of rents and are chargeable to value added tax. The rent payable under a full repairing lease is wholly exempt, even though part of it is payable for maintenance and repairs. Where in addition to rent, a separate charge is made for maintenance and repairs, this is chargeable to valued added tax. Similarly, where an owner does work which is the legal obligation of a tenant, the service is chargeable to value added tax. The respective obligations of owners and tenants for this purpose are as set out in the tenancy agreement, but where not covered by the agreement are prescribed in SI 1948/184. The value added tax position, where costs are recovered by landlords from tenants in connection with farm repairs can be complex and has been the subject of a Customs and Excise guidance note to local offices.

9.3   SUPPLIES

9.3:1   Taxable supplies

For VAT purposes, a supply is taxable only if all the following conditions are satisfied:

1 It is made by a *'taxable person'*, defined as a person who is, or is liable to be, registered, because his turnover exceeds the *de minimis* limit.
2 It is made *'in the UK'*. Services are located 'in' the UK, if the supplier 'belongs' here (VATA 1983 s 6(5)). This is a test peculiar to VAT. A supplier 'belongs' in the UK, if:
   (a) he has a business here; or
   (b) his usual place of residence is here; or
   (c) the establishment 'concerned with' the supply is here.
   A company has 'its usual place of residence' where it is legally constituted.
   The rules, which seem complex, are designed to tax international trading, which is outside the scope of this book.
3 It is made in the *'course of business'* (VATA 1983 s 2(1)).
   For this purpose, a 'business' is more widely defined than for income tax purposes, but, obviously, includes any trade, profession or vocation; a club or other association providing services to members for a subscription; admitting persons to premises for a consideration (for example to an historic house: see para **9.2:4**); and supplies made by organisations which would not be liable to income tax. The profit motive is not a pre-requisite for this purpose. Land-ownership, which may not qualify as a trade for income tax, is undoubtedly a 'business' for VAT.
   The term 'business' does not, however, include the services of employees; voluntary services to the community; investors hiring out investment assets; and activities designed for pleasure and social enjoyment. After an activity has been classified as a business, any supply made in the course of carrying it on is likely to have been made in the course or furtherance of that business (VATA 1983 s 47(1)). Thus a supply may include the disposition of assets or liabilities of a business; the sale of a business as a going concern; and anything done in connection with the termination of a business, transaction which would be of a capital nature and therefore not liable to income tax.
   Where goods forming part of the assets of a business are transferred by the person carrying on the business, and those goods cease to form part of those assets, there is a supply regardless of the fact that there is no consideration. This rule may apply to gifts of farmland of farm assets amongst members of a family. The supply takes place when the assets are transferred, and the value of the supply is the cost to the donor of making the gift. There is no requirement to charge at full market price save in particular circumstances, as follows:

A Where the supply is not a gift but there is some consideration receivable in money but the amount is less than open market value.
B Where the person making the supply and the person to whom it is made are connected persons (TA 1988 s 839) and VATA 1983 Sch 4 para 1(1)).
C The person to whom the supply is made is not entitled to recover the input tax on the supply.

In these circumstances Customs and Excise must give notice within three years after the time of supply that the value is to be market value (VATA 1983 Sch 4 para 1(2)). There is an exclusion from this rule where the supply is made by an employer to his employees and consists of food and drink or accommodation.

9.3:2 Self-supply

The normal rule is that a value added tax 'supply' implies two parties: one who 'furnishes or serves' the goods or services; and one who receives those goods or services. However, there are specialised circumstances in which a self-supply can become chargeable to value added tax. Where a business provides for itself services used in the construction of a building work; or altering or enlarging the floor space of a building by 10% or more, those services are subject to value added tax at the standard rate. Liability arises only if the value of such services is not less than £100,000 (VAT Self-supply of Construction Services Order SI 1989/472).

The value of the supply is the open market value of the goods and services supplied for the construction of the building or work (SI 1989 472 4(1)).

A different category of self-supply may occur where a developer constructs a commercial building and lets it on an exempt tenancy or occupies it as a partially exempt person. This does not apply to residential buildings; nor if construction were commenced for 1 August 1989; nor if a standard rated sale of the freehold had occurred before the occasion on which the taxable self-supply is deemed to arise.

That deemed self-supply is deemed to arise on the date when the building owner moves into occupation of the building; or alternatively when he first makes an exempt supply by granting a lease of it. The deemed self-supply arises only within the period ending ten years after completion of the building.

Again the value of the supply is the total of the acquisition cost of the owner's interest in the land and the value of the standard rate taxable supplies made in connection with the construction of the building. There is a *de minimis* limit of £100,000. It is possible to envisage circumstances in which these complex and burdensome provisions will apply to farm and land-owners developing a building on their land either for their own use or for occupation by a tenant.

Yet another form of self-supply arises where a relevant residential building ceases to be used for this qualifying purpose. If it is sold or let within ten years of its date of completion, that transaction is treated as a business supply taxable at the standard rate. Similarly, where the use changes, and a person in the past has benefited from zero-rated supplies related to the building, but he begins to use it for a non-residential purpose, he is treated as making a taxable self-supply of the building. The value of the supply is the amount which would have been chargeable on the original zero-rated supply. Thus the effect is to bring him within the scope of charge to value added tax (VATA 1983 Sch 6A para 1(4)(5)).

9.3:3 Apportionment of input tax

One of the most complex situations under value added tax is where, as on most estates, there are some outputs which are exempt, and others which are standard or zero-rated. In such cases, input tax must be distributed to either exempt or taxable outputs. With effect from 1 April 1987, input tax directly attributable to existing or future exempt outputs ('exempt input tax') is disallowed unless it falls within one of the following *de minimis* limits:

(a) £100 per month on average;

or

(b) both £250 per month on average and 50% of all input tax;

or

(c) both £500 per month on average and 25% of all input tax.

If the amount of exempt input tax is below any one of these limits, that input tax will be treated as attributable to taxable supplies and can be fully recovered.

Alternatively, an application can be made to the local VAT office to apply for a different method (eg, the standard method, which was the normal method of calculation before 1 April 1987) and this method will be permitted providing it produces a further reasonable result (see Part V of VAT General Regulations).

Another form of *de minimis* relief is available when expenditure is incurred, for example legal or professional expenses, in granting leases or tenancies or licences to occupy land or premises.

Normally, the input tax attributable to these exempt supplies would be non-recoverable. Where in such circumstances, however, the input tax attributable to all such supplies is less than a £1,000, and no exempt input tax is incurred in respect of any exempt supply other than the one exempt supply in question, the VAT on exempt inputs can be fully recovered (SI 1985/886 reg 31(1)(*b*)).

9.3:4   Value added tax as a deductible expense

In practice, problems sometimes arise as to the treatment of value added tax in income tax and corporation tax computations. In computing the income tax liabilities of an exempt person for value added tax, the value added tax on deductible items will also be deductible. Capital allowances will be given on the cost plus value added tax. In computing the liabilities of a taxable person, for example a retailer taxable at the standard rate, or a farmer taxable at zero-rate, both income and expenditure are treated as exclusive of value added tax, and capital allowances are based on a value added tax exclusive cost. For partly exempt persons, a combination of these principles is applied, and Inspectors of Taxes will approve any basis which produces a reasonable result (see also Section **9.6:15**).

9.3:5   Bad debt relief

Some form of relief for the value added tax element in bad debts written off has been available since the introduction of value added tax. The original legislation provided that a number of stringent conditions had to be met, but this version has now been replaced for supplies made after 25 July 1990 (FA 1990 s 11(9)). If a tax payer has written off all or part of the money due to him as a bad debt in his accounts and a period of time has elapsed since the date of supply he can make a claim for refund of value added tax. It was originally enacted that a period of two years needed to have elapsed, but this period was reduced to one year in the Finance Act 1991 s 15.

The rules enacted in the Finance Act 1989 are more generous than the earlier version, in particular, it is not necessary for the debtor to be in liquidation to secure the relief.

False claims for bad debt relief can give rise to prosecution of liability to penalties.

9.4 THE OPTION TO TAX

9.4:1 Introduction

The Finance Act 1989 introduced a new sub-system into the value added tax regime, designed to permit recovery of input tax, as permitted by the EEC Sixth Directive Article 13C. There is an important special application for owners of agricultural land.

When a farmer or landowner makes a 'supply' of his land either by selling it or letting it, he has the right to elect to waive the exemption (VATA 1983 Sch 6 Group 1) normally applicable and to charge VAT at the standard rate. This is called 'the option to tax' (VATA 1983 Sch 6A paras 2–4).

Once the option to tax has been exercised the exemption is immediately lost. In *Devoirs Properties Ltd v Customs and Excise Comrs* MAN/90/1061 (unreported), a property company exercised the option to tax by writing to the local VAT office but received no acknowledgement. It then failed to charge VAT on rents, contending that failure to respond to the option invalidated it. It was held that the Commissioners were not required to take any steps to complete the effect of the election and the only action required was that of the taxpayer. The Appeal was dismissed.

The consequences and implications of exercising the option are wide ranging, particularly having regard to the way in which farming is carried on or the way in which a landed estate is composed. At this early stage in the lifetime of the rule, it is difficult to predict precisely how it will operate, but it is clear that an election has many advantages and disadvantages, short- and long-term, to be weighed in the balance before it is made. It is possible to enumerate a series of factors to be taken into account.

9.4:2 Factors to be taken into account in making the election

(1) TIMING

The election was available from 1 August 1989, and if made before 1 November 1989 could be made retrospectively back to 1 August 1989. Otherwise the election takes effect from the beginning of the day on which it is made, or some specified later date, and must be notified to Customs and Excise within 30 days.

(2) IRREVOCABILITY

The election once made is irrevocable as regards the land within it. Hence, whilst an election may seem beneficial at the present time, changes in farming, family, or financial circumstances may render an election disadvantageous.

(3) SCOPE

In the first draft of the Finance Bill an election applied to all farmland in ownership and all farmland subsequently acquired. Clearly, that required a virtually impossible judgment for the future.

The final form of the law permits the election on a farm by farm or estate by estate basis. Where the land includes a building, the election applies to the whole building and the land within its curtilage.

As regards agricultural land, the election applies automatically to any other agricultural land in the same ownership which is not separated by land, which is not agricultural land; or by agricultural land in separate ownership. For the purpose of determining what is a 'separation', land is not taken to be *separated* by a road, railway, river or some similar dividing route; and land is in *separate ownership*, where the individual owner making the election has no interest in, right over or licence to occupy it (VATA 1983 Sch 6A para 3(4)(5)).

There are a number of problems here: first, it is clear that where an estate is in single ownership and, is within 'a ring fence', the election will apply both to owner occupied and to tenanted land within the estate. Secondly, where farms in one ownership are separated by land in separate ownership, more flexibility is secured, but the rules apparently foresee an attempt to secure this flexibility by artificial separation of ownership and seek to negate such an attempt.

Thirdly, it is not certain what exactly is 'agricultural land' since there is no definition of it. Whether woodlands could serve as a separating element is not clear.

It will be apparent from this bald summary of the Scope of Election rule that the value of it may depend on the particular topography or layout of an estate. This must be carefully reviewed before making an election.

(4) TENANTS' BURDEN

Before an option is exercised, it will be essential to contemplate the effect on tenants whose rent will be increased by (at present) 17½%. Following election, VAT may be added to rent unless the lease etc specifies otherwise (VATA 1983 s 42) (see example below). Zero-rated tenants, ie farmers will, be able to recover the VAT that they pay. Tenants of commercial buildings, who are standard rate payers, should be in a similar position. Tenants carrying on a financial services business, for example a building society, will presumably not be able to recover the VAT and the imposition of VAT on their rent will represent an additional charge. However, any proportion of rent attributable to farmhouses or cottages will not be liable to VAT (VATA 1983 Sch 6A para 21).

Correspondingly, input tax on expenditure incurred on residential premises remains irrecoverable.

(5) SALES OF FARMLAND

Sales of farmland to which an option applies will be liable to VAT, and so also will gifts save where a business is transferred as a going concern (see para **9.6:1**). As with rents (see (4) above) proceeds of sale apportioned to residential premises remain exempt and corresponding input tax remains irrecoverable.

(6) SURRENDERS OF TENANCY

Where a tenancy is to be surrendered and tax is to become payable (see para **9.1:3**), there will be a positive incentive to exercise the option to tax, in order to recover the input tax.

(7) IMPROVEMENT EXPENDITURE

Where an estate is acquired in a run-down condition, or generally, improvement expenditure is needed, there can be a 'self supply'. The option to tax should be considered.

(8) ALTERNATIVE LAND USE

Diversification will inevitably increase the standard rated supplies, for example on holiday lettings, sporting and caravan park rents. The option to tax reduces the burden of partial exemption calculations.

(9) MARKETABILITY

As a generalisation, however, it seems that the option to tax is likely to be valuable only in a limited and specialised set of circumstances, and it should be borne in mind that one effect may be to make the property less marketable.

Another may be to create two markets: one in 'elected' and another in 'non-elected' land. This is already occurring in various parts of the country.

Example: The option to tax

Effect on Rent of £1,000 pa

Lease allowing VAT addition

	£ pa
Rent per lease	£1,000
Add: VAT @ 17½%	175
Due from tenant	£1,175
VAT payable	175
net rent	£1,000

Lease excluding VAT addition

	£ pa
Rent (inc VAT)	£1,000
VAT payable	149
net rent	£851

9.5 FARMER'S FLAT RATE SCHEME

9.5:1 Introduction

With effect from 1 January 1993, farmers will have the choice of remaining registered for value added tax, or deregistering and becoming a 'flat rate' farmer (F(2)A 1992 s 16).

The principal consequence of deregistration is that a deregistered farmer does not need to account for VAT on the sale of his farming goods or services nor is he able to recover VAT paid on inputs, including input VAT on capital expenditure. To compensate for this exclusion, he is able to charge VAT registered persons a fixed flat rate percentage as an addition to the price paid to him for goods and services, and he is permitted to retain the amount he receives.

Those who pay this flat rate addition to the farmer will be able to reclaim it as input VAT in their VAT returns, providing they themselves are registered for VAT. When a flat rate farmer sells to a non VAT registered person, and this includes another flat rate farmer, he is not able to add the flat rate addition to the sale price of his goods or services, nor charge VAT.

No flat rate addition may be made when non-agricultural goods or services are supplied.

9.5:2   Qualification for entry

A farmer who is VAT registered may elect to deregister and become a flat rate farmer. Farmers whose turnover is below the registration threshold, which is currently £36,600 pa, may adopt the flat rate scheme, if they otherwise qualify for voluntary VAT registration.

The flat rate percentage addition has been set at 4%, but there is an entry restriction: where the benefits of the flat rate scheme would be £3,000 or more pa by comparison with what would have been the input tax if registered for VAT, election for the scheme is not available. However this restriction is not applied to small farmers whose annual turnover is £70,000 or less.

In consequence it has been announced, (Hansard Vol 215 Cols 819/820) that up to 90% of farmers with an annual turnover of up to £300,000 will be able to join the scheme.

9.5:3   Scope of scheme

It is clear that a wide range of farming activities will qualify for inclusion into the option scheme ranging from crop production, stock farming, forestry, fisheries and processing products derived essentially from agricultural production. Supplies of agricultural services which normally play a part in agricultural production are considered to be eligible. A list of qualifying activities and qualifying services is set out in section **9.5:6** and section **9.5:7** below.

9.5:4   Operation of scheme

Flat rate farmers will not be registered for VAT, so that they will not account for VAT on their sales, nor make a claim for VAT paid on inputs, ie business purchases. They will charge VAT at a flat rate percentage to VAT registered persons when supplying their agricultural goods and services. This flat rate addition will be retained by a flat rate farmer to compensate him, wholly or partly, for the VAT which he has elected not to reclaim. VAT registered persons will be able to reclaim the flat rate addition as if it were input VAT.

9.5:5   Administration

The detail of the scheme is regulated by statutory instrument (see SI 1992/3220, 3221 and 1992/3103). Regulations have been made permitting the Commissioners to 'certify' applications for inclusion and specifying the form and manner in which applications must be made. Penalties are imposed for failure to comply. To prevent farmers opting in and out of the scheme, the regulations specify a minimum period of time (3 years) which must elapse between two certifications.

9.5:6   Agricultural production activities qualifying for scheme

The following activities qualify for the scheme:

I Crop production
(a) General agriculture, including viticulture.
(b) Growing of fruit (including olives) and of vegetables, flowers and ornamental plants, both in the open and under glass.
(c) Production of mushrooms, spices, seeds and propagating materials; nurseries.

II   Stock farming together with cultivation
(a) General stock farming.
(b) Poultry farming.
(c) Rabbit farming.
(d) Beekeeping.
(e) Silkworm farming.
(f) Snail farming.

III   Forestry

IV   Fisheries
(a) Fresh-water fishing.
(b) Fish farming.
(c) Breeding of mussels, oysters and other molluscs and crustaceans.
(d) Frog farming.

V   Where a farmer processes, using means normally employed in an agricultural, forestry or fisheries undertaking, products deriving essentially from his agricultural production, such processing shall also be regarded as agricultural production.

9.5:7   Agricultural services qualifying for scheme

Supplies of agricultural services which normally play a part in agricultural production shall be considered the supply of agricultural services, and include the following in particular:

(a) field work, reaping and mowing, threshing, baling, collecting, harvesting, sowing and planting;
(b) packing and preparation for market, eg drying, cleaning, grinding, disinfecting and ensilage of agricultural products;
(c) storage of agricultural products;
(d) stock minding, rearing and fattening;
(e) hiring out, for agricultural purposes, of equipment normally used in agricultural, forestry or fisheries undertakings;
(f) technical assistance;
(g) destruction of weeds and pests, dusting and spraying of crops and land;
(h) operation of irrigation and drainage equipment; and
(i) lopping, tree felling and other forestry services.

9.5:8   Factors to be taken into account in making the election

In making the decision as to whether to become a flat rate farmer, the following factors would need to be taken into account:

(1) An estimate or forecast of the amount of the flat rate addition recoverable, by comparison with the amount of VAT which has been recovered in the past under the ordinary system.
(2) Whether administrative savings will be secured, for example not having to render VAT returns, keep records, and possibly incur penalties for late or inaccurate returns. The saving is likely to be greater where, for example, there are partial exemption calculations to be made and an apportionment of input tax.

(3) The proportion of sales of agricultural goods and services which are regularly made to non-registered persons, because the flat rate addition cannot be added to sales invoices for that category of sales.

(4) Whether a farmer has been taking advantage of the option to tax in respect of his land and buildings (VATA 1983 Sch 6A para 2). This will have permitted him to add VAT at the standard rate and it is an irrevocable option applying automatically to all agricultural land in the same ownership.

The option to tax is irrevocable, and it is not easy to envisage the circumstances in which that option will be preferable to the new flat rate scheme election.

(5) Farmers who are registered and decide to deregister will not have to account for output tax on stocks and other physical assets on hand, even where they have secured a deduction for input tax when acquiring them.

(6) Above all there is the commercial consequence of deregistration, ie whether farming goods and services will become more or less competitive in the market taking cash-flow into account.

9.6   SPECIAL CATEGORIES

9.6:1   Value added tax – business assets

The sale of business assets where a business or part of a business is transferred as a going concern is not a supply for the Value Added Tax (VAT Special Provisions Order SI 1981/1741 para 12(1)). However, where 'goods' which form part of the assets of a business are separately transferred or disposed of this may be treated as a supply. This is so, even where there is no consideration receivable (VATA 1983 Sch 2 para 5(1) and (3).

Similarly, there is a taxable supply when an interest in, right over, or licence to, occupy land forming part of the assets of a farming business is granted without consideration (VATA 1983 Sch 2 para 8). The value of the supply is treated as the cost to the person making the supply (VATA 1983 Sch 4 para 7(b)). The object of this exceptional basis or charge is to ensure that the input tax originally allowed to the donor is recovered.

The actual sale price will be substituted if any consideration is received, even though the consideration be in an amount less than market value (VATA 1983 s 10(2)). Alternatively, market value may fall to be substituted if, as in the corresponding income tax situation, the donor and donee are connected parties (VATA 1983 Sch 4 para 1(1)).

In the context of a zero-rated farming business, the effect of this rule can only be advantageous. However, where the 'option to tax' has been exercised (VATA 1983 Sch 6A para 3(4) see **9.4**, a gift of farmland will attract VAT at the standard rate. This is a new hazard to be considered when rearranging the ownership of farmland amongst members of a family in the course of an inheritance tax planning exercise. Another factor to be borne in mind is that business asset disposals and other transactions in 'goods' forming part of the capital assets of a business are included for the purpose of determining whether the registration threshold has been reached.

9.6:2 Surrender of farm tenancies

It has been confirmed by HM Customs and Excise that the surrender of a farm tenancy is not regarded as a supply (VATA 1983 Sch 2 para 5(1)), provided there is no consideration for the surrender. It is also being confirmed that the prospect of future savings of other taxes, for example inheritance tax, is not regarded as consideration for this purpose. Nor will the subsequent continued occupation of the land by the former tenants under the surrendered tenancy be regarded as consideration.

9.6:3 Value added tax and sporting rights

In general, the grant of any right to take game whether by licence, lease or otherwise, is taxable. This applies to freeholds, leaseholds and other disposals of sporting rights. Where there is a grant of an exempt interest in, right over or licence to occupy, land, which includes shooting and fishing rights, the consideration must be apportioned between sporting value and the balance. Customs and Excise have indicated that sporting rights for this purpose will be regarded as 'valuable' so requiring an apportionment unless:

1 On a freehold sale, the value of the rights is less than 2% of the sale proceeds;
2 On a lease where the value of the rights is less than 5% of the rent (VATA 1983 Sch 6 Group 1 Note 7).

A supply for value added tax purposes is one made in the course of, or furtherance of, a business. Land ownership in the general sense used in this book is undoubtedly a 'business' for value added tax purposes. However, the sale of a private house by a residential owner occupier would not attract value added tax on any shooting or fishing rights which were included in that sale.

Problems arise where the landowner enters into arrangements with a number of persons. These arrangements may fall into various categories:

(i) The landowner makes an outright grant of shooting rights to a syndicate which thereafter manages and controls the shooting activities, eg the syndicate employs keepers, rears the game and arranges the shooting programme. Any consideration for the grant paid by the syndicate to the landowner is taxable at the standard rate assuming the landowner is a taxable person. If he himself is a member of the syndicate but makes no charge or a reduced charge for grant of the shooting rights in return for paying less than a full share of the syndicate expenses, the amount of the taxable consideration must include the share of the syndicate expenses that he would otherwise have to pay.

If the landowner is a taxable person and in the course of his business supplies goods or services, eg ammunition or gamekeepers, to the syndicate, these supplies will attract value added tax which will form part of the syndicate's expenses recoverable from its members. So far as the syndicate itself is concerned, the position is that where a group of private persons form a syndicate simply to share the expenses of a shoot the syndicate would not normally be deemed to be carrying on the business and would not therefore be considered to be making taxable supplies to members. If, however, it in turn provided shooting facilities for a consideration to others (not members) the syndicate would be regarded as making supplies in the course of business.

(ii) A landowner has the shooting in hand and manages and controls the shooting activities, eg decides who shall take part and settles the contributions paid by the guns which may or may not be sufficient to cover expenses; he employs keepers and rears game, reserves to himself the shot game and maintains a proper account of income and expenditure on the shooting activities. In such cases the landowner is regarded as making supplies in the course of a business carried on by him and the contribution paid by each gun is a consideration for the right to take game and therefore taxable at the standard rate if the landlord is a taxable person.

In *Lord Fisher v Customs and Excise Comrs* [1979] VATTR 227 Lord Fisher invited friends to shoot with him on the basis that they would make stated contributions towards costs. The London Tribunal on 30 October 1979 decided he had made taxable supplies but that this was done in course of a shoot for pleasure and social enjoyment and did not amount to business for value added tax purposes. No value added tax was chargeable. This decision was upheld by the High Court ([1981] STC 238).

During 1991, representations have been made to Customs and Excise that charging value added tax on Sporting Rights, included in a sale of freehold land is contrary to European Community Law (the EC 6th VAT Directive Article 13(B)). Following these representations, value added tax will continue to be charged only on Sporting Rights sold, leased or licensed separately from land. Where land is sold freehold and the sale includes Sporting Rights to take game or fish, value added tax will no longer be chargeable. Where value added tax has been charged on sales since 1 April 1989, claim for refund with interest may be made provided the refund is in turn passed on to purchasers.

Where land including Sporting Rights is leased (rather than sold freehold), valued added tax will continue to be chargeable on the proportion of rent attributable to the Sporting Rights, if the Sporting Rights are 'valuable'. 'Valuable' Sporting Rights are those where the rental value exceeds 10% of the total rent under the lease. It is understood that this proportion of 10% is intended to represent a *de minimis* exclusion, and may be reviewed from time to time. At the time of writing, the law and practice is about to be changed, as from a date not yet announced.

9.6:4   Grazing rights

A supply of grazing rights is zero-rated as animal feeding stuffs. If, however, care of animals is provided for in the relevant agreement other than merely incidental care, the entire supply is treated as liable to value added tax at the standard rate. All other forms of 'keep' of customers' animals which are provided on a headage basis, including livery and agistment, are similarly regarded as liable. To avoid charge, separate agreements for grazing and service should be arranged.

9.6:5   Stud farms

The provision of stud services and food and keep for animals for a single payment has been held to constitute a single supply taxable at the standard rate.

9.6:6   Protected buildings

Protected buildings enjoy a small privilege for value added tax. Zero-rating permitting recovery of value added tax paid is accorded to:

(a) sales of long leases of substantially reconstructed protected buildings; and
(b) certain approved alterations to protected buildings.

The expression 'substantially reconstructed' is statutorily defined as 'a virtually new building ... using certain preserved features of the existing building or where there has been a total internal conversion – for example where the shell of a listed warehouse has been preserved and flats are constructed using that structure'.

In *Vivodan Ltd* EDN/90/134, it was held that the supply fell outside provisions of Group 8(a) of Sch 5, and was not entitled to be zero-rated. It was held that the building in question was not 'reconstructed' in the normal sense of the word, in that there were no structural alterations to the main building, albeit one extension had been demolished and another extension underpinned. Work had consisted of an overhaul of the roof and general repairs with the stripping out and replacement of electrics and plumbing, repointing, replacement of some windows and partitions. Despite all that, it was held that if there had been a reconstruction of the building it was not a 'substantial' one in that the approved alteration did not amount to 3/5ths by reference to cost of the total reconstruction. The only item which could be described as an approved alteration was the underpinning of one of the extensions.

However, zero-rating is only available if the building is to be used as a residential building after the work has been carried out or is to be used by a charity for a relevant charity purpose. If the work was not an approved alteration; or it was an approved alteration on a non-domestic building; or it was non-approved on a non-domestic building the work will attract VAT at the standard rate. Sales of protected buildings which have not been substantially reconstructed but which are to be used for a residential or charitable purpose are exempt.

It is not easy to perceive the logic of this detailed categorisation, particularly as repairs and maintenance (as opposed to approved alterations) remain standard rated.

A 'protected building' is one which has been listed under the Town and Country Planning Acts by the Secretary of State by the Environment; or is a building treated by the local planning authority as within the curtilage of a listed building; or is listed as a scheduled monument under the Ancient Monuments and Archaeological Areas Act 1979.

Gifts to residential housing associations are not within the scope of value added tax. On sales at an under value, the consideration receivable is an exempt supply.

9.6:7 Woodlands

A sale of land with standing timber is exempt from value added tax. However, sales of timber itself are standard rated, and a grant of a right to fell and remove timber is also standard rated (VATA 1983 Sch 6 Group 1 Item 1(*h*)).

There is a small exemption when timber is sold as domestic fuel when it becomes a zero-rated supply (VATA 1983 Sch 5 Group 7 Item 1). In practice woodland owners may make no taxable supplies during a long period whilst trees mature. In these circumstances it is possible to make a voluntary registration providing the woodland is managed on a commercial basis with a continuing intention to make taxable supplies in due course. (VATA 1983 Sch 1 para 11(1)).

9.6:8 Firewood

A supply of firewood in the form and at a price that is compatible for the wood to be held out as firewood to a domestic user is zero-rated. A supply to a wholesaler is not considered as a supply for domestic use and is therefore standard rated (C & E leaflet 701/19/90).

9.6:9   Holiday accommodation

Seasonal or annual pitch rentals are normally exempt (VAT Act 1983 Sch 6 Item 1(e)). It is assumed the site owner grants the caravan dweller a licence to occupy giving the licensee a legally enforceable right for a specific area for a continuous period which must not exceed one year.

Rents from holiday accommodation in a cottage, flat or caravan are standard rated for value added tax. Holiday accommodation includes any accommodation advertised or held out as such. Where holiday accommodation is offered at a lower rate during the off-season it can be treated as residential accommodation providing the let is for more than four weeks. This applies only in holiday resorts (VATA 1983 Sch 6 Group 1 Item 1(c)).

Holiday accommodation in caravans includes those drawn by motor cars; or those which remain static on a particular emplacement. Tents similarly include those pitched by the user and those provided by the site owner.

There have been a number of cases concerning 'time share' holiday accommodation. The general principle seems to be that a distinction needs to be made between (for example) shares in a time share company which are an exempt supply; and the holiday accommodation secured by acquisition of that share which is a standard rated supply. In such circumstances, the price paid has to be apportioned. However a share in a freehold reversion under a time sharing agreement is a standard rated supply. The grant of facilities for parking a vehicle are similarly standard rated.

9.6:10   Land drainage and agricultural water supplies

Certain systems used to be eligible for zero-rating but since FA 1989, zero-rating applies only in special cases where the supplies are made in the course of construction of dwellings or civil engineering work necessary for the development of a permanent park for residential caravans. Otherwise agricultural drainage schemes are standard rated. This appears to be so even where the drainage might be correctly regarded as a farming input.

9.6:11   Straw

When straw is used as an animal feed it is eligible for zero-rating. Where used for some other purpose, for example crop protection, composting or animal bedding, the supply is standard rated. HM Customs and Excise have issued guidelines to resolve the problem of determining the use to which the straw is to be put at the time supply is made. Supplies are to be zero-rated, unless the straw is held out for sale as a non-animal feeding purpose. Straw which is advertised or labelled as non-food stuff; sold in small bags for pet bedding; sold for market gardening or other composting purposes; sold to known industrial packers, or sold as gardening material will be standard rated.

9.6:12   Freshwater fish farming

Customs and Excise rejected the claim that carp should be zero-rated as food for human consumption, but the claim was upheld by the VAT Tribunal.

9.6:13 Farmhouses

Where, as is usual, a farmhouse is used both as a private residence and as farm business premises, value added tax on farmhouse expenditure is apportioned as between the business and non-business use, and only the former proportion is recoverable.

Where the farm office premises are separate and distinct the apportionment presents no problem, but in most cases the whole of the premises are used for both purposes. At one time one third of business purposes was the normally accepted business input fraction but, more recently, Customs and Excise have begun to investigate individual cases with a view to imposing a lower recovery fraction, apparently because one third contravenes the EC 6th VAT directive (see *Mac-Donald v Customs and Excise Comrs* [1982] CMLR 477).

The apportionment does not need to be made on an area basis, there is some authority for its being made on respective amounts of use. It follows that where a farmer is absent from the farm for a period of the year, the business use fraction will be lower.

In a partnership business where there are two or more farmhouses occupied by partners, and therefore likely to be used in the business, the appropriate input tax deductions may be claimed on both or all of them.

There may also be 'duality of purpose' so far as repair and maintenance etc work is done on farm cottages occupied by farm workers. In particular, renovation work to a farm cottage occupied by an employee who was a member of the family required an apportionment of these renovation costs (*AC Eccles & Co v Customs and Excise Comrs* EDN/85/71 (unreported)).

9.6:14 Farmland development

Another VAT trap for the unwary is where a farmer or landowner becomes a 'developer'. Zero-rating is lost if an owner carries out reconstruction, conversion, alteration or extension of an existing building. This rule applies only to commercial and other non-residential buildings. However if the residential use of a development ceases within ten years of a new house being completed and there is a sale or a new tenancy is granted, the zero-rating benefits are clawed back.

Another development category is where a freehold of a new or partly completed building is sold, being one not intended for residential or charitable purposes (VATA 1983 Sch 6A paras 5, 6). For this purpose, new buildings are those sold within three years of completion. In such a case, the VAT incurred on inputs will be recoverable, so that the net effect may be simply to increase the purchase price in the eyes of a would-be acquiror.

The only situation envisaged is a sale of the freehold. The grant of a lease remains VAT exempt, and fails to secure a corresponding recovery of input tax. However, in such circumstances the grantor may be making a 'self supply'. (VATA 1983 Sch 6A paras 5, 6). The effect of this deeming provision is to permit recovery of the VAT paid for his interest in the land plus the cost of constructing the building.

9.6:15 Capital goods

The 'capital goods' scheme implement EC Directive 6 Article 20(2). In the UK, it is regulated by VATA 1983 s 15(3) and VAT General Amendment Regulation No 4 1989. What follows is necessarily a brief summary designed to alert readers to an unfamiliar and potentially dangerous VAT sub-system. The object of the

Scheme is to secure that the proportion of input tax deducted in respect of a 'capital item' is not finally determined in the year of supply, but is subject to adjustment over its subsequent 'period of use'.

The Scheme applies also to certain computer equipment, but this analysis is confined to its relevant application: land and buildings of £250,000 or more in value (including certain extensions and self-supplies) but excluding rent. The subsequent 'period of use', during which detailed records must be kept is ten years, the purpose of this test being to ascertain in what proportion the business has become partially exempt, or more or less partially exempt during this period.

In general terms, the adjustment formula applies to restrict deductible or reclaimable input tax in the same proportion. Instead of input tax being related wholly to taxable supplies, it is treated as relating partly to exempt supplies, and becoming partly non-deductible.

The same principle may apply in reverse. If the capital item is sold during the period of adjustment, the adjustment calculations are finalised by what has been regarded as a balancing charge or allowance (by analogy with the income tax system of capital allowances (see section **5.2**)). There is a similar result if a business is transferred as a going concern.

The following particular applications need to be borne in mind:

(a) The system applies only to land and buildings acquired after 1 April 1990 when the scheme came into force.

(b) An estate owner making a land purchase where a vendor has exercised his option to tax (or where VAT is due for other reason) should consider his intended future use of the land and buildings, in the light of the scheme application.

(c) So should a farmer in a similar position contemplating a variation in his future land use to activities which involve taxable and tax exempt supplies.

(d) Adjustments in VAT under this Scheme are taken into account in arriving at amounts which qualify for income tax capital allowances. Changes in VAT are added to or deducted from unrelieved expenditure and future writing down allowances are thus based on a revised amount.

9.6:16   Fuel and power

Supplies of fuel and power for domestic or residential use, previously zero-rated, become standard rated from 1 April 1994 at 8%. From 1 April 1995, the full rate of 17½% (at present) will be applied. Supplies for business use, previously standard rated, remain chargeable at the standard rate. 'Fuel and power' includes gas, electricity, coal and other solid fuels and heating oils.

9.7   PLANNING AND ADMINISTRATION

The general principles of tax planning as set out in chapter 15 apply to value added tax with some modifications. As a point of departure, the value added tax rate of 17½% still hardly justifies complex schemes. Any scheme which is within 'the new approach' doctrine (see section **15.1:2**) will be caught if it is a series of steps which has no business effect taken solely with a view to avoid value added tax.

Value added tax planning involves making maximum use of various reliefs and exemptions under the Acts. Like income taxes, it requires examination of the different ownership structures available to carry on an activity; and for examination of particular contracts and transactions so that the value added tax consequence is known before completion.

Value added tax planning may involve a change of accounting practices as regards timing of bills or rental demands, having regard to cashflow implications. Earlier repayment of VAT inputs can improve cashflow of a smaller business.

Value added tax administration offers a number of important choices to the tax payer, and the correct exercise of these choices is an important element in planning. For example, a business owner who wishes to register for value added tax but who is below the registration limit (£37,000 with effect from 16 March 1993) can register as a voluntary trader. Registration permits the recovery of VAT on inputs and eliminates an unnecessary expense. Tax-payers may elect to adopt a cash accounting scheme (VAT Cash Accounting Regulations SI 1987 /1427) which enables businesses to account for tax only on the basis of cash actually paid and received. It applies to businesses whose taxable turnover does not exceed £350,000 (from 16 March 1993). For this purpose, taxable turnover includes zero-rated supplies, but excludes supplies of capital assets in the business and VAT itself.

Principally the scheme is advantageous for businesses which normally provide long-term credit facilities to customers or which suffer persistent bad debts, because bad debts are automatically relieved. Businesses which are zero-rated are unlikely to benefit from the scheme, and there are disadvantages for businesses which are able to deduct input tax when expenditure is incurred but before payments are made.

Another relief is available under an annual accounting scheme (VAT Annual Accounting Regulations SI 1988/886). This permits authorised businesses to submit only an annual return. The taxable turnover limit is again £300,000. There are also schemes for businesses which cannot record the precise amount of output tax, perhaps because the transactions are too small. (For example a sweet shop.)

These special schemes for retailers permit them to calculate tax on an estimated basis, instead of keeping detailed records. They apply standard mark up of prices according to the type of goods or business. There are three different types of such schemes with respective limits of £750,000, £125,000 and £100,000 (Schemes B2, C and D).

Value added tax has its own penalty regime. A serious 'misdeclaration penalty' is imposed where there is an under declaration of, or over claim of, tax and there is no 'reasonable excuse' for the error. 'An insufficiency of funds to pay any tax due is not a reasonable excuse' (FA 1985 s 33(2)(a)). What is a 'reasonable excuse' has been the subject of various precedent cases. It is possible to distinguish between the insufficiency of funds itself which cannot qualify as a 'reasonable excuse'; and the underlying cause of the insufficiency of funds, which may so qualify (see *Customs and Excise Comrs v Salevon Ltd* [1989] STC 907).

The question may arise as to how the insufficiency of funds has been created. In *Customs and Excise Comrs v Steptoe* [1992] STC 757 the inability to pay VAT was due to the failure of a customer to pay for work done and reluctance to press for payment which might have destroyed a relationship with an important customer. This was accepted as a reasonable excuse.

Voluntary disclosures without penalty may be accepted by Customs and Excise.

The Commissioners will be given powers in 1993 to mitigate penalties as they see fit, and appeals against their decision to a VAT tribunal will become possible. These charges will be by Treasury Order.

9.8   CHECKLIST OF VAT RATES

	Sales of freehold	*Rate*	*Ref*
1)	New dwelling houses sold by developer	Zero	**9.1:2**
2)	'New' commercial buildings	Standard	**9.1:3**
3)	All other domestic and commercial buildings	Exempt	

	Leases	*Rate*	*Ref*
4)	Grants: new dwelling houses sold by developer (21y+)	Zero (premium) thereafter Exempt	**9.1:2**
5)	Grants: 'new' and old commercial buildings	Exempt	**9.1:3**
6)	Grants: domestic and non-commercial buildings	Exempt	**9.1:3**
7)	Assignments	Exempt	
8)	Surrenders (and assignments to landlords)	Standard	**9.1:3**

	Construction and repairs	*Rate*	*Ref*
9)	New dwelling houses	Zero	**9.1:2**
10)	New commercial buildings	Standard	**9.1:3**
11)	Repairs, alterations, maintenance, demolition	Standard	**9.2:3**

	Miscellaneous	*Rate*	*Ref*
12)	Sporting rights	Standard	**9.6:2**
13)	Private shoots	Exempt	**9.6:2**
14)	Timber	Standard	**9.6:6**
15)	Firewood	Zero	**9.6:6**
16)	Grazing rights	Zero	**9.6:3**
17)	Protected buildings	Zero	**9.6:5**
18)	Holiday accommodation	Standard	**9.6:7**
19)	Drainage	Zero or Standard	**9.6:8**
20)	Stud farms	Standard	**9.6:4**
21)	Fish (for human consumption) farming	Zero	**9.6:9**

Chapter 10

Stamp duty

10.1 INTRODUCTION

The object of this section is not to equip farmers, landowners and their advisers with a detailed knowledge of the law and practice of stamp duty, still less to explain methods of saving duty. The topic is included as a reminder that stamp duty is payable on all conveyances and transfers of property, and is therefore an additional cost to be borne well in mind, when making purchases and sales of farm land, either for ordinary commercial reasons, or in connection with rearrangements of ownership undertaken for tax planning reasons as described in later sections of this book.

Stamp duty is imposed by the Stamp Act 1891 (see also Stamp Duties Management Act 1891). Strictly, it is not a tax on individuals or on particular transactions, but upon instruments, that is written documents. If a transaction need not be carried out by written instrument, there is theoretically no need to pay stamp duty, but in practice, the legal and commercial risks usually make a written document indispensable. An oral agreement is less easy to evidence, and doubts may arise as to the precise terms. Moreover, in some cases, writing is essential in order that a transaction be legally valid, in particular the creation or disposition of a legal interest in land.

10.2 SCOPE OF CHARGE

Stamp duties are charged on 'instruments' transferring 'property' (Stamp Act 1981 s 1). For this purpose an instrument is defined to include all written documents. If a transaction is effected without a document, that is by oral promise, or by delivery of goods, there is no need for any stamp duty. If, on the other hand, the transaction requires more than one instrument, duty need not be paid more than once.

An instrument includes every written document (Stamp Act 1981 s 122). The term 'property' is not defined for stamp duty purposes, but it has been held that it does not include a licence to do something on or with property remaining in the possession of an existing owner. 'Property' is not restricted to real property, and includes goodwill, debts, the benefit of a contract, an option, and a contingent interest. It is not necessary that any beneficial interest should pass under the instrument. Stamp duty charges on property other than land and buildings are to be abolished late during the tax year 1991–1992. The date will coincide with the date of abolition of the stamp duty on transactions in shares. That will depend on the date of introduction of paperless share dealing under the Stock Exchange's new automated share transfer system, known as 'Taurus'.

The amount of duty is based on the 'consideration'. Interest on the amount due is to be ignored, and if the consideration is not expressed in cash, the rules of valuation apply as for other forms of taxation. 'Consideration' is inclusive of VAT.

Where consideration is payable in instalments there are detailed rules. If the period for payment does not exceed 20 years, the total throughout the period is taken. If the period exceeds 20 years, the total for the next 20 years is taken.

Stamp duty on voluntary gifts, ie where there is no consideration, was abolished in the Finance Act 1985.

Wills, other testamentary instruments and deeds of family arrangements are exempt from stamp duty (see FA 1985 s 84(1)). However, a deed of family arrangement is not exempt if made for monetary consideration.

10.3 RATES OF CHARGE

There are certain instruments chargeable to fixed duty at 50p, for example deeds (including partnership deeds) and covenants, but for land, etc the duties are *ad valorem*, that is on a sliding scale based upon particular amounts, as follows:

Head	Amount on which duty charged
Conveyance on sale of land	Consideration for the sale
Lease of land	Annual rental or premium on lease, or both
Life insurance policy	Sum assured
Contract note	Duty repealed (FA 1985 s 86)
Voluntary gift	Duty repealed (FA 1985 s 82)

For conveyance or transfer of freeholds, and premiums on leases, the scale is as follows:

Consideration £	Rate on full consideration
0–60,000	nil
60,000 +	1%

These rates apply to documents executed on or after 16 March 1993, provided they are not stamped before 23 March 1993.

For leases, the scale is as follows:

TABLE OF STAMP DUTIES ON LEASES

	If the term does not exceed 7 years or is indefinite	If the term exceeds 7 years but does not exceed 35 years	If the term exceeds 35 years but does not exceed 100 years	If the term exceeds 100 years
	£p	£p	£p	£p
Not exceeding £5 pa	Nil	0.10	0.60	1.20
Exceeding £5 and not exceeding £10 pa	Nil	0.20	1.20	2.40
Exceeding £10 and not exceeding £15 pa	Nil	0.30	1.80	3.60
Exceeding £15 and not exceeding £20 pa	Nil	0.40	2.40	4.80
Exceeding £20 and not exceeding £25 pa	Nil	0.50	3.00	6.00
Exceeding £25 and not exceeding £50 pa	Nil	1.00	6.00	12.00
Exceeding £50 and not exceeding £75 pa	Nil	1.50	9.00	18.00
Exceeding £75 and not exceeding £100 pa	Nil	2.00	12.00	24.00
Exceeding £100 and not exceeding £150 pa	Nil	3.00	18.00	36.00
Exceeding £150 and not exceeding £200 pa	Nil	4.00	24.00	48.00
Exceeding £200 and not exceeding £250 pa	Nil	5.00	30.00	60.00
Exceeding £250 and not exceeding £300 pa	Nil	6.00	36.00	72.00
Exceeding £300 and not exceeding £350 pa	Nil	7.00	42.00	84.00
Exceeding £350 and not exceeding £400 pa	Nil	8.00	48.00	96.00
Exceeding £400 and not exceeding £450 pa	Nil	9.00	54.00	108.00
Exceeding £450 and not exceeding £500 pa	Nil	10.00	60.00	120.00
Exceeding £500 for any sum of £50 and also for any fractional part thereof	0.50	1.00	6.00	12.00

10.4   PROPERTY SUBJECT TO A DEBT

A farm may be conveyed subject to a mortgage debt, the purchaser taking over the obligation to repay the mortgage loan, and the cash consideration being accordingly reduced. In such circumstances the stamp duty payable on the sale will reflect the amount of the debt taken over by the purchaser. If there is no cash consideration and taking over the debt represents the whole of the price payable, the debt will be the total amount on which stamp duty is calculated.

It is the amount of the debt that is taken into account, not its value, so that the fact that a debt is bad does not reduce the amount of duty. This rule is subject to another, whereby the stamp duty chargeable is limited by reference to the value of the property transferred if this is less than the amount of the debt (see SP 6/90).

10.5   PROCEDURE

The stamp duty procedure differs from all other taxes. No liability to pay duty is imposed by statute upon any person, nor, consequently is any person under any obligation to make a return that an instrument has been written. It is the practical consequences of failing to stamp which are the automatic sanction, in particular, the inability to sue on certain contracts, and for land, the inadmissibility of an unstamped instrument in evidence. There are fines and penalties for failure to stamp, and late stamping in certain other special cases.

In practice liability for duty falls on a purchaser of land. There is a due time for payment of duty, which for conveyances of land is 30 days after execution. An instrument is stamped by being presented (with the duty) at the counter of a stamp office, or by handing in at a money order post office, or through the post. The document is impressed by a die showing the amount of duty. More than one stamp may be needed to make up a total.

In recent years, the value of agricultural land has increased to levels which make stamp duty by no means a trivial consideration. In special cases, there are technical methods of avoiding duty, but more generally, the correct approach is to ensure that no more dutiable transactions occur than are necessary. If there is a choice of securing the same result by different methods, stamp duty can be a determining factor. For example, a purchase of land should be made direct by a son, rather than by a father with a second separate sale to the son afterwards. The effect of creating two sales can be to pay duty at an effective rate of 2% instead of the statutory 1%.

Chapter 11

Community charge and council tax

11.1 INTRODUCTION

This section explains the system of local government financing charges which was introduced with effect from 1 April 1990 (Local Government Finance Act 1988), now repealed. There were three new categories the *'personal community'* charge; the *'standard community'* charge; and the *'non-domestic rate'* (or *'uniform business rate'*). It describes the relationship of the community charge (or 'poll tax') with income taxation.

There was a fundamental difference between the community charge and the former system of local rates. Rates were a graduated charge expressed as a percentage rate payable (not by all citizens), but those occupying rateable property, calculated in accordance with the 'rateable value' of that property. The ascertainment of this rateable value was a complex process based on rental value, theoretically repeated at five-year intervals. Thus, in theory, rating was a progressive and indexed form of taxation. In practice, the periodic revaluations were not undertaken and rateable values became obsolete. This was used to justify the introduction of a new non-progressive, non-indexed system, which, predictably, was received without enthusiasm. Agricultural land and buildings were wholly exempt from local rates but farm cottages and sporting rights were rateable.

The *personal community charge base* was made up of individuals rather than property, although this principle sometimes seemed to be lost. The 'individuals' were adults of voting age (18 years or over) solely or mainly resident at a particular address on a specified date. There were detailed exemptions and rebates outside the scope of this book.

The general consequence is that although residences may be used for business purposes, it did not follow that any part of the personal community charge was deductible in calculating income for tax purposes. Thus where premises were used partly for residential and partly for business purposes, as a farmhouse, the apportionment to produce a deductible business element was no longer made. In a sense, therefore, the community charge was an additional cost to the agricultural sector.

The *standard community* charge was badly named. Its base was domestic property which was not the sole or main residence of any person (see para **11.3** below). Non-domestic property was subject to the *uniform business rate* (see para **11.4** below).

11.2 EMPLOYEES

An employer may decide that although the personal community charge was not based upon the occupation of premises, he would, nevertheless, pay it on an employee's behalf. The reason might be because, in the past, he paid the rates of an employee's cottage or other residence, and if he failed correspondingly to pay the community charge, the relationship between the parties was to that extent being varied.

If a farmer did so decide to pay his employee's community charge, the consequence for income tax was that an employee's personal expense was being borne by his employer, so that the payment represented additional remuneration in the hands of the employee. Both income tax and national insurance were chargeable on this remuneration, which would not necessarily have been so with payment of rates.

If, as a second stage, the employer also paid the tax and national insurance liability arising on the community charge benefit, those payments would themselves bear tax and national insurance, so that a further grossing up exercise was required in order to calculate the total amount involved.

The principle needs to be illustrated by an example:

> If an employee who is a basic rate tax payer and whose national insurance contributions represent 9% of his emoluments, faces a community charge of £500, his employer would need to pay him £758 to return the employee to the position he would have been in before the community charge. If the employee's spouse's community charge is also to be paid by the employer the amount will fall to be doubled.

However, in making the decision as to whether to subvent an employee, the farming employer needed to bear in mind that the amounts so paid would form part of the remuneration payable to employees and would therefore be income tax deductible as expenditure paid wholly and exclusively for business purposes.

Whether or not payments of spouses or other dependents, community charges similarly qualify depends on whether it can be contended that such payments were made under an employee's employment contract. It may be advantageous to pay a salary increase to an employee (deductible) rather than pay his non-employee dependents, community charges which are likely to be challenged. Alternatively, he might make a once and for all lump sum cash payment, perhaps into an employee's pension scheme.

11.3   THE STANDARD COMMUNITY CHARGE

The standard community charge, unlike the personal community charge had as its tax base residential property which was not the sole or main residence of any person. A person who used standard community charged premises for business purposes was permitted to deduct, for income tax, an appropriate proportion of the charge depending upon the proportion of business use. This might be arrived at on a time basis or on a physical proportion of use basis, or both.

The charge was calculated as a multiple of the personal community charge for a particular area.

11.4   ADMINISTRATION

The personal and standard community charges were fixed by the local authority which was called 'The Charging Authority'. This authority could also prescribe the methods of payment, which might be in instalments.

There was a comprehensive appeals procedure which enabled aggrieved parties to present their case to a valuation and community charge tribunal. This was empowered to hear appeals on the contents of the community charge register, liability for community charge, and other related issues. However, there were various aspects which could not be appealed before the tribunal, for example the amount of the community charge, matters relating to joint and several liability, the appellant's financial circumstances, some of which were regarded as 'enforcement aspects' and dealt with by the Magistrates' Courts.

Unpaid community charges were the subject of a summons, and proof of liability was required. If satisfied, the court made a liability order, and thereafter there were a number of enforcement powers against the debtor. These were:

attachment of earnings;
attachment of state benefits;
distraint;
imprisonment;
insolvency;
and a charging order.

There was joint and several liability of husbands and wives and couples living together as husbands and wives.

11.5   THE UNIFORM BUSINESS RATE

Rating continues for non-domestic property, and on some domestic property which is used partly for business purposes. The business rate remains a qualifying deduction in calculating income tax profits, and where premises such as farmhouses are used partly for business purposes and partly for residential purposes, the business rate is deductible to the extent that the part of the premises on which they are paid is in fact used for business purposes.

The old rules for valuing property and for calculating its rateability remain in force or have been effectively re-enacted. In general, the rateable value is:

'. . . an amount equal to the rent at which it is estimated the hereditament might reasonably be expected to be let from year to year, if the tenant undertook to pay all usual tenant's rates and taxes and to bear the cost of repairs and insurance and the other expenses (if any) necessary to maintain the hereditament in a state to command that rent' (LGA 1988 Sch 6 para 2(1)).

Agricultural land and buildings are exempt (LGA 1988 Sch 5 para 1) as they were under the former system. For this purpose 'agricultural land' is:

(a) Land used as arable meadow or pasture ground only.
(b) Land used for a plantation or a wood or for the growth of saleable underwood.
(c) Land exceeding 0.10 hectare and used for the purposes of poultry farming.
(d) Land which consists of a market garden, nursery ground, orchard or allotment.
(e) Land occupied with and used solely in connection with the use of a building which (or buildings each of which) is an 'agricultural building' (defined below).

It is clear that agricultural land does not include:

(a) Land occupied with a house as a park.
(b) Gardens other than market gardens.
(c) Pleasure grounds.
(d) Land used mainly or exclusively for sport or recreation.
(e) Land used as a race course.

A building is an 'agricultural building' if it is not a dwelling house and:

(a) It is occupied together with agricultural land and is used solely in connection with agricultural operations on the land; or
(b) It is or forms part of a market garden and is used solely in connection with agricultural operations at the market garden.

It is clear that borderline cases will arise, both as regards the nature of the operations; the nature of the occupation; and the relationship between the occupation and the operations. At the time of writing, limited guidance is available from the cases, but a farm shop selling only produce raised on the farm was held to be rateable (*Fletcher v Bartle* [1988] RA 283) because retail sales were not the same activities as the activities carried on on the associated land.

Livestock buildings are classified as exempt agricultural buildings even if the above tests are not satisfied, provided:

(a) The building is used 'solely' for keeping or breeding livestock; or
(b) It is occupied together with agricultural land and used also in connection with agricultural operations on that land and that other use, together with the keeping and breeding of livestock, is its sole use; or
(c) It is a building other than a livestock building (not a dwelling house) occupied with livestock buildings and is used in connection with the operations carried on in those buildings (eg a feeding store).

'Livestock' for this purpose includes any mammal or bird kept for the production of food or wool or for the purpose of its use in the farming of land. Animals kept for exhibition and game birds raised for sporting are not 'livestock' (*Cook v Ross Poultry Ltd* [1982] RA 187).

A list of rural activities showing whether or not rateable and the authorities is attached. These precedents should be treated with caution as many of the decisions were reached on the basis of specialised facts.

11.6   SPECIAL ACTIVITIES

The following brief summary of liabilities on special farming or related activities may serve as a checklist:

Nature of activity		*Liability*
Caravans (sole or main residence)		occupier's personal charge
Caravans (not sole or main)		owner's standard charge
Holiday caravans let		uniform business rate
Other holiday accommodation		uniform business rate
Studs and stables		uniform business rate
Grass drying plant		exempt
Farm shops		uniform business rate
Bee keeping		exempt (LGFA 1988 Sch 5 para 6)
Fish farms	('the breeding or rearing of fish, or the cultivation of shellfish for the purpose of . . . transferring them to other waters or producing food for human consumption')	exempt
Sporting rights	('any right of fowling, of shooting or taking or killing game or rabbits or of fishing')	uniform business rate ('when severed from the occupation of the land on which the right is exercised')
Charities		80% relief
Non-profit making bodies		discretionary relief

11.7   THE COUNCIL TAX

The council tax replaced the community charge with effect from 1 April 1993. It is an annual tax, close to the former system of local rates, in that it is based on the value of domestic property relative to other domestic property in the area. Individual property values as determined by valuation are categorised into various bands and charged out at a specific rate in the pound.

There are however reliefs for certain classes of occupiers. The person liable to pay the council tax is the individual corresponding to the first category in the following sequence:

(a) a resident who has a freehold interest (ie the owner-occupier);
(b) a resident who has a leasehold interest;
(c) a resident who holds a statutory tenancy;
(d) a resident who has a licence to occupy, eg a worker living in a tied farm cottage;
(e) any other resident;
(f) non-resident owners of property.

If a property is vacant and is not the sole or main residence of any individual, then the non-resident owner will be liable to pay the tax. Where a property is a second home or is unoccupied, 50% relief is due. Other reliefs are due if there are fewer than two residents in a property.

11.8   VALUATION AND ADMINISTRATION

The basis of valuation for council tax is the sale price which might have been expected, if the property had been sold in the market on 1 April 1991, subject to certain assumptions. These are, principally, that the sale was with vacant possession and the property was in a reasonable state of repair, that the size, layout and character of the property, and its locality were the same on 1 April 1991 as on the date the valuation was made.

The council tax is fixed by the local authority which notifies the valuation band, ie, the range of values attributable to the property into which the property falls. The authority also prescribes methods of payment, which may be by instalments. There is a comprehensive appeals procedure, which permits appeals against the banding.

11.9   DEDUCTION FOR INCOME TAX

Where property, for example a farmhouse, is used partly for domestic and partly for non-domestic purposes, the different parts may be subject to council tax and uniform business rate. However, it is more likely that farmhouses will be subject only to council tax.

The Revenue has announced that a deduction may be claimed in calculating trading profits for that part of the council tax which is attributable to the trade of farming. The appropriate proportion is to be determined by reference to the particular facts of the case concerned, and the former conventional 1/3rd of expenses deductible has ceased to be acceptable by the Revenue. The Revenue has explained that this change in their practice results from their view that farmhouses are now used only to a limited extent for business purposes, and that most farmhouse expenditure relates to domestic circumstances of the farmer and his household. This will apply to council tax, as it applies to the other outgoings on the farmhouse.

11.10   EMPLOYEES

When an employer pays council tax on behalf of an employee, or a member of an employee's family, the cost will normally be deductible in computing the employer's farming profits. That is provided the payments are part of the employee's remuneration, which will usually mean that they are payable under the terms of his employment. It has been confirmed in an Inland Revenue Press Statement issued with the 1993 Budget that where the provision of living accommodation in itself does not give rise to a benefit in kind the payment of council tax by the farming employer will be similarly treated. Thus the position returns to that which existed under the former local rating system, and reverses the position which obtained during the period of community charge.

However, payment of an employee's council tax is treated as earnings for the purposes of national insurance contributions (see chapter 12). Such a payment is regarded as the settlement of a personal debt due from the employee.

Chapter 12

National insurance contributions

12.1 INTRODUCTION

Reductions in the rates and impact of income taxation have increased the relative importance of the system of social security contributions, which cannot unreasonably be regarded as a form of supplementary taxation. It is conventional to calculate the burden of NIC as increasing personal income tax by 9% of earnings. The farming industry naturally bears the double cost of farmers' own contributions and those of their employees. The Table (see below) shows that the various percentages involved are not trivial, so that it has become worthwhile considering what opportunities exist for minimising these costs. Hence this brief summary is included as an introduction to the subject.

The four categories of contributions under the Social Security Act 1975 s 1 are as follows:

Class 1

This category relates to employments (see section **12.2**) and is divided into two forms: primary contributions made by employees themselves; and secondary contributions from employers.

Class 2

These are contributions paid by the self-employed (see para **2.2**) at a flat rate.

Class 3

These are voluntary contributions paid to provide or supplement entitlement to future benefits.

Class 4

These are graduated contributions paid by 'self-employed' persons. They vary in accordance with profits and are assessed and collected via the tax system (Social Security Act 1975 s 9). The contribution is payable on the same date as the related tax. One half of Class 4 contributions is deductible in computing income tax liabilities.

Employers should bear in mind that the National Insurance Regulations (Social Security (contributions) Regulations 1979 (SI 1979/591) as amended by the Social Security (contributions) Regulations 1990 (SI 1990/605)) impose obligations to submit returns showing details of national insurance paid for employees. These correspond to the PAYE regulations, and there are similar penalties for negligently incorrect returns and for delay (Social Security Act 1990 s 17 and Sch 5).

12.2 NATURE OF EARNINGS

'Earnings' for the purposes of social security contributions does not have the same meaning as for income taxation. It is defined as 'remuneration or profit derived from employment', but there are a number of exceptions relating to what would be called under the income tax rules: 'benefits in kind'. Under the social security legislation the wording is: 'any payment in kind (other than a security) or by way of the provision of board or lodging or of services or other facilities' (Social Security Contributions Regulations 1979 reg 19).

Thus national insurance contributions are limited to cash remuneration or to payments to employees which are capable of being converted into cash. Where a farmer supplies accommodation to employees, that accommodation may be treated as income for taxation purposes (see section **5.5:1**). It does not follow that national insurance contribution is payable simply because taxable income is so created.

In the same way an employer's contributions to an approved pension scheme are considered to be a payment in kind and are therefore not chargeable to national insurance contributions. Board and lodging, or luncheon vouchers, and the supply of other services are thus all exempt.

However, employer's contribution is chargeable on the provision of company cars and petrol to employees. The measure of the charge is the scale used for income tax benefits. This innovation was announced in the Budget 1991. Also payment of council tax by an employer is treated as the discharge of a debt due from the employee and is liable to national insurance contribution. This is so, irrespective of the income tax treatment.

It is unrealistic to suggest that an employer can merely convert cash payments to his employees into one or other of the exempt categories of payments, so reducing his liability for national insurance contributions. Clearly, employees require to be paid cash wages, and reduction of national insurance contributions is subject to overriding commercial considerations. But in very limited circumstances the possibility of savings along these lines should be considered.

Another possible saving route is by converting employees to a self-employed basis, bearing in mind that not only the national insurance contribution but also a different tax regime will be involved (see section **2.2**).

12.3   RATE TABLES

National insurance

NATIONAL INSURANCE CONTRIBUTIONS   from 6 April 1993
Class 1 earnings

Rate applied to all earnings

CLASS 1   **Contracted in**

All earnings up to	Employee	Employer
−£ 55.99pw	NIL	NIL
−£ 94.99pw	(2% on first	4.6%
−£139.99pw	£56 plus	6.6%
−£194.99pw	9% between	9%
−£420.00pw	£56 and £420)	10.4%
Over £420pw	No further payment	10.4%

Contracted out

All earnings to	Employee		Employer	
	On first £56pw	On excess to £420pw	On first £56pw	On excess to £420pw
−£ 55.99pw	NIL	NIL	NIL	NIL
−£ 94.99pw	2%	7.2%	4.6%	1.60%
−£139.99pw	2%	7.2%	6.6%	3.60%
−£194.99pw	2%	7.2%	8.6%	5.60%
−£420.00pw	2%	7.2%	10.4%	7.4%
Over £420.00pw	No further payment		£0–56	10.4%
			£56–420	7.4%
			above £420	10.4%

CLASS 2   1993–94
Small earnings exemption   £3,140
Weekly   £5.55

CLASS 3   1993–94
Weekly   £5.45

CLASS 4   (50% income tax deductible)
Annual earnings – upper   £21,840
– lower   £6,340
Rate   6.3%
Maximum   £976.50

Chapter 13

Woodlands

13.1 INCOME TAX

13.1:1 Introduction

The changing systems of forestry taxation can only be understood in the context of non-fiscal considerations. In Britain, trees have long been more than ornaments on the landscape, or a shelter for wildlife. That timber is a diminishing world resource has become a truism. Substitute materials are costly. Britain currently imports some 90% of its requirements the value of which is about £4½ billion per year.

Supplementary arguments are that wood substitutes, for example steel and cement, are more expensive to produce and consume more energy. The geography of this country makes it suitable for forestry. Finally, conservationists favour forestry as part of the preservation of the beauties of the countryside.

For all these reasons, the tax regimes for woodlands have been traditionally benevolent. Tax reliefs have represented a form of government subsidy supplementing cash grants available to owners who enter into dedication agreements with the Forestry Commission.

This benevolence was demonstrated most notably in 1963 when the income tax liability of woodlands remained under Sch B for assessment on an arbitrary amount of notional income, instead of being transferred to Sch D so as to secure assessment on actual or commercial income. The key factor taken into account at that time was that forestry is a long-term activity, in which half a century might elapse between planting and the flow of income. When major changes were made in the taxation of income from land in 1963, it was thought unfair to upset the taxation of woodlands, because owners had planted under one tax regime and were entitled to continuity.

Although similar arguments were mounted in the Budget debates for 1988, they were not accepted by government. It was contended that commercial woodlands had become a tax shelter, and the Chancellor's stated objective at that time was to take commercial woodlands out of the income tax system altogether.

The change in treatment which took place makes it necessary to distinguish carefully between the basis before 15 March 1988 and the basis after the date. However the impact of the change was temporarily diminished by transitional provisions effective until 1992–93. Expressed briefly, the effect of the change was to extinguish the possibility of offsetting the costs of planting and management of woodlands against an owner's other taxable income. It is too early to evaluate the economic effects of this change, but clearly it is a substantial one. Whether it be regarded as the extinction of a tax shelter, or the extinction of a valuable tax incentive depends very much upon one's point of view.

13.1:2 Income tax: pre-15 March 1988

The general principle was that income tax was chargeable under Sch B in respect of the occupation (not ownership) of woodlands in the United Kingdom managed on a commercial basis and with a view to profit. This was subject to a right to make an election for Sch D (see section **2.1:3**). Under Sch B, tax was chargeable on the assessable value, which was ⅓ of the annual value, or a lesser proportion if the occupier were in occupation for only part of the year. The annual value was defined as in other contexts; the rent which might reasonably be obtainable on an annual letting, if the tenant paid tenant's rates and taxes, and the landlord undertook to pay for repairs, insurance and any other expense necessary to maintain the land in a state to command that rent. The annual letting envisaged was of the unimproved land.

So long as this basis continued, no income tax was payable on cash received, nor, on the other hand, was tax relief due for cash paid as operating expenses, or on buildings or equipment which might have otherwise qualifed for capital allowances (see section **5.2**).

Grants from government sources, for example under the Forestry Acts 1967, were also income tax exempt.

It was said that the average value of land on the Sch B basis was 15 pence per acre. Assessments were often trivial in amount and were not in practice made by inspectors, presumably because the administration costs would have exceeded the tax collectable.

13.1:3   Election for Schedule B

The woodland occupier had an important option: to elect to be assessed under Sch D in place of Sch B. This election substituted the Sch D basis of computation, the actual profits arising from the woodlands calculated as if they were the profits or gains of a trade. The effect of the Sch D election was not to treat the woodlands as a trade. If that had been so, the value of growing trees would have been treated as stock in trade so affecting each year's profit calculation. Growing trees were not so treated (*Coates v Holker Estates Co* (1961) 40 TC 75).

The normal basis of assessment for woodlands, for which an election had been made was the profit (if any) of the year preceding the year of assessment, although where a newly established estate was involved, it was doubtful if a period before the date of planting could be so used. A cash basis, ignoring debtors and creditors, was often acceptable.

The value of the Sch D election derived from the treatment of losses, which could be set against the total income of the tax payer in the same way as losses of a trade under Sch D. Losses were computed in the same way as trading losses, and writing down allowances on capital expenditure could be claimed.

Losses not set off against total income for the current or succeeding year could be carried forward and set against future woodland profit. Writing down allowances were similarly treated. The three-year carryback of loss reliefs (see section **2.6:3**) was not applicable.

An election needed to be made in writing to the inspector not later than two years after the end of the first chargeable period for which it was to take effect (TA 1970 s 111(2)). Once made, an election was irrevocable, so long as the elector remained the occupier. However, an owner could sell, donate or let the land to some other person, so that the right of election arose to the new occupying purchaser, donee, or tenant.

Thus Sch B was advantageous during the period of maturity of an estate when timber sales were occurring, and the proceeds would otherwise have been treated as Sch D income. On the other hand, Sch D was advantageous during the initial period of planting, and during periods of growth, when the cost of maintenance and thinnings often exceed the thinnings income. Having made a Sch D election, the owner could not revert to Sch B. However, it was possible to revert back to Sch D by arranging transfer of the occupation by sale or gift into the hands of a relative, trustee or family company. The election ceased to apply in the hands of a new owner who enjoyed the income on the tax exempt Sch B basis.

This category of scheme was repeatedly attacked as an abuse and led to the Finance Act 1988 reform which abolished the right to elect for Sch D treatment; abolished Sch B; and abolished corresponding rights of deductibility of interest on loans taken out to acquire interests in commercial woodlands.

13.1:4   Income tax: after 14 March 1988

The objective of Finance Act 1988 was to take woodlands out of the income tax system. The compensation was increased grants designed to make up for the cancellation of the loss relief. Details of the Woodland Grants Scheme which came into effect on 15 March 1988 are outside the scope of this book but, in general, grants are based upon the stipulated amount per hectare planted, payable in three instalments: 70% on completion of planting; 20% after five years; and 10% in the tenth year. There are reductions and supplements in particular cases.

The importance of the pre-15 March 1988 rules is that they continued in effect under transitional provisions until 5 April 1993 (FA 1988 Sch 6 Para 4(7)). The tests for the benefit of transitional relief were as follows:

1 The occupier must have been in occupation of the woodlands on the key date of 15 March 1988, irrespective of whether or not he had made an election to be taxed under Sch D.
2 Alternatively the occupier qualified if he had entered into a contract to occupy or to plant new trees before 15 March 1988; the contract must be evidenced in writing.
3 Alternatively the occupier must have applied for a grant under a forestry commission scheme in force on 15 March 1988, his application being received before 15 March 1988.

These transitional rules were particular to the occupier on the transition date. If the occupier disposed of his interest before 1993, the acquiror did not acquire the benefit of the Sch D election, unless the succession was on death (FA 1988 Sch 6 para 4(1)(*b*)).

Where an occupier had validly elected for Sch D treatment, but had applied for and received a grant under the new scheme during the period, the Sch D treatment ceased in the following period. For the period in which the grant has been made, only expenses not covered by the grant were deductible.

These transitional rules applied to capital expenditure, so that writing down allowances were due, but there was no recapture of those allowances by balancing charges as at 5 April 1993 when the transitional period came to an end.

13.1:5   Scope of woodlands exemption

Although the Finance Act 1988 exempts an occupier from income tax liability in respect of the value of his occupation of woodlands, the question arises as to whether certain categories of profits may be taxable under some Schedule other than Sch B. For example, income from shooting rights over woodlands may be liable under Sch A. Similarly, if an occupier fells the timber and subjects it to manufacturing processes, liability will arise under Sch D Case 1.

There are a number of precedents which apply to determine how far a Sch B assessment exhausted the taxable capacity of forestry operations. Expressing the issue in a less technical form: if the occupier cuts timber and sells it, no liability arises, because the profit on sale is 'franked' by the Sch B assessment. But if he cuts timber, strips it, trims it, and manufactures it into packing cases, which he sells, does not the operation extend beyond the growing and harvesting of trees? These were the facts in the precedent case of *Collins v Fraser* (1969) 46 TC 143 in which earlier cases turning on the same problem were reconsidered.

It was held that if the activity was simply to make the produce of soil marketable, the profit from it could be treated as franked by the Sch B assessment. If not, liability (under Sch D on the manufacturing profit) would arise, and it could be said that the operation had an additional 'taxable capacity'. Unfortunately, the outcome of *Collins v Fraser* is not reported, but it appears that the Revenue argument would have been upheld.

Identifying the occupier on whom tax is chargeable may present problems. The basic rule is that any person having the use of land should be deemed to be the occupier of it (TA 1970 s 92(4), now repealed), a somewhat uncertain identification, where, for example, a landowner allows another person to enter and fell timber. This was the position in *Russell v Hird* [1983] STC 541, where a syndicate purchased the timber, felled it, constructed roadways, provided machinery, maintained fences and ditches, and cleared land, ready for replanting. However, there was no timber manufacturing process undertaken.

The syndicate claimed to be assessed under Sch B, so as to exclude any Sch D liability. The Commissioners found as a fact that they were indeed the occupiers. The court upheld this view, on the basis that occupation depended not only on legal rights, but what was actually done on the land. The protection of Sch B was therefore established.

However, this decision was reversed in FA 1984 s 51, which enacts that a person who has use of woodlands for felling, processing or removing timber, or clearing or preparing land for replanting shall not be treated as an occupier for Sch B purposes. Thus, timber merchants effectively revert to Sch D Case I with effect from 13 March 1984. The principle of taxable capacity is also discussed at section **4.1** to which reference should be made.

13.2 CAPITAL GAINS TAX

It is convenient to mention the capital gains tax treatment here. Profit from the sale of the trees themselves is exempt from capital gains tax. Profit on the sale of the solum, ie the land, remains liable to capital gains tax, and in making the calculation, the appropriate elements of the cost and sale prices relating to the trees are excluded. Roll-over relief and general relief for gifts are available for capital gains tax under the provisions described in sections **7.4** and **7.5**.

13.3 INHERITANCE TAX

13.3:1 Deferral relief

The economic justifications for forestry income tax reliefs have been described in section **13.1**. For inheritance tax stronger justification can be asserted since the event of death may lead to premature felling of trees to raise cash to pay the tax bill. This was recognised under estate duty, in that the value of timber was not aggregated with free estate for the purpose of arriving at an effective duty rate. Non-aggregation has not been reproduced under inheritance tax; instead, relief takes the form of possible deferral of payment of tax, until the natural occurrence of events calculated to produce the cash required (IHTA 1984 s 125ff).

This relief applies only to transfers made on death. The person liable can elect within two years of the date of death, although the Revenue has discretion to accept later claims. The effect of election is to exclude the value of the timber (but not the solum) from the deceased's estate for all purposes. In order to qualify for election, the only test is that the deceased was the beneficial owner for five years before his death, or had become so entitled by gift or inheritance (IHTA 1984 s 125). Formerly, there was a condition that the woodlands must be subject to a dedication agreement, but this was repealed in FA 1977. Nor is it a requirement that income tax liability must be under a particular Schedule; nor that the woodlands be managed on a commercial basis with a view to profit. However, trees growing on 'agricultural' property are excluded. Relief may be claimed by lessees and life tenants, but not owners who are discretionary trustees.

The effect of election is twofold. First, no inheritance tax is payable on the timber until it is sold or given away, or otherwise disposed of (IHTA 1984 ss 127 and 128). A disposal of an interest in the timber is treated as a disposal of the timber itself. This is an anti-avoidance proviso. Secondly, if the disposal is a sale for full money's worth (ie at market value), tax is then chargeable on the net cash proceeds of sale. If not, tax is chargeable on the net value at the time of disposal. In determining 'net value' selling expenses may be deducted. So may expenses of replanting within three years of disposal, so far as these expenses have not been allowed for income tax. There is a discretion to extend the limit, which will be exercised if delay in replanting was due to circumstances outside the owner's control.

The rate of charge is found by treating the taxable proceeds or value as the top slice of the deceased's estate. For this purpose, all previous sales or disposals are included in arriving at the estate, and may therefore increase the rate. If a second death occurs before the timber has been sold, no tax is chargeable on subsequent disposals by reference to the first death. It is also possible to contemplate exceptional circumstances in which there are two charges to inheritance tax. That would be where there is a lifetime transfer, which is itself chargeable, and which also triggers off tax due on a previous death, when an election has been made. In those circumstances, the tax payable by reference to the death is deducted, in calculating the amount of the chargeable lifetime transfer.

A further complexity is added in that woodlands qualify for business property relief, whether transferred in lifetime or on death, and whether or not a deferral election has been made (for disposals after 26 October 1977). For disposals before that date, deferral relief and business property relief were alternatives.

Clearly, the problem in deciding whether or not to elect lies in estimating the increase in value which will take place between the date of death and the time of ultimate sale. The greater the increase, the longer the period of time before sale, and these two factors may be regarded as self-cancelling. In the case of trees which are immature on death, there will be a significant gap between the value then, and the value on ultimate sale, and an election may not be beneficial. Where, at death, the trees are relatively mature, and little further accretion of value is forecast, election may be beneficial. Consideration should also be given to the possibility of electing for mature parts of an estate and not for immature parts.

13.3:2 Estate duty

Where property is subject to a deferred estate duty liability, it is not normally entitled to potentially exempt transfer treatment. Under the old estate duty and capital transfer tax rules, when estate duty arose on the death of a woodland owner, the tax could be deferred until the personal representative felled and sold the timber, so raising the cash to pay the tax.

This deferral disappeared under inheritance tax. The woodland transfer became immediately chargeable to inheritance tax, and the estate duty charge was cancelled. (FA 1986 Sch 19 para 46). However, it appears that the legislation was defective in that it denied PET treatment to all property comprised in a single transfer, any item of which, however small, was woodlands, subject to the deferred estate duty. By a concession (5 December 1990) the PET treatment becomes available to all parts of a transfer other than the woodlands subject to a deferred charge.

13.3:3 Woodlands and business property relief

Woodlands qualify for business property relief, providing, of course, the woodlands are run as a business on a commercial basis. This may need to be evidenced by the presentation of separate woodland accounts, which, conceivably, might not have been prepared since the change in income tax treatment taking final effect on 5 April 1993 (see section **13.1:4**). These accounts might be necessary to demonstrate the commercial basis of woodlands, where this is the only commercial operation within an estate, all the other parts of which are let to tenants.

The question arises as to whether the new rates of business property relief enacted in F(2)A 1992 are applicable to the deferred tax chargeable under IHTA 1984 s 125 and following sections (see section **13.1:1**). It appears that the new rates are not so applicable. IHTA 1984 s 126 which is the charging section for the deferred tax does not refer to a 'transfer of value' or to a 'chargeable transfer'. Thus there is nothing to secure that business property relief as such applies. The deferred charge, therefore, is apparently to be reduced by 50%, as is enacted by s 127(2). This relief has not been increased by the 1992 Act.

The implication is that the election to defer has lost its value since 100% business property relief was introduced, and there is no benefit in making such an election, provided it is clear that the tests for 100% business property relief will be satisfied.

Chapter 14

The countryside and the national heritage

14.1 INTRODUCTION

It has been an oft expressed aim of government to:

> 'maintain and enhance all aspects of our heritage, including our country-side, historic buildings and their contents, and major works of art. Nor are preservation and improvement the sole objectives; our heritage is there to be enjoyed . . . by as many people as possible'. (A National Heritage Fund (Cmnd 7428)).

This approach has helped determine the tax treatment, the central feature of which may be described as a bargain between the Exchequer and the owner. The former undertakes to defer (not exempt from) capital taxation, so long as the latter performs his side of the bargain. He gives two separate undertakings: to maintain and preserve the property; and allow public access to it. So long as he performs these functions, tax that would otherwise be payable hangs in suspense. If he breaks his undertakings, then the deferred tax may become payable. This regime may be regarded as the contemporary version of that originally devised for heritage property, when estate duty was first introduced by Sir William Harcourt in 1894.

It has been accepted by owners, and their representative body 'The Historic Houses Association', because it offers an opportunity for some 3,000 country houses and their contents to remain in private ownership, during a period when burdensome taxes and maintenance costs seem to create massive problems for them. There is a consensus view that continuing private ownership is better than public ownership and any relief is better than no relief.

On the other hand, the future contingent liability to taxation may be said to create a locked-in effect, with loss of flexibility. Given the overriding urge to retain the property in a family, this may seem a price worth paying.

At the time of writing, it does not appear that the system described in this section has been very popular or very successful.[1]

1 For a comprehensive guide see: 'Capital Taxation and the National Heritage' issued by the Board of Inland Revenue (IR 67), December 1986. Price £5.20.

14.2 DESIGNATION FOR INHERITANCE TAX

14.2:1 Introduction

The first attempts to produce a workable regime for inheritance tax were made in FA 1975, but there were substantial variations made the following year.

14.2:2 Scope of relief

The following events may be the subject of a claim for conditional exemption, that is designation of a property:

On death: all transfers of property.

Lifetime: transfer to a person other than an individual, in particular a transfer to discretionary trustees or to a company; or transfer to an individual, where there is retention of benefit (see section **8.1:5**).

Transfer: to an individual where the donor dies within the seven-year period.

Exemption cannot be claimed for a gift which is exempt as a gift to a spouse or to charity. As to the property itself, there are the following categories:

(A) WORKS OF ART

These include pictures, prints, books, manuscripts, works of art, scientific collections or other things not yielding income of national, scientific, historic or artistic interest.

(B) LAND OF OUTSTANDING SCENIC, HISTORIC OR SCIENTIFIC INTEREST

This can include land of outstanding horticultural, sylvicultural or arboricultural interest, but generally this class does not extend to buildings on the land unless they contribute to scenic interest. Before granting the exemption, the Board consults the following bodies as appropriate:

Scenic	England and Wales	Countryside Commission, England and Wales
Scenic	Scotland	Countryside Commission, Scotland
Scenic	Northern Ireland	Ulster Countryside Committee
Scientific	Great Britain	Nature Conservancy Council
Scientific	Northern Ireland	Nature Reserves Committee (NI)
Forestry		Forestry Commission
Botanic		Royal Botanic Gardens, Kew

Scenic
A high standard is required, and a starting point is whether the land is in a National Park or designated Area of Outstanding Natural Beauty (AONB). This is not an absolute test.

Scientific
This includes flora, fauna, geological or physiographical features.

Historic
This includes association with a particular historical event, earthworks and archaeological sites, sites scheduled as ancient monuments and gardens.

(C) BUILDINGS OF OUTSTANDING HISTORIC OR ARCHITECTURAL INTEREST

The following tests are relevant but not conclusive:

(i) receipt of grant under Historic Buildings and Ancient Monuments Act 1953 s 4;
(ii) listing under Town and Country Planning Acts, Grade I rather than Grade II (land adjoining an historic building essential for protection of the character and amenities of the building is also eligible for exemption).

(D) WOODLANDS

Land qualifying as of outstanding scenic, historic or scientific interest, often includes woodlands as an element justifying conditional exemption. In such circumstances undertakings are required as regards the management, thinning, felling, and replanting of woodlands so as to conserve the heritage elements. A management plan with these objectives agreed with an advisory body will often serve as such an undertaking.

(E) AMENITY LAND

Essential amenity land is land that is essential for the protection of the character and amenities of an outstanding building. The factors taken into consideration include the need to protect the views from an outstanding building to landscaped parkland, and the views of the building from elsewhere, and the prevention of development close to the building. Exemption granted to essential amenity land may include buildings on it providing they make their own contribution.

Undertakings (see section **14.2:3** below) need to be given for the essential amenity land and for the building which the land protects.

Amenity land need not physically adjoin the building it serves; there may be other essential amenity land lying between the building and the amenity land.

(F) ASSOCIATED PROPERTIES

'Associated properties' may be a building, an area of essential amenity land, or an object historically associated with a building. Conditional exemption may be claimed for associated properties. There are special rules linking the tax privileges attaching to associated properties with properties which are the subject of conditional exemption.

14.2:3   Undertakings

Undertakings have to be given to the Board by applicants. There are variations as between works of art on the one hand, buildings and land on the other, but the general effect may be summarised as follows:

  (a) works of art must be kept permanently in the UK; temporary absences for overseas public exhibitions need to be individually approved;
  (b) reasonable steps must be taken to preserve the property;
  (c) reasonable steps must be taken to secure public access to it;
  (d) as regards land, representatives of the appropriate body (eg Nature Conservancy Council) must be allowed on to it after reasonable notice;
  (e) any relevant body must be provided with details of footpaths, signposts, access routes over land for use by foot either at all times, or during reasonable periods of the year;
  (f) the land must be managed in a way which safeguards its essential features;
  (g) as regards buildings, (b) above applies, plus the continued association of exempt objects with the buildings;
  (h) as regards buildings, (c) above also applies. For smaller buildings, reasonable access means at least 20 days a year during the summer months, plus the Spring and Summer Bank Holidays; for larger buildings, liable to attract and able to handle larger numbers of visitors, greater access is required. (Access means access to the interior of the house, not only to the grounds and appropriate publicity of openings will be required.)

14.2:4   Breach of undertakings: chargeable events

The conditional exemption is lost if a condition is breached (IHTA 1984 s 32). As a large amount of tax can become payable, it is important to examine closely what constitutes breach. Where it appears there has been a breach, due notice will be given, and an opportunity tendered to rectify matters. Generally, the authorities appear to be showing considerable sensitivity to the issues involved.

Breach of an undertaking is one of a series of possible 'chargeable events'. The others are:

(a) sale of property, other than to a public collection;
(b) gift of property, other than to public collection etc;
(c) death of a person beneficially entitled, unless this results in a fresh conditionally exempt transfer, or the undertakings previously given are renewed by the recipient;
(d) other disposals, save where the property is offered and accepted in lieu of tax by the Treasury.

Where there is a chargeable event, the charge will be upon the sale proceeds if there has been a sale, or the market value in other circumstances. Liability falls upon the person beneficially entitled to the proceeds.

It is possible to envisage problems arising in practice. It has been suggested that when a property is burned down, that might be a disposal 'by sale or gift or otherwise'. It is understood that the practice is for the Board not to claim if the insurance proceeds are applied to rebuild, repair etc, the property. Certainly, that seems an equitable course, if the property can be reinstated in its former condition. Generally, it is Board policy not to claim tax on conditionally exempt property which has been destroyed, unless it is shown an owner failed in his undertaking to preserve.

Where some modest part of the designated property is sold, for example associated contents, the Board may direct that no chargeable event shall be deemed to occur. In such cases the practice is to ascertain whether the heritage property as a whole has been materially affected by the disposal.

Under the Housing and Urban Development Act 1993, leaseholders of long leased flats and houses are able, subject to various eligibility criteria, to collectively purchase the freehold of their properties. Where there is such a disposal which is solely attributable to leasehold enfranchisement or earlier leasehold reform laws, the inheritance tax effect is limited to the part of the property which is sold, and if the disposal does not affect the heritage entity as a whole, conditional exemption of the remainder is not lost.

14.2:5   Amount of charge

The sale proceeds or market value as the case may be will be charged at a rate derived from the circumstances of the person who made the last conditionally exempt transfer, or any other maker of a conditionally exempt transfer within the last 30 years as the Board of Inland Revenue may select (IHTA 1984 s 33). This, apparently, is to counter avoidance by the insertion of an impecunious owner in an ownership chain.

The charge will be at lifetime rate, if the conditionally exempt transfer was a lifetime gift, and at full rate if the conditionally exempt transfer was a death. In both cases, it will be assumed that the conditionally exempt property is charged on top of the transferor's accumulated total of taxable gifts as a top or next slice (IHTA 1984 s 33(1)).

Because the sale etc, proceeds form part of the cumulative total of that person's transfers, creation of the charge may affect the rates at which other transfers are charged.

If the last conditionally exempt transferor be alive, the rate charged on subsequent transfers of all his property will be affected. If not, the rate charged upon subsequent sales etc of other heritage properties may be affected, assuming that those heritage properties were also designated.

There is a further rule, where at the time of sale etc, the property is comprised in a settlement made within 30 years of the date of sale, or has been so comprised within five years preceding the chargeable event. In those circumstances, the settlor who made a conditionally exempt transfer of property can be included as a person who made the last conditionally exempt transfer before the chargeable event.

It is difficult to predict how these extremely complex rules will work in practice. Some years must necessarily elapse, during which property passes down the generations, before the effect can be evaluated. In the meantime, it is worth noting that if a chargeable event occurs, some liability will arise to recapture the tax deferred on the transfer initiating designation. That is, the status of conditional exemption cannot be secured without some tax being put into suspense.

14.2:6   Conditional exemption and inheritance tax

The introduction of inheritance tax permitting potentially exempt lifetime transfers (see section **8.1:2**) has changed the emphasis of the conditionally exempt regime, and diminished its importance. Conditional exemption under capital transfer tax represented a system whereby property could be passed down to the next generation without an immediate tax payment being required as an entry price. Under inheritance tax, the freedom to make lifetime transfers to heirs and individuals generally has rendered unnecessary the difficult decision of whether or not to seek conditional exemption during lifetime. However, conditional exemption can be valuable in special circumstances:

(a)   where a transferor fails to survive the seven-year period between gift and death (see chapter **8**);

(b)   where a gift has failed or is vulnerable by reason of retention of benefit (see section **8.1:5**);

(c)   where gifts of say, works of art are liable to capital gains tax, and no hold-over relief is due (see section **7.5**);

(d)   where a maintenance fund seems advantageous.

The two sub-systems (conditional exemption and PETs) do not readily fit together; the general rule is as follows: where there is a transfer of value of heritage property, any possible qualification for conditional exemption is to be disregarded in determining whether or not the transfer is a potentially exempt transfer. Any claim for conditional exemption is deferred until death, assuming that death occurs within seven years of making the potentially exempt transfer, and that it fails to qualify for that reason. If the seven-year period is completed, the question of conditional exemption never arises on death and the claim is then made by personal representatives, provided that:

(a)   qualifying circumstances to support the claim exist as at the date of death (and not the date of transfer);

(b)   in particular the property has been retained by the transferee until the date of death;

(c)   or failing that, the property had between the date of transfer and the date of death been disposed of to a public collection; or to the Revenue in payment of tax.

Owners and their personal representatives should bear in mind that their land is capable of becoming the subject of a claim either in its own right, or as adjoining an historic building. There is no objection to claims under both headings being simultaneously put forward for the same land. However, as in many cases, the value of the land will be far greater than that of the historic building itself, and because land is a more marketable commodity, the Board tends to adopt a strict attitude towards it. In the Board's view the amount of land needed to 'protect' an historic house is often limited. One qualification is that the acreage is capable of being seen from the house or from which the house can be seen.

14.3   MAINTENANCE FUNDS

14.3:1   Introduction

The concept of maintenance funds is modelled on endowment: that in order to preserve the national heritage, tax privileges must be conferred, not only on the heritage assets themselves, but also upon funds the income from which is to be applied to preserve heritage assets in a decent state of repair. The ability to set up such a fund should serve as an encouragement to make use of the national heritage reliefs.

14.3:2   The requirements

The main features are as follows:

(a) Until FA 1980 the fund needed to be created by settlement upon irrevocable trusts with an approved custodian trustee. The current position is that the trust must provide that for a period of six years from the date when the property is settled, both the property itself and the income from it may be used only for:

  (i) the maintenance, repair or preservation of the heritage property for which the fund has been set up; or
  (ii) for making provision for public access to it; or
  (iii) the maintenance, repair or preservation of the property which has itself been put into the settlement; or
  (iv) for defraying the expenses of the trustees.

  Any income which is not so applied and which is not accumulated, must be distributed to one of the bodies listed in IHTA 1984 s 25(1), Sch 3 (see section **14.6**) or to a charity which is wholly or mainly concerned with the maintenance, repair or preservation of national heritage property.

  The trust must also stipulate that throughout its whole life and not only for the first six years, the income from the settled property may be applied only for the above purposes. In addition, it is important that the transfer into the fund takes immediate effect and the conditions must be satisfied within 12 months; must not be defeasible; nor must the transferor have less than the full interest in the property transferred. Nor must the trustees of an existing maintenance fund acquire a reversionary interest by purchase.

(b) Under the pre-FA 1980 regime, the trusts became 'purpose trusts', that is they were established for non-human beneficiaries, but the objects were not charitable. They were analogous to trusts designed to maintain a tomb or monument for the benefit of animals. In consequence, they became subject to the perpetuity rule limiting the period of trust to the perpetuity period: 80 years or lives in being plus 21 years. After that the funds had to go to national heritage institutions or to a heritage charity and under no circumstances could they be returned to the settlor or his family. All this was changed by FA 1980.

(c) After the property has been settled in the maintenance fund for six years, it may be withdrawn from the settlement for any purpose whatsoever. However, income tax and inheritance tax charges may arise on withdrawal as explained below. It should be noted at the outset that there will normally be no inheritance tax or capital gains tax liability and only a reduced charge to stamp duty if property is distributed out of a maintenance fund to an individual who, within 30 days, resettles it on trusts of a new fund in accordance with a direction. Nor will there be an income tax charge if the whole of the property distributed out of the first maintenance fund goes into a new fund.

(d) The property included in a maintenance fund must be of an appropriate character and amount. Non-income producing assets are likely to be regarded as unsuitable particularly if their own maintenance may make excessive demands on the resources of the fund. Tenanted farmland surrounding a mansion house and managed as one estate with a mansion house is likely to be deemed appropriate as would a portfolio of stocks and shares.

(e) There are obligations to supply information, eg annual statements of accounts and a report.

(f) Maintenance funds may be created from funds held in a life interest in possession trust after the death of a life tenant, without an inheritance tax liability arising. The period of time allowed for the property to pass to the maintenance fund is two years from death extended to three years, if an application under the Variation of Trusts Act 1958 is needed (IHTA 1984 s 57A).

14.3:3   Tax reliefs

The privileges obtainable are not trivial:

(a) Inheritance tax exemption is secured in respect of the original transfer of assets to trustees of the fund, and in respect of capital distributions from the fund (IHTA 1984 Sch 16).

(b) Hold-over relief for capital gains tax has been preserved. This is particularly valuable since the withdrawal of general hold-over relief from March 1989.

Capital gains arising on the disposal of fund assets are chargeable to capital gains tax in the normal way (see section **14.4**).

(c) There is a special treatment designed to prevent the trustees' income from being exhausted by income tax. For any year of assessment, the trustees may elect that their income be treated as that of the settlor, and therefore become part of his total income available to be reduced by loss or other relief. Alternatively, the trustees' income may be treated as not deemed part of the settlor's income, and so be liable at the basic rate plus the additional rate (TA 1988 s 691). The effect of this rule is to limit the liability of the trustees to the latter rate, which at the time of writing would be 35%.

Maintenance funds are permitted only where the income is to be applied to buildings or land or objects associated with buildings, and contents as such do not qualify. Until some alleviation is tendered that represents another deterrent.

It is not difficult to perceive why the authorities have adopted so stringent an approach: there is natural anxiety to prevent maintenance funds and the national heritage reliefs as a whole from creating a tax haven or shelter, capable of attracting investment moneys for that reason alone. In that the authorities have been successful, but the penalty so far as maintenance funds is concerned has been to tender a regime at what many advisers feel to be far too high a price to be worth acceptance.

The position when capital is withdrawn after six years (or the earlier death of a settlor) is as follows:

(A) INHERITANCE TAX (IHTA 1984 SCH 4)

Property paid out for approved heritage purposes	No liability
Property paid to individual, who within 30 days (or two years if distribution is after a death) puts it into new approved fund	No liability
Property paid out to settlor, spouse, or widow/widower at certain times	No liability unless coming from previous fund
Property paid out to anyone else	Chargeable (IHTA 1984 Sch 4(8)). There are complex rules to fix the rate.

(B) INCOME TAX (TA 1988 s 694)

Chargeable on accumulated income of fund not used for heritage purpose, unless the property is withdrawn for a heritage purpose, or is resettled within 30 days into a new approved fund.

(C) CAPITAL GAINS TAX (FA 1980 s 82)

There is a roll-over relief when property is taken out and settled in a new approved fund, otherwise liability arises.

(D) STAMP DUTY (FA 1980 s 98)

On resettlement only one charge to duty is made, although there will be two separate conveyances.

14.4 CAPITAL GAINS TAX RELIEFS

It has already been explained that a gift of an asset is treated for capital gains tax purposes as a sale at the market value of the asset as at the date of the gift (see section **7.1**). Hold-over relief for capital gains tax has been preserved.

The effect of the relief is to put the capital gains tax into suspense until the donee disposes of the asset, without in turn qualifying for capital gains tax relief.

This relief is available for transfers of property to a maintenance fund (see section **14.3**). However, gains arising on disposal of maintenance fund assets by the trustees are chargeable in the ordinary way. The effect of this deserves consideration. On a disposal to maintenance fund trustees, the trustees are treated as acquiring for a consideration that gives rise to neither gain nor loss, which would be historic cost to the settlor.

That historic cost will also be historic cost to the maintenance fund trustee, so that the fund may sustain liability representing the accretion of value in the hands of the original settlor, many years earlier.

Gifts to charities, and certain national heritage bodies, are similarly exempt from capital gains tax (see section **14.6**).

14.5   INCOME TAX: HOUSES OPEN TO THE PUBLIC

14.5:1   Introduction

The conditions for designation (see section **14.2**) include an undertaking that a building of outstanding architectural or historic interest will be made accessible to the public, but this is not the most significant factor encouraging owners to open their doors. Most owners contemplate the step as a means of raising cash to meet maintenance and repair bills. Apart from entrance fees, car-parking charges, profits from the sale of 'refreshments' and other entertainments, opening is encouraged by the Historic Buildings Council. Grants are available, subject to opening. All this compensates for the loss of privacy.

The income tax treatment of the profit or loss arising on the opening assumes considerable importance. Any profit is often destined to meet capital costs, and a loss needs to be subvented from other taxed income. The 'profit' or 'loss' which emerges from a set of financial accounts can be a somewhat arbitrary figure. That will be because an historic house is often a private residence as well as a source of income, and adjustments need to be made to reflect the residence element. Because general upkeep costs are often high, the outcome can be determined by what adjustments are made, and accepted by the Inspector of Taxes. Apportionments may be necessary for other reasons, because, for example, part of the upkeep cost is included as a deduction in computing the profits of the farming business, in respect of which the house qualifies as a farmhouse. A copy of a note agreed between the Inland Revenue and the Historic Houses Association will be found at Appendix III.

14.5:2   Computation of liability

There are several different methods of computing liability, which may be summarised as follows:

(A) OWNER OCCUPATION

If the historic house is maintained wholly as a private residence, then no income tax liabilities arise, and obviously no relief can be claimed for the cost of upkeep.

(B) SCHEDULE A

Liability arises under this Schedule in respect of profits from land, including rents, annual receipts, and other receipts (see section **4.2**). Deductions may be claimed for maintenance, repairs, insurance and management. An excess of expenditure over income (which is more usual for an historic house) may be carried forward, but may never be set against other classes of income either for the current or future year. This treatment would apply where the admission fee merely gave access to a viewpoint or empty building and is therefore disadvantageous.

(C) ONE ESTATE ELECTION UNDER SCHEDULE A

This exceptional treatment is still found in practice (see section **4.4:2**). At the end of 1962–63, there was a change in the rules of Schedule A, and as a special transitional measure, owners of a number of properties were allowed to retain an advantage they had enjoyed under the former rules. Under a 'one estate' election, income and outgoings on owner-occupied and let properties were aggregated in one calculation. The usual benefit is that the expenses on the house can be offset against rents receivable from tenanted farms. Deficiencies may be carried forward to future years. No new 'one estate' elections can be made.

(D) SCHEDULE D CASE VI

The Revenue often contends that the activities of historic house ownership fall short of trading, and the profits (if any) should be treated as 'other profits or gains'. This may be because the house is maintained mainly as a private residence; or because the historic features are not significant; or because there are insufficient openings; or because there is insufficient organisation or prospect of profit; or because the other tests of 'trading' are not, in the Inspector's view, satisfied.

Under this class, deductions are more restricted than under Case I, and generally are limited to the additional expenses incurred by openings. Losses are allowable only against other Case VI profits, or may be carried forward only against Case VI profits.

(E) SCHEDULE D CASE I

In order to qualify within this most advantageous class, the house must be maintained wholly or mainly as a show place; managed on a fully commercial basis; open on a substantial number of days a year, with proper accounts and a systematic organisation. The investment of capital is helpful as showing a trading motivation.

Where the tests are satisfied, losses may be set off against total income (unearned or earned) for the current or succeeding year, or carried forward against future years' profits from the same source. Generous writing down allowances may be claimed and these are deductible as are losses. The general effect is to make the net cost of ownership fully tax deductible.

(F) 'HOBBY TRADING RULES'

The effect of this rule is to limit the value of Case I treatment as described above. Loss relief is denied if the trade is not carried on on a commercial basis and with a view to profit. In practice, the Revenue tends to invoke this rule after losses have been sustained for five or six years in succession. Writing down allowances are treated in the same way as losses (see section **2.6:5**).

14.6   GIFTS TO PUBLIC BODIES AND CHARITIES

14.6:1   Introduction

Most owners of national heritage property and contents have as an objective the preservation of that property in their own ownership and occupation. The process of designation, and the creation of maintenance funds have been established to secure such an objective, as described in the earlier sections of this chapter. There are, however, occasions when it may be desirable for ownership to be conceded, and the property or corresponding value to be handed over to the State or to an official body. Inheritance tax exemptions are available, and are briefly enumerated in sections **14.6:2–14.6:4.**

14.6:2   Gifts and bequests of national heritage property

Such gifts may be made under a general exemption if to a suitable non profit-making body individually approved by HM Treasury (IHTA 1984 s 26(1)). This exemption applies to land of outstanding scenic, historic or scientific interest; buildings of historic, architectural or aesthetic interest, together with land used as grounds; objects kept in and given with the building; works of art and similar objects of national scientific, historic or artistic interest; and property given as a source of income for upkeep of these items. The Treasury may call for undertakings as ensure reasonable public access and the preservation of the property. Generally, this form of relief follows the lines laid down for designation. Conditional or defeasible gifts are excluded.

14.6:3   Gifts and bequests of property (not necessarily national heritage property)

Such gifts and bequests to national museums, universities, the National Trust and certain other bodies are exempt (IHTA 1984 s 25 and Sch 3).

14.6:4   Gifts to charities

Gifts to charities and other bodies in the UK are exempt (IHTA 1984 s 24) subject to a number of conditions: they must take immediate effect; be not defeasible; be an entire interest; and no right of occupation may be retained save on commercial terms. 'Charity' has the same meaning as in the income tax Acts generally, and means any body of persons or trust established for charitable purposes. In turn 'charitable purposes' has the same meaning as in other parts of English law, and whether a particular purpose is or is not charitable is often a complex question, to be decided in the light of a long series of precedent cases. In this connection, the transferor's motives and opinions are immaterial, and the court will look to the benefit of the community as a whole, for the overriding test as to whether an object is charitable is whether or not it is made for public benefit. This is, however, insufficient in itself, and the purpose must be publicly beneficial in a way which the law deems charitable. In the leading case of *Income Tax Special Purposes Comrs v Pemsel* [1891] AC 531, 3 TC 53, HL four general charitable heads were distinguished:

  (a) relief of poverty;
  (b) advancement of education;

(c) advancement of religion;

(d) other purposes of a charitable nature beneficial to the community, not falling under any of the three preceding heads.

It is the last of the four heads which will be of most relevance to owners of heritage property. Promoting the preservation of land and buildings of beauty and historic interest for the benefit of the nation was held to be a charitable purpose in *Re Verrall, National Trust for Places of Historic Interest or Natural Beauty v A-G* [1916] 1 Ch 100, [1914–15] All ER Rep 546. The improvement of agriculture was similarly held to be a charitable purpose in *IRC v Yorkshire Agricultural Society* (1927) 13 TC 58. Thus it is open to owners of heritage properties to contemplate the establishment of a charitable trust as a distinct alternative to a combined designation and maintenance fund. Such a trust would be wholly exempt from both income and capital taxation, subject only to the proviso that if the trustees carry on a trade, for example farming or showing the house to the public, the profit may be taxable, even though it be wholly applied to the objects of the trust.

The choice of a charitable trust as the vehicle to preserve a heritage property is unlikely to be made simply for tax reasons. One reason for preferring a trust would be that there were no suitable descendants in prospect who would accept the responsibility of ownership and management, and therefore trustees were required to serve as a substitute. There would be no objection to an existing owner serving as one of a number of trustees, although the trust deed would need to provide for replacement after his death.

Alternatively a charitable trust might be selected, because of reservations as to the stability of the designation process, or fears that the law might be changed under future governments of different political complexions. One tenable view is that designation represents a first step towards nationalisation, and the use of a charitable trust, with independent trustees, might seem to offer better fortification for an historic country house and its surrounding farmlands.

A Housing Association may be a qualifying charity attracting the tax benefits described above. A Housing Association is a non-profit making society, trust or company, whose object is the construction, improvement or management of houses (Housing Associations Act 1985 s 1(1)).

Gifts of land to registered charities or charities exempt from registration are similarly exempt from capital gains tax. Sales at under-value are not wholly exempt but are chargeable on the actual consideration. That is the computation is based upon the consideration receivable less the cost or 1982 value plus indexation and costs of sale.

Gifts or sales at undervalue to Housing Associations without a charitable status attract the substitution of market value (see section **7.1:1**).

The IHT consequences similarly differ as between gifts to registered charities and gifts to associations without charitable status. In the former case, any unconditional gift is exempt from inheritance tax (IHTA 1984 s 23). Two conditions must be satisfied. First, the donor must give his entire interest in the property. Secondly he must not reserve any benefit. Thus, a donor cannot grant a lease out of the freehold; nor can he continue to occupy the land without paying a full market rent to the Housing Association.

These conditions are also applicable to the bounty element in a sale made at a price less than market value as at the time of the sale.

14.6:5   Property in lieu

The Revenue has power to accept specific heritage property in whole or part satisfaction of an estate duty, capital transfer tax, inheritance tax, or interest thereon due on other taxable property.

Under this arrangement, no capital taxation is payable on the property accepted in lieu of tax. The amount of tax which is to be deemed satisfied is fixed by agreeing a special value for the property given in satisfaction. This value is found by establishing an agreed value for the item, and deducting a proportion of the tax payable on it. This arrangement is known as the 'douceur'.

The value of the property in question may be determined as at the date the item is offered or as at the date it is accepted. If the former, interest on the tax ceases to run from the offer date (FA 1987 s 60).

Chapter 15

Tax planning I: choice of medium

15.1 OBJECTIVES OF TAX PLANNING

15.1:1 Introduction

The objective of tax planning may be described as reduction of taxes to the legal minimum; or the maximisation of post-tax income and capital; or as a continuous attempt to reconcile the demands of the Exchequer with the economics of farming and landownership. That the burden of taxation is a severe one should have emerged from chapters 1 to 7 of this book. The vulnerability of the industry to taxation has been described in the introduction; the question now arises as to what positive strategies are available, and how to set about finding and putting them into operation.

The demands of the Exchequer are always particularly exigent at death, for it is axiomatic that death is a good point in time to levy tax. The argument is that heirs inherit bounty, and therefore will be less disinclined to part with a share to the State. As a result inheritance tax has been the biggest single menace, and it follows that alleviating the burden of that tax is the biggest single objective. If inheritance tax were the only tax, the problem would be less acute. Often, the combination of capital and income taxes presents the most intractable difficulties, for income taxation tends to leave too small a net residue to pay for living expenses; to provide working capital; to finance improvements and development; and (finally) to fund inheritance tax.

Capital gains tax is more intrusive on the occasion of a particular transaction, most obviously a sale of land. Its impact is also felt on the disposal of a farm or estate at the end of a working career, when capital gains tax is applied abruptly to value increases accruing over a long period, perhaps a lifetime. In one sense 'tax-planning' means a continuous awareness of the taxation aspects of all such capital transactions and a readiness to try to adapt them for tax reasons.

In another sense, tax planning means embarkation upon formal systematic exercises designed to investigate whether a farm or estate is owned and operated in the most tax-efficient manner. If not, what practical changes should be made.

A review of this kind should have been undertaken by every farmer and landowner of substance in conjunction with his professional advisers by the age of say 40, or earlier if family circumstances are appropriate. It is convenient to visualise such exercises as consisting of three separate steps (see section **15.1:3**).

15.1:2 Anti-avoidance law and practice

Tax planning as described in the previous section is still a valid and proper activity. There is no general anti-tax avoidance provision in English law, but at the present time, there is uncertainty as to the limits of permissible avoidance.

Until 1981, it was a truism that every tax payer was entitled to arrange his affairs so as to attract the minimum amount of tax. This was the doctrine laid down by Lord Tomlin in the *Duke of Westminster v IRC* (1935) 19 TC 490. The rule was that if a particular transaction avoided tax, the Revenue could not seek to substitute for the transaction a different transaction which would have attracted tax.

However, in the early 1980s the courts adopted what has been called a 'new approach'. This approach has derived from a series of precedent cases in the

House of Lords particularly *Ramsay v IRC* (1983) 54 TC 101 and *Furniss v Dawson* [1984] STC 153. This is not the place to describe those cases and the new approach in detail, but henceforth all tax planning must be conducted with a recognition of the new approach and its implications.

Since this approach emerges from a series of cases, the judgments in which sometimes conflict with one another, it is impossible to summarise the principles involved. However, the following statement from the judgment of Lord Brightman in *Ramsay* has become the classical text:

'First, there must be a pre-ordained series of transactions, or, if one likes, a single composite transaction. This composite transaction may or may not include the achievement of a legitimate commercial (ie business) end . . . Secondly, there must be steps inserted which have no commercial (business) purpose apart from the avoidance of a liability to tax – not "no business effect".'

The new approach undoubtedly applies to inheritance tax as well as to income, capital gains and corporate taxation. The onus is on the Revenue to state what fiscal consequences derive from the alleged composite transaction. In *Fitzwilliam v IRC* [1990] STC 65) it was held that there had not been a single composite transaction, so the rule did not apply. Those who contend there is no application to inheritance tax base their argument on the fact that inheritance tax has its own anti-avoidance rule (IHTA 1984 s 268).

The tax planning discussed in this chapter does not involve artificiality, and it will have been observed that commercial and farming considerations have been emphasised throughout.

Mostly, tax planning in this book means strategic planning over long periods of time during which fiscal and commercial elements blend indissolubly into one another. Nevertheless, the 'new approach' needs to be taken into consideration, particularly on the occasion of the sale of land. There may be a temptation to structure multiple sales via a series of legal entities, and this temptation should be resisted. One of the uncertainties is whether the new principle can be invoked where the timing of a transaction has been influenced by taxation factors, and another uncertainty is how strong the commercial motives must be to displace the new principle.

In farming, many of the legal structures used are traditional in the industry, and ante-date tax pressures. Clearly, that represents a significant line of defence.

15.1:3   Practical tax planning

(A) THE FIRST STEP

The first step (see Appendix IV) towards finding a protective strategy is always to assemble on paper the relevant financial data, which becomes raw material for a tax plan. Total asset values at a current date are summarised to disclose the total value of the farm or estate plus other non-agricultural assets, so as to form some crude estimate of the amount of contingent inheritance tax payable in the event of immediate death of one or all estate owners. It is important not to omit non-agricultural assets, generally liable at higher rates than agricultural assets, and which, when included, can significantly increase the rate chargeable across the board. Similarly, funds held in trust need to be included to get the true measure of the problem. Major debts and other liabilities fall to be deducted.

This summary of assets and liabilities must be examined as representing a set of current values capable of being varied by technical changes to produce a lesser sum in tax payable.

(b) THE SECOND STEP

The second step is to consider what changes might produce a different result, having regard to non-taxation factors, in particular how the estate owner wishes his estate to devolve amongst members of his family on death, and how far he is willing or able to transfer to them shares of farm ownership and income during their lifetimes. These transfers may well be determined by family and farming considerations, as to what practical contributions members of the family respectively make; their ages, marital circumstances and attainments; their ability to farm or manage an estate; what future contribution they intend; whether, for example, care of the estate is to become a full-time career, and a variety of similar factors, beyond the scope of this book to evaluate.

Capital tax reductions are most readily achieved, by spreading out assets and income amongst members of a family, but donation can be disadvantageous if it leaves a donor or, more importantly, his widow, impoverished in favour of later generations. A potential donor's income requirements after retirement should be considered well in advance to make sure they have been provided for by a pension scheme, or other funding arrangements. The cost of providing a pension is usually deductible for tax, so that tax planning includes pension planning (see section **16.4**). Personal security may seem an obvious consideration, but is still, in practice, overlooked.

Another disadvantage of donation is that it may solve the donor's problems, but create new problems for recipients. If children have, in the past, been well-provided for, or are otherwise well-endowed, there may be a case for making gifts which skip a generation, into the hands of infant grandchildren, or to trustees for their benefit (see section **15.7:4**). If a later generation of grandchildren has not yet formed, there may be a case for delaying donation until later.

(c) THE THIRD STEP

Armed with the assembled data and the non-taxation factors, an estate owner can embark on the third step, which is to examine the technical alternatives, and choose between them.

He will have a theoretical choice of different ownership structures; a partnership with his wife; a partnership with his children; a limited company; a landlord/tenant relationship, all of which will produce different tax bills both current and future, even though farming assets and profits remain unchanged. Traditionally, farmers and landowners start off as sole traders, but at some time contemplate taking members of their family into *partnership*. Farming is a family business so partnership is a useful legal mechanism for regulating shares of ownership, and shares of profits, and for working together. When business expands, some farmers contemplate incorporating into a *private limited company*. There are other alternatives: *joint ventures* are becoming popular using the expression to mean owning and running a farm jointly between two or more farmers, both contributing resources and enjoying profits without the partnership relationship.

Although *trusts* have not been widely used to carry on farming businesses, much farm land is still owned by trustees as landlords and is farmed either by beneficiaries under the trust; by the original settlor; or by tenants unconnected with the settlor's family. The object is to compare and evaluate these different media, weighing the current advantages and disadvantages.

It is natural to suppose that the status quo is the inevitable arrangement, and that there are no alternatives. This can never be so, although there may be a strong case for not making costly, gratuitous or frequent ownership structure changes (or any), unless real advantages can be shown to follow. Research may be required to demonstrate that tax reductions can be achieved without impairing business efficiency or family security.

Also, the creation of a new structure, for example a partnership, may require payment of some additional tax at the outset as an entry price. The question then arises as to whether it is worth a payment of £x now, in order to secure a saving of a multiple of £x on death at an unknown date in the future. The answer will involve predictions as to the growth in value of the farming business, and of the value of agricultural land, a notoriously unpredictable item. In the end, competing pressures will need to be balanced-off one against the other.

This chapter considers in turn four different sets of ownership structures and arrangements, without making any final decision as to which is 'best'. That will depend on the circumstances of the farmer. A specimen exercise is set out in Appendix IV.

Finally, a subsidiary benefit from tax planning exercises is that they instil a consciousness of the requirements of tax planning which is helpful to farmers and estate owners contemplating particular transactions.

15.2 INHERITANCE TAX

15.2:1 Grant of tenancy to family partners pre-10 March 1981

The strategy described in this section was widely adopted during the years 1974 to 1981, but the former tax consequences have been substantially varied by FA 1981 and by the introduction of inheritance tax (see section **15.2:3**). However the strategy which was very widely used and all its former tax consequences continue to remain important (see section **15.2:3**). The most obvious benefit was that the grant of a tenancy to a family farming partnership converted the value of farmland from vacant possession value to tenanted value for the purposes of capital transfer tax. There was evidence to suggest that at that time tenanted land was worth approximately 60% of the comparable land with vacant possession, although this was a relationship which varied from time to time and in different parts of the country. This reduction became a major goal to be achieved in the face of certain difficulties.

A partnership is not, of course, a legal entity in England and a tenancy to a partnership operates as a tenancy to individual partners, or to the first four named in trust for all upon statutory trusts. The fact that a landowner wishes to let land to himself and, say, his wife and son, presents no difficulties. He can be landlord and tenant, provided he alone is not both.

For inheritance tax purposes the value of the property is the price which it might reasonably be expected to fetch if sold in the open market at the time (IHTA 1984 s 160). The land will be valued as tenanted if there is security of tenure evidenced by a payment of rent; or a written agreement; or where there is a licence under the Agricultural Holdings Act 1948 s 2(1) which requires that a licence to occupy land for agricultural use must be treated as a tenancy.[1]

The general rule is that the lease should be in writing and signed. The specific agreement may be in the partnership deed or separate from it. Mere 'occupation' does not suffice. Precise terms are obviously helpful since any ambiguity or uncertainty may be construed in favour of the Revenue rather than the owner. On completion, the value of the land is instantaneously reduced in value, with major tax consequences.

The very act of granting a tenancy causes a reduction in value of the land-owner's estate and the critical question before 1981 was whether this in itself triggered off liabilities. Inheritance tax is chargeable on any disposition which reduces a transferor's estate irrespective of whether the transferee's is augmented in value (IHTA 1984 s 3). Since there was a reduction equal to the difference between vacant possession and tenanted values, then prima facie there was a transfer. Hence the terms of the tenancy needed to be arranged to take advantage of the let-out provisions (IHTA 1984 s 10) for commercial bargains as follows:

(a) there must be no intention to confer gratuitous benefit; and
(b) the transaction must be at arm's length between unconnected persons; or
(c) the transaction must be such as might have been expected to be made between persons not connected with one another.

In a family partnership, (b) could not be satisfied. Therefore (c) must be satisfied and therefore the rental must be a rack-rental, a conclusion which at the time this strategy was being widely used, carried undoubted income tax disadvantages.

1 There are a number of cases which illustrate and interpret s 2: see *Verrall v Farnes* [1966] 2 All ER 808 (payment of rent not essential); *Goldsack v Shore* [1950] 1 All ER 276 (legally enforceable contract required); *Bahamas International Trust Co Ltd v Threadgold* [1974] 3 All ER 881 (exclusive licence needed).

15.2:2 Revenue practice: tenancies granted pre-10 March 1981

The Revenue practice on family tenancies during the 1980s was a determining factor in the structure and form of many tenancies still in existence. The Revenue took the view that IHTA 1984 s 10 should not be applied in selected cases of 'bad bargains'. The relevant circumstances encountered were said to be many and varied but these circumstances included the terms of a partnership as well as those of a tenancy. The Revenue might attack where the grant of a tenancy was closely followed by a transfer of the reversion so that it was apparent that the second transaction was in mind at the time of the first.

In construing 'intention', the Revenue view was that an individual intends the natural consequences of his acts, so that it was possible to infer intention from ensuing events. In the case of a farmer who let land to his son the Revenue view was that if the son be a professional farmer, ie be qualified to farm, that might justify the father taking him into partnership. The Revenue also accepted that no liability arose where the tenancy had been granted to a member of the family in the normal course of managing a tenanted estate by an owner who made a regular practice of granting tenancies. In the case of an owner-occupier, however, the Revenue inquiry was directed to why he was giving up owner occupation and whether he had contemplated alternative arrangements. Where the tenancy had been granted before the coming into force of capital transfer tax the Revenue would not have claimed liability, since tenanted value would already have been established by that date.

This practice gave rise to uncertainties. Because of the commercial disadvantages of non-family tenancies there was a danger that the question might be raised as to whether any owner would ever grant a tenancy on any terms. A partnership tenancy might have been said to deprive an owner of vacant possession for a longer period than an individual tenancy. One answer to this was that because of succession rights under the Agriculture (Miscellaneous Provisions) Act 1976 there was no longer any difference between individuals and partnerships.

Another problem at the time was that the rack rent so desirable at that time for capital transfer tax reasons effectively converted partnership profits (earned income) into rent (investment income) creating liability to the income investment surcharge in the hands of an owner at an additional 15%. On a rent of say £20,000 per annum, that could be £3,000 a year, which seemed at that time, a heavy price to pay for capital transfer tax benefits in the future. (Since abolition of investment income surcharge in FA 1984, this problem no longer arises.)

It was suggested that the easiest way to avoid the problem was to transfer the land itself to the partnership, so that it became a partnership asset. The disadvantage might have been that the land so held ceased to be 'tenanted'. Partnership land is valued as vacant, less a discount of say 10% to 20% reflecting the cost and difficulty faced by a partner in securing vacant possession.

There were other possible solutions to be considered, in particular that of waiving the rental to avoid the income tax liability. In principle, a waiver is only effective if made without consideration and reasonably to avoid hardship (TA 1988 s 41). On the other hand, it is possible to contemplate a waiver occurring so that the recipient never became entitled in the chargeable period (TA 1988 s 15) to the rents or receipts. If that was so, it would follow that the test in the Schedule A charging rule would not have been satisfied and no liability would have arisen.

15.2:3   Grant of tenancy after 10 March 1981

It is necessary to understand the tax planning strategies widely adopted before 10 March 1981 for three separate reasons.

First, arrangements made then may fall to be scrutinised by the Capital Taxes Office on the death of a farmer who, during his lifetime, granted a pre-1981 tenancy over his farm to a family farming partnership of which he was a member (see section **18.4:1**).

Secondly, it may seem desirable to bring to an end such a tenancy, and the reasons for its existence need to be understood before taking that step.

Thirdly, tenancies created during that period were usually designed to qualify the landowner for full-time working farmer relief (see section **8.4**), the predecessor of agricultural property relief (see section **8.5**). Because this relief is now given at the rate of 100%, the original qualification may determine whether or not a farm property will be completely exonerated from inheritance tax.

FA 1981 varied the law and practice in two major respects:

(a) A grant of tenancy of agricultural property in the UK, Channel Islands or Isle of Man for use for agricultural purposes, made at any time, whether before or after the passing of the Act, was declared not to be a transfer of value if for full consideration in money or monies worth (IHTA 1984 s 16). This eliminated the uncertainty which had existed as to the legal effects of a grant.

(b) It might have appeared that the grant of tenancy to a family farming partnership would reduce relief from 50% to 20% (the rates of relief applicable at the time). However, there was a transitional provision which granted relief at 50% on the first transfer of property to those whose family farming partnership secured the favourable 'double discount' under the pre-FA 1981 Revenue practice.

Thus those who had adopted the pre-1981 strategy of granting a tenancy to family partners secured reliefs, which as explained (see section **8.4:1**) now have an enhanced continuing value.

15.2:4 Preservation of transitional relief

The 1981 double discount is an unrepeatable relief conferring a privileged status worthy of careful preservation and maximisation. Before FA 1981, creation of a family partnership plus a tenancy involved risks of attack on the grounds that the grant of the tenancy, even at arm's length, had been a diminution of the grantor's estate giving rise to immediate capital transfer tax liability.

Those who ran this risk have got their reward and cannot now be attacked (IHTA 1984 s 16(3)). In order to retain and maximise the prize of the double discount various disciplines are required:

(a) If an owner's right to vacant possession is restored, the double discount will be lost. Where a partnership is composed of the landlord and one other individual, say his wife or son, the death of the second partner could terminate the partnership and possibly the joint tenancy. Landlord and tenant would become one and only one person. One person cannot contract with himself, so the tenancy might thus be prematurely ended. It is theoretically desirable therefore that any family farming partnership be comprised of three persons. It may be that this danger can be countered by constituting the partners as tenants in common, or by inserting other stipulations in the partnership deed, for example, covenants to grant a fresh tenancy in the event of a sole surviving tenant.

(b) The introduction of a third partner may be desirable: where the only tenants are husband and wife (IHTA 1984 s 161) (see section **15.3:5**). Then the tenancy and reversion are related property. Since the tenancy has little value, the whole vacant possession value will be allocated to the reversion, so that the strategy will have failed to that extent, even though the 100% relief under the double discount rules will have been preserved.

(c) If a landowner sells the land he was farming on 10 March 1981 and buys other land, double discount does not attach to the new land even though all the other tests are satisfied.

(d) Another factor is whether the double discount 'trump card' should be played and consumed on a lifetime gift or retained in hand and only played at death. Testamentary gifts to a spouse preserve relief. Lifetime gifts do not.

(e) The double discount is given only within the alternative limits prescribed by full-time working farmer relief (FA 1975 Sch 8). The applicable limit is usually now 1,000 acres, since £250,000, the alternative, will represent a much smaller acreage and be less advantageous. If land in excess of 1,000 acres is owned, and a lifetime gift is contemplated, it might seem theoretically desirable to give land 'in excess of 1,000 acres' retaining the 1,000 acres for a gift on death. This is not permissible, because agricultural property relief is applied automatically, without a claim being made, and will continue to be applied until the 1,000 acres is consumed, leaving land 'in excess of 1,000 acres' to pass on death, qualifying for relief at 50%.

15.2:5   Pre-inheritance tax family farming tenancies and gifts

Before the introduction of inheritance tax, there was an advantage to be secured by arranging for a gift of land to a member of the family *before* signing a contract of sale to a third party. The result was that the lifetime transfer of value was reduced by agricultural property relief, which would have been lost had the sale been made before the gift of the sale proceeds.

The position under inheritance tax is that there may now be a significant advantage in postponing a gift until *after* a sale has been completed. If the proceeds of the sale are to be reinvested in land, it may be easier for the donor rather than the donee to maintain the relief, since the replacement tests during the period before donation are easier to satisfy than the tests applicable after donation (see section **8.5:9**).

15.2:6   The effect of 1992 reliefs

This section explains how the new rates of relief for agricultural and business property enacted in F(2)A 1992 have, at a stroke, changed inheritance tax ownership structure strategies.

(1) The new rates have made the relief more valuable and thus it is clearly more important to secure full qualification. The difference between the two rates, (100% for vacant possession land and 50% for tenanted land) is greater than the former difference (50% and 30% respectively). Similarly, the difference between 50% relief for tenanted land and no relief at all is greater than 30% and nil relief. These may seem self-evident propositions, but they do explain to some extent why the emphasis has changed.

(2) The former relationship between inheritance tax and capital gains tax has been changed. The correct comparison is no longer between tax liability at 50% × 40% = 20% (inheritance tax); and at 40% less indexation reliefs (capital gains tax) as was the position before the 1992 change. Instead the comparison is between nil (inheritance tax) and 40% less indexation reliefs (capital gains tax). Thus where there is a choice as to which rate of tax to pay, inheritance tax will seem the least burdensome! This topic is explored further in section **15.2:7** below.

(3) The balance is changed as between property capable of being relieved by agricultural or business property reliefs and property which does not qualify for either relief. This issue is now important when the question arises as which property should be the subject of lifetime gifts to members of a succeeding generation.

(4) The strategy for Wills and Deeds of Variation has been changed because property which is now wholly exempt from inheritance tax by reason of business property relief has become freed of tax and can be redirected down to members of succeeding generations, instead of being directed into the hands of a surviving spouse.

15.2:7 Lifetime gifts of agricultural property

During the years before the enhancement of business and agricultural property reliefs, in F(2)A 1992, there were substantial incentives to encourage property owners to make gifts of their qualifying assets to their sons and members of the next generation generally during their lifetimes. Gifts have been a traditional method of passing value down generations so as to endow with assets younger members of a family at the time of their accepting management responsibilities on the farm or estate.

Amongst the incentives available there were the following:

(a) The application of the business and agricultural property reliefs reduced the amount of inheritance tax potentially at risk as a result of making the gift.
(b) If qualifying business or agricultural assets were selected as the subject of the gift, hold-over relief for capital gains tax was available (see section **7.5**).
(c) Landlords entitled to transitional or 'double discount' relief under the now repealed full-time working farmer rules (see section **8.4**) were also entitled to capital gains tax hold-over relief.
(d) Such gifts could be structured to take advantage of the annual exempt amount for capital gains tax purposes; and/or the first slice exemption for inheritance tax.
(e) A suitable trust could be interpolated into a gift to create a chargeable transfer or for family reasons.
(f) It was possible to make calculations of the capital gains tax on a non hold-over qualifying gift for comparison with the inheritance tax immediately payable on a chargeable transfer so as to ascertain which was the less onerous payment both now and in the future.

All these considerations are now overshadowed by the fact that where property qualifies for 100% business or agricultural property relief, inheritance tax is not in itself a valid reason for gifting it before death. It is arguable that the exoneration is as likely to be secured by the donor as by the donee. Indeed, assuming that the donor will, at death, have retained the property in question for a longer period than will the donee at his death, there is less chance of the detailed tests failing to be satisfied (see section **8.3:5**).

However, it is the incidence of capital gains tax which argues strongly *against* lifetime transfers. If the property be retained until death the donee takes with the market value as at the date of death as his future cost base. If the property passes as a lifetime gift, the donee takes with the donor's original cost base continuing as his (the donee's) future cost base. Thus if the value of the property concerned has risen during the lifetime of the donor, he will, on death, pass on the property at its uplifted value without liability to capital gains tax. If he makes a lifetime gift of the property, it is a reasonable assumption that that uplift will be chargeable to capital gains tax sometime in the future.

If on the other hand the value of the property has fallen since its base date and it be retained until death, then the donee will take with a lower base cost and this loss in value of the property will never be relieved against any other capital gains.

If this property be gifted during lifetime and hold-over relief claimed, the donee will take with the original donor's cost base as his cost base and the loss in value may thus be relieved on a future sale.

It may be argued that these are very theoretical considerations, and they should not be allowed to deter a possible donor from endowing his son with the farm or estate, in respect of which he is accepting management responsibilities. It is also arguable that the 100% inheritance tax relief may not endure future political changes and that therefore there is much to be said for taking advantage of it at the present time.

15.2:8   New family farming tenancies

In the light of the enhanced business and agricultural property reliefs enacted by F(2)A 1992, two separate problems present themselves. First, there is the question of whether it remains, on balance, beneficial to set up a family farming partnership plus tenancy now. This question is, of course, considered only from the taxation standpoint. The second question is whether existing family farming tenancies should, in the light of the new reliefs, be brought to an end. That is inevitably a more difficult question, because the answer may depend upon the precise advantages and disadvantages being secured under an existing structure, and the tax cost of making a change.

In order to answer the first question, it is necessary to analyse a series of fiscal consequences:

(a) One major result is to exchange relief at 100% of vacant possession value, for relief at 50% of tenanted value, which cannot be beneficial, and which no longer depends upon the relationship between the two values.

(b) Any such tenancy will need to be for full consideration in money or monies worth, if not to rank as a transfer of value. This may create income taxable rent, at a time when there is no taxable farm profits. That rent payable may reduce entitlement to capital gains tax retirement relief (TCGA 1992 Sch 6, para 10) (see section **7.6:6**).

(c) The grant of a tenancy within three years of transfer might fall to be designated one of a series of associated operations which could be disadvantageous (see section **15.3:2**).

(d) There is the possibility that such a tenancy might destroy an owner's entitlement to agricultural property relief, because of failure to complete the stipulated seven years ownership required for tenanted land.

(e) There is also possible loss of roll-over and retirement relief for capital gains tax (see **7.4:2** (c) and **7.6:5**).

(f) The creation of a tenancy inevitably gives the tenanted land a lower cost base for capital gains tax purposes on any future sale, after a death intervening.

In all these circumstances, it follows there is now an overwhelming case against establishing agricultural tenancies unless there are excellent family or other reasons for doing so. Other alternatives should be carefully considered:

(a) It may be better to create a partnership without the grant of any tenancy to it. If the land be retained by the owner partner and farmed by the partnership as licensee, there will be entitlement to 100% agricultural property relief against vacant possession value. That seems to be the position, but strictly it depends on whether it can be said that it is his

'interest in the land' which carries the right to vacant possession, and not a right to terminate the partnership agreement.
(b) There are numerous other forms of tenure, eg grazing licences; share farming; contract farming etc.

15.2:9 Lifetime gifts of land where sales are in contemplation

Where sales of land are in contemplation, it is necessary to consider carefully the sequence to be adopted, that is as to whether the gift should precede the sale, or whether the sale should precede the gift (see section **15.2:5**).

15.2:10 Reservation of benefit and business and agricultural property reliefs

It is arguable that the retention of benefit trap has become less dangerous since the enactment of 100% business and agricultural property reliefs. The argument is that if a potentially exempt transfer fails because of some reserved benefit element, the 100% relief will extinguish any inheritance tax which may be due (see section **8.1:6**). The tests as to whether business and agricultural property relief is available will be applied at the date of death rather than at the date of gift, which may or may not be advantageous. By that date the conditions for 100% relief may have ceased to be satisfied, and there may have been a substantial value change. Moreover, the continued existence of the 100% relief over successive generations cannot be guaranteed.

Taking all these factors into account, it is recommended that if the retention of benefit rule cannot be satisfied for family reasons, it is probably better that the potentially exempt transfer should not be attempted, at least not solely for tax planning reasons.

15.2:11 Alternative landholding arrangements

One principal effect of F(2)A 1992 has been to increase the tax advantage of owning land either with vacant possession or the right to obtain it within the next twelve months (IHTA 1984 s 116(2)(a)). If this vacant possession condition is satisfied, the land is capable of being transferred free of inheritance tax to the next generation.

This section summarises the tax consequences of adopting alternative arrangements, where a landowner will not himself be working the land. Clearly these arrangements will become increasingly popular, in view of the increased inheritance tax advantage to be secured:

(A) CONTRACT AND SHARE FARMING

The inheritance tax consequences are studied in sections **17.4:2** and **17.4:3**. In general the vacant possession condition should be satisfied providing the agreements between the parties are correctly drafted.

(B) LAND RETAINED BY OWNER PARTNER AND FARMED BY PARTNERSHIP AS LICENSEE

When there is no tenancy agreement granting rights of occupation over land, the question nevertheless arises as to whether the partners other than the landowner will obtain contractual rights to share occupation of the land by virtue of a partnership or any other agreement. If that were so, the question would obviously arise as to whether the landowner would be entitled to obtain vacant possession within twelve months according to the stipulations included in any such agreement. Thus, it is arguable that the vacant possession condition can be satisfied by correct drafting of a partnership agreement, for example by stipulating that the landowning partner has the power to dissolve the partnership and revoke an implied licence to occupy the land within a period of 12 months.

Whilst this may be theoretically satisfactory there are dangers. Apart from the practical disadvantages involved, which might be substantial, it will be open to the Revenue to contend that such a stipulation would be an artificial one introduced amongst parties not at arm's length with one another.

(c) GLADSTONE V BOWER TENANCIES

The period permitted under the precedent in *Gladstone v Bower* [1960] 2 QB 384 is a fixed period of more than one but less than two years. This period does not confer on the landowner the right to vacant possession or the right to obtain vacant possession within 12 months. However, its principal advantage is that it has offered an arrangement for letting land without conferring any security of tenure. It is clear that such a letting is 'an agricultural holding' (*EWP Ltd v Moore* [1992] 1 QB 460, CA).

In order to retain 100% inheritance tax relief, a *Gladstone v Bower* tenancy may be granted, for say, twelve months and one day, so that the vacant possession condition will be satisfied two days after the tenancy has commenced. If this is unacceptable to a prospective tenant, it may be advantageous to effect a life insurance policy to cover the first 12 months of the tenancy, during which a 50% inheritance tax liability will continue to exist.

(d) MINISTRY CONSENT TENANCIES

Tenancies approved by the Ministry of Agriculture or Secretary of State for Wales do not confer security of tenure but may be for not more than one year (AHA 1986 s 2) or for not less than two but not more than five years (AHA 1986 s 5).

The s 2 tenancies are undoubtedly satisfactory from the stand-point of the vacant possession condition, and should be preferred if the tenant is prepared to accept them.

15.3   FAMILY FARMING PARTNERSHIPS

15.3:1   Introduction

A further set of problems arise as to what partnership terms or stipulations need to be included (or must be excluded) in order to satisfy the tests in IHTA 1984 ss 10 and 16. Admittedly, it is the grant of a tenancy rather than the creation of the partnership which creates the reduction in value, but the Revenue view has been that the two sets of relationships need to be looked at together, not each in isolation.

The question is sometimes put as to whether new partners can come in with a very low profit share, eg 5%, or whether this would be uncommercial. The answer seems to depend on what is ordinary practice locally. A low participation might be appropriate for a young partner to give him a chance to experience ownership on a modest level. Again, the participation might be determined by the new partner's capacity to invest capital or contribute farming skills. It is also possible to contemplate a new partner coming in, as an income partner with a nil capital contribution, and enjoying only a share of future profits and losses. Whether this would be 'commercial' obviously depends upon the facts of the case, and the past record of farming results.

15.3:2 Chargeable transfers: associated operations rule

The partnership terms must impose appropriate obligations on all partners, and a new entrant son should be an active, not a sleeping, partner which might evidence wish to confer benefit. Now supposing all these tests are satisfied, the effect of IHTA 1984 s 268 must be considered. The Revenue will regard the associated operations rule as applicable if there is a transfer of the freehold reversion to let property made within three years of the grant of a tenancy at a rack-rent. If the tenancy be not at a rack-rent, it will regard the associated operations rule as applicable to any transfer at any time. The absence of a rack-rent, at the outset, is fatal, because the full consideration test would not be satisfied.

The need for a rack-rent throughout the tenancy is not so certain. It is arguable that there might be a claim because the rent chargeable should have been increased at the date of rent reviews but had not been. On the other hand, it is equally arguable that market value would be unaffected by this failure to act, since a potential purchaser for value would be able to review the rent after purchase, and increase it.

The associated operations rule should also be considered when it is desired to vary the partners' shares within three years from the commencement of the partnership.

15.3:3 Existing family farming partnerships plus tenancies

The question arises as to whether under current legislation it is, on balance, beneficial to set up a family farming partnership plus a tenancy and this is considered in section **15.2:8**. This section analyses the problem of whether to bring to an end an existing family farming partnership tenancy, the incentive being the 100% agricultural property relief for vacant possession land enacted in F(2)A 1992. Clearly there is now no continuing net advantage in having reduced the taxable value of farmland from vacant possession value to tenanted value, so long as the former qualifies for 100% relief and the latter only 50% relief.

At the outset it must be conceded that many family farmers will be naturally reluctant to vary arrangements, which are working well from farming and business stand-points, simply to secure a future tax advantage. This view will be reinforced by recognition that any change in the partnership arrangements is likely to involve legal costs, and may create liabilities to other taxes. The different forms that such liabilities may take need very careful review. In the first place, liability to capital gains tax may arise on changes in the framework of the partnership or on its total dissolution (see section **6.1:5** and **15.3:8**).

That liability may be capable of reduction because, in certain circumstances, acquisitions or disposals of partnership assets in accordance with bona-fide commercial arrangements may fall to be treated for capital gains tax purposes as having occurred at their actual sale prices, without any substitution of market value. Also such disposals may be treated as taking place at a consideration which gives rise to neither gain nor loss (SP D12 para 4).

Again, various capital gains reliefs may be claimed by individual partners:

(a) hold-over relief on transfers of business assets;
(b) retirement relief (see section **7.6**);
(c) roll-over relief etc (see section **7.4**).

The possibility of capital gains tax arising on the termination of a tenancy should also be considered. The tenant will be making a disposal of an asset, which may be regarded as having a significant capital value.

Where the parties are connected parties, market value considerations may fall to be substituted. Thus, on the termination of a tenancy, a landlord may be deemed to have made a payment to the tenant to secure vacant possession by way of surrender of the tenancy, ie its disposal. The individual partners will be liable for fractional shares of the deemed consideration receivable in accordance with the principles described in section **15.3:8**. The entitlement to the reliefs mentioned above, particularly hold-over relief, should be carefully considered. For more detailed treatment of the capital gains tax consequences for the landowner, see section **7.7:2** and for the tenant see section **7.7:3**.

The major deterrent may be VAT, since usually the parties in a family farming tenancy will be connected persons for the purposes of VAT. Then, the VAT will be recomputed on the basis of market value where there has been no consideration paid or, where the consideration is for less than full market value or, where the consideration does not wholly consist of money (VATA 1983 s 10 (1) and Sch 4 para 1(1)). This last category of deemed consideration may be applied where some new arrangement between the parties is to be put in place. One solution which has been suggested is to transfer the whole farming business to the landowner as a going concern on the basis that this will be exempt from VAT (see VAT Special Provisions Order SI 1981/1741 Art 12(1) and section **9.5:1**). The contention would be that the tenants interest should be treated as one asset of the farming business, and on the transfer would be surrendered and merged with the freehold reversion, so obtaining vacant possession of the land. Such a step would require great care, since it might involve loss of capital gains tax and inheritance tax relief.

As regards inheritance tax see section **7.7:8**.

15.3:4   Alternative configurations

It will be apparent from the above (section **15.3:3**) that reducing land values from vacant possession value to tenanted value has ceased to be an advantageous strategy.

In general, the grant of a tenancy to a partnership was designed to devalue an asset for tax purposes without making a lifetime transfer, an event which would have created an immediate tax liability under capital transfer tax.

This is no longer an objective under inheritance tax, since lifetime transfers create no immediate liability.

The case against tenancies seems to have been reinforced, and one of a variety of other configurations may be advantageous.

CONFIGURATION A

Land retained by an owner and farmed by a partnership as licensee, the consequences of which are that there will be 100% agriculture property relief against vacant possession value, providing all the tests are satisfied, in particular, whether it is the landowner's interest in the land which carries the right to vacant possession, and not his right to terminate the agreement.

CONFIGURATION B

Alternatively, the land may be transferred to the partnership and be included in the partnership balance sheet, so that each partner becomes a joint tenant. Each partner will be entitled to agricultural property relief at 100% against his share at vacant possession value, taking account of the fact that the property is jointly owned.

Partnership property is subject to the retention of benefit rule. Where the father takes a substantial share of income profits, and the son a share of the capital gain flowing from the value of the land, or where the father receives a disproportionate proportion of the profits, or sole rights of occupation, there is vulnerability to attack in accordance with retention of benefit considerations.

This point was raised during the 1986 Finance Bill debate, when the Financial Secretary to the Treasury gave the following reply:

'Furthermore the Inland Revenue tell me that in their view the gifts with reservation rules will not apply to an unconditional gift of an undivided share in land merely because the property is actually occupied by all the joint owners including the donor. Nor will the rules be applied to the partnership example mentioned, provided that any profits and losses of the partnership are shared between the partners according to their respective interests in the partnership assets.'

This seems to introduce a new test: that for the gift of land to be effective, profit sharing ratios must be equal to asset owning ratios. This seems a very artificial formula.

One attraction of Configuration B is that land is undoubtedly being transferred with vacant possession, so that if the potentially exempt transfer fails because the donor dies within seven years, the vacant possession value will attract agricultural property relief at 100% (see section **8.5**) above.

If, on the other hand, a tenancy is granted before a transfer, the associated operations rule will reimpose vacant possession value so that entitlement to agricultural property relief will be limited to 50%. This is because the 100% relief is conditional upon factual vacant possession as opposed to the deemed vacant possession imposed by the associated operations rule.

CONFIGURATION C

This envisages the gift of the land with vacant possession to a son (or other member of a younger generation) and the creation of a tenancy as a second step. It will be the son who grants the tenancy to the family farming partnership including himself and the father. On this configuration the tenancy must be granted on arm's length terms, and must remain on such terms, because the occupation of land on non-commercial terms is undoubtedly a retained benefit. This retained benefit will continue until the arrangement becomes an arm's length one, so eliminating the reserved benefit and setting the seven-year exemption period running.

The disadvantage of Configuration C is that it creates an obligation for a member of the elder donating generation to pay a share of rent, at a time when income is likely to be restricted. Unless there is some exceptional family reason for adopting it, it is difficult to see what overall advantage is secured.

15.3:5   Death of a partner

The situation which emerges on the death of a partner may be illustrated by the following example:

Example

A the owner of Blackacre lets it to himself and his son as joint tenants retaining the freehold reversion. A and his son farm in partnership, until A dies, bequeathing the freehold reversion to his son in his will.

It seems therefore that on A's death, his son becomes the freeholder and also the sole surviving tenant. In these circumstances the Revenue may well decline to treat the existence of the tenancy as diminishing the unencumbered freehold value of the property. The argument is that the tenancy merges with the freehold and is extinguished by operation of the law.

There are certain expedients for remedying this situation. (The possibility of a deed of family arrangement should also be considered, see section **18.3**.) In particular, it is possible that the letting be made to the partners as tenants in common. Alternatively, there is the possibility of a covenant in the partnership agreement by the landlord that in the event of his becoming sole surviving tenant, he will grant a fresh tenancy to the persons then becoming partners.

Lastly, the Capital Taxes Office has confirmed that the former practice under estate duty will continue to apply under inheritance tax. Under this practice, the position was dependent upon whether in the particular circumstances of the case the surviving partner's tenancy would be protected under the Agricultural Holdings Act 1948. If so, the Office would not seek to draw a distinction solely on the ground that the surviving partner became entitled to the freehold under the deceased owner's will or intestacy (see also section **18.2:1**).

15.3:6   Related property

Yet another set of problems arise, where the tenancy is to be granted to a spouse or trustee. Property comprised in the estate of a spouse is treated as related property (IHTA 1984 s 161(1)). The rule is that related property is to be valued for inheritance tax purposes as an appropriate proportion of the value of the whole combined property, if by doing so a higher value is produced. To clarify this elusive concept, suppose a husband and wife each hold 40% of the shares in a company. Neither has a controlling interest with the automatic accretion of value that control confers. However the related property rule applies, and the value of 40% transferred is to be calculated as half of what would be the value of 80% – a proportion which would carry with it the control element.

Suppose again that the unencumbered freehold value of Blackacre (see **Example** in **15.3:5**) is £100,000 and the owner grants a tenancy at a rent to his wife, estimated to be worth £10,000. In consequence, he now holds the freehold subject to the tenancy, the value of which is now £60,000 in the open market.

For inheritance tax however, the value of the freehold is calculated as follows:

$$\frac{60}{70} \times 100,000 = £85,714$$

It may be arguable that the value of the tenancy is negligible, assuming the tenancy be from year to year and non-transferable. On that supposition, the value of the freehold reversion would be:

$$\frac{60}{60} \times 100,000 = £100,000$$

That is if the reduction in value secured depends upon the value of the tenancy created.

This rule applies only to spouses' property. It has no application to property forming part of the estate of children or other relatives. From this standpoint, therefore, it is advantageous to introduce a son as partner.

15.3:7 Partnerships: retention of benefit

In 1975 the Revenue published a Statement of Practice (17 January 1975) for capital gains tax explaining the treatment of partnership transactions, both as regards disposals to third parties and as amongst individual partners. A supplement was published on 12 January 1979 dealing with capital sums on retirement.

Generally, each partner is treated as owning a fractional share of each partnership asset, with market values to be substituted for balance sheet values, whenever there occur asset share transactions amongst persons connected with one another, otherwise than by the partnership itself.

The treatment of partnership assets for capital gains tax purposes is not matched for inheritance tax where a partnership interest is treated as a single asset. Where there is a gift, for example a share of a capital account is debited to one partner and credited to another, the question arises as to whether there is a gift with reservation.

In order to answer this question it is necessary to scrutinise the terms of the farm partnership agreement. The shares of partnership capital may carry particular rights under the partnership deed. Subject to that, the difficulty is that there will be common possession and enjoyment of partnership assets by continuing partners, so that the 'benefits' after the gift may appear identical with those before the gift. If this is so, it seems to follow that benefits will have been retained, and the gift will fail for inheritance tax purposes.

It is possible to envisage a whole range of transactions in which these assumptions may nullify a gift. A farmer may take a son into partnership; he may bring a new partner into an existing partnership; or vary the partnership profit sharing ratios.

Similar problems may arise from the assumption of partnership liabilities. If in the course of a gift of a share of a partnership to a son, the son indemnifies his father to discharge the debts of the partnership, the question arises as to whether this indemnity is a retained benefit. Sole occupation of the farmhouse by a father could obviously represent a retained benefit; similarly, a disproportionate share of profits. Faced with these problems, it may be that a tenancy will need to be established to perform a new function in regulating the relationship between the parties.

The purpose of this tenancy will not be, as hitherto, to devalue land. It will be to secure the right of the donor to continue farming the land or alternatively to continue to receive income. By segregating the ownership of the land, with entitlement to income, from the ownership of the business with entitlement to profits, the reservation of benefit problem may be resolved. The landowner will be receiving his proper commercial return *qua* landowner, and the tenant his return *qua* tenant.

The legal rights respectively comprised in a lease and a reversion upon a lease will make it easy to identify the respective economic returns, eliminating the possibility of a retained (non-economic) benefit.

If this new function for a tenancy is to be attempted, care will be needed to retain the commercial terms established at the outset and not to allow them to fall into disrepair.

It cannot be claimed that the use of a family farming tenancy as this form of defensive mechanism is a very elegant or ambitious one. If the uncertainties surrounding the operation of the retention of benefit rule are resolved, such a mechanism may become superfluous.

It will have emerged from what has already been said that whilst, at the outset, the concept of a family partnership may look attractive, there are a number of dangerous tax pitfalls. The dangers are re-emphasised when one begins to consider the secondary consequences of such a step – consequences so far as income tax and capital gains tax liabilities are concerned. It is not possible to try to envisage all the consequences that may flow from the creation of a partnership, since much may depend on the personal circumstances of the members of the family. However, it may be worth noting that the more the partnership reflects the commercial state of things already existing before its inception, the more likely it is to succeed in its aims. The higher the element of artifice, the weaker it will be.

15.3:8   Family farming partnerships and capital gains tax

The application of capital gains tax to partnerships is uncertain and difficult. One of the uncertainties arises from the general rule that any partnership transactions are treated as transactions by the individual partners and not by the firm as such (TCGA 1992 s 59). The effect of this formula is to treat gains made by the partnership as attributable to the partners in the proportion in which they have agreed to share assets of the partnership. This may or may not be the same share as has been agreed for dividing income profits of the partnership.

Secondly, tax law fails to envisage transactions amongst partners and this gap has been filled by a Statement of Practice (SP D12 dated 17 January 1975) giving the Revenue view as to how partnership transactions should be treated for capital gains tax.

Thirdly, transactions involving partners are complicated by the fact that partners by definition are connected persons (see section **7.1:1**) and therefore market value should be substituted for any actual consideration receivable.

This substitution of market value as the consideration is however not always applied. It is subject to an important exception in relation to acquisitions or disposals of partnership assets pursuant to bone-fide commercial arrangements (TCGA 1992 s 286 (4) re-enacting CGTA 1979 s 63(4)).

Nor is market value to be substituted if, (although the partners are relatives), consideration receivable is not less than the amount which would have been receivable had the parties been at arms' length with one another (SP D12 para 7). Nor is market value to be substituted where the consideration cannot be valued (TCGA 1992 s 17(1)(b)).

Another source of complexity is that transactions amongst partners may take place in one of two ways that is, internally, by an adjustment within the partnership capital accounts, or externally, by payments and receipts outside the ambit of those accounts, privately as amongst the partners. As regards the former, disposals are not treated as having occurred merely because a partnership asset is re-valued and a partner is credited in his current or capital account with an amount equal to a fractional share of the increase in value. However, on a later change in profit sharing, the partner may be treated as disposing of a fractional share for a consideration equal to his share of the re-valued amount, which may be more or less than the historic base cost.

Thus, a re-valuation of partnership assets is not itself a disposal giving rise to capital gains tax but may increase capital gains tax liabilities at a later stage (SP D12 paras 5 and 6).

Capital gains tax, however, may arise simply because there is a change in partnership sharing ratios, including those arising from new partners entering or old partners leaving the partnership. The disposal consideration is treated as a fractional share of the balance sheet value of each chargeable asset, subject to there being no payments made outside the framework of the partnership accounts. Where there are payments made outside the framework of the partnership accounts, for example, payments for assets not included in the partnership balance sheet, those payments are also subject to capital gains tax, and a separate calculation may need to be made.

There are further detailed provisions dealing with the possibility of annuities paid to a retiring partner, mergers between two or more existing partnerships, and the acquisition of partnership shares in stages which appear to have little application in the farming industry. Possible liability to capital gains tax should be borne in mind when contemplating the dissolution of a family farming partnership, where the land farmed, cottages etc, is owned by the partnership and shown in the partnership balance sheet.

It is unusual for a farming business to create goodwill as a separate asset, other than that reflected in the value of the land. However, milk quota is treated as a chargeable asset and liability to capital gains tax may arise on the dissolution of a partnership owing milk quota (see section **2.4:2**). Liability may similarly arise where other forms of compensation are involved.

15.4 CAPITAL GAINS TAX

15.4:1 Introduction to capital gains tax planning

At the present time, capital gains tax is imposing great pressure on farmers and landowners. The reasons deserve exploration. First, there is the historic reason: that agricultural land is being held for long periods over which land values have been increasing. Many farmers own land with a trivial historic cost base, so that virtually all sale proceeds will be liable to capital gains tax at 40%.

Secondly, in response to financial pressures in recent years, farmers have been scrutinising holdings to find a disused farm building, strip of land, or surplus acreage which can be sold to reduce obligations. These transactions inevitably give rise to capital gains tax liabilities and it is frustrating to find that a large proportion of proceeds are destined for gains tax.

Thirdly, capital gains tax was at one time considered capable of reduction by so-called 'artificial' transactions. These can now be negatived by the Revenue under the *Ramsay* doctrine although scope for planning does remain, using reliefs, or by arranging transactions in a commercially justifiable pattern. (See for example section **15.2:5**.)

The relentless pressure of capital gains tax has encouraged enactment of a range of statutory and extra-statutory reliefs and exemptions (see section **7.2**). The correct approach is to arrange transactions in forms which maximise value of these reliefs, bearing in mind that many are *annual* reliefs, the value of which can be multiplied when a transaction is spread over more than one tax year. The roll-over relief (see section **7.4**) is probably the most useful relief, but cannot be claimed when proceeds of sale are used to repay borrowings.

No substantial disposal, exchange or gift should be undertaken without previously computing the contingent capital gains tax and considering availability and interaction of reliefs at the time of transaction and in the future. At one time, owners were advised to defer transactions on the assumption that capital gains tax would be repealed by the present administration. This now seems unlikely. The official view is that indexation relief has mitigated the pressure.

15.4:2   Grant of tenancy

One view is that the grant of a tenancy on any terms is a part disposal for capital gains tax. The argument is that such a grant involves a part disposal for capital gains tax purposes because it creates new rights over the land enjoyed by the tenant whilst the landlord retains some residual rights under the lease. That would seem to apply irrespective of whether there were a premium and a ground rent; or, on the other hand, if there were no premium and a rack-rent. However, it is enacted (TCGA 1992 Sch 8 para 2(1)) that where there is a premium there is a part disposal, and it is possible to infer from that sub-paragraph that where there is no premium there is no part disposal. On this first view, that is a false piece of reasoning and the correct conclusion is that the general definition of part disposal in TCGA 1992 s 37(1) is wide enough to embrace the grant of a lease at a rack-rent and is not modified or over-ridden by TCGA 1992 Sch 8 para 2(1) (see section **7.7:8**).

15.4:3   Part disposals: liability to tax

The practical effects are important. In most cases, the part disposal creates no liability. That may be because the consideration receivable for it and the historic base cost of what is disposed of are both nil, in which case the tenant similarly secures an asset with a nil historic base cost. Alternatively it may be that the Revenue does not pursue any theoretical liability which exists.

There is a view that TCGA 1992 s 37(3) would entitle the Revenue to treat as consideration the capitalised value of the rent payable under the tenancy. If this were so, one would not only have consideration for the part disposal, but a value for A in the $\frac{A}{A+B}$ equation, which is applied to apportion the cost base, where A = consideration for the disposal; and B = value of property undisposed of.

If there be a premium receivable, there is undoubtedly a part disposal. If the transaction be not one at arm's length between unconnected persons (ie is between father and son) there may be a deemed premium with the same practical result. This will be the position when any family partnership is formed.

An alternative view is that the 'asset owned' or 'interest enjoyed' by the landowner is not the land itself, but a freehold interest therein, so that the only part disposal which can occur of a freehold interest is where a joint tenancy or tenancy in common (of the freehold) is created. Therefore, TCGA 1992 s 42(1) would not apply generally. On this supposition, it is possible to argue that on the execution of a lease, what happens is:

(a) there is no disposal (part or otherwise) of the freehold (unless a premium is paid, in which case TCGA 1992 Sch 8 para 2(1) deems there to have been a part disposal of the freehold);

(b) a new asset is created and retained by the landowner, ie the right to receive rent during the period of the lease; and

(c) another new asset is created in the hands of the tenant, ie the right to occupy the land during the period of the lease; at the outset, on a rack-rent basis, this asset is valueless (no consideration is paid to the landowner for this asset, and its acquisition was at no cost to him, so there is no gain and no loss).

If less than a rack-rent be charged, the question of whether or not a premium may be imputed will, of course, depend upon the connection between lessor and lessee, or other 'arm's length' considerations.

Whichever view be adopted, the Revenue seems to accept in practice there is no need to capitalise a rack-rent for capital gains tax purposes and that a tenancy at a rack-rent has no capital value. All that it is possible to say is that a rack-rent is the safer course. This is the principal practical conclusion and remains true, irrespective of whether the grant of a tenancy in itself is or is not a part disposal.

15.4:4 Disposal in a series of transactions

Granting a tenancy first and transferring the tenanted land after three years was effective for capital transfer tax (now inheritance tax), but was never equally effective for capital gains tax. The step is caught by a rule regarding the effect of a series of transactions (TCGA 1992 s 19, see also TCGA 1992 ss 29, 30).

15.5 INCOME TAX

If, as is likely, the person formerly carrying on the business – the father – becomes a partner, then, although the cessation rule normally applies, it will be possible to elect for the continuation basis of assessment. Another useful by-product will be the increase in the amounts of profits chargeable to income tax at lower rates, and correspondingly the decrease in those chargeable at higher rates. The following thresholds are worth noting:

(a) a marginal rate of 40% is reached by a married man at £28,715 per annum taxable income, so from that point onwards, the small company rate of 25% is more attractive;

(b) children's personal thresholds are now £3,295.

15.6 COMPANIES

15.6:1 Introduction

At some stage, most farmers have considered forming a company. The utilisation of the private company structure involves reconsideration of some tax-planning matters already covered, and some new factors intervene. The general principles of corporation tax are summarised in section **6.3**.

15.6:2   Agricultural property and business property relief

There will be no loss of agricultural property relief, or business property relief, if the agricultural land be owned by a farming company (see sections **8.3:1** and **8.5:2**). The relief is effectively given on shares or debentures held by a qualifying shareholder. Nor will relief be lost if the land be retained by a qualifying shareholder with occupation by his company. However, if the shareholdings are arranged so that qualifying control be lost, problems will arise. 'Control' is an expression which is statutorily defined (IHTA 1984 s 169). A company is controlled by a transferor if he has control of voting power on all questions, a power which if exercised would yield a majority of the votes capable of being exercised.

In counting votes for this purpose, the related property rule applies, and votes held by a spouse may be attributed to a transferor. Where shares are held by trustees of a settlement, and there is a life tenant in possession, he is deemed to hold the voting power for these purposes.

The different sets of circumstances foreseen by the legislation, and the consequences are set out in section **8.5:2**.

15.6:3   Inheritance tax reliefs and company shareholdings

The new rates of business and agricultural property reliefs enacted in F(2)A 1992 have made it important to consider how shares in a family farming company should be held to secure maximum possible reliefs. Now that it is possible to secure a 100% relief on a controlling shareholding in an unquoted company, past planning strategies may need to be varied or indeed reversed. For example, in the past, it was advantageous to fragment the share capital of a company into small holdings, because each small shareholding would be worth less than its proportionate part of the total value. However, if the shareholdings are arranged so that control be secured by all shareholders (and this can be done having regard to the related property rule), exemption can be secured for the total value of the family farming company.

In order to achieve this result, one course of action is for small shareholdings which have been distributed amongst members of the family to be aggregated in the hands of the senior member so as to produce a shareholding of 51%. However, this course of action may be unattractive, not only for tax reasons, but also because it appears to take from junior members of the family rights which have in the past been accorded to them. In such circumstances alternative courses of action to secure the necessary result deserve consideration. It may be possible to vary the voting powers of shares as prescribed in the articles of association of the company. It is not unusual to find special voting rights reserved in relation to particular decisions, eg rights effecting one class of shares, or rights arising on a winding up. These are categories of rights which may be disregarded in determining control, but a review of voting rights can secure the required result without need for share transfers.

An alternative course of action may be to issue new shares for modest consideration but with the necessary rights attached to secure voting control. Care needs to be taken to ensure that value does not pass out of shares in such a way as to give rise to a capital gains tax liability (see TCGA 1992 ss 30–34).

15.6:4   Non-voting shares

Holders of voting shares attract business property relief at 100%, whilst non-voting shares attract relief at 50%, even when both categories are held by the same shareholder. This can lead to a loss of relief:

Example

The shareholdings in *Farmers Ltd* are as follows:

Shareholder	Voting	'A' (non-voting)	Total	% Relief
Mr AF	120	500	620	50
Mrs AF	120	500	620	50
B	190	–	190	50
C	190	–	190	50
D	190	–	190	50
E	190	–	190	50
Totals	1000	1000	2000	

A rearrangement takes place to produce the following results:

Shareholder	Voting	'A' (non-voting)	Total	% Relief
Mr AF	130	400	530	100
Mrs AF	130	400	530	100
B	185	50	235	50
C	185	50	235	50
D	185	50	235	50
E	185	50	235	50
Totals	1000	1000	2000	

Such rearrangements can increase the value of the relief without substantially transferring value amongst the parties. However, in this case, relief will not be due for two years (IHTA 1984 s 109A). Consideration may need to be given to varying the rights of different categories of shares to secure a similar result.

15.6:5   Sole surviving tenant

The sole surviving tenant problem (see section **15.3:5**) is automatically surmounted when a company is used as a tenant. On the death of a controlling shareholder, the company shares and the land retained may either devolve together, or to separate beneficiaries under the will or intestacy rules. Whatever be the devolution, it does not appear that the reduction created by the existence of the tenancy can be lost, since the corporate tenant is, of course, a legal person separate and distinct from any person upon whom the freehold reversion devolves.

Another problem may arise where the tenant of farmland is a company controlled by the owner of the same land. In *Henderson v Karmel's Executors* [1984] STC 572 it was held in such circumstances the land should be valued as subject to a tenancy. Despite the fact that the individual shareholder had the control of the company, and hence the ability to procure that vacant possession could be given to a purchaser, it was impossible to say that the asset owned by the company at Budget Day 1965 was an encumbered freehold. The effect of this judgment was to impose the lower tenanted value as the base cost so increasing capital gains tax on sale of the land. This is consistent with the general Revenue view that a farm tenancy has real and inextinguishable value.

In the *Henderson* case, tenanted value as at the base date increased capital gains tax liabilities. However, the precedent is useful where the tenant is a company in that it represents an authority in favour of tenanted value, which might decrease inheritance tax liability on the death of the landowner and controlling shareholder.

15.6:6   Valuation

The use of a company involves the valuation of the shares in it for inheritance tax purposes, rather than the valuation of the underlying farming assets, 'underlying' in the sense that they will have become assets in the company's Balance Sheet, whose direct ownership will not change on the death of the shareholder. Unquoted shares are subject to valuation rules similar to those for other forms of property, and there is no legislation governing the precise factors to be taken into account in determining value. The past dividend record, historical earnings, the current going-concern value of the underlying assets, and the break-up value of those assets, may all, in appropriate circumstances, fall to be taken into account. Although the shares may be subject to restrictions which preclude sale in the open market, an open market sale is to be contemplated. Prospective purchasers would be assumed to have access to all information a prudent purchaser would require.

If an assets basis be adopted and the excess of assets over liabilities falls to be calculated, the contingent capital gains tax liability on the sale of the company's assets should be taken into account. This is disputed by Inland Revenue Shares Valuation Division whose view is that it is wrong to make allowance for such liabilities, unless it is clear that the company is to sell its assets in the near future. Similarly, in the Revenue's view, the costs of liquidation are not a proper deduction, unless liquidation is a likely possibility. It is clear that capital gains tax liability on a notional sale of the company's shares by a shareholder would not fall to be deducted.

15.6:7   Capital gains tax and other factors

The existence of these two sets of capital gains tax liabilities should be borne in mind and care should be taken not to transfer more assets with growth potential to a company than is necessary. Indexation relief may be said to help reduce this factor. Other pitfalls to be kept in mind are the related property rule, so far as the company's shares are concerned, and the rule in IHTA 1984 s 3A(6) which treats transfers of value made by companies as chargeable transfers made by the participators (shareholders), and which prevents them from being potentially exempt transfers.

A company can in addition be used as a channel to smooth out an irregular flow of profits from one season to another. This is done by regulation of the salaries and fees which become payable to directors and employees. It is arguable that since profit averaging for farming, this advantage is of less importance than it was. But averaging is subject to inflexible rules and companies, in this respect, are not. Directors' emoluments fall under Schedule E and PAYE and tax is payable earlier than for a Schedule D partner's profit share.

Formerly, the ownership of a farming business via a company was subject to one particular disadvantage. The sale of the shares in the company failed to qualify for capital gains tax roll-over relief, whereas the sale of the business itself, or a partnership interest in the business, would have qualified. This disadvantage has been removed in FA 1993 which provides, subject to certain provisos, that the sale of shares in a qualifying unquoted trading company may attract roll-over relief (see **7.4:3**).

15.6:8   Trading losses

However, there is an important disadvantage in the separate income and corporation tax treatments of the company on one hand and its directors on another. Trading losses sustained by the former cannot be utilised by the latter.

15.6:9 Cessation rules

In the short term, the cessation provisions will apply to any firm or business carried on, and this may make timing of the changeover a critical factor. The extinction of accumulated loss reliefs brought forward from past years may be another significant factor in deciding whether the corporate form is beneficial. Where the consideration for transfer of a farming business to a limited company consists wholly or mainly of shares, some carry forward of losses may be secured (TA 1988 ss 385, 386).

15.6:10 Transfer to a company: capital gains tax

For capital gains tax purposes, deferral of whole or part liability is usually obtainable under TCGA 1992 s 162, where a person carrying on a business transfers that business as a going concern, together with all the assets of the business, wholly or partly in exchange for shares issued by the company to the transferor. The requirement that all business assets must be transferred in order to secure the deferral may seem relevant when deciding whether or not to transfer agricultural land. However, where land does not appear in the business Balance Sheet, it may not fall to be regarded as a business asset for this purpose (see section **7.4**). As regards the meaning of 'going concern' see section **7.4:2**(G).

Where a business is carried on by a company, and the land retained in the ownership of a shareholder or director, the entitlement to roll-over relief on the sale or gift of the land is now not lost merely because the land will have ceased to be an asset of the business. Where, similarly, land is let by an individual to a family partnership, in which he is a partner, roll-over relief is also given (see section **7.4**). As regards retirement relief, see section **7.6:7**.

15.6:11 Annual inheritance tax exemptions

The shares in a family farming company represent useful currency in which a donor can utilise his annual exemption of £3,000 for inheritance tax. The formalities of transfer are less costly than for land, and a whole shareholding, when fragmented into small parcels, produce modest values. On the other hand, partnership interests can be transferred with equal facility.

15.6:12 Profit averaging

The fact that profit averaging (see section **2.5**) is not applied to companies is sometimes expressed to be a disadvantage. However, since companies are not liable at a progressive scale of tax, there is no need for averaging, and the complaint seems misconceived.

15.6:13 Losses on shares

Where a company fails, investors who subscribed for shares may obtain relief for their losses against their personal income tax on other income (see section **2.6:2**).

15.6:14 Summary: choosing the right medium

We are now in a position to summarise the tax planning consequences of the steps described above.

The question is sometimes put: which form is generally more advantageous – partnership or company? There is no absolute answer and much depends on family and commercial circumstances, and the balance of advantages amongst various competing considerations:

(a) The ownership of a company is capable of greater fragmentation than is a partnership, and this, together with the fact that a company is a natural commercial entity, seems to confer a handling advantage.

(b) National Insurance costs and benefits may also need consideration (see chapter 12).

(c) A partnership enables an owner to spread both income and capital around members of his family, so that there will be more reliefs to be set against it, than if the same income and capital were all bunched together in his own one single pair of hands. As there are personal reliefs and reduced rates for income tax, so there are annual exemptions and for inheritance tax.

(d) A partnership also conveys the facility of an owner being able to grant a tenancy converting the value of his land from vacant possession value to tenanted value. This is an obsolete strategy.

(e) A limited liability company can be used to secure the two advantages described above, and one other as well, emerging from the nature of the corporate structure. In particular, the use of a company puts shares into the hands of a farmer in place of the underlying company assets. The shares are always worth less because owning them does not entitle an owner to deal with the assets as freely as if he owned them direct. So incorporation reduces taxable value. The reduction depends upon the rights attaching to particular shares and the proportion of the whole they represent. The discount increases as the proportion reduces.

  This advantage has as a corollary the disadvantage of 'two-tier capital gains tax'. The company pays on its gains when it sells its assets, and the shareholders pay on their gains when they come to sell their shares. However this disadvantage need not inhibit those who see their families retaining the family farm for ever and a day.

(f) The government's initiative to encourage the small business sector has given rise to recent legislation directed towards limited companies as the natural small business medium. For example, there are alleviations of taxation when companies divide up into two or more separately owned companies (TA 1988 s 213). Companies are now permitted to buy back their own shares (TA 1988 s 219) without this mechanism inevitably being treated as an income taxable distribution to shareholders. This specialist legislation may make companies marginally more flexible and attractive.

(g) A company as an operating medium permits the setting up of an approved Pension Scheme for directors and employees in a form whereby the whole employer's pension contributions usually become deductible for corporation tax purposes. An ordinary annual contribution by an employee may also be wholly deductible in computing his income for Schedule E. Moreover, an employer's contribution to an approved scheme is not treated as income or benefits in the hands of the employee. An Exempt Approved Pension Fund is itself entitled to exemption from income taxation on its investment income and from capital gains taxation. All approved schemes may produce both pensions and capital sums on retirement (TA 1988 s 590). These provisions compare favourably with the facilities available to self-employed individuals, and those not eligible for such schemes for whom relief may be limited to 17½% of net relevant earnings, generally remuneration earned, but not remuneration from pensionable employment.

Moreover, company pension schemes permit the setting-up of a self-administered fund; that is, one where the management of the fund can be 'captive'. The owner or chief executive of the farming company can become a trustee of the fund, so acquiring the power to direct and review its investment policy. In certain circumstances, and within limits, a captive fund can acquire farm assets as an investment, or can lend cash back to the farming company as working capital. Captive funds are subject to close scrutiny by the Inland Revenue Superannuation Fund Office, but represent a valuable mechanism, adding flexibility to the operations of a farming company, with attendant risks as to the value of the pension ultimately payable to a farmer-director.

(h) The progressive reductions of corporation tax rates during the financial years 1983 to 1986, together with a 25% small company rate, have further tilted the balance in favour of incorporation. Use of a company will permit profits in the band between £28,715 pa and £250,000 pa to be taxed at a 25% rate instead of at 40% applicable to the same profits in the hands of a married individual taxpayer.

(i) In July 1987, the Revenue published 'Disincorporation', a consultative document putting forward suggestions for improvements in the law which would facilitate change from operating a business as a company to operating it as a sole trader or partnership.

In this document, two of the disadvantages mentioned above, double capital gains tax and extinction of loss relief, were mentioned as candidates for change.

If these proposals are ever enacted, companies would undoubtedly become significantly more advantageous. If the cost of corporate status and compliance with company law were also to be reduced as promised in this document, that would give additional encouragement.

15.7 TRUSTS

15.7:1 Introduction

Trusts have become widely used as ownership vehicles for farms and estates in Britain. That is because farming is fragmented into relatively small business units, owned by individuals and families rather than by corporations, and since the nineteenth century, trusts have been the traditional medium for family ownership.

Since farming is a long-term activity spanning succeeding generations, it is convenient to invoke a trustee to give ownership continuity. Under a trust, the beneficiaries can change, but the trust property can remain vested in a trustee, so that no transfer occurs on a death. That made trusts useful media for the avoidance of taxation chargeable upon the event of death, and under estate duty, trusts and trustees flourished. Under inheritance tax, 'the broad principle to be applied to settled property is that in general the charge to tax should be neither greater nor smaller than the charge on property held absolutely'. That was the statement of intent ('neutrality principle') contained in the government White Paper of August 1974 (Cmnd 5705), and if it had been totally put in practice, there might be no need for a chapter in this book on the topic. At the time of writing the taxation of trusts is again under review. A consultative document was published at the time of the Budget 1991. The stated aim of new legislation is that of bringing the taxation of trusts more closely into line with the taxation of individuals.

In some critical respects, trusts are very disadvantageous and many trusts have been broken or varied for tax reasons. On the other hand, some advantages remain in specialised forms of trusts, and this section is mainly devoted to describing the possibilities and limitations of new trusts rather than the updating of old ones.

For inheritance tax, the definition of a settlement is a wide one and means any disposition of property, whereby the property is held in trust for persons in succession; or to accumulate the income therefrom, with power to make payments at discretion; or is charged with payment of an annuity or similar periodic payment. A lease of property for life or for lives is also to be treated as a settlement, unless the lease was granted for full consideration in money or money's worth. A foreign settlement is treated as a settlement if it would have satisfied the above tests had it been regulated by English law, or if under foreign law the administration of property is governed by provisions having equivalent effect.

There is a correspondingly wide definition of settlor: any person by whom the settlement was made directly or indirectly and any person who has provided funds directly or indirectly for the purpose of or in connection with the settlement, or has made with any other person a reciprocal arrangement for that other person to make the settlement. A settlement can thus have more than one 'settlor'.

15.7:2   What is a trust?

A trust has been defined as; 'the relationship which arises, wherever a person called the *trustee* is compelled in equity to hold property . . . for the benefit of some persons . . . who are termed beneficiaries . . . in such a way that the real benefit of the property accrues not to the trustees, but to the beneficiaries or other objects of the trust'. (Keeton's definition).

Expressing this in a less technical form, a trust may be said to be a collection of legal rights and obligations brought into being by a specific legal process. According to this process, an individual, the settlor, transfers to a legal person (the trustee) rights or property for the benefit of one or more third parties who are called beneficiaries. Trusts may be set up for objectives quite separate from tax saving, and the non-fiscal consequences of a trust should be very carefully considered beforehand.

The non-tax-saving objective is usually to hold property for members of a family who are minors; who are not yet born because they are the next or future generations; because they are in some way disadvantaged or disabled; or alternatively for some charitable or similar purpose. This is not meant to be an inclusive list but it should convey that trustees act in a fiduciary or guardianship role holding value for the benefit of those who may not have the capacity to hold it and invest it themselves. There are other objectives which may be viewed as of an investment or a fiscal nature, depending upon the precise circumstances. For example, trusts may be designed to segregate income from capital and to allocate income to one member of a family and capital to other members.

A trust is created by a Deed of Trust and a Trustee is a separate legal person who may be either an individual or a trust company acting in accordance with the obligations of the trust as set out in the deed constituting the trust. If individuals are selected as trustees there may be any number between one and four. If a corporate trustee is selected, only one is normally needed. It is usual to set up a trust designed for the benefit of a future generation and a trust which has only a short-term life is unlikely to be worthwhile. On the other hand, a trust cannot be made to last indefinitely because of the 'rule against perpetuities'. It is usual to regard the maximum duration of a trust as being 80 years, or alternatively a life in being at the date of the trust plus 21 years.

The selection of trustees is clearly an important element in the setting up of a new trust. A settlor can appoint himself as a trustee, but it usually inadvisable to do so, because it blurs the distinction between the two functions, and can suggest that the trust property has not been alienated.

Additional or replacement trustees may be appointed in accordance with provisions in the Trust Deed. Alternatively existing trustees may appoint, and in the last resort the Court can make an appointment. Trusteeship endures for a lifetime; or the period of the trust; or until retirement or removal. Removal is in accordance with the Trust Deed; appointment of a replacement under the Trustee Act 1925 s 36; or by action of the Court.

Land cannot be held by less than two trustees or by more than four. Alternatively land may be held by a Trust Corporation.

It will be recognised that this section represents a very brief summary of a complex part of English law, and many of the general rules stated above need to be modified in particular cases!

15.7:3 Inheritance tax regime for trusts

It will be recalled that a potentially exempt transfer is a chargeable transfer to another individual or to the trustees of a maintenance and accumulation settlement; or to a trust for disabled persons (see section **8.1:3**).

Accumulation and maintenance trusts were accorded certain privileges under capital transfer tax and this new rule has further enhanced the attractions of this specialised class of trust. The criteria for accumulation and maintenance trusts are described in section **15.7:7** below, but the general intention of such trusts is that the trust fund be applied for the education and maintenance of infant children.

By comparison, gifts to discretionary trusts cannot qualify as potentially exempt transfers, and inheritance tax becomes immediately chargeable. In these circumstances, it is not easy to identify particular situations in which discretionary trusts can still be attractive.

There may still be a case for creating a discretionary trust to consume a donor's nil rate band. Gifts up to the threshold of £150,000 can be made without attracting immediate inheritance tax liability, and it is arguable that there is an advantage in consuming the nil rate band by such gifts before attempting potentially exempt transfers. The argument is that if the PETs are made first, and these transfers fail because the donor does not survive the seven years, the liabilities attaching to the subsequent chargeable transfers may prove to be at higher rates than was originally calculated.

It should be borne in mind that where tenanted agricultural land qualifying for agricultural property relief is used as the currency for a nil rate band discretionary trust, the value may be increased by 50% APR (see section **8.5:1**).

If the donor includes himself as a member of the discretionary class in a discretionary trust, he will be treated as having reserved a benefit. Such an inclusion is unlikely for income tax and capital gains tax reasons (FA 1988 s 109 and Sch 10). There is no similar problem so far as the inclusion of a widow is concerned.

The circumstances in which a discretionary trust may be selected are various. It may still be good planning to settle on discretionary trusts an asset which has little present value, but which is expected to appreciate in value in the future. Shares in a family company which is at an early stage of its development might represent an appropriate example.

The regime for discretionary trusts described below (see section **15.7:6**) is of course important for discretionary trusts already in existence at the time of the introduction of inheritance tax.

15.7:4   Life interest trusts under inheritance tax

Where a settlor makes a gift of property in trust, so that he retains income from the property during his own life, but with capital passing after his death to another person or persons, the gift to trustees is not a chargeable event. Nor can there be a reserved benefit. The subject matter of the gift will be the value of the property passing to the remainderman under the trust, and inheritance tax will be chargeable on that event, at that time.

Life interest trusts under which property was settled on *another person* or *persons* for his or their lives were originally disadvantageous. This transfer did not qualify as a potentially exempt transfer under the Finance Act 1986. Tax was chargeable then and the death of the life tenant was an event giving rise to inheritance tax. This double charge was eliminated in F(2)A 1987 s 96.

A gift by an individual into a life interest in possession trust, or the assignment or termination of a life interest during lifetime, is now treated as a potentially exempt transfer.

There are anti-avoidance provisions to prevent property being routed through a life interest trust into a discretionary trust, with the object of reducing future inheritance tax liability of the discretionary trust.

Clearly such a life interest trust can be useful, if it is necessary to make available to an individual income during his or her lifetime, and at the same time determine the devolution of the land or other trust assets after that individual's death. Such trusts may also be useful where there are no qualifying candidates for an accumulation and maintenance trust, and a discretionary trust would be too costly in immediate tax.

15.7:5   Occasions of charge to inheritance tax

The four occasions when settled property may become the subject of a charge to inheritance tax are as follows:

(a) With certain minor exceptions, property is chargeable to inheritance tax on the initial gift to a discretionary trustee.

(b) Tax is charged on the value of settled property when an interest in possession comes to an end, eg on the death of a life tenant. The interest is taxed as part of his total estate, but tax is normally payable by the trustees of the settled property.

(c) Where there is no interest in possession, tax is chargeable whenever property ceases to be held on discretionary trusts, either when the settlement comes to an end, or there is a distribution to beneficiaries out of capital.

(d) For discretionary trusts, there are also provisions for periodic charges once every ten years. This represents an attempt to apply the principle of neutrality already described (see section **15.7:1**), ie to produce the same result as for unsettled property where liability can be expected once in a generation.

The charge to inheritance tax on a gift into trust represents a significant deterrent, as it requires immediate payment of cash, to secure a possible saving at some indeterminate date of death in the future. Cash to pay the charge would need to be found from other resources, and the loss of working capital would rarely be justified. Borrowing costs at current rates inhibit the ability to borrow to finance this entry cost.

A second factor is the general loss of operating flexibility sustained by the relevant assets being locked into trust. Trustees may carry on a trade of farming but conflicts sometimes arise between the duty of the trustees to preserve the assets of the trust, on the one hand, and the ordinary risks of commercial ventures on the other. Although the terms of a trust deed may stipulate that trustees may deal with assets as if they were absolute owners, it may be difficult for corporate trustees, eg a clearing bank trust corporation, to apply such a clause in practice. Trustees need to be more conservative than absolute owners, and this may not conform with farming policy. It is easier for trustees to become owners of a tenanted estate.

There is, thirdly, a contingent inheritance tax liability on all settled funds, though in a sense the same could be said of free estate. The periodic charge tends to make the contingency seem more immediate than the death of an estate owner, although the comparison needs to be supported by actuarial calculation.

Attention needs to be paid to the incidence of other taxes. The application of income tax to trustees is important, since, in the past, some trusts were set up with income tax saving in mind. Where there is a tenant for life who enjoys all the income of the trust property, that income is fully taxable in his hands as part of his total income. Where the trustees receive the income of a discretionary trust and pay tax on it at the basic rate plus 15% additional rate, and the trustees pay over the net, it is so treated in the hands of beneficiary and will be grossed up to arrive at the full amount of his income.

Where trustees accumulate the income, the treatment varies depending whether the beneficiaries have a vested interest in it. If they do, generally speaking the income is treated as their income year by year as it arises. If beneficiaries have a contingent interest, then the income is treated as theirs only in so far as it is paid over, or applied for their benefit, for example to pay maintenance or education costs. In so far as income is accumulated, income tax liability is reduced to the basic rate plus additional rate, which may represent a considerable saving on rates applicable to the same income in the hands of the individual settlor.

Thus whether or not to create a discretionary trust may be a question of weighing current inheritance tax on setting up against future savings, a difficult equation. The position will be further complicated by the incidence of capital gains tax, which requires separate consideration. Generally, the three first occasions of charge to inheritance tax, initial gift to trustees, coming to an end of interest in possession and distribution out of trust property, are also occasions of charge to capital gains tax, (except death) capable of being relieved by hold-over relief on gifts (FA 1981 s 78).

Thus, until the capital taxation of trust property is made less severe there can rarely be cases where it will be advantageous to transfer a farm or farmland into trust. However, many existing trusts will remain in being because of the high taxation cost of varying them under the present regime, although the future of those, in turn, will fall to be reconsidered after the law is changed. The remaining question is whether specialised trusts can be helpful, eg where the fund is comprised neither of a farming business, a farm estate nor farmland, but other assets, particularly cash; or where the setting up cost for both capital taxes can be acceptably small.

15.7:6 The regime for discretionary trusts

The current system had a long germination period. The consultancy process between government and interested bodies commenced with the August 1980 Orange Consultation Paper, and continued for some two years. The government seemed to conclude that the charging structure originally proposed was generally correct, subject to major changes in the balance of it.

The original structure included an entry charge when a discretionary trust was created; an exit charge – when a trust was terminated or distributed; and (thirdly) a periodic charge at ten-yearly intervals between these two events, as a supplementary liability to compensate for the theoretical immunity from taxation on death during the discretionary trust period, and to secure parity of treatment with property held absoutely. The exit charge was reduced by a credit for tax payable on a periodic charge, providing that the distribution occurred within 20 years of the relevant periodic charge anniversary. For settlements created before 17 March 1974, there were transitional reliefs for termination or distribution before 31 March 1983.

THE TENTH ANNIVERSARY CHARGE (IHTA 1984 s 64)

The regime retains this structure but reverses the emphasis: entry charges remain unchanged; 'the periodic charge' has become a main charging provision, instead of being an interim liability to be credited against the ultimate exit charge. The 'periodic charge' now described as the 'principal charge to tax' is imposed every ten years at 30% of the full lifetime scale rate, on the date in a year corresponding to that in which the settlement commenced. A settlement 'commences' when property becomes comprised in it. Property in which the settlor or his spouse has an interest in possession immediately after becoming comprised in the settlement is to be treated as not having become comprised on that date although this does not affect the date of ten-year anniversaries.

The periodic charge is made on what is called 'relevant property'. Property in which the settlor or his spouse has an interest in possession is not treated as relevant property; nor is income which has neither been distributed to the beneficiaries nor accumulated. This latter exclusion follows from the change in Revenue practice dated 10 November 1986 (SP 8/86). Periodic charges are not subject to any 'grossing up' calculation.

THE EXIT CHARGE (IHTA 1984 s 65)

The 'proportionate charge', a form of exit charge, is a time-based proportionate charge, the rate of which is calculated by taking the rate applicable to the last periodic charge, and multiplying it by the appropriate fraction – which is so many fortieths as there have been complete successive quarter-years since the date of the last periodic charge.

The amount on which tax is charged is the amount of reduction in the value of 'relevant property', that is, settled property in which there is no 'qualifying interest in possession.' (See Inland Revenue Press Release 12 Feb 1976 which gave the Revenue interpretation of this expression, subsequently withdrawn in the light of *Pearson v IRC* [1980] STC 318, where elucidates the meaning of '*interest in possession*'). This reduction will have occurred because property ceases to be part of the settled fund, or because the trustees have made a disposition which reduced value. If the tax is paid out of the settlement funds and not out of property which has been distributed, the diminution in value falls to be grossed up. The grossing-up calculation is based on a special system by reference to the hypothetical transfer (see below). Where a distribution or other chargeable event occurs within the first quarter after the settlement commences or within the first quarter after a periodic charge, there is no liability.

Where a distribution is made in the early part of the decade after the last periodic charge and the number of time-expired quarters is small, the effect of the time basis proportion formula may emerge as similar to the earlier system of crediting periodic charges against later exit charges. However, where distribution is made towards the end of the decade since the last periodic charge, the effect of the new system will be disadvantageous, because there will be a larger number of quarters, and the proportionate charge will not be much smaller than the next periodic charge. Under the earlier regime, the whole of the last periodic charge would have been available as a credit. However, in making this comparison it should be borne in mind that exit charges are imposed under the new rules at 30% of the lifetime rate scale; whereas under the old rule the 30% reduction was confined to periodic charges, and exit charges were made at the full scale rate (see below).

The computation of liability requires two stages. First, the amount of the property to be charged needs to be ascertained. Secondly, the rate of charge needs to be calculated and applied. This rate does not derive from the amount of property to be charged, but is separately calculated having regard to a hypothetical chargeable transfer, and certain hypothetical past transfers.

THE RATES OF CHARGE

For both classes of charge, 'periodic' and 'proportionate', the rate is 30% of the lifetime scale. The maximum rate at which the exit charges and periodic charges can be made is therefore 30% × 20% = 6%. For business property and agricultural property with vacant possession, qualifying for relief at 50%, the maximum rate will be 3%. For agricultural property not with vacant possession, the maximum rate after 30% relief will be 4.2%. For exit charges, the appropriate fraction is three-tenths of another fraction; the denominator of the latter fraction is 40, and the numerator is the number of complete successive quarters in the period beginning with the day on which the settlement began, or the day of the last ten-year anniversary, and ending with the date before that on which the exit charge arose. When this principle applies, the scale rate is therefore computed as follows:

$$\frac{1}{40} \times 30\% \times 20\% \text{ (life-time rate)} = 0{\cdot}15\% \text{ rising to:}$$

$$\frac{40}{40} \times 30\% \times 20\% = 6\% \text{ with intervening steps of } 0{\cdot}15\% \text{ per quarter.}$$

The calculation of the rate of charge involves certain hypotheses to arrive at an effective rate, which is applied to the relevant property to be charged.

The effective rate calculation differs in detail depending upon whether the calculation is being made for the purpose of arriving at a rate to be applied to:

(a) a proportionate charge before the first periodic charge; or
(b) a periodic charge; or
(c) a proportionate charge after a periodic charge.

There are also differences in detail depending upon whether the settlement was made before or after 27 March 1974, when CTT (now IHT) came into operation.

Where the proportionate charge falls before the first periodic charge, the amount of the notional chargeable transfer is the total of:

(a) value of relevant property in the settlement immediately after commencement; plus
(b) value of property in any related settlement.

The rate of charge is fixed on the cumulative principle, after taking account of the point on the progressive scale reached by the settlor on the occasion of the initial settlement.

For the periodic charge; and where the proportionate charge falls after a periodic charge, the amount of the notional chargeable transfer is the total of:

   (a) value of relevant property immediately before the ten-year anniversary; plus
   (b) value of non-relevant property comprised in settlement immediately after it became so comprised; plus
   (c) value of property comprised in any related settlement.

Again the rate of charge is fixed on the cumulative principle taking account of hypothetical previous chargeable transfers, the amount being the total of:

   (a) value of chargeable transfers made by settlor in ten years before (but excluding) the settlement; plus
   (b) value of any earlier exit charges (subject to variations as to which see below).

The tax rate produced by these assumptions is then applied to the relevant property being charged.

There are various methods of arriving at the cumulative totals – that is, of identifying what past transfers must be taken into account in determining what rate on the progressive lifetime scale shall be applied to a current transfer. The position differs depending on whether the settlement was made before or after 27 March 1974, when IHT came into operation. Since there have been, in practice, so few settlements made since that date, it is the method for pre-IHT settlements that assumes more importance.

For exit charges before the first periodic charge and periodic charges, the hypothetical cumulative total is based on distributions and exit charge amounts during the previous ten years. The value of non-relevant property in the settlement and the value of property in related settlements (b) and (c) above are not taken into account, nor is the value of chargeable transfers made in the ten years before the settlement.

However, distribution payments made before 9 March 1982 are taken into account as being the equivalent of exit charges. For exit charges after a periodic charge, the rate to be adopted is that of the last periodic charge, without any element of progression, but subject to recalculation in certain special circumstances.

For post IHT settlements, there are three different alternative treatments. For exit charges before a first periodic charge, the cumulative total is based on the settlor's own individual ten-year cumulative total. For the periodic charge this total is the starting point, but to this should be added amounts on which exit charges were imposed in the previous ten years plus any distribution payments. For exit charges after a periodic charge, the pre-IHT settlement system applies. It is not easy to perceive the logic of all these different rules.

The former 'full-time working farmer relief' was not accorded to discretionary trustees. The agricultural property relief is so accorded, so here there is a distinct improvement. The conditions to be satisfied by trustees do not differ from those to be satisfied by an absolute owner. (Where there is an interest in possession, the tenant for life is treated as if he were the absolute or legal owner, and the agricultural property relief is granted to him, providing that he satisfies the necessary tests, and not to the trustees even though they are strictly the legal owners of the trust property.)

Clearly, the inheritance tax regime for trustees is now less severe. The more modest rates combined with the trustees' ability to secure agricultural property relief and the availability of roll-over relief for capital gains tax on both property going into and coming out of the trusts, may together convince trustees' families and their advisers that they should retain some property in settlement.

For income tax, there is a small advantage. Discretionary trustees are currently liable at 25% plus 10% 'additional rate' on their income. A trustee is not an individual so is not liable to higher rate tax, nor entitled to any personal reliefs.

15.7:7 Accumulation and maintenance trusts

One form of specialised trust, which remains distinctly useful, is the accumulation and maintenance trust (IHTA 1984 s 71). This form has been granted taxation privileges so long as the fund is intended to be spent on the education and maintenance costs of children. The special criteria are as follows:

(a) there must be no interest in possession in the settled property;
(b) the income must be applied for the maintenance, education or benefit of the infant beneficiaries;
(c) in so far as it is not so applied, it must be accumulated by the trustees to be applied in a future year;
(d) one or more beneficiaries must become entitled to the settled property or to an interest in possession in it by the age of 25 years (it is worth noting that the entitlement at 25 may be to the income only, with the capital held in trust until a later age);
(e) either, not more than 25 years must have elapsed since creation of the settlement, or the latest time when the above conditions were satisfied; or all the actual or potential beneficiaries are grandchildren of a common grandparent, or children, widows, or widowers of such grandchildren, who were themselves beneficiaries, but died before the time when had they survived, they would have secured a vested interest.

If all these tests are satisfied, the trust property is not relevant property and the charges applicable to discretionary trusts (see section **15.7:6**) cannot arise. Nor is there liability when a beneficiary becomes beneficially entitled to trust property, or an interest in possession in trust property. This may be on his entitlement on attaining a specified age, or it may be before attaining a specified age.

Nor is there a charge on the death of the beneficiary before or after attaining a specified age.

Great care is needed in drafting accumulation and maintenance trusts so as to avoid importing powers of appointment or statutory powers under the Trustee Act, which inadvertently destroy the reliefs.

The exemption from inheritance tax on distributions by the trustees, and from the periodic, charge has made accumulation and maintenance trusts seem relatively attractive, and they are now recommended as quasi-discretionary trusts, that is, where the object is simply to accumulate for infant members of the family, and those still unborn.

That is because the deterrents are reduced to one: the exclusion of adult members of the family, producing a relatively narrow permitted range of beneficiaries. In practice, this exclusion usually limits accumulation and maintenance trusts to modest amounts of value. It makes accumulation and maintenance trusts inappropriate as ownership media for a whole farm or estate.

Accumulation and maintenance trusts are more often constituted of cash, invested in a portfolio of securities. These will yield income convenient for distributions to pay, for example, school fees. It is arguable that accumulation trusts are tax-efficient media, the use of which can increase net spendable income, so releasing farming profit for reinvestment. However, that is a very different purpose. So far as direct ownership of a farm is concerned, it is impossible to conclude that any form of trust is always advantageous but an accumulation and maintenance trust can be a useful vehicle in many different circumstances.

Charitable trusts often attract interest (IHTA 1984 s 23), until it emerges that the ultimate destination of the fund must be to charity and not to heirs or family generally (see section **14.6:4**). Finally, although it may be advantageous to set up a new trust to own a farm or farmland at the present time, it does not follow that all existing trusts should be broken. On the contrary, the price (in tax) of breaking a trust can be as daunting as the price of setting one up.

15.7:8   Trusts and business and agricultural property reliefs

The 100% rate relief for agricultural and business property enacted in F(2)A 1992 has had the effect of making discretionary trusts more efficient as farm ownership vehicles. Where entitlement to 100% business property relief or agricultural property relief is available, there will be no charge to inheritance tax on the initial gift to a discretionary trustee. Nor will there be at this time any charge to capital gains tax (TCGA 1992 s 165 and Sch 7(1)).

If there are distributions out of a discretionary trust during the first ten years of the life of the trust, they will be taxed at the 'effective rate' (see section **15.7:6**). This will be calculated by reference to the value of the property at a date immediately after commencement of the trust, ie after the property had been settled on the trustees. Thus, trustees will need to hold the property for two years (owner-occupied property) or seven years (rented property) in order to qualify. A distribution of owner-occupied property within two years will not secure any relief and a distribution of tenanted property made within seven years will similarly not secure relief. That conclusion is dependent upon the ownership qualifications of the trustees (IHTA 1984 s 68).

It is also worth noting that other assets which have ceased to qualify for relief, eg cottages no longer used for farm employees could lose the benefit of relief even though they had secured relief at the time they were settled on trust.

Where there is a trust with an interest in possession, the tenant for life is treated as if he were the absolute legal owner and provided he satisfies the necessary tests, the agricultural property relief is granted to him and not to his trustees, even though they are strictly the legal owners of the trust property.

The ability to secure 100% agricultural property relief and the availability of hold-over relief for capital gains tax on both property going into and coming out of trusts may together make discretionary trusts (in particular) popular again, when family circumstances are appropriate. There is a small advantage for income tax. Discretionary trustees are currently liable at 25% plus 10% 'additional rate' income. A trustee is not an individual so is not liable to higher rate tax, nor is he entitled to any personal reliefs.

15.7:9   Capital gains tax regime for trusts

Trusts are liable to capital gains tax, in accordance with special rules briefly summarised here.

In the first place, capital gains tax may arise on the creation of a trust, because the disposal by way of gift or a transfer otherwise than at 'arm's length' is treated as a sale at market value as at the date of the gift (TCGA 1992 s 17).

Secondly, when the trustees dispose of trust assets they become liable to capital gains tax at the sum of the basic rate and the additional rate, ie 35% for 1993–94. Trustees have a special annual exemption of £2,900 of gains. This annual exemption does not apply where a settlor has retained an interest in the trust, because the gains are then his gains not the trustee's gains. As regards roll-over relief see section **7.4:2**(E).

Thirdly, when the trust ends, or property is transferred out of the trust because of an advance to beneficiaries, trustees are deemed to have disposed of the assets concerned at the market value to which the beneficiary becomes entitled. When this occurs, the assets in question cease to be subject to the trust capital gains tax regime, and become subject to the regime applicable to the individual beneficiary. Assets cease to be part of a trust, even though they may not pass to an individual beneficiary but become subject to a different separate trust. This also may create a deemed disposal and capital gains tax liability.

When an individual dies there is no general liability to capital gains tax on his free estate. Similar treatment is given to trust property in which a deceased person had a life interest in possession. On the death of the person having the life interest and enjoying the income from the property, there is a deemed disposal and reacquisition by the trustees of property remaining subject to the settlement. Although there is no charge to capital gains tax, the base cost of the assets is uplifted to their market value at the date of death.

Under a concession announced 17 February 1993, interests in possession which are not life interests will be treated similarly. For example, a beneficiary may have an interest in possession which terminates when he reaches a specified age. If, in such a case, the property continues to be held in trust, there is no charge to capital gains tax, but the base cost of the trust assets is uplifted. It was stated when this concession was introduced that it would affect only a small number of taxpayers (see *Simon's Tax Intelligence* 1993, p 290).

When a discretionary trust comes to an end and inheritance tax becomes payable, any capital gains arising on a distribution to a beneficiary may be held-over until the assets distributed are ultimately sold. The liability to capital gains tax at that time will depend upon the beneficiaries position (TCGA 1992 s 260).

Chapter 16

Tax planning II: farm finance

16.1 INTRODUCTION

Sooner or later, every farmer and landowner needs to borrow: either short-term, as a temporary expedient; medium-term, to provide working capital; or long-term, to acquire additional land or other assets. There is evidence that borrowings are increasing. The Agricultural Mortgage Corporation (AMC) is the biggest single lender, a company owned by the clearing banks and the Bank of England, set up for the purpose of providing loans to agriculture in England and Wales. The Scottish equivalent is the Scottish Agricultural Securities Corporation.

About 80% of all long-term finance from institutional sources comes from the AMC, which makes fresh advances of between £25m and £50m per annum. The main clearing banks are also big lenders and in the mid 1980s were estimated to be lending approximately £5.5 billion. This was mainly on an overdraft basis, to finance the production cycle, 'from seed time to harvest', but the concept of seasonal lending is now somewhat out of date, and it appears there is a solid core of borrowing throughout the year, with some small increases during summer months, reducing in the autumn. Over-borrowing has closed down many farms.

This chapter examines the taxation treatment of farm finance: including the borrowing costs. The true economic cost of borrowing, and therefore the practicability of it may depend upon whether interest payable is deductible in computing profits for income or corporation tax purposes. A borrowing at 20% per annum has a true cost of 12% if the interest is payable out of profits suffering tax at 40%, and the interest is fully deductible for the current year. The longer the delay between date of payment of the interest, and due date of payment of the tax against which the relief is given, the less the true value of the relief. The combination of high interest rates and high tax rates have made full and early tax relief a critical factor, and care is needed in making financing arrangements so that maximum tax advantages can be secured.

A similar principle applies to inheritance tax. In general, a transferor's liabilities are taken into account in valuing an estate transferred on death. Therefore, total inheritance tax may depend on maximising the effect of a liability, ensuring it is deductible against assets not already otherwise relieved.

Thirdly, there is the larger question of the contingent liability to tax: its incidence as a future debt. Traditionally, tax planning includes not only tax reduction, but also some funding of the reduced liabilities, often in the form of a life insurance policy. The principle is simply expressed: on the death giving rise to the inheritance tax bill, the policy will mature, producing the cash to pay the tax bill, so preserving the farm or estate assets from sale to meet the Chancellor's demands. The arrangements made will have ensured that the policy proceeds will not themselves be liable to tax because they will have arisen in another pair of hands. In practice, the arrangements tend to be complex, to secure the tax-free status of the policy, and also because life assurance is an expensive commodity and a farm or estate may not be generating adequate income needed for development to meet the proprietor's living expenses and to finance future tax obligations.

Where the proceeds of an insurance policy arise in the hands of a younger generation, it is assumed that the cash will be used to buy as much as possible of a farm or estate from the personal representatives, so effectively securing continuity down the generations. It must be recognised that by the relevant time, circumstances may have changed and the cash proceeds may never be so applied. There will not normally be any obligation on beneficiaries so to apply them. When such arrangements are being considered, thought should be given to the terms of the will, so that the beneficiaries of the policy proceeds and the future heirs of the farm or estate are either one and the same persons; or at least matters are arranged so as not to create conflict amongst different branches or members of the family.

16.2 THE INTEREST DEDUCTION

16.2:1 Introduction

The tax treatment of interest paid has fluctuated over past years, and a historical resumé is needed.

(A) FINANCIAL YEARS UP TO AND INCLUDING 1968–69

Interest, other than 'short' interest, was inadmissible as a deduction in computing the profits of a trade. That was because interest and other annual payments were generally deductible as charges on income. On making payment, the payer deducted and withheld tax at the standard rate, so effectively ensuring the recipient was taxed and giving himself relief. The principle of deduction at source was applied without limit, and irrespective of the purpose of the borrowing in respect of which the interest was payable, and whether or not a trade was carried on. The deduction was effective against total taxed income.

(B) 1969–70 TO 1971–72

The principle of deducting and withholding tax was abandoned for interest. Instead interest became fully deductible, where payable for the purposes of the trade, profession or vocation. Otherwise, interest was not deductible, unless the loan was for a specified qualifying purpose (see section **16.2:2**).

(C) 1971–72 TO 1973–74

All interest became deductible, save for the first £35 of interest paid by an individual per annum. However, this restriction did not apply to 'protected' interest, other than overdraft interest. 'Protected' interest is that payable on loans for a specified qualifying purpose (see section **16.2:2**). The machinery of deduction at source was not revived.

(D) THE CURRENT POSITION (26 MARCH 1974 ONWARDS)

The position has been restored to what it was from 1969–70 to 1971–72, with some major differences. First, interest paid on a bank overdraft or on a credit card arrangement does not qualify for relief. Secondly, money borrowed to purchase or improve land or buildings qualifies only if the property is a principal private residence; or a property which is let (TA 1988 s 353).

The general effect of the current rules may be summarised as follows: farmers carrying on a trade will have no difficulty in securing the deduction of interest as a business expense. That will include interest on the farm overdraft, or money borrowed for a specific purpose, for example the purchase of another farm, new machinery, or to pay wages.

The only recorded difficulty is that the Revenue may contend that bank overdraft interest is not deductible as a business expense when the farm capital account is overdrawn. The Revenue argument is that this interest would relate to private expenditure (drawings) and the interest is therefore not money laid out for the purpose of the farming business.

16.2:2   Specified qualifying purpose

When the borrower is not carrying on a trade, but is liable, eg under Schedule A, then the purpose of the loan is the qualifying test, and the following purposes qualify:

(A) THE PURCHASE OF AN INTEREST IN LAND, HOUSES OR FARM BUILDINGS

Relief for interest on a borrowing is given to purchase property which is to be let commercially (TA 1988 s 354) or used as the principal private residence of the borrower. Relief for interest on a borrowing to purchase property of a dependent relative or former or separated spouse was abolished as from 6 April 1988 (FA 1988 s 44(1)). Relief to purchase a principal private residence is from 6 April 1991 restricted to the basic rate of income tax. It is also limited to interest on a loan of up to £30,000. The amount of £30,000 is not a maximum per person but per residence (FA 1988 s 42). Interest on borrowing to purchase let property is deductible only against rent receivable from that property, but if the rent for a current year is inadequate to absorb relief, the excess may be carried forward and applied against rent of future years (TA 1988 s 355(4)). Property must be let at a commercial rent for more than 26 weeks in any 52-week period, which includes the time at which the interest is payable. When not so let, the property has to be available for such letting, or used as the owner's only or main residence, or unavailable because it is undergoing repairs (TA 1988 s 355(1)(*b*)).

Caravans and house-boats are included under this heading. The caravan must be a 'small' caravan not exceeding 22 feet in length and 7 feet 6 inches in width. The treatment of interest to be paid should be borne in mind when land is owned by a member of a partnership and let to that partnership on the lines described in section **15.2:1**.

The interest paid by a landowner may create problems when the land is owned by a member of a partnership and leased to that partnership on the lines described in section **15.2:1**.

If there is any tenancy agreement providing for a rack-rent to be payable, the loan interest will be deductible from the rent receivable. If the interest exceeds this rent, the excess will be deductible against other rental income in that year, or may be carried forward against future rental income.

If there is no tenancy agreement, and the rent is in practice paid by the partnership and reduces the partnership profit before allocations amongst the partners, the payments may be deducted as if they were payments of rent payable by the partnership to the landowning partner. This permits the deduction in the computation of the partnership profits. The interest (treated as rent) in the hands of the landowning partner is then extinguished by his interest payment.

If there is no tenancy agreement, and the interest is not in fact paid by the partnership, it will not be deductible in computing the partnership profits nor will the landowning partner be able to secure a deduction from his taxable income.

Comparable treatment is available where a shareholder or director in a farming company borrows money to purchase land farmed by the company. If there exists a tenancy agreement at a commercial rent between the landowning shareholder/director and the company, the interest is deductible from the rent, provided it is not overdraft interest.

If there is no tenancy agreement, but the company pays the interest, the interest payments by the company are not treated as rent but as emoluments payable to a director taxable on him under Schedule E. This creates the deduction in the company's computation of taxable profits, but the interest payment made by the director will not be correspondingly deductible against the additional emoluments, as it will hardly be an expense incurred 'wholly, exclusively and necessarily in the performance of the director's duties'.

Where the company pays neither the rent nor the interest, it will secure no deduction. The interest payable by the director will, therefore, be unrelieved.

Clearly, these last two configurations represent traps to be avoided. It should be borne in mind that the determination of a rent on an uncommercial basis may produce secondary consequences, for example as regards the retention of benefit for inheritance tax purposes (see section **8.1:5**).

(B) THE IMPROVEMENT OF LAND

Relief for interest on loans for improvements is abolished for loans taken out after 5 April 1988 (FA 1988 s 43).

Relief was given on the same tests as for the purchase of land but it should be noted that the repair or maintenance of land, houses etc, was not a qualifying purpose. This seems a curious anomaly, the effect of which was to make revenue expenditure more costly than capital expenditure, and a distortion of income tax principles. It followed that, where practicable, the burden of repairs should be allocated to tenants (this was also advantageous for VAT purposes).

(C) THE PURCHASE OF PARTNERSHIP INTERESTS

Interest is allowable where the loan is applied to purchase an interest in a farming etc, partnership, or to contribute cash as capital to a partnership (TA 1988 s 362). Throughout the period from the loan to the time of payment of interest, the individual must have personally acted in the trade, profession or vocation carried on by the partnership, so that borrowing made by sleeping partners fails to qualify. This rule has been varied for interest paid after 10 March 1981. From that date, interest paid by sleeping partners is eligible for relief. Interest paid by limited partners is still excluded (TA 1988 s 362(2)(a)).

In the Revenue view, the individual has to be a member of the partnership throughout the period dating from the application of the proceeds of the loan until the date the interest is paid. Thus, after the individual has ceased to be a member of the partnership, relief is denied. That would be the position even where the partner leaving the partnership was unable immediately to withdraw all his capital.

Interest on loans for the purchase of plant and machinery for use in the partnership business is allowable, but only for three years after the end of the year of assessment in which the debt was incurred (TA 1988 s 359).

Where capital is recovered from the partnership, it is treated as having been applied to repay the loan and the interest relief is reduced accordingly. For this purpose, the recovery of capital has a wide meaning, and includes the receipt of consideration for sale, the repayment of a loan or advance; consideration for the assignment of a debt.

(D) THE PURCHASE OF SHARES IN CLOSE COMPANIES

Similarly, interest qualifies for relief on a loan used to buy ordinary shares in a family company (see section **6.2**); to lend money to such a company, to be used wholly and exclusively for its business; or in paying off a loan, the interest on which would itself have qualified for relief (TA 1988 s 360).

The borrower must have a material interest in the company (5%), but the rule requiring the borrower to work for the company, corresponding to the rule requiring personal activity in a partnership, has been abolished in relation to interest paid after 26 March 1980. Where a borrower has not so worked, and the company is an investment company, it is a condition that no property used by the borrower is held by the company. This is an anti-avoidance rule.

The capital recovery provisions applicable to partnerships apply also to close company share purchase borrowings.

(E) PAYMENT OF CAPITAL TRANSFER TAX OR INHERITANCE TAX

Borrowings by personal representatives of a deceased person are sometimes needed to pay tax before estate assets can be realised, and before a grant of representation (TA 1988 s 364).

(F) TO PURCHASE LIFE ANNUITY

Interest qualifies for relief providing at least nine-tenths was applied by a borrower aged 65 years or over to purchase a life annuity secured on his only or main residence (TA 1988 s 365).

(G) PURCHASE OF PRIVATE RESIDENCE BY REPRESENTATIVE OCCUPIERS

See section **5.5:3**.

In a tax-planning context, the importance of the interest deduction rules lies partly in its interaction with other sub-systems offering capital tax advantages. It will have been noted that there is no special class of interest relief where the loan is applied to purchase land to be farmed by a partnership or company, but which is to be excluded from the partnership or company Balance Sheet. The former benefit of this arrangement is described in section **6.1:3**, but the price payable for it might have been loss of valuable interest relief, because of the inadequacy of rental income.

Again, it should be noted that the effect of a substantial borrowing by a farmer may be to extinguish the profitability of the farm, at least for a period, until additional profits are created out of the new land or business bought with borrowed money. During the interim period, the interest paid might have reduced profits to a level which fell below 75% of earned income, the relevant test for the purposes of full-time working farmer relief (see section **8.4**).

Similarly, if losses arise for five years in succession, the losses may fall to be disallowed as uncommercial (see section **2.6:5**) on the grounds that no reasonably competent farmer would have burdened himself with so substantial a debt. Thus it is what might be called the secondary consequences of the interest deduction rules which need to be borne in mind, when devising a tax plan. For example, it may be advantageous to secure that interest payable is relieved as a charge against total income rather than as a deduction in calculating the net profits (or losses) of a farm.

16.2:3 Costs of obtaining finance

The incidental costs of obtaining loan finance represent a deductible expense in arriving at the taxable profit of a farm business. These costs may include fees and commissions paid, advertising etc, but the premiums payable on a life insurance policy required as a condition of obtaining loan finance are not regarded by the Revenue as qualifying incidental costs.

16.3 LIABILITIES UNDER INHERITANCE TAX

As a general principle, the value of an estate transferred for the purposes of inheritance tax is its net value (IHTA 1984 s 5(3)). That means that liabilities as at the date of transfer may be deducted in arriving at the chargeable amount. A future liability is not so deductible; nor one not incurred for money or money's worth, for example, future payments under a voluntary convenant.

It is a second general rule which may give rise to tax-planning considerations: that a liability which is specifically charged on a particular property is primarily set against the value of that property (IHTA 1984 s 162(4)). It follows that where a farm or land is itself charged as security for a mortgage, only the net amount, that is the value of the farm less the mortgage debt at the date of transfer, will become the base upon which agricultural property relief is calculated. The same principle applies to business property relief.

It is therefore desirable that borrowing should, where practicable, be secured on property which does not attract reliefs. This arrangement is particularly recommended where tenanted land is available as collateral security, or alternatively marketable securities or life policies may be offered as prior security. Then in so far as the value is matched by the collateral security, the reliefs will remain unscathed. This strategy is not always accepted readily by the Capital Taxes Office. Moreover, for the purposes of business property relief (see section **8.3**) and as regards payment of tax by interest-free instalments (see section **19.4**), the rule for measurement of the net value of a business requires deduction of liabilities incurred 'for the purpose of the business', irrespective of the asset on which they are secured (IHTA 1984 s 227).

The same principle makes ineffective the annual release of mortgage debts as a method of utilising annual exemptions to make gifts in a family. Under such a scheme, a landowner agrees to sell to a purchaser land at market value, the purchaser paying a deposit of the customary proportion, say 10%, and interest at a commercial rate. The mortgage of land should be formally registered, and the conveyancing should follow ordinary practice.

Then at annual intervals, the vendor releases the purchaser from mortgage loan repayments in such amounts as fall within his annual exemptions of £3,000 per annum. Such releases should be voluntary and not in accordance with prior agreement or arrangement. Alternatively, the vendor could make regular annual cash payments to the purchaser, each of which being applied after an interval to repay part of the outstanding mortgage loan.

This method often seemed preferable to making corresponding transfers of parcels of land for a number of reasons. First, annual conveyancing costs are avoided. Secondly, the value of small parcels of land may be uncertain, depending upon their location within the estate or farm. Thirdly, because an asset is being transferred as a whole at the outset, any future accretion of value passes at once to the purchaser. This method is particularly attractive where future accretions are clearly in prospect, whether for reasons of planning, farm development or mere inflation.

However, there could be considerable disadvantages, particularly where the sale is by father to son. At the outset, there will be a capital gains tax liability, the mortgage being the equivalent of a payment of cash by the son. This will make it impossible to claim the hold-over relief (TCGA 1992 s 262). Should the father die shortly after the initial transaction, the outstanding mortgage debt may be a substantial asset in his estate and one not eligible for business property relief or agricultural property relief. The attempt to reduce this value by an agreement to accept a nil or low rate of interest over the terms of the loan could itself amount to a transfer of value.

Even if the plan be carried through to completion, the Revenue may contend that the sale, mortgage and subsequent releases amount to a series of associated operations (IHTA 1984 s 268).

Thus, it will generally be preferable for the purchasing son to pay cash, with the price if necessary being reduced to ensure he can finance his borrowing from commercial sources. Capital gains tax payable should be limited by reference to the cash received with the balance being held over. Furthermore, the cash received in place of the mortgage debt would give the father greater opportunities for other planning, for example purchase of an annuity, funding life policies, gifts to other children etc.

16.3:1 Non-deductible liabilities

Under inheritance tax, there is a major prohibition against 'loanbacks' revived from the old estate duty rules. The mischief which is the subject of the anti-avoidance rule may be regarded as a form of reservation of benefit (see section **8.1:5**). Where property is given, but income from that property retained, benefit is reserved. So similarly where property is given, but that property or a corresponding amount is borrowed back, deduction of the debt in determining the value of the estate immediately before death is disallowed.

Similarly if the property is bought back for value but the purchase price is left outstanding, that price becomes a non-deductible debt.

Calculations of the disallowance may be needed to take into account the value of any consideration for the loan (for example, interest) being property derived directly or indirectly from the donor.

Repayment of a loan which is classified as a non-deductible debt for the above reasons, is treated as a transfer of value. Thus, the repayment will be an exempt transfer if the repayer survives a further seven years.

16.4   FUNDING INHERITANCE TAX LIABILITIES

16.4:1   Introduction

It has already been noted that inheritance tax represents a contingent liability upon all farms and estates, and that life insurance is the traditional medium for funding that liability in advance, so that personal representatives or beneficiaries under a will or intestacy can find sufficient cash to pay inheritance tax without recourse to sales of land or other business assets. The object of the exercise is to produce cash at the right point in time – the date of death of the life insured – the cost of so doing having been arrived at by actuarial calculation. This is the attribute of life insurance policies which makes them uniquely appropriate as funding media, rather than any tax exemptions or privileges.

Where a policy has been taken out by an individual on his own life and for his own benefit, the proceeds of the policy payable on his death form part of his taxable estate in the ordinary way. Consequently, there is no tax advantage to be gained by such an arrangement, and the blandishments of brokers and others are to be strongly resisted.

Where a policy is assigned to another person by the original life insured, or taken out from the outset for the benefit of another person, usually a dependant, the value of the policy itself on death is excluded from the life insured's estate, which is as might be expected since neither he nor his estate has any entitlement to the proceeds. Instead, the assignment or payment of the premiums constitutes a transfer of value, at the time the policy is assigned or when each premium is paid.

The value is obviously the amount of premium actually paid, but where an existing policy is assigned, the value adopted is the greater of the value of the policy at that time or the premiums previously paid under the policy (IHTA 1984 s 167). Special rules are applied for modifying this artificial basis of valuation where sums have previously been paid out under the policy or where the value of the policy, and the benefits payable on death, are determined by the value of underlying investment units (IHTA 1984 s 167(4)).

Where a policy is taken out by an individual on the life of another person, again, on the death of the life insured, the proceeds do not form part of his taxable estate. However, in the hands of the proposer, the policy represents an asset in his estate and will form part of his estate on his death before that of the life insured. In these circumstances, when such a life of another policy forms part of an individual's estate on death, the artificial valuation rules are not applied and the policy is valued, for tax purposes, at its open market value.

This summary will suffice to prove the point that life insurance policies enjoy no special tax privileges, and indeed, can suffer some disadvantages created by the artificial valuation principles. How best then to use life insurance as a tax planning mechanism, bearing in mind the other demands for cash which are likely to exist? The following represent the principal strategies available.

16.4:2 Using lifetime exemptions

The classic strategy is to pay premiums of amounts within the lifetime exemption limits to fund policies written in favour of dependants either absolutely; or under the Married Women's Property Act 1882 s 11; or otherwise in trust.

Four separate lifetime exemptions are available for this purpose: the £3,000 per annum annual exemption (IHTA 1984 s 19); the exemption for gifts in consideration of marriage (IHTA 1984 s 22); the £250 outright gift annual exemption (IHTA 1984 s 20); and the normal expenditure out of income exemption (IHTA 1984 s 21). The first two exemptions call for no particular comment except that where the £3,000 annual exemption is being used to fund annual policies, the amount of the loss to the donor's estate for tax purposes is the premium paid. As regards the annual £250 small gifts exemption, it must be remembered that this exemption is only available for outright gifts. Consequently, if the exemption is being used in order to fund the payment of premiums for a life policy, the correct procedure is for the donor to gift the cash outright to a beneficiary who then in turn uses the funds to meet premiums for the policy on the donor's life.

As regards the 'normal' expenditure out of income exemption, the question often arises as to whether the payment of premiums can be said to be 'normal'. Under estate duty, the payment of one premium alone was evidence of habitual expenditure, providing the policy would endure for at least three years, and this practice continues for inheritance tax.

It is important that the scale of premiums is not such as to lower the donor's standard of living and raise doubts as to whether the gifts were 'out of income'. One view is that amounts up to one-sixth of income are acceptable from this standpoint, but this will inevitably be challenged by the Revenue if the donor habitually used all his income for living purposes, or maintained substantial personal overdrafts. Gifts by a wife may be more acceptable than those by her husband since her income could be regarded as available unabated. This is on the assumption that her husband has the responsibility to maintain her and the family as a whole.

There are several practical advantages in funding a policy of insurance to mature on death rather than making straightforward outright gifts to a donee. First, donees do not immediately find themselves with funds capable of being spent. Instead, the amounts gifted are held 'in limbo' until the death of the life insured, the time when the funds are needed to meet inheritance tax liabilities. Secondly, if death strikes prematurely, the full sum assured will be payable under the policy, and this sum will substantially exceed the amount actually paid in premiums, whereas only a relatively trivial share of the farming business could have been handed over assuming the annual exemption rate of donation. Finally, it is possible for the proposer to write the policy in a form which could effectively take away the benefits from the children, and return them to himself or his widow. This gives added flexibility, which would be helpful if the profitability of the farm declined, or the proposer was doubtful about his financial security at the time of his retirement.

16.4:3   Joint life last survivor policies

Joint life last survivor policies are useful to pay the inheritance tax arising on the death of the surviving spouse. His or her estate may have been enlarged by the receipt of assets from the spouse dying earlier, so that, although liability was avoided on the earlier death, a substantial tax bill is likely to arise on the second death. By leaving an estate to a surviving spouse, either absolutely, or for his or her lifetime, an important advantage is secured: the deferral of payment until the second death in the generation. In these circumstances, a joint life last survivor policy will mature on the second death to provide funds available to meet this increased tax liability.

From the income tax standpoint, joint life policies can be qualifying policies, so that the proceeds are not subject to higher rate tax. In addition, such policies can cost less than equivalent policies written on the single lives of each of the husband and wife, since the premiums have to fund a whole life element effectively for the younger of the two lives.

16.4:4   Life of another policies

Providing the proposer pays the premiums from his own resources, and providing he or she has an insurable interest, there will be no tax payable on the policy proceeds on the death of the life assured. Spouses have an unlimited insurable interest in each other's lives, and children have such an interest to the extent that they have a pecuniary interest in the lives of their parents. Family relationships as such are insufficient. Employers, employees, partners, trustees and mortgagees have such an insurable interest depending upon the precise nature of the financial relationship between the parties.

In practice, the absence of an insurable interest need not be an insurmountable obstacle, and can often be overcome by the life assured taking out the policy, paying one or two initial premiums, and then assigning it to a beneficiary. Inheritance tax on the assignment on the basis of the premiums paid, should be within annual exemptions (see section **16.4:2**).

16.4:5   Term insurance policies

A term policy is one which insures the risk of death only within a stipulated period. After that, the policy expires and has no value. The cost of premiums for such a policy is modest by comparison with whole life and endowment policies.

Term policies have become particularly useful under inheritance tax, as there will be a need to protect against the possibility of a donor dying within seven years from the date of a gift. Since liability for inheritance tax on a potentially exempt transfer falls primarily on a donee, it is usual for the donee to protect himself against the potential liability by taking out a decreasing seven-year term insurance policy, under which the sum assured would be sufficient to pay the potential tax liability.

In addition, where a potentially exempt transfer fails because the donor dies within seven years, there will be increased inheritance tax liability on the residual estate passing on death. Here again, a seven-year term policy can provide funds in the hands of the executors or beneficiaries under a will to pay additional tax produced by the cumulation of the failed potentially exempt transfer.

Where a chargeable transfer has been made, a comparable term insurance policy can be useful to protect the donee against additional inheritance tax payable following the death of the donor within the statutory period.

16.4:6   School fees

School fee policies can be on an annual or single premium basis and are designed to mature at the age or ages when children's education bills become payable.

Parents setting up such a policy may pay the premiums without inheritance tax liability ever arising, on the grounds that the policy is destined to meet maintenance, education, etc costs which are not treated as transfers of value (IHTA 1984 s 11). Parents who have no liability to inheritance tax on the premiums should forgo their surrender rights, to avoid the proceeds on death becoming an asset of the estate. Grandparents have no need to do so.

16.4:7   Conclusion

It hardly needs to be added that this survey of different types of policies is not exhaustive, and much more sophisticated arrangements exist. The limitation is likely to be the capital cost at outset or the annual premium cost. When contemplating such schemes, the alternative of a pension financing arrangement should also be studied. Pension arrangements for company and other employees; purchased life annuities; personal pension plans for self-employed persons; all may carry with them income tax reliefs (TA 1988 Part XIV). In particular, capital sums paid on death before retirement under both company and self-employed pension schemes can be arranged to be paid free of inheritance tax, whilst the cost of providing the capital sum by annual premiums is fully deductible for income tax purposes.

In the end, both insurance and pensions represent forms of investment outside the family, and success or failure may depend on the skills of the life company's portfolio investment manager. The spread of investments into land, government securities, equities, etc comprised in that portfolio may serve as a counter balance to the particular risks of farming a particular farm. On the other hand, the withdrawal of cash to fund the policy or pension may starve the farm of working capital and increase farming risks. There is naturally no absolute answer and a reconciliation is required.

Chapter 17

Tax planning III: business development

17.1 ACQUISITIONS AND NEW ACTIVITIES

17.1:1 Introduction

At the time of writing, it is Government policy to encourge farmers to diversify out of agriculture, and to find land alternative uses other than the production of food stuffs sold into European surpluses. 'Alternative land use' covers a whole range of possible activities and investments, some of which bring in new tax regimes and therefore new tax problems. In order to understand the nature of these problems, the starting point is to recognise that the income tax statutes classify the tax base into rigid categories, according to the nature of the source from which the income is received. Each category has its own detailed treatment, as regards scope of charge; rate of charge; basis of assessment; person chargeable; and relief given (see section **2.1:4**).

In order to determine the tax rules applicable to any source of income, that source needs to be allocated to its correct category. Thus it follows that when a farmer changes the nature of his land use, for example from owner occupier to tenanted landowner, he is effectively selecting a different tax category which gives him a new tax treatment in many respects. What is true of income tax is true of other taxes: capital gains tax, etc. Because farming has attracted a range of important reliefs, giving up farming and switching to another activity is likely to be disadvantageous. The principal reliefs are: income averaging (see section **2.5**); agricultural buildings allowances (see section **5.2:4**); agricultural property relief (see section **8.5**); zero-rating for value added tax (see section **9**); exemption of woodlands (see section **13**) (see check lists sections **17.1:2** and **17.1:3**).

There is another applicable discrimination to be noted. The two activities: farming under Case I of Schedule D; and rents receivable under Schedule A have already been distinguished in chapters 3 and 4. The differences of treatment have already been noted. To recapitulate: a farmer ceasing to be an owner-occupier and transferring his livelihood under Schedule A may be giving up:

(a) more generous deductions for trading expenses;
(b) the preceding year basis on which his assessments are calculated hence tax payment deferral;
(c) better systems of allowances for capital expenditure;
(d) relief for farm losses;
(e) deductibility of interest payable;
(f) special reliefs for capital gains tax; retirement reliefs; roll-over relief; and hold-over relief;
(g) special reliefs for inheritance tax; business property relief; interest-free instalment basis etc.

Activities other than food production may change the value added tax basis from zero-rate to standard-rating (see section **9**). Agriculture is derated and not subject to the unified business rate (see section **11.5**).

17.1:2   Check-list of special agricultural reliefs vulnerable to alternative land use

Relief	Nature of tax	Effect	Reference section
profit averaging	income tax	averages income fluctuations	2.5
excess maintenance expenditure	income tax	offsets landowning expenses	4.3:3
one estate election	income tax	offsets mansion house expenses	4.4:2
agricultural buildings and works	income tax	deduction for new buildings	5.2:5
hold-over relief	capital gains tax	defers tax (let land)	7.5:3
agricultural property relief	inheritance tax	deduction for agricultural land	8.5
zero-rating	value added tax	nil rate VAT	9.2:3
exemption	business rate	exoneration	11.5
exemption	woodlands taxation	exoneration	13.1:5

17.1:3   Check-list of business reliefs vulnerable to alternative land use

Relief	Nature of tax	Effect	Reference section
preceding year basis	income tax	delay in payment	2.1:5
capital allowances	income tax	deduction for capital expenditure	5.2
trading losses	income tax	offset of losses reducing tax on investment income	2.6
trading losses	capital gains tax	offset of losses	2.6:4
family partnerships	income tax	spreading income	6.1

Relief	Nature of tax	Effect	Reference section
deduction of loan interest	income tax	reduces cost of finance	**16.2**
roll-over relief	capital gains tax	defers tax	**7.4**
hold-over relief	capital gains tax	defers tax	**7.5**
retirement relief	capital gains tax	reduces tax	**7.6**
business property relief	inheritance tax	reduces tax	**8.3**
interest free instalment payments of tax	inheritance tax	defers tax	**19.4:3**

17.1:4 Secondary effects

There are less obvious secondary effects to be considered. When a tax payer changes from farming to some other category of activity, eg carrying on a bed and breakfast business, letting land to a caravan park, or to a rural crafts workshop, he may lose reliefs enumerated. He may well secure equivalent reliefs which are valuable. These new reliefs may not come to life until after a period of time in the new activity has elapsed, because many tax reliefs demand a qualifying period of time.

For example, agricultural property relief for owner occupiers requires the property transferred to have been occupied for the purposes of agriculture throughout the period of two years ending with the date of transfer (see example below).

The interaction of agricultural property relief with the system of potentially exempt transfers can also create problems. A transferee must retain the farmland from date of transfer to date of death, using the land for agricultural purposes. If not, and the PET fails because of death within the seven-year period, agricultural property relief is lost.

> Example: loss of agricultural property relief
>
> Giles acquires Blackacre Farm in 1990 and he continues farming there as an owner-occupier until 1992. After completing two years' farming, Blackacre qualifies for agricultural property relief at the rate of 100%.
>
> In the same year, Giles gives up as an owner-occupier, and he grants a tenancy over Blackacre to Green. After ceasing to be an occupier he gives up agricultural property relief at 100%. Giles dies in 1996. He fails to qualify as an owner-occupier and he also fails to qualify for relief at 50% as an owner of tenanted land because he has not been an owner for the period of seven years before his death.

17.1:5 Property development

Although planning consent for residential development may be difficult to obtain, there is no doubt that in terms of the value involved, this would be the most substantial category of diversification, giving rise to the most substantial tax problems. The augmentation of value which is created by planning consent, representing the difference between agricultural value and development value, can raise massive problems despite the repeal of development land tax. There still remain four consequential forms of taxation: liability under Case 1 of Schedule D (see section **5.7:2**); liability as an artificial transaction in land (see section **5.7:3**); liability to capital gains tax (see section **7.1**); and liability to inheritance tax on lifetime gift or death. If a landowner becomes a 'developer' land previously held as a farm asset may be 'appropriated' to stock in trade. On this change of status, capital gains tax arises on a deemed disposal at market value (TCGA 1992 s 161). It is notorious that the impact of capital taxation can substantially destroy the value of a sale, and where this has been undertaken for refinancing purposes, that can be disastrous.

In most cases, the farmer will sell his land to a professional developer and this may be the bargain which needs to receive scrupulous attention. The timing and sequence of events will be critical in computing the tax liability, and the possibility of progressive and deferred sales should be considered. In the nature of things, developers are often only too ready to defer completion of transactions, and this readiness needs to be capitalised, not passively accepted. However, deferred consideration may fail to qualify for roll-over relief (see section **7.4** and for use of options **7.8**).

Sales of small parcels of land should be structured to take account of annual exemptions and deferment reliefs. Gifts amongst members of a family can sometimes increase the value of those exemptions, and may be useful in distributing the accretion of value amongst members of a younger, rather than an older, generation.

17.1:6   Business expansion and development

The expansion and development of a farming business itself may involve several different tax aspects, including some discussed in earlier chapters as follows:

Form of expansion and development	Tax factors	Textual reference: section
acquisition of additional plant or buildings	claims for capital allowances	5.2
acquisition of additional land or other assets	claims for capital gains tax roll-over relief	7.4
raising of additional finance	sales and lease-back	7.7
cost of borrowing to make acquisitions	deductibility of interest	16.2
use of corporate structures as aids in financing	exchange of income tax for corporation tax	15

This section approaches the question of farm development from a different standpoint: as to how new business acquisitions can be related to or integrated with long-term inheritance tax-planning and farming business succession programmes. One principle to be examined is that whenever new business activities are contemplated, the desirability of vesting ownership or part ownership in the hands of the younger generation should be contemplated at the same time. At the time of acquisition, what is being acquired will be at its lowest value. A new farm may be in a run-down or unworked state. During early years of ownership, accretion of value is likely to be most rapid, and it is desirable that this new value accrue to the younger generation, since if this occurs the effect is to pass value down the generations without a taxable transfer ever taking place.

This process may be emphasised and accelerated by various factors. First, the new business may be acquired with the aid of borrowing from the Agricultural Mortgage Corporation or from a farmer's own bankers. That borrowing will reduce the amount of cash needed to be given by father to son to serve as the son's share of cost of acquisition. As the borrowing is progressively paid off, the son's equity automatically increases in value, so maximising the value effectively transferred.

Consideration should always be given to establishing a new operation in the form of a limited company (see section **6.2**) separate and distinct from the partnership or company through which existing operations are conducted. It will be possible to allocate to the younger generation a controlling interest in a new company, whilst retaining a minority interest in the hands of the older generation. At the outset, the relationship between the majority and minority interests should fall to be established on a strictly arithmetical basis, but with the passage of time, the value of the majority stake should increase more rapidly than that of the minority stake.

Example

Suppose a second farm, Whiteacre, be acquired by the Black family owners of Blackacre, for £200,000 of which £120,000 be found by borrowing, leaving £80,000 to be found from existing resources. Then it would be possible for Black senior to give his son £45,000 in cash to acquire a 56% interest in Whiteacre. After the expiry of ten years and repayment of the borrowing, and excluding retained profits, that 56% interest would be worth at least £112,000.

In the event, the accretions of value will inevitably occur more rapidly, as the initial borrowing is repaid, and as interest costs are reduced. The process will be accelerated as the valuable contracts and connections of Blackacre are used to assist the development of Whiteacre but clearly there are limits to this principle.

When arranging the shareholdings of a new company, entitlements to agricultural property relief and business property relief need to be considered (see sections **8.3** and **8.5**).

17.1:7 Capital gains tax roll-over relief: new businesses

Where alternative land use involves the cessation of one business and the commencement of a new business, the question arises as to whether assets used in the new business, when sold, will qualify for roll-over relief. The test is that the asset disposed of must have been used throughout the period of ownership only for the purposes of 'a business'. However the rule is relaxed where a person carries on two businesses 'successively' and they are treated as one. Hence, relief is not lost where, for example, land was originally used for farming purposes but has become an asset of a new business after the cessation of the farming enterprise (TCGA 1992 s 152(8)).

It is important to note that if there is an interval between the cessation of one trade and the commencement of another, the two trades are treated as being carried on 'successively', providing the interval does not exceed three years (SP 8/81). If the disposal and acquisition take place during the intermediate period, relief is not lost, provided the asset is not used for any other purpose before the commencement of the new business, and is used for the new business after it has commenced (SP 8/81(2)). The time limits in this practice statement are subject to the overriding limit that the acquisition of the new asset must take place within the four-year period commencing one year before and ending three years after the disposal of the old asset.

17.1:8   Capital gains tax reliefs: retirement

Where alternative land use involves the cessation of one business and the commencement of a new business, the question arises as to whether disposal of the new business, or new business assets will qualify for retirement relief (see section **7.6**).

Maximum retirement relief is due where a tax payer has carried on a qualifying business for a period of ten years. Where the business has been carried on for less than ten years, a proportion of the full amount of relief is due, computed on a time apportionment basis.

For this purpose, it is not necessary that the business carried on throughout the ten-year period should be the same business as that carried on when the capital gains tax disposal takes place. Thus a change of business from, say, farming to, say, a caravan site ending in a disposal of the latter business on retirement would not affect the retirement relief due.

However, there would be a reduction of relief if there were a time gap between the two business periods. If that time gap were greater than two years, the earlier period in business would cease to qualify for relief, even though it fell within the ten-year period.

If the time gap between the two businesses were less than two years, the earlier business period would continue to qualify, but the intervening period would not qualify for relief and a proprotionate reduction in the maximum relief would fall to be made (FA 1985 Sch 20 para 14(5)).

On the change of land use, therefore, preservation of retirement relief requires that the interval of time between the two activities be reduced to a minimum. Accounting dates should be selected which demonstrate this fact, and so as to preserve continuity.

Where farming ceases, and all the other retirement relief tests are satisfied, there is nothing to prevent a claim for the relief merely because it is intended to use those assets not sold but retained in some alternative activity. In these circumstances there will be retirement relief on one disposal, and then a claim for relief on a subsequent disposal, when there may be relief restrictions having regard to the previous disposal (FA 1985 Sch 20 para 15). In such cases, the rules are extremely complex.

Another exceptional situation, is where there has been a change in the nature of the business, but the new business has not been carried on throughout the last year prior to the disposal in respect of which retirement relief is claimed. One of the important tests for relief is that the business disposed of must have been carried on for at least one year.

In satisfying this test, no credit is given for periods during which an earlier business was carried on. It follows that any alternative land use business should be carried on for at least a year before an ultimate disposal in order to qualify for retirement relief.

17.1:9   The set aside scheme: income tax

The set aside scheme was authorised by the European Communities Act 1972 and its object is to cut back UK agricultural production having regard to the

European Community surplus. Under the scheme, farmers are entitled to receive various categories of payments as compensation for ceasing to farm agricultural land. They are permitted to put the land to alternative use providing that this qualifies under the regulations (SI 1988/1352; SI 1989/1042; SI 1990/1716; SI 1991/1847; and SI 1991/1993). These regulations set out the requirements and restrictions of the scheme, conditions of eligibility, method of application etc. None of the regulations refer to the taxation of payments received.

The scheme is constructed on a voluntary basis. Those choosing to participate withdraw land from agricultural production, being at least 20% of the land used for growing certain relevant arable crops in the base year 1987–88. There are three basic categories of permitted use of the set aside land with certain sub-categories:

(a) permanent, rotational or grazed fallow;
(b) permitted non-agricultural use;
(c) woodland.

Each category attracts different rates of payment. The income tax treatment of the set aside receipts does not, however, depend upon the use to which the set aside land is put.

Set aside has been a voluntary scheme (SI 1988/1352). Those choosing to participate withdraw land from agricultural production, and either leave it fallow or convert it to woodlands, or to a non-agricultural use.

In general, a farmer who receives set aside payments while continuing to farm, will be assessable under Schedule D Case I in respect of those payments. He will be treated as continuing to farm, even if he sets aside the whole of his farming land to fallow so that, effectively, the set aside payments become his only income receipts. The reasoning is that in order to fulfill a condition under the set aside scheme that a farmer must 'keep set aside land in good agricultural condition', he would need to engage in such acts of husbandry as would provide evidence that his farming activity had continued. Set aside may thus depend on whether the land is maintained so as to permit it to be returned to agricultural use.

Where, however, a farming business ceases and a new non-agricultural trade commences, the question will arise as to whether the income from set aside will continue to be regarded as compensation for loss of agricultural earnings. In such circumstances, the treatment of the set aside payments will depend upon the facts of the particular case.

If the appropriate tests are satisfied, receipts may fall under Schedule A or Schedule D Case III. For this to be so, the first test is that the set aside payment be an annually recurring one. If the obligation is capable of exceeding and likely to exceed one year, the payments will be regarded as annually recurring.

The second test for income under Schedule D Case III is that it be pure income profit in the hands of the recipient. Case III may apply if an owner gives or sells land, but retains the right to the set aside payments.

It is understood the Inland Revenue view is that the giving up of the right to farm does not constitute the provisions of goods or services. However, the acts of husbandry which a farmer needs to undertake to maintain the land in good agricultural condition may be regarded as a provision of service. For the application of this test, reference needs to be made to *IRC v City of London Corpn (as Conservators of Epping Forest)* ((1953) 34 TC 293) and *Campbell v IRC* ((1968) 45 TC 427) which elucidate the meaning of 'pure income profit'.

Moreover, there is a third test: that the monies be received under a legal obligation. That implies an element of valuable consideration given before an agreement is enforceable. In the case of set aside, the giving up of rights of certain use of the land is considered to constitute valuable consideration for this purpose. If what were receivable could be regarded as a fixed maximum sum, divided into annual capital instalments, it would be incapable of falling within Schedule D Case III (see section **2.1:4**).

As regards set aside woodlands, it is understood the land concerned is treated in the same way as other woodlands; that is, no change in the basis of computation of liability is envisaged. (For the effect of set aside on inheritance tax see section **17.1:11**).

17.1:10   Set aside: capital gains tax

If land set aside is left fallow under the set aside scheme, roll-over relief (see section **7.4**) and retirement relief (see section **7.6**) will normally continue to be allowed against disposals.

If the land is put to some use other than trade or business use, for example is let to produce Sch A rental income, these reliefs will be lost. If, again, the farming business ceases and a new different activity commences on the land, there will be two sets of tests. The first test in that event is whether the new use of land amounts to use in a trade. If so the reliefs may be preserved, subject to more detailed continuity tests (see sections **17.1:7** and **17.1:8**).

17.1:11   Set aside scheme: inheritance tax

Set aside land is still regarded as 'farm land' for the purposes of agricultural property itself. It is merely that the part of the land has become fallow whilst the remainder of the land continues in production. If there are buildings upon the set aside land, they will continue to qualify for relief so long as they are still used in the farming business so that it can be said that their occupation is 'ancillary' to the occupation of land for the purposes of agriculture.

If, however, buildings are converted for some other use, it may be possible to regard them as having a retained agricultural value on which the relief is due; and a non-agricultural value, over and above the agricultural value.

This would allow the relief to be preserved in part during the operation of the set aside scheme.

17.1:12   Tax strategy

A farmer who contemplates giving up farming in whole or in part and in undertaking some activity which falls under the heading 'alternative land use' will need to bear in mind specific strategies.

(I)   THE NATURE OF THE NEW ACTIVITY

The farmer will first examine whether his activity can qualify as farming given the definition which exists (see section **2.2**). If he is merely switching to alternative crops of an experimental nature eg Evening Primrose; or alternative stocks such as deer breeding etc these activities will qualify as farming, so that he will retain the fiscal privileges already enumerated.

Second, if his activity amounts to a trade or business, according to the definition already described, he will retain the privileges attaching to businesses.

The most difficult step for him is to contemplate giving up all trade or business, and exchanging business profits for rental income. This would be so if he were renting out his land for country sports and pastimes, for a golf course, to an owner of a caravan site, or to occupiers of redundant buildings as rural craft workshops.

(2) THE TAXPAYER

He should ask himself whether it is correct for the existing taxpayer to carry on the new activity contemplated. He should analyse the consequences if the new activity were to be carried on by another member of his family; by a new partnership; or by a separate limited company. The facts of his existing farm operations will help determine the operating structure which he selects. He will need to analyse the consequences of segregating the new activity into the hands of a new separate taxpayer or retaining the new activity in the hands of the existing taxpayer, probably himself. This may depend upon the current and forecast future results of the existing farming business. If his farm is a profitable one so that he is a higher rate taxpayer, it will be advantageous to segregate the new business into a company or into the hands of members of his family paying a lower rate.

If on the other hand his farm is showing losses for tax purposes, it will be advantageous to create an operating structure whereby the profits or rent from the new activity can be aggregated with the farm losses.

(3) FINANCE

The farmer will wish to consider how his new activity is to be financed, as regards the payment of interest and the repayment of the capital debt. He will wish to arrange for his financing costs to be fully tax deductible.

(4) TIMING

It will be necessary for him to consider the correct sequence of transactions, for example as regards transfers of assets into the hands of different members of his family. It might be necessary for him to make the gifts as a first step in order to secure hold-over relief; and to set up the new enterprise thereafter. It may be desirable for the new activity to be established progressively for commercial reasons; so that assets need to be transferred to it progressively. The dates of cessation of one activity and commencement of a new activity may need to be selected.

(5) PRESENTATION

Whether an activity on a farm is or is not part of a farming business; and whether an activity is or is not farming are questions which may be of fact and degree. Where there are various categories of alternative land use, some eg alternative crops may qualify as part of an existing farming trade, if that trade is continuing on a substantial scale.

The form of the financial accounts and income tax returns submitted to HM Inspector may determine the treatment of alternative land use activities. If the accounts presented are in the same conventional form as previous accounts, a challenge is less likely. If the form of the accounts changes, the tax treatment may change also. Taxpayers have a statutory obligation to make a complete and correct return, but they also need to present the best case to the Revenue so as to preserve their deductions and reliefs.

(6) SCALE OF ACTIVITY

It is important to contemplate in advance what is to be the scale of the new activity and how that scale will relate to the scale of the farming business previously carried on.

If the scale of the new activity is very small, for example, the mere letting of a disused building for a modest annual rental, the rent and the relevant expenses will probably all be capable of being included in the annual farm accounts. They will not fall to be treated as a new and different source of income on *de minimis* principles.

If however the new activity is relatively big with an infrastructure: finance, management, marketing etc it may be substantial enough to qualify as a separate trade or business in its own right. For example, if farming is abandoned and the whole farm converted into a caravan site, the trade of caravan site owner will probably have been commenced. There is a third possibility. If the scale is intermediate it may fail on both the above accounts. The Revenue will seek to disentangle it from the farm accounts, but it will not amount to a trade or business but will be a source of property income under Schedule A; or miscellaneous profits and gains under Case VI of Schedule D. That may secure the worst of both worlds.

17.2   SPECIALISED ENTERPRISES

17.2:1   Stud farming

The activity of stud farming may or may not be a trade under Case I. Fees receivable for the services of a stallion have been repeatedly held to be chargeable under Case VI (*Malcolm v Lockhart* (1917) 7 TC 99). Similarly, monies received from the sale of nominations to a stallion in respect of shares held in a thoroughbred owning syndicate have also been held to fall under Case VI. (*Benson v Counsell* (1942) 24 TC 178). However, if the breeding of horses can be held to be part of the farming business, liability falls under Case I. (*Lord Glanely v Whightman* (1933) 17 TC 634). Stallions owned for breeding purposes are not deemed to be plant for the purpose of writing down allowances (*Earl of Derby v Aylmer*) (1915) 6 TC 665)).

As explained above, (see section **2.2**) the effect of liability under Case VI as opposed to Case I is generally disadvantageous.

17.2:2   Fish farming

The question arises as to whether fish farming: the breeding and sale of fish is within the meaning of 'farming' for taxation purposes. The answer appears to turn upon the meaning of 'husbandry' (see section **2.2** above). The Revenue view is that husbandry is a term which carries with it some relationship with land or dependance upon land. Thus, where fish farming is carried on in tanks, it is contended that that is not 'husbandry'. On the other hand, where fish are bred in natural lakes and rivers, they are within the definition quoted above. Seafishing is clearly not farming within the ordinary meaning of the word.

Treatment seems to vary from one tax district to another and farmers setting up for the first time may wish to present their accounts and computations to the

Inspector in a form which substantiates that their business qualifies for the various agricultural reliefs described in this book.

17.2:3 Commodity markets dealing

An arable producer may deal in the commodity markets by, for example, selling his crop before it is harvested for a fixed future price. This is an accepted technique of risk reduction. A more sophisticated mechanism is to trade in commodity options: such options give the right to buy or sell a specific quantity and quality of the selected commodity at a specific price on or before a specific future date.

Commodity markets trading for example in wheat, potato or other futures is treated as a part of a farming business, and any resulting profit or loss will be included in the farming profit or loss under Schedule D Case I.

The treatment of non-farmers, eg land owners, liable under Schedule A, is less certain. There are authorities determining that a purchase and sale of commodities can be a trade or an 'adventure in the nature of a trade', and one isolated transaction is sufficient for this purpose (*Wisdom v Chamberlain* ((1968) 45 TC 92)). Options, on the other hand, fall within the capital gains tax regime (TCGA 1992 s 144) (see section **7.8**).

17.3 EROSION OF FARMING INTERESTS

17.3:1 Introduction

The system of arranging for an older generation's interests to be progressively eroded in favour of a younger generation represents a structural change capable of being applied both to shares in partnerships and shares in companies.

17.3:2 Partnerships: transfer of shares

Where a partnership is involved, it is possible to invoke the principle of *A-G v Boden* [1912] 1 KB 539. A father who had taken his sons into partnership disposed of his own shares to his sons, the sons paying nothing for goodwill. The agreement secured that the sons should devote the whole of their time to the business, whereas the father should henceforth devote only such time as he thought fit. The benefit that accrued to the father was held to constitute consideration for the transfer of goodwill, and no estate duty was payable on the value of the goodwill on the father's death.

This mechanism is considered equally apt for inheritance tax, and when what passes is not goodwill as such, but shares in a farming partnership. However, a series of reservations need to be noted. First, it is open to consideration whether the whole transaction passes the test set out in IHTA 1984 s 10 (for a discussion of the principles involved, see section **8.1**). It may be arguable that on the specific terms of a revised deed, no intention to confer gratuitous benefit can be adduced. However, where a family relationship is involved, it would be necessary to contend that the arrangement was such as might be expected in an ordinary commercial transaction.

It has been suggested that the difficulty might be overcome by a 'Boden' scheme bring carried out in several stages, for example where a father first agrees to work full-time, and after a period, disposes of part of his interest and contracts to work such time as is necessary: then later disposes of a further part of his interest and contracts to work such time as he thinks fit. The relevant fractions of a working week or the number of working days could also be stated, but it is doubtful whether such stipulations would add commerciality, and indeed, they might reduce it.

As regards possible retention of benefit, see section **8.1:5**.

17.3:3   Limited company: deferred shares

Where it is desired to use the limited company framework, a similar effect can be achieved by the mechanism of ordinary deferred shares. Such shares rank equally with ordinary shares as to votes, and as to participation in the net surplus of the company in a winding up, but they carry no rights to dividends until the end of a stipulated period, usually five or ten years. The intention of quoted companies issuing such shares is usually to transform the otherwise anticipated dividend into a capital gain.

Absence of dividend rights must place deferred shares at a discount by comparison with ordinary shares, the discount becoming reduced as the date when entitlement to dividends approaches. The amount of the discount will vary with the length of the deferred period, and the profitability of the company.

The mechanism proposed may take a variety of forms, but one approach is to reorganise the capital of a company to create a bonus issue of deferred shares into the hands of existing shareholders. Then these shareholders (the older generation) give or sell the deferred shares to the younger generation, whose interest in the farming company progressively increases.

Again, reservations fall to be expressed. The most obvious danger flows from the associated operations rule in IHTA 1984 s 268, already referred to (see section **15.3:2**). The question arises as to whether the reorganisation of shares of a company is an 'operation'. One precaution would be for the deferred shares to be sold at an arm's length value rather than given away.

The strategy is particularly apt where the farm to be owned by the company is a newly acquired one. Then in the circumstances envisaged in the previous subsection, there will be a future accretion of value, as borrowings are repaid and the connections of an existing farm are used to develop the business of the newly acquired one. This process of value accretion can be emphasised by the use of deferred shares. Moreover, where the company has been incorporated with a class of deferred shares at the outset, the dangers might be reduced.

When creating shares with restricted rights, regard should be had to the question of whether business property relief is affected. This would apply, for example, to non-voting shares, which would forfeit that relief, and are therefore unlikely to be a useful mechanism.

17.4   CONTRACT FARMING

17.4:1   Introduction

The relationships amongst parties so far considered include that of partnership and landlord and tenant. It is arguable that the latter is a balanced and valid arrangement, the landlord contributing fixed capital at a low cost, the tenant working capital and skills. However, the enactment of succession laws giving special rights to tenants, and the denial of capital tax and other reliefs to landlords, have upset the balance and made landowners reluctant to re-let when land falls vacant. A partnership is not always an acceptable alternative. The element of unlimited liability is a deterrent. Unless the land is included in the partnership Balance Sheet, the business property relief is reduced from 100% to 50% (IHTA 1984 s 105), but this is probably less significant than the fact that partnership seems to imply a closer relationship than the parties require for their respective purposes.

In these circumstances, it is possible to enter into a farm contractorship agreement, the tax advantages of which need separate consideration. The general basis of such an agreement is usually that one party ('the owner') contracts with another ('the contractor') who undertakes to work the farm owned by the owner, in accordance with the owner's instructions and policies. In consideration, the contractor receives a flat management fee, and a commission based on the profitability of the enterprise.

It is possible to arrange to share out the profits of the enterprise in a variety of ways, but it is usual to reserve a slice of profits for the owner corresponding to the rent he would have received, had he let the farm in the ordinary way. It is desirable that the agreement operate for a limited period only, so that this rental equivalent can be reviewed in line with current market rents. On the other hand, it is important that the agreement be not construed as a tenancy agreement, and for this reason, it might be better not to stipulate three-year reviews, as creating an obvious analogy with three-year reviews of agricultural rents (in England and Wales).

In so far as the profits of the farm are to be divided between the owner and the contractor, it will be important to stipulate the basis on which those profits are to be calculated, when payments out are to be made, and how disputes between the parties are to be arbitrated.

It will also be important to draft the agreement to avoid its being construed either as a tenancy agreement; or as a partnership agreement; or as creating the relationship of employer and employee, all of which might create tax consequences other than those intended. It must also be added that the agreement must be drafted so that the owner does not inadvertently purport to transfer ownership of or an interest in farm property to the contractor. It is for consideration whether explicit disclaimers of these effects should be included in the text of an agreement. To do so might be to admit a drafting failure.

There are a number of supplementary advantages. First, where a farmer has sustained over a period trading losses on which he has been denied relief (see section **2.6:4**) a contractorship agreement producing a modest profit may be advantageous.

Normally, it will be the commercial advantages of a contractorship arrangement which are dominant. For example, where a tenanted farm has fallen vacant due to the death, retirement or other circumstances of the tenant and the landlord does not wish to farm the land himself because he lacks the capital to do so, but nonetheless wishes to retain vacant possession having in mind that one of his family may wish to pursue a farming career in the future.

In these circumstances the contractorship agreement will probably be for a relatively short period, but usually not less than three years.

17.4:2   Taxation consequences

(a) INCOME TAX

It should follow that both owner and contractor will be carrying on (separate) farming businesses under Schedule D Case I, and both will prepare accounts, and make income tax returns accordingly. The expressions 'management fee', 'commission share' and 'interest on capital' may be apt for the contractorship agreement, but it does not automatically follow that they should be used in the farm accounts, where they may be misleading designations. The danger of the contractor being treated as an employee so transforming his profit into Schedule E income with consequences under PAYE and National Insurance, is increased if he works solely under the Contractorship Agreement.

(b) CAPITAL GAINS TAX

If the landowner is treated as a farmer under Schedule D Case 1, he will become entitled to roll-over relief and retirement relief (see sections **7.4** and **7.6**).

(c) INHERITANCE TAX

If both owner and contractor are carrying on separate farming businesses, business property relief at the rate of 100% will be available on the business assets of both parties.

Agricultural property relief (see section **8.5**) should be due at the rate of 100%, as the owner should be regarded as farming the land. However, relief depends upon whether it can be said he has the right to vacant possession, which will in turn depend upon the construction of the share farming agreement.

Certain special problems may arise where the agreement between the parties is in the nature of a grazing rent (see section **5.1:2** above). The general effect of a licence under AHA 1986 s 2 is that the licensee does not enjoy any security of tenure. The owner's right to retain vacant possession ensures that the land is valued as vacant possession land with relief at the rate of 100%, and the two-year owner occupation test, rather than the seven-year test (see section **8.5**) is applied.

A problem has been known to arise where land is subject to seasonal grazing agreements. It has been suggested that in such cases the land is not *occupied* for the purposes of agriculture. This may be relevant in determining whether occupation has continued *throughout* the two or seven-year periods stipulated (IHTA 1984 s 118). Farming requires occupation of farm land (ICTA 1988 s 832). The word 'occupation' is not statutorily defined and the tests for occupation are uncertain. In particular, it is not determined whether there can be more than one occupier of particular land, and although there are a number of precedent cases, the general principle is undecided, and Revenue practice varies (see also section **5.1:2**).

(d) VALUE ADDED TAX

Suppliers should render separate invoices to each of the parties involved in share farming in respect of items purchased by them, so that each party can reclaim VAT through his own separate VAT account. If it is not possible to secure separate invoices addressed to the landowner and the operator, the invoice payer should submit a separate VAT invoice to the other party so as to secure reimbursement of the agreed share of the expense.

Suppliers should be dissuaded from issuing invoices in the joint names, since this is an undesirable indication of a partnership.

Each of the parties will be responsible for his own VAT return in the ordinary way.

17.4:3 Share farming

The distinguishing feature of 'share' farming is that the parties respectively providing the land, fixed equipment, machinery, labour and input costs, agree to share the gross output or product arising, ie share of the sale proceeds of whatever commodity eg milk, grain, meat, wool etc marketed, rather than the net output. The shares of gross output form the basis of a starting point of the separate accounts prepared for the separate independent businesses. The shares will be calculated in the proportions contributed, as determined by an annual budget.

In 1991, following a change in policy, the Revenue declined to accept that both the landowner and the operator could be treated as carrying on farming businesses under Schedule D Case 1. Apparently, this argument was based upon the proposition that there could only be one occupier of land receiving farm income save where the land was jointly occupied by persons each of whom enjoyed the same occupation rights, for example as in the case of joint tenants farming in partnership (see *Dawson v Counsell* (1938) 22 TC 149). This could have applied both to share and contract farming.

However, the Revenue has now abandoned this contention, and has accepted that *both* the owner and the operator can be regarded as carrying on a farming business provided the following conditions are satisfied:

(a) The agreement between the parties is in fact operated in accordance with its terms.

(b) The landowner takes an active part in the share farming business at least to the extent of concerning himself in the details of farming policy, and exercising his right to enter on to the land for some material purposes, even if only for the purpose of inspection and policy making.

In addition, it is strongly recommended that:

(c) There should be separate bank accounts for landowner and operator, with no right of access by each party to the other party's accounts.

(d) Separate financial accounts should, of course, be prepared, in a form which would demonstrate that the parties are carrying on their businesses in accordance with the terms of the share farming agreement.

(e) That agreement should, by its terms and conditions, illustrate the contributions of expertise, working capital and the assumption of risk by the landowner.

If the agreement merely stipulates a guaranteed return for the owner against his contributions of land and buildings that will not point to a trading activity.

The landowner whose farm is operated under a share farming agreement may have difficulty in establishing a Case I trade, particularly if his share farming is not part of a larger farming operation carried on elsewhere. Much depends upon whether his functions as a share farmer extend beyond the functions of a landlord. The contributions of expertise, working capital and the assumption of risk point to a trading activity. Contributions of land and buildings against a guaranteed annual return do not.

The inheritance tax reliefs will be subject to corresponding tests.

17.4:4   Share farming and the herd basis

The herd basis treats animals kept for production or reproduction as if plant or machinery. The advantages and the effects of the herd basis are described in section **3.2** above.

However, additional problems arise where a herd is owned in connection with a share farming agreement. At the outset, it is necessary to distinguish between the situation in which:

(a) the herd is owned by one party in a share farming agreement; and
(b) where the herd is jointly owned.

Where the animals are not jointly owned, each party to the agreement can make an election for the herd basis to apply to his animals, if he is eligible to do so. Entry into the share farming agreement does not in itself provide an occasion permitting an election to be made (see section **3.2:3**).

Where the animals are owned in undivided shares, both parties can jointly elect for the herd basis to apply, but both parties must be eligible to make an election. Again, entering into the agreement will not in itself provide the opportunity to make an election. Where there is an existing herd basis election by either party to a share farming agreement, and that party transfers a herd into undivided ownership, the Revenue view is that a trading receipt arises and the exemptions in TA 1988 Sch 5 para 3 are not applicable. That view rests on the construction of para 3(8) which requires either the sale of the whole of the herd or the sale of part of the herd 'on a substantial reduction being made on a number of animals in the herd'.

Whilst the Revenue's view is that the receipt from the sale of the 'share' is a trading receipt, there is allowable as a deduction against that receipt any part of the cost of that share not previously allowed.

It follows that the two sub-systems, the herd basis and the share farming basis, do not fit together well, and great care is needed to avoid weakening or destroying the advantages of the herd basis when entering into a share farming agreement.

17.4:5   Conclusion

Agreements in the form described are now being quite widely used. Where a farm is tenanted, it is difficult to see how such an agreement could be substituted for the landlord and tenant agreement in force. Thus utilisation of contract farming agreements may tend to be confined to cases where an owner has vacant possession, would in the normal course install a farm manager, but sees a contractorship agreement as giving more incentive to the individual concerned, and therefore likely to be better for all parties in the long-term.

They have become more popular during a period when farming capital is more scarce, as a method of dividing the financing of a farm between two parties, whilst avoiding a partnership relationship.

17.5   ESTATE MANAGEMENT COMPANIES

17.5:1   Introduction

So far long-term tax planning techniques have applied mostly to land with vacant possession. One important tax planning technique available to the estate owner is to create a private estate management company in his own or family ownership to undertake the function of estate management, which would otherwise have been performed by the owner himself. The share capitalisation of such a company can be very small, since it will not have any assets transferred to it.

17.5:2 Structure

The effect sought is as follows: the income of the company will be comprised of a management fee payable to it by the estate owner, under an agreement for the company's management services. That fee may constitute the company's only income. It will render those services via the agency of the individual owner or other members of his family, who will become directors or employees of the company. It is not envisaged that they will be 'full-time' employees, but they must render some services.

They will be remunerated by fees or salary, the amounts of which will be deductible in computing the corporation tax profit of the company. Such salary will of course, be assessable as such upon the recipients. The general effect will be to convert the rents into salary. This was particularly valuable when rents were subject to the investment income surcharge at 15%, abolished in FA 1984. The expenses of the company will be limited to such small items as audit fees, so that on the face of it, this may appear to represent a very attractive strategy.

17.5:3 Amount chargeable for remuneration

There are however limitations. The important question is as to what amount can reasonably be charged for remuneration without invoking a challenge from the Revenue. That the Inspector is entitled to question the true nature of the remuneration emerges from *L G Berry Investments Ltd v Attwooll* (1964) 41 TC 547 which determined that the amount is limited to that payable upon a reasonable commercial basis as between unconnected parties. What is reasonable is a question of fact in any case.

One useful guide will be amounts charged by professional surveyors or land agents for management services including rent collection. Such a fee would normally cover: collection of rents; supervision of tenants; making estate payments; keeping necessary estate cash accounts; specifying and supervising all necessary running repairs and maintenance by estate workers or outside contractors; ordinary management of estate woodlands; estate income tax; rates; maintenance of ordnance maps etc. For all these services a fee equal to 10% of the rent roll might be expected.

The following are amongst the services not normally covered by such a fee: valuations (including dilapidations and tenants' rights); new lettings and rent reviews; sales and purchases of properties; preparation and supervision of woodland plans and accounts and sale of felled timber and underwood; new and additional building works; improvements and other architectural services; general control and accounts of home farm and/or market gardens; surveys, plans, attendance at valuation and other courts, tribunals, inquiries or arbitrations. All these services may be regarded as justifying additional fees.

17.5:4 Other factors

There are a number of other factors to be borne in mind when deciding whether an estate management company is justified (including VAT payable on fees).

First, profit which is not drawn out as directors' emoluments will fall to be taxed at the company's corporation tax rate, which may be more or less than the rate at which the same income would have been taxed in the hands of an individual recipient.

Again, the mechanism of a company may offer some flexibility in the general arrangement of affairs. If the estate owner's wife assists in the management of the estate, it will be reasonable for her to become a director and receive part of the company's income as remuneration. Thus advantage could be taken of the wife's independent taxation provisions.

In suitable cases, the earned income so created could form the basis of utilisation of the retirement annuity relief, by taking out a personal pension plan with an insurance company. Within the prescribed limits the premiums would be deductible in computing profits (see section **16.4:7**). A company can sometimes usefully own a motor car or other plant or equipment. Finally, since rents tend to increase over the years, this in turn justifies an ascending scale of remuneration.

For large companies, for example, those undertaking estate contribution and repair work in addition to management, the effects of a company upon capital gains tax and other taxes may need consideration. It will have been noted that there is no requirement to transfer the estate itself to the company, so as to create an estate owning company. That is not usually attractive, because of the locked-in effect created, and the entry price payable.

17.5:5   Taxation consequences of estate owning companies

An estate management company will not normally own substantial assets. One which manages an estate which it owns is a very different proposition. From the standpoint of income or profit taxation, the effect could be to limit liability on the estate rent-roll to the small companies' rate of corporation tax, at the present time 25%, which might seem advantageous. There would be greater scope for payment of directors' and employees' salaries and fees and expenses along the lines suggested for a management company, and without so stringent a set of limitations applicable.

(A) INHERITANCE TAX

From the inheritance tax standpoint, some reduction in value created by the act of incorporation would be secured (see section **15.6**). As for business property relief, the position is at least arguable. Business includes a profession or vocation, but excludes a business carried on otherwise for gain, or a business which consists of property dealing, or the making or holding of investments. There is little doubt that the Revenue would take the view that estate ownership is excluded as the 'holding of an investment', and it would be for the taxpayer to contend that there was a sufficient degree of active management and control to escape from the exclusion. The point is a tenuous one.

(B) CAPITAL GAINS TAX

A similar problem arises for capital gains tax. When property is transferred to a company by the estate owner this would normally be a disposal at current market value giving rise to a gain.

The question is whether the roll-over relief provisions (TCGA 1992 s 162(1)) could be invoked. The capital gain is deferred where a person who is not a company transfers to a company a business as a going concern, together with the whole assets of the business, or together with the whole of the assets other than cash, wholly or partly in exchange for shares issued to the transferor by the company. There seems to be no reason why an agricultural estate should not qualify as a business for this purpose, so that it is at least possible for an estate owner to incorporate himself without paying capital gains tax as an entry price. Other capital gains tax factors involved in the use of companies are described in detail in section **15.6**. However, a major deterrent is usually described as 'two-tier' capital gains tax which refers to ultimate potential double liability: first, when the company disposes of its assets; and secondly, when the shareholders dispose of their shares in the company. Where it is contemplated that an estate will continue to be owned by a family down the succeeding generations, less weight may be attached to this deterrent, although the possibility of a forced or unexpected sale at some time in the future cannot be wholly disregarded. Indexation of capital gains tax is a factor, in turn mitigating this deterrent.

17.6 RESIDENCE AND OTHER INTERNATIONAL FACTORS

17.6:1 Introduction

The tax systems described in this book are those applicable to persons 'resident', 'domiciled', and 'carrying on a trade' in this country. Each of those expressions has a technical meaning. It is beyond the scope of the book to examine those meanings in detail, and to expound the general incidence of UK taxation upon persons resident and domiciled and carrying on a trade abroad. However, there are four aspects particularly relevant to farming and landownership, which cannot be omitted:

(a) Emigration has become an established routine, adopted by refugees from the UK tax system, and the effect of going to live permanently abroad but retaining agricultural land and interests in this country needs examination.

(b) Many of those farming in this country have at some time contemplated the challenge of farming abroad instead or in addition.

(c) Over the past decade, overseas buyers have come to own a proportion of farmland in Great Britain. Estimates vary, but Northfield suggested 1% of the total area was so owned (200,000–300,000 hectares – say half to three-quarters of a million acres) (Report of the Committee of Inquiry into the Acquisition and Occupancy of Agricultural Land 1979, Cmnd 7599 para 410). Foreigners buy farmland for sporting or investment purposes, and find it relatively cheap by comparison with prices elsewhere. Northfield did not think it necessary to recommend restricting overseas purchasers, but thought the situation needed 'close monitoring' (Cmnd 7599 para 34). The UK taxation of foreigners includes special features.

(d) There is the contentious practice of seeking to avoid UK taxation by transferring the ownership of assets abroad. Transfers to foreign companies and trusts are also made to avoid a possible reintroduction of a system of exchange control in the UK. The question arises as to whether these advantages are capable of being secured in the case of agricultural land, farming businesses or interests.

17.6:2   Emigration

The Taxes Acts have clear territorial limits (for a summary of the law and practice on residence (see *Simon's Taxes* Division E5): to be liable to income taxation the person to be taxed must either be resident in the UK; or the source of his taxable income must be located here. Emigration usually implies becoming a non-resident. The word 'residence' is not defined in the statute: there is no single overriding test, and the question is one of fact. The Revenue has its own code of practice, which takes account of a variety of relevant factors; past history and way of life; physical presence during a year of assessment; whether a home is maintained here; purpose of absence and of visits back; number and extent of visits. The rules are complex, but, briefly, absence must include a full tax year, and visits must not exceed a quarter of the year, if non-residence is to be secured.

Emigration may also imply abandonment of UK ordinary residence, and of domicile. Ordinary residence means habitual residence, taking one year with another. Domicile has a more permanent status than residence, and it may be said that an individual is domiciled in the country where he has his permanent home and intends to remain. An individual can have only one domicile at a time, and there is a presumption of law against a change of domicile. Domicile is relevant for inheritance tax. Again, either UK domicile, or transfer of assets physically situated in England is sufficient to establish liability.

We are now in a position to examine the effect of emigration upon a farmer or landowner. Although he may become non-resident, he will remain liable to income tax on the profits of his farm in this country; or the income from his estate here. That is because he will be carrying on a trade here, or the source of his income is located here. In order to escape UK income tax, he will be obliged to dispose of his farming interests here and commence farming abroad. If such sales are in contemplation, they should be deferred until after emigration, since an individual who is neither resident for a year, nor ordinarily resident is not liable to capital gains tax. To secure exemption the individual must also not be carrying on a trade through a branch or agency here, so no such exemption will be available to a farmer, as opposed to an estate owner.

Similarly, an emigrant who acquires foreign domicile will remain liable to inheritance tax on assets situated in this country (property situated outside the UK, if transferred by an individual domiciled outside the UK, is excluded property, ie not liable to inheritance tax, IHTA 1984 s 6(1)).

17.6:3   Farming abroad

An individual resident in the UK who acquires a farm abroad, and farms it alone or in partnership with others is liable to income tax under Schedule D Case V on the income from a foreign possession (TA 1988 s 18(3)). Rents receivable from land abroad are taxed on a similar basis. The computation will follow Case I principles (TA 1988 ss 65–67), but it should be borne in mind that liability will arise to taxation in the country where the farm or land is situated. Double taxation relief may be claimed to secure relief for the foreign tax against the UK tax (see generally *Simon's Taxes* Vol F).

Those contemplating farming abroad should consider incorporating an overseas company as a vehicle for ownership and trading. Another alternative is an overseas partnership, that is a partnership managed and controlled abroad. If the company is non-resident, because its day-to-day management and control are situated abroad, and its trading is wholly abroad, its profits will not be liable to UK tax. Nor will any relief be due against UK tax for any losses which it may sustain. Clearly, careful planning will be needed to take into account the anticipated trading results, financing costs and other factors in combination.

The sequence of events may need to be carefully planned, since a saving of UK taxation may be critical in securing adequate financial resources to sustain an overseas venture.

The fact that farming is carried on overseas, or that overseas land is owned will not reduce inheritance tax nor capital gains tax. Roll-over relief is not lost if a farmer sells a farm in the UK, and uses the sale proceeds to buy a farm abroad. Care is needed to ensure the identity of the ownership structure. For example, if the UK farm were farmed by an individual, and the overseas farm by his company, roll-over relief would be lost. However, agricultural property relief is not due on the value of agricultural property overseas (IHTA 1984 s 115(4)).

Business property relief is not affected, even though the business assets transferred be situated abroad.

An individual who personally carries on a business in another country exposes himself and his estate to the capital taxes of that country. On his death his estate may be liable to local death, succession or gift taxation, and this should be avoided, where practicable, by incorporating a company as a vehicle to carry on the business. It may be desirable for this company not to be a UK company, nor one resident in the territory where the farm is located, but in a third, low tax, territory. Specialist advice on such structures is obviously required.

17.6:4 Overseas buyers

The expression 'overseas buyers' is generally used to mean individuals resident and domiciled overseas acquiring agricultural land and commencing to farm in the UK. The taxation effects follow the principles already described in section **17.6:2**.

(A) INCOME TAX AND CORPORATION TAX

Liability arises on profits of trade carried on in the UK; or on rents or other income from real property situated in the UK. A tenant paying rent to a person whose place of abode is outside the UK, must deduct income tax from the rent, and pay the tax deducted to the Revenue (TA 1988 s 43(1)).

(B) CAPITAL GAINS TAX

Liability arises on the assets of a trade carried on through a branch or agency in the UK (TCGA 1992 s 10). No liability arises on other assets, providing the owner is not resident or ordinarily resident.

(C) INHERITANCE TAX

Liability arises on land or other assets situated in the UK, but there is no liability on overseas assets. Property situated outside the UK, if transferred by an individual domiciled outside the UK, is excluded property, ie not liable to inheritance tax (IHTA 1984 s 6(1)). All these liabilities may be affected by the incidence of overseas taxation and the grant of double taxation relief in the overseas buyer's country of residence. If the overseas buyer comes permanently to live and personally farm in the UK, then his tax treatment will not differ from that of any other UK resident individual, who may never have set foot overseas. If he comes intermittently to this country, his visits must on average be limited to one quarter of the year, since otherwise, he will fall to be classified as 'resident'. Mere foreign nationality has, in itself, no effect on taxation liabilities.

Most overseas buyers tend to accept the liability to income taxation but seek to avoid liability to capital taxation by incorporating an offshore company to own the farming business and carry on the trade in the UK. Then the death of the shareholder will not in itself create a transfer of any UK assets. Nor would the sale of shares in that company create liability to UK capital gains tax. The tax planning arrangements of overseas buyers naturally tend to be determined by taxation and currency laws of their own countries.

17.6:5   UK tax avoidance

It is open to any UK resident to carry on a trade or business in the UK through the medium of an offshore or tax-haven company, situated, most obviously, in Jersey, Channel Islands, Switzerland etc. A non-resident company which is trading in the UK would remain liable to UK taxation, irrespective of its residence, so no avoidance would be achieved.

Where such a company is not trading in the UK, the position is more complex. There are elaborate provisions for preventing avoidance of income tax by transactions resulting in the transfer of income to persons abroad (TA 1988 s 739, see *Simon's Taxes* E1. 751–766). Where assets are transferred, so that income becomes payable to a non-resident person (eg a company) and an ordinarily resident individual has 'power to enjoy' then the income of the non-resident person is deemed the income of the resident individual. There are corresponding provisions for capital gains tax (see TCGA 1992 ss 13–14, FA 1981 s 80 and FA 1991).

Chapter 18

Tax planning IV: death

18.1 WILLS AND INTESTACIES

18.1:1 Introduction

This chapter sets out principal planning guidelines, but does not offer comprehensive advice on the making of wills generally, nor on all the taxation aspects, for which the reader is referred to a more general work. The aspects selected for detailed consideration are those which are relevant to the estates of farmers and landowners. The making of a will involves a variety of problems, economic, legal, actuarial and practical, and any will represents a forecast of future events and values. It may be helpful to catalogue difficulties, admittedly easier to enumerate than to solve.

18.1:2 Problems of making a will

(A) ECONOMIC

A will operates as from date of death. The process of inflation and changing land values have made it imperative for all wills to be regularly reviewed, since otherwise an intention may be frustrated by changes in the value of currency. For example, a pecuniary legacy of £20,000, which at the date of will seemed ample to safeguard an individual's future, may prove pitifully inadequate at date of death.

(B) LEGAL

It is important to make a will, since otherwise property devolves under the law of intestacy. That law changes from time to time, but the intestacy rules may produce a pattern of devolution very different from that which an owner would have wished; one which effectively disregards the responsibilities he implicitly accepted when he inherited the property; and one which is grossly disadvantageous from the tax standpoint. It is therefore extremely important that all farmers and landowners should make wills, and keep them under regular review.

(C) ACTUARIAL

At risk of stating the obvious, it must be added that dates of death cannot be predicted, and that the sequence of deaths in a family is equally unknown. For tax purposes, it is often necessary to make assumptions as to which death will come first, and for this purpose age and health are obvious factors to take into account.

(D) PRACTICAL AND FAMILY PROBLEMS

Farmers naturally wish to leave their land to those members of a family who have manifested a desire to live on it and work the estate. However, at the time a will is made, children may still be too young for their inclinations and aptitudes to have manifested themselves. In such circumstances a trust may be helpful and trustees can be given discretionary powers, helpful in preserving the continuity of a family farm or estate. A settlor can also give his trustee an informal 'letter of wishes', offering guidance on future distribution of family assets, and relating those assets to management responsibilities. Such letters of wishes are not binding, but are persuasive.

A separate but related difficulty may arise from the relatively large capital values involved in a landed estate, where there is but modest income available for upkeep. A testator may recognise he is bequeathing a successor a massive problem, and that he must ensure that capital is not isolated from income needed for maintenance and upkeep. This may require a particular allocation amongst individuals, one not altogether in line with other aspirations, for example to leave cash to daughters and land to sons, or to leave income to a widow during her lifetime, or to leave specific legacies to deserving beneficiaries.

The advantages of 'generation-skipping' should be borne in mind. Where the immediately succeeding generation is already well endowed, it can become apparent that further gifts to that generation will create a massive inheritance tax liability when the estate passes from the hands of that generation to the grandchildren. In these circumstances, it may be helpful to select as heirs members of the grandchildren generation, so effectively passing the estate down the line with maximum saving. There are limits to the application of this principle, and much depends upon the ages of the parties. The application will be most justified where the generation to be skipped is already middle-aged, and the succeeding generation is adult and the career patterns are emerging.

Health and life expectation are factors which should also be taken into account. Gifts to grandchildren can be made in trust, where the grandchildren are minors, and the advantages of accumulation and maintenance trusts as set out in section **15.7:7** should be studied. A relatively modest share in a farm partnership or company can be usefully gifted by will, particularly where the grandchild is already participating in the farming business as an employee.

18.2 TAXATION CONSEQUENCES

18.2:1 Introduction

Once the existence of these practical problems and others has been recognised, it will be apparent that any will involves compromises between competing pressures. When tax considerations are taken into account additional pressure is added. The tax factors can again conveniently be catalogued as a series of problems to be solved.

18.2:2 Interspouse exemptions

Gifts from one spouse to another are exempt from tax, providing they are living together and both are domiciled in the UK (IHTA 1984 s 18: inheritance tax; TCGA 1992 s 58: capital gains tax). On a superficial view, it seems to follow that both spouses should make wills leaving the entire estate to the other, so deferring all tax until the second of two deaths. However, the rule thus baldly stated can never be correct, for it overlooks the fact that each testator has a first slice exemption. If each spouse's estate is aggregated in the hands of a surviving spouse after the first death, then only one will be utilised. However, there are factors which seem to make testamentary gifts advantageous. For example, one major advantage of a death-time transfer is that the capital gains tax base henceforth will be uplifted to the market value at the date of death, so that future saving is achieved without any 'tax-price' being payable (see section **18.2:7**).

All these factors need to be balanced out but so far as first slice exemption is in issue, the correct planning formula is to ensure that on the first death value passes down the generations, in an amount sufficient to consume it.

It follows that to take advantage of the first exempt slice, some measure of estate equalisation between spouses should have occurred during lifetime. If it has not, and if the poorer spouse dies first, the first exempt slice utilisation may be lost.

18.2:3   Legacies

Where there are included in a will specific legacies and a residuary estate, the question arises as to who bears the tax paid by the personal representatives. Should it be deducted from the specific legacies or should it be borne by the beneficiary of the residuary estate?

The statutory rules are that personal or movable property situated in the UK, eg leaseholds, stocks and shares, tenant's capital, are given free of tax. That is, the tax on legacies of this class of property is borne by the residual estate (see Administration of Estates Act 1925 Sch 1).

Land, wherever situated, and personal property situated overseas, are given subject to tax, but all these principles are subject to contrary provision being explicitly made in the terms of the will. However, specific gifts which do not bear their own tax may fall to be grossed up to arrive at their value.

These principles must be borne in mind in drafting the will, since a testator has a choice as to the class of gift which he gives: either (a) a specific legacy bearing its own tax; or (b) a specific legacy free of tax (tax borne by residuary estate); or (c) share of residue. There is certainly some sense of satisfaction to be derived from knowing a beneficiary has received a gift unencumbered, but the grossing up procedure can be complex, particularly where some legacies are tax-free, and some are subject to tax, and particularly where the residue goes not to an exempt spouse but to a non-exempt recipient. It is better to avoid mixing these two classes of legacies, since this produces complex calculations.

Where a legacy is made subject to tax, it may not be possible to ascertain the amount of tax until a late stage in the administration of the estate, and actual payment of the legacy may be accordingly delayed.

18.2:4   Trusts

Reference should be made to section **15.7** for a summary of the advantages and disadvantages of trusts generally. At one time, it was common practice for wills to include secret or implied trusts, eg 'to X to distribute amongst my family in accordance with a letter of wishes which I have handed to him'. Whilst this may be satisfactory for relatively small legacies to children and individuals other than direct heirs, it is of doubtful value under inheritance tax, since it can create a double charge, once on the death and once on the distribution out of the trust so created, after the expiry of two years from the date of death (IHTA 1984 s 143).

18.2:5   Annuities

It is generally undesirable to charge an estate with the payment of an annuity, and better to make a gift of a sum with which an annuity can be purchased.

18.2:6 Wills and business and agricultural property reliefs

The new rates of business and agricultural property reliefs enacted in F(2)A 1992 have significantly changed the strategy to be adopted in framing wills of qualifying property.

It has already been noted that property qualifying for 100% relief is likely to be retained by a testator until death, so as to preserve the capital gains tax uplift to market value occurring then (TCGA 1992 s 62). It is envisaged that on death, many estates will consist of qualifying property and non-qualifying property, the general objective being that both categories should devolve to surviving spouse and direct descendants so far as possible unscathed by tax. The terms of the will will be drafted so as to avoid double relief, ie any overlap between the 100% relief for qualifying business or agricultural property, other reliefs or exemptions, eg gifts from one spouse to another and each spouse's first slice exemption from inheritance tax.

Timely transfers between spouses may be necessary. For example, if one spouse's estate were to consist wholly of 100% relieved business or agricultural property, the ability to transfer to the next generation £150,000 worth of non-qualifying property will have been lost. Similarly, if all qualifying property is bequeathed in a will to the surviving spouse, the opportunity of passing property down the generations without liability to inheritance tax will have been lost.

Example 1

		£
GILES ESTATE	Blackacre Farm	£1,000,000
MRS GILES ESTATE	1 Acacia Ave (non-agriculture property)	£250,000
	Portfolio of shares	£150,000
	Total	£400,000

INHERITANCE TAX

IHT on Giles' death	nil
IHT on death of Mrs Giles	£400,000
less first slice exemption	£150,000 −
	£250,000 @ 40%
IHT =	£100,000

Example 2

GILES ESTATE	Blackacre Farm	£1,000,000
	Portfolio of shares	150,000
		£1,150,000
MRS GILES ESTATE	1 Acacia Ave	£250,000

INHERITANCE TAX

IHT on Giles' death (100% BPR & first slice exemption)	nil
IHT on death of Mrs Giles	£250,000
less first slice exemption	£150,000 −
	£100,000 @ 40%
IHT =	£40,000

18.2:7   Capital gains tax planning

The need to reduce inheritance tax liability in a farming family creates pressure
to transfer assets down the generations during a lifetime. For capital gains tax
purposes, however, it is arguable that one of the most effective forms of planning
is for an older generation to remain possessed of assets pregnant with chargeable
capital gain until death, and to transfer them by Will.

This is because there is no capital gains tax on death and because beneficiaries
take assets at market value as at the date of death. Thus it is correct to regard
death as a tax free event occasioning a valuable uplift in the future value of assets
for capital gains tax purposes. It can be said: death 'washes' assets 'clean' of
accrued gains. Clearly these two strategies are in conflict.

The choice between paying capital gains tax on a lifetime gift; or inheritance
tax on death is not always a simple one particularly if it is impossible to hold over
tax on a gift (see section **7.5**). The lost opportunity to uplift value on death will
not necessarily increase liability to tax at any time, if assets are to be retained long
term in a farming family. That is, if no sales are in prospect. Thus if hold-over
relief *is* available lifetime gifts may be the preferable strategy.

Another situation needs to be envisaged: where a gift is a potentially exempt
transfer, and the donor dies within the seven-year period (see section **8.1:3**) the
result may be doubly disadvantageous. The property comprised in the inter vivos
gift will become chargeable to inheritance tax, but the effect of the lifetime gift will
be to forfeit the value uplift for capital gains tax purposes.

It is impossible to lay down precise rules designed to avoid this disadvantageous result. Clearly, much depends upon the age and health of the prospective
donor, and the contingency of death within the seven-year period is one against
which it may be possible economically to insure.

Where assets are showing, not a gain but an accrued loss for capital gains tax
purposes, so that at the date of death, the probate value is likely to be lower than
historic cost, the above considerations do not apply.

18.2:8   A planning exercise

The writing of a will should be combined with a detailed planning exercise
designed to demonstrate the burden of tax on death, and how that tax is to be
funded (see Appendix IV).

18.3   DEEDS OF FAMILY ARRANGEMENT

If no will is made, or a will is written in a form which fails to conform with the
principles set out in section **18.1**, the damage done can be repaired by making use
of a very valuable relief designed to permit redistribution of a deceased's estate
(IHTA 1984 s 144), described as 'alteration of dispositions taking effect on
death.' If, within two years of the date of death, the beneficiaries entitled under
the will or intestacy so agree in a formal document, the estate or part of it can be
redistributed. The effect of redistribution is twofold:

(a) the redistribution itself is not treated as a chargeable transfer; and
(b) the tax chargeable on the death is recalculated as if the estate had been
    distributed under the will or intestacy in the form adopted by the
    redistribution.

A wide range of circumstances can be covered, making the relief serve as a form of post-mortem tax planning. Most obviously, on the death of a grandparent, a son can renounce his inheritance in favour of the grandchildren, so effectively skipping a generation, where this has not been provided by the will.

Gifts can be switched from a widow to children so utilising exempt slice as described under the appropriate headings in section **18.1**.

A similar effect can be secured by a disclaimer of interest in settled property, if not made for consideration.

Again, similar relief is accorded to distributions by the trustees of a discretionary will trust, within two years of the date of death. There must be no interest in possession in the trust property. This form of relief will help an estate owner to create a flexible set of dispositions, if he is minded to do so. He can leave his estate to trustees, giving them directions that they should have regard to the requirements of his widow, but leaving to them decisions as to how much should go to her, and how much to the children. This permits the personal circumstances of the parties, which could not be known at the time of making a will, to be taken into account. Similarly, the division of an estate amongst members of a family can be achieved in the knowledge of then current tax reliefs and exemptions, and individual requirements and capacities, rather than those operative at the time of making a will. Other advantages of a discretionary will trust are that the trustees will have the power to distribute without a court order, where there are minor or unascertained beneficiaries; or without the consent of uncooperative or untraceable adult beneficiaries. There is also freedom from liability to stamp duty.

It is important to recognise that so long as the discretionary trust is brought to an end within two years from the date of death, distributions of the property by the trustees are treated as having been made by the deceased as at the date of death.

As to capital gains tax, the Revenue view is that much depends on by whom a power of appointment is exercised; and when it is exercised. If executors and trustees under a will are the same individuals, it is necessary they identify in which capacity they are acting. The Revenue view is that these are separate and distinct bodies of persons for tax purposes.

When a power of appointment is vested in and exercised by executors, this is considered not to be a variation of a testamentary disposition, so that no capital gains tax can be said to arise (TCGA 1992 s 62(4)).

When, on the other hand, an appointment takes effect only after an asset is assented to trustees, or after it has fallen into residue, the position is different. A beneficiary is, in the Revenue view, to be treated as becoming absolutely entitled as against the trustee, so giving rise to liability to capital gains tax (TCGA 1992 s 71(1)).

A new application for Deeds of Family Arrangement has been created by the enhancement of business and agricultural property reliefs enacted in F(2)A 1992. The new rate of reliefs applies to deaths on or after 10 March 1992, but where a tax payer died before this date, and his estate includes assets qualifying for the new 100% relief, it may be possible (subject to the time limit) to execute a Deed of Variation to direct the qualifying assets to the deceased's spouse. After an interval of time, the spouse may then choose to donate the assets to the beneficiaries under the will, a transfer to which the 100% business or agricultural property relief will apply.

Care must be taken to ensure that the surviving spouse has owned the property for the specified qualifying period. However, when a person becomes entitled on the death of his or her spouse, he or she may add the deceased's period of ownership to his or her own for the purpose of satisfying the two year ownership requirement (IHTA 1984 s 104).

Whilst this relief can be most valuable as an adjunct to tax-planning, it should not be regarded as an excuse for inactivity. An estate owner with small children may have reservations about the appointment of trustees to exercise what he regards as parental responsibilities, or he may have no suitable trustees available. Also a discretionary will trust must increase legal costs.

18.4   DEATH OF A FARMER: FAMILY TENANCIES

18.4:1   Introduction

The purpose of this section is to examine what attitude will be adopted by the Capital Taxes Office on the death of a farmer who, during his lifetime, *granted a tenancy* over his farm to a family farming partnership of which he was a member (see section **15.2:1** above). Where, however, 100% agricultural or business property relief is due under FA 1992, the issues discussed in this section may not arise.

It is clear that in certain circumstances the CTO will resist the tenanted valuation and seek to substitute VP value. The Capital Taxes Office will ask for evidence that a tenancy existed. It will also ask for sight of the relevant tenancy agreement, and if none be presented, or if no rent had been paid under such an agreement, the CTO will normally refuse to concede tenanted value.

Moreover, the grant of such a tenancy might be regarded as having given rise to CTT liabilities, on a transfer of value which may not have been correctly returned by the farmer or pursued by the Revenue at the time of grant. There may have been neglect to make a true and correct return at the time of grant, which will have given the CTO the power to make an assessment for a tax year which would otherwise be out of time, and/or to recover penalties (see section **19.3:1**).

In order to analyse the position, it seems desirable to distinguish four separate historical periods within which a grant might have been made.

PERIOD A: UNTIL MARCH 1974

The period during which liability on death was to estate duty, ending 26 March 1974. No retrospective liability can arise as regards grants of tenancy made in this period. However, the CTO will review the later history of such a tenancy, to see whether there was a cessation by surrender and a grant of a new and different tenancy. The question then arises as to the date of grant of this new tenancy, and into which period it falls.

PERIOD B: 26 MARCH 1974 TO 10 MAY 1981

During this period the grant of tenancy to a family farming partnership appeared to convert the value of the land from vacant possession to tenanted value. The critical question was whether the reduction in value created liability as at the date of creation of the tenancy. This depended upon whether the transaction had been arranged to take advantage of the let-out provisions (then FA 1975 s 20(4)(b)) for commercial bargains as follows:

(a) there must be no intention to confer gratuitous benefit; and
(b) the transaction must be at arm's length between unconnected persons; or
(c) the transaction must be such that might have been made between persons not connected with one another (IHTA 1984 s 10).

In a family farming tenancy (b) could not be satisfied. Therefore (c) needed to be satisfied, imposing the need for a rack-rental which carried income tax disadvantages during the investment income surcharge period (FA 1971 s 32; FA 1980 s 18(1)(b)).

However, (a) also presented a major problem, since the absence of intention to confer a gratuitous benefit would inevitably be a difficult fact to prove.

Thus Period B cases can be sub-divided into:

(1) Those with no rack-rental payable at the outset.
(2) Those with a rack-rental payable at the outset, which was waived or allowed to lapse during the tenancy.
(3) Those with a rack-rental at the outset and that rack-rental having been kept up by periodic rent reviews.

A separate question arising on tenancies created during this period is whether there is (or was) entitlement to transitional relief (see section **15.2:3**). That seems to call for separate review of the terms of the tenancy during the period since its creation until the date of death or conceivably some intermediate date, to see whether the transitional relief tests were satisfied.

PERIOD C: 10 MAY 1981 UNTIL 18 MARCH 1986

During this period the question of whether or not the grant of a tenancy was a transfer of value was regulated by statute. A grant of tenancy of agricultural property *made at any time* whether before or after the passing of the Act, was not to be a transfer of value if made for full consideration in money or money's worth. This implied a full rack-rent, but the question of intention of the grantor no longer needed consideration. The rack-rent sub-categories set out above seem to be applicable. The question of transitional relief does not arise for grants within this period (see section **15.2:3**).

PERIOD D: 18 MARCH 1986 ONWARD

During this period the concept of retention of benefit intervenes, and liabilities to inheritance tax will exclude consideration of retrospective liabilities to CTT.

18.4:2 Grant of tenancy to family partners and transfer of freehold reversion by deceased during the seven-year period

A death within the seven-year period will produce an additional problem arising from the fact that a potentially exempt transfer has failed to be converted into an exempt one. In such circumstances the CTO will look back to see if liability arises on vacant possession land under the associated operations rule. That will occur if:

(a) the 'lease' was not for full consideration in money or money's worth (ie at a rack-rent); or
(b) if the interval of time between grant of tenancy and gift of reversion is less than three years.

In these circumstances, the land will be valued as vacant possession land (for consequences as to AP relief see section **8.5:8**).

Chapter 19

Procedure: tax returns; assessment; collection

19.1 INTRODUCTION

So far, this book has described the law and practice regulating the calculation of farmers' and landowners' tax liabilities annually for income taxes, and after the occurrence of particular transactions (and on death) for capital taxes. There is a separate aspect of taxation: the legal process whereby income, capital gains or capital transfers are to be reported to the Revenue; and 'assessed' to tax, so that the amounts properly due can be demanded and collected. The process is a complex one, for at each step, rights and obligations are allotted to taxpayers and Revenue officials, so that non-compliance, whether accidental or deliberate, can be costly and damaging. The penalties for non-compliance range from prosecution for a criminal offence to payment of tax lost to the Revenue with interest over the period involved. The whole process can be best envisaged as a series of stages, occurring in sequence of time, although in practice, the sequence may vary, and stages may overlap one another.

19.2 INCOME TAX, CORPORATION TAX AND CAPITAL GAINS TAX

19.2:1 Stage I: returns

The principal obligation on all taxpayers, individual and corporate, is to deliver to the Inspector of Taxes a return of income for each year (TMA 1970 ss 7, 8). The time allowed is one year after the end of the relevant year of assessment. The return form asks for amounts of income and capital gains under various classified sources together with a declaration that to the best of the taxpayer's knowledge, the particulars given in it are correct and complete. A return form is required to be completed and despatched within 30 days but this time limit is not strictly enforced.

There are provisions whereby a taxpayer who discovers his original return was incorrect, and whose omission was not fraudulent or negligent, may correct it without penalty, provided his correction is made within the stipulated time limit and before proceedings against him have begun (TMA 1970 s 97). The question of what is fraudulent or negligent is considered later. Inspectors issue two different versions of return forms, one simplified designed for PAYE taxpayers, and a fuller version. Return forms in the Welsh language are available at tax offices in Wales.

Certain classes of taxpayers are subject to special rules as follows.

(A) THE TAXABLE UNIT

    (a) *Income tax*

        Income tax applies to individuals, trusts and partnerships. So far as individuals are concerned, the taxable unit may be the individual alone; husband and wife; or husband and wife and minor children. Certain children's income derived from parents is aggregated with parental income.

Until 1988, the system of taxation of married couples was based upon the assumption that the income of a married woman belonged to her husband. Thus her husband was primarily responsible for making returns of his wife's income, although he had no statutory right to obtain from her the necessary information. The liability to pay tax on wife's income fell on the husband and only in very limited circumstances could the wife be assessed. There were special rules for elections to be made to treat wives as if they were separate individuals.

In 1988, the Chancellor of the Exchequer announced 'Quite simply, that is no longer acceptable'. Under independent taxation which began in 1990–91, wives are taxed as individuals and are liable to make returns of their income and gains to pay the tax liabilities arising as if single individuals. A wife issued with a return form must either sign and take responsibility for it or appoint her husband as agent on her behalf. However, the appointment of an agent does not diminish the wife's responsibility for the correctness of her return.

A husband receives a 'married couples' allowance which has been treated differently for different tax years. For 1992–93, the allowance was given firstly to the husband and was transferable to the wife only insofar as it could not be applied against the husband's total income after all other deductions had been made against it. However, in the computation of total income for this purpose mortgage interest paid (MIRAS) is not to be deducted. From 1993–94, a married woman may, herself elect to receive half the married couple's allowance, or both spouses may elect for the whole allowance to be transferred to the wife (F(2)A 1992 s 20 Sch 5 para 2). The election to transfer is irrevocable.

(b) *Capital gains tax*
With effect from 6 April 1990, capital gains on husband and wife are taxed separately in the same way as income (FA 1988 s 104). The rate of capital gains tax on each spouse's gains is calculated by treating the gains as the top slice of his or her income. Each spouse has a separate annual exempt amount (currently £5,500), which is not transferable to the other spouse if not fully exhausted. Similarly, allowable losses by one spouse are not transferable to the other, nor are losses established before 6 April 1990 brought forward.

Provided spouses are living together, transfers of assets from one to the other are still treated as if the amount of consideration were such that neither a gain nor a loss arises to the spouse making the disposal. The acquiror's acquisition is treated as having occurred when the disposer acquired it where acquisition was before 1 April 1982 (FA 1988 Sch 8 para 1).

This is helpful where a half-share transfer can be conveniently made before ultimate sale of an asset, so as to utilise both annual exempt amounts, one of which might otherwise be lost. There are limits to this tactic: the no gain/no loss transfer is only available where the spouses are living together. Moreover, there is a vulnerability to the anti-avoidance doctrine, so that this may be regarded as an 'artificial scheme'. It is best to make any such transfer well before the envisaged ultimate sale.

For jointly held assets, eg farmland in joint names, gains are apportioned between spouses in accordance with their respective beneficial interests in the land at the time of its disposal. Normally the Revenue will assume that the spouses hold the assets in equal shares, but if this is not so, and ownership is unequal, eg 70/30, that fact should be reported to the Revenue when submitting the return of the disposal. Where the division of ownership is uncertain, it is obviously sensible to have regard to the tax exemptions available before reporting a particular division of ownership. In particular, it may be that one spouse has been acting merely as a nominee for the other and has no beneficial interest in the land. This is a fact which may need to be substantiated by the conveyancing deeds.

If a special division of income in unequal shares is returned for income tax and income tax has been so charged, it is likely that the same division will be applied for capital gains tax, subject to some special reasons for a different division being applicable.

(c) *Inheritance tax*

For inheritance tax, husbands and wives and treated as separate tax payers, but transfers between them are exempt (see section **8.1:3**).

(d) *Stamp duty*

Stamp duty is not chargeable on gifts, but applies on sales by one spouse to another.

(e) *VAT*

VAT can apply on, for example, land sales between spouses.

(B) PARTNERSHIPS

The partner first named in the partnership agreement is responsible for making returns for the partnership as a whole (TMA 1970 s 9). If there is no written agreement, the precedent acting partner is responsible, and he must give the names and addresses of all the partners.

(C) COMPANIES

The company secretary or person acting as secretary is responsible for making the return (TMA 1970 s 10).

(D) PERSONS ACTING FOR OTHERS

The Revenue has wide powers to obtain information from individuals relating to the affairs of other individuals. Employers are obliged to give information concerning remuneration of employees (TMA 1970 s 15); bankers etc, are obliged to give information concerning interest paid without deduction of tax (TMA 1970 s 17); taxpayers carrying on business are required to give details of fees and commissions paid to others (TMA 1970 s 16), and generally persons receiving taxable income belonging to others are required to report the fact (TMA 1970 s 13).

(E) FAILURE TO MAKE RETURNS

When an Inspector raises a query on a return form, in particular when he asks for confirmation that the return submitted is complete and correct in all respects, it is often because he is trying to reconcile the information received from another source. Such requests for confirmation should not, therefore, be treated lightly.

The submission of an income tax return sets in motion the annual process of tax collection. Those who contemplate instructing a tax accountant or other professional adviser should do so before submission of a return form and not afterwards. Once the return is made, the scope for negotiation, for example, for claiming that an item is exempt or that it represents a capital rather than an income receipt, is reduced.

In practice, it is not necessary that the amount of farm profits be entered on the face of the return form, but an entry connecting up the return form with the farm accounts sent separately is necessary and by convention, the usual entry is 'see accounts to follow'. It is obviously prudent to keep a copy of each return form, if only for reference in completing the return for the following year.

If a taxpayer fails to make a return, the Inspector can withhold his personal allowances for a year and can impose penalties. A taxpayer is under a statutory duty to report a new source of income, even if no return form has been sent to him. From 6 April 1990, the penalty for failure to make a return is 100% of the unpaid tax.

The Inspector of Taxes has wide powers to obtain information from third parties about the affairs of any taxpayer. He can call for documents but some information is supplied to him automatically (see **19.2:1**(D)). One such document which has been of considerable help to Inspectors in detecting incorrect returns is a notification from a bank paying interest of more than £15 pa. This leads Inspectors not only to inquiries about interest omitted from tax returns, but also about the source of cash paid into that particular bank account.

There is also a power to obtain information from other government departments, and taxpayers should bear in mind that their income tax returns to the Inland Revenue department, and their value added tax returns to the Customs and Excise department are likely to be correlated at some time.

In the normal course, the farmer's annual tax return is supported by a set of farm accounts which are prepared in conventional form, disclosing the balance of net profits (or net loss!) on the profit and loss account; together with a balance sheet showing the net assets (or net liabilities!) of the farming business. It is normal for such a set of accounts to be prepared by a qualified accountant, and to be certified by that accountant as 'true and correct in all respects'.

The submission of duly certified accounts is not a statutory requirement, but has been required as evidence to support the amount of net profit entered in the tax return.

The Revenue has introduced a simplified requirement for small businesses with effect from April 1990. 'Small businesses' are those individual farmers and farm partnerships with annual turnover of less than £15,000. Full certified accounts are not required, and instead the farmer or landowner needs merely report his total turnover; total business purchases and expenses; and the resulting net taxable profit.

It is assumed that farmers will continue to keep accurate and complete trading records, so as to arrive at the figures disclosed, and the Revenue 'will continue to investigate business accounts . . . where it has reason to believe that profits may have been understated'.

This simplified basis is useful for landowners receiving a relatively modest amount of rents from property, where a statement of income and expenditure has been accepted in the past.

19.2:2   Stage II: assessment

Responsibility for the formal act of 'assessment' is placed on the Inspectors of Taxes and the Board of Inland Revenue, according to statutory procedures (TMA 1970 s 29). Assessment, in the practical sense, means examination of returns and accounts, and transfer of the amounts therein (or rejection of the amounts, and the substitution of others) to documents of record, copies of which, incorporating notices to pay are sent to taxpayers.

Generally, non-delivery of a return does not prevent the Inspector from making an estimated assessment on a particular source of income. A large proportion of assessments on farming businesses are estimated in the first place, to secure submission of accounts. The fact that the amount shown in an assessment is manifestly a round-sum estimate (and a hopelessly inaccurate one) does not in itself invalidate an assessment.

In practice, the amount of an assessment may have been agreed before the assessment is made, by submission of accounts and/or other information. Inspectors have separate powers to call for production of books, accounts and other documents (TMA 1970 ss 20–20D), but in the ordinary course, issue of an estimated and excessive notice of assessment is considered sufficient to elicit accounts.

There are important time limits governing the making of assessments (TMA 1970 s 34). Ordinarily, an assessment may be made no later than six years after the end of the tax year to which it relates. During 1987–88, therefore, the last year of assessment for which a notice may be issued is 1981–82. However, the six-year rule is extended to 20 years (FA 1989 s 149) where there has been a loss of tax due to 'fraud' or 'wilful default' (TMA 1970 s 36); or neglect (TMA 1970 s 29(3)). 'Fraud' and 'wilful default' imply a degree of deliberation on the part of a taxpayer. Conscious carelessness is wilful default (*Clixby v Pountney* (1967) 44 TC 515).

'Neglect' is defined as negligence or failure to give information, make a return or furnish documents. A failure to prepare and submit accounts may amount to neglect, entitling the Revenue to claim penalties and interest. 'Neglect' is also relevant in relation to capital gains tax. Inspectors tend to take a strict view of time limits, and will not accept that capital gains tax computations should be deferred whilst trading accounts are being finalised. In order to establish more precise meanings for these terms, it is necessary to study the body of case law. Generally, this gives little hope of escaping extended time limits on semantic grounds.

Apart from the general power to make assessments, Inspectors have special powers to make additional assessments, if they discover (TMA 1970 s 29(3)) profits have not been assessed, or are undercharged, or excessive reliefs have been given. What constitutes a discovery for this purpose is important, since if no limits were imposed, Inspectors could continue making assessments, and finality would never be achieved. Discovery means, inter alia, the finding out of new relevant facts, because an admission is made or for other reasons. Whether it means coming to a different conclusion on the same facts is not certain.

There are various rules determining who shall be assessable, but generally, it is the person entitled to or receiving the relevant profits or income (as to partnerships, see section **6.1**). Where a husband and wife are living together, her income is no longer deemed his for tax purposes. Minors, that is children under the age of 18, are assessed in the names of their parents or guardians (TMA 1970 s 73). Deceased persons are assessed in the names of their executors or administrators. Death, in itself, does not excuse taxation (TMA 1970 s 74).

19.2:3   Stage III: examination

All business accounts are subjected by Inspectors to a systematic examination, in accordance with the tax district plan. Each annual set of accounts received is classified into the following categories:

(a) *'A' cases*
   This means that the farm accounts will be accepted for that particular year without detailed scrutiny.
(b) *'B' cases*
   This means the accounts will be reviewed with a view to disallowing inadmissible deductions, and correcting other apparent error. Substantial profit cases are reviewed regularly.
(c) *'E' cases*
   This means that the case has been selected for detailed examination with a view to challenging the accuracy of the results for a particular year and probably for earlier years so as to create liability to interest and penalties.

Investigation of farm accounts is often triggered by one or more of the following factors, and it is worthwhile reviewing the following checklist before submitting accounts:

(a) Information received by the Inspector from other sources, most usually interest on an undisclosed bank account; reports following a VAT visit; other information from third parties.
(b) A low level of drawings from the business particularly in the light of ordinary living costs.
(c) Capital introduced into the business from an unexplained or doubtful source.
(d) Gross margins low by comparison with similar businesses.
(e) Accountant's certificate drawing attention to incomplete records.
(f) Reconciliation between accounts and returns reveals that there are unexplained items, for example dividends, or acquisitions of investments.
(g) Absence of full accounts or returns in past years and acceptance of estimated asssements.
(h) Where transactions are admitted to take place in cash at local cattle markets etc.
(i) Unexplained change of accountant or tax agent.
(j) Personal observation by the Inspector of farm shops, caravan sites, or other alternative land use.

A signal that an Inspector is about to commence a detailed investigation, can often be detected. It may take the form of a letter requesting confirmation that a particular set of farm accounts or a particular client's return is complete in every respect. Alternatively, the Inspector may request that the accountant and his client call at his office at some proposed time for a 'brief discussion'. Alternatively, an explanation that a client's file is not available, 'due to its having been sent to another office' may be a signal that a specialised investigation department is being consulted.

If an investigation is anticipated, it is prudent for the farmer and his advisers to consider carefully at the outset whether any omissions have or have not occurred. An early voluntary disclosure can save both penalties on unpaid tax and professional costs.

19.2:4   Stage IV: appeal

Taxpayers who do not wish to accept an assessment may appeal against it (TMA 1970 Pt V). Appeal sets in motion a further stage in the process, which can continue for many years. To exercise a right of appeal does not mean the taxpayer is personally aggrieved, nor that he is claiming hardship, nor that he wishes to go over the head of an Inspector to his superior officer, as is sometimes supposed. It means that because he wishes to challenge some feature of the assessment, he requires it kept open, until his appeal is settled by agreement with the Inspector or by a tribunal. Appeals must be made within 30 days of the date stated on the notice of assessment, but this limit is not strictly enforced and there are provisions for late appeals due to absence, sickness or other reasonable cause (TMA 1970 s 49). To be 'reasonable', the cause should be similar in nature to absence or sickness. When appealing, it is necessary to state the grounds, and, by convention, it is sufficient to say that the assessment is estimated and incorrect, or to indicate what aspect is in dispute.

Although notices of appeal are delivered to Inspectors, an appeal lies to the General Commissioners (TMA 1970 s 44 (usually)) or to the Special Commissioners (TMA 1970 s 46), the two statutory bodies, respectively lay and professional, set up to hear appeals. Notice must be given of an election to be heard by the Special Commissioners (in Northern Ireland, the county court). If the appeal cannot be settled by agreement with the Inspector, because of a dispute on the principles involved, or because the taxpayer remains silent and fails to pursue his appeal, the Inspector will arrange for a personal hearing of the appeal before the Commissioners and, in the absence of representations by the taxpayer, will procure the Commissioners' determination of the appeal and confirmation of the assessment.

Pending determination of an appeal, the tax shown payable remains payable on the due date (TMA 1970 s 86), subject to an application to postpone payment, on the grounds that the tax shown will exceed the amount of ultimate liability. Applications to postpone payment have to be made at the same time as an appeal, and should say why the tax is excessive. Such applications may or may not be agreed by the Inspector, and can be heard and determined by the Commissioners separately from the appeal itself.

There is a special penalty (interest on unpaid tax) for having postponed payment of tax, which ultimately is found to be payable when the appeal is settled (see section **19.2:5**).

19.2:5   Stage V: personal hearing

If an appeal cannot be settled by agreement with the Inspector, it must be heard by one of two sets of appeal commissioners. There can be no other outcome, and an appeal cannot legally 'lapse' although with the consent of the Inspector it can be withdrawn (TMA 1970 s 54).

The General Commissioners are the Revenue equivalent of lay magistrates, and the Special Commissioners the equivalent of stipendiaries. Both bodies are concerned only with tax appeals, and both are advised by a Clerk, usually a solicitor, or retired tax Inspector. Two General Commissioners constitute a quorum. One Special Commissioner may sit alone (FA 1984 Sch 22 para 2).

Proceedings before General Commissioners are usually informal. The appellant is invited to state the grounds of his appeal, that is, his side of the dispute (if any) with the Inspector. If the dispute is a matter of fact, the appellant can advance his case by calling witnesses to testify on his behalf. There is no oath swearing before the Commissioners and the formal rules of evidence are not always observed. When a witness gives evidence, the Inspector is entitled to cross-examine.

After the conclusion of the appellant's statement, the Inspector gives his account of events, or explains why the appeal has been brought before the

Commissioners to adjudicate. After that, the appellant has a right of reply. He is not permitted to recite his tale a second time, but must confine himself to answering points made by the Inspector.

If the dispute is substantial, the Commissioners consult their Clerk, and may ask the parties to withdraw. After that the finding is announced forthwith, usually that a particular assessment should be confirmed, discharged, or varied either upwards or downwards. Commissioners have the power to increase, as well as reduce an assessment on appeal (TMA 1970 s 50(7)). There are no costs before the Commissioners, that is, if the appellant employs an accountant, solicitor or barrister to represent him, as he may do (TMA 1970 s 50(5)), and wins, he must nevertheless bear the professional costs himself. If he loses, he does not pay the Inspector's costs. The procedure for appeal hearings is at present under review. It has been proposed there should be an award of costs where either party has acted unreasonably. Changes of nomenclature are also in prospect.

On the announcement of the Commissioners' findings, one or both parties may express dissatisfaction with it (TMA 1970 s 56(1)). This is the formula for indicating the losing party intends to pursue the matter further, into the High Court. Dissatisfaction must be expressed immediately, and the next step in the chain of procedure which follows, is for the aggrieved party to ask the Clerk to Commissioners for a case to be stated for the opinion of the High Court (TMA 1970 s 56(2)). This document records the facts of the appeal, according to the evidence given, and the Commissioners' findings. Copies are sent to both appellant and the Revenue, and the final agreed version is the basis for the ultimate High Court hearing (TMA 1970 s 56(6)). From the High Court, there is the possibility of further appeal to the Court of Appeal and thence to the House of Lords. Certain appeals may go direct from the Special Commissioners to the Court of Appeal. Obviously such appeals involve considerable costs, and are unlikely to be considered, unless the tax in issue is substantial. An appeal can be pursued into the courts only on a question of law. On matters of fact, the Commissioners are the final arbiters. Questions of fact are determinable by evidence, whilst questions of law are not.

In practice, many appearances before Commissioners do not derive from a dispute, but are because the appellant or his accountant has been dilatory in following up his appeal with accounts, or other relevant information, and a personal hearing is the Inspector's mechanism to secure the material he has requested. The question then is whether the Commissioners will be prepared to adjourn the appeal, that is, allow the appellant more time, or whether they will simply confirm the assessment. Their course of action will be much influenced by the Inspector's attitude. If the Inspector's patience is exhausted, he will apply for confirmation, and few bodies of Commissioners are minded to refuse such an application if supported by persuasive and detailed accounts of the appellant's failure to act.

An appellant who is summoned to a personal hearing, and who knows that he cannot comply with the Inspector's requirements is best advised to communicate with the Inspector before the time set for the hearing, explaining the difficulty, asking for more time, and offering a date on which the missing information is expected to be forthcoming. In these matters there is a wide degree of variation between one body of Commissioners and another and between one Inspector and another. Some Commissioners rely on a process of precept, in which they make a formal order for the appellant to supply certain information, subject to penalties for non-compliance.

It is often a question of strategy as to whether a dispute with the Inspector is worth pursuit to personal hearing. The most likely occasion is where the amounts of tax are substantial; or the Inspector's attitude seems obstinately unfair; or where the issue is one of fact and evidence. In such circumstances, professional representation will be indispensable.

19.2:6   Stage VI: collection

The final stage in the process is collection of the tax due as finally determined (TMA 1970 Pt VI). This is the duty of Collectors of Taxes, who issue demands, and are in charge of proceedings where necessary for non-payment. Collectors have no powers to vary demands without reference to the Inspector.

Different categories of tax have different due dates of payment, and these may conveniently be summarised as follows (TMA 1970 s 86; FA 1980 s 61):

Class	*Due date*
Income tax payable in one sum	1 January in the year of assessment; or 30 days after issue of the notice of assessment, if the notice is issued after that date.
Income tax payable in two instalments on the profits of trades and professions	1 January and 1 July in the year of assessment; or 30 days after issue of the notice of assessment, if the notice is issued after those dates.
Capital gains tax	1 December following the end of the year in which the gains accrue.
Corporation tax	Nine months after the end of the acounting period, or one month after issue of notice of assessment if later.
PAYE deducted from salaries and wages	14 days after the 5th of each month.

The Revenue can enforce deduction of tax at source through the mechanism of Pay As You Earn and operates a specialist enforcement system for casual and temporary employees, including agricultural gang masters, those supplying casual labour for farmers at harvest and other peak times. Gang masters are employers of their teams, and should operate PAYE on the wages paid to the individual employees. The Agricultural Compliance Unit is responsible for enforcing the PAYE and National Insurance Contribution deductions, and, where appropriate, for requiring names and addresses of recipients under the Revenue statutory powers. Interest and penalties on under-paid tax can be imposed.

In 1984, an informal agreement was reached between the Inland Revenue, the Social Security Department, the Ministry of Agriculture and the National Farmers Union to the effect that PAYE was not applicable to wages paid to a daily casual harvest worker employed for a period not exceeding one day and with no agreement for further employment. These were cases where the worker was paid in cash at the end of the day. Since then, it has emerged that the Revenue's view of 'no agreement for further employment' is a broad one. It includes written and oral contracts but does not include those instances where there is a mere expectation of future employment.

19.2:7   Stage VII: interest

Where there is delay in making a tax return, and in consequence an assessment is made late or is inadequate, interest is payable (TMA 1970 s 88). This interest is computed on the unpaid tax as from the date on which the tax should have been paid (see section **19.4:2**.) The Revenue has discretion to mitigate the interest, and it is the practice to do so only where the delay is not 'substantial'. 'Substantial' means a delay of thirty days from the date of issue of the tax return; or later, by 31 October following the end of the tax year in which the income or chargeable gain arose. The problem usually arises in connection with a return by individuals of capital gains, in which circumstances the Revenue does not press for interest providing sufficient information has been given to allow an adequate estimated assessment to be made. That is usually the sale price of the asset disposed of (SP 6/89.)

Interest is chargeable on overdue tax. There are complex provisions for determining the date from which interest should run, which is known as the 'reckonable' date (TMA 1970 s 86(3)). Generally, the reckonable date is the original due date for payment, unless there has been an application to postpone payment on an assessment under appeal, and that application produces a later due date. But there are limits to the time allowed, and if the appeal defers finality of the assessment for more than six months after the normal date in the year when tax would be payable, then the reckonable date is a date six months after the date when tax would normally fall due.

RATES OF INTEREST

The following rates of interest take effect from 6 March 1993:

Interest charged on late payment of income, corporation and capital gains tax	6.25%
Interest in respect of the above taxes overpaid (repayment supplement) The formula used is (Base Rate + 2.5%) − income tax basic rate (TMA 1970 s 90)	6.25%
Interest charged on inheritance tax paid late	5.00%
Interest paid on inheritance tax overpaid The formula used is (Basic Rate + 2% − basic rate tax − 1%)	5.00%

These rates do not apply to interest deemed received on loans which constitute benefits in kind. The official rate of interest for that purpose from 6 March 1993 onwards is 7.75%.

Interest charged is not itself deductible against any tax, and the repayment supplement is not taxable.

19.3   INHERITANCE TAX

19.3:1   Introduction

The administration of inheritance tax follows a pattern similar to income taxes, and therefore the outline given below is more summarised to avoid repetition. There is a primary obligation to make a return to the capital taxes office:

(a) by a transferor of a lifetime chargeable transfer;
(b) by trustees on transfers or distributions of settled property;
(c) by personal representatives in respect of a deceased person's estate (IHTA 1984 s 216(1)).

The rules requiring delivery of accounts are modified for 'excepted' estates. These are estates where the total value of the property is less than £125,000 from 1 July 1991; where there is no trust property; not more than £15,000 out of the total is property situated outside the United Kingdom; and the deceased person died having been domiciled in the United Kingdom and having made no lifetime gifts chargeable to inheritance tax or capital transfer tax within the seven years before his death.

Clearly these regulations, which are designed to avoid administration in cases producing no tax, can be very useful. However, it is important to ensure before taking advantage of them that there have been no earlier lifetime transfers which have not been properly reported.

Before personal representatives can obtain a grant of representation giving them powers to act, they must deliver an account, usually a provisional one, and pay tax on that provisional basis.

There is an obligation on transferees to report potentially exempt transfers which have failed, and also gifts with reservation. The return must be delivered not later than 12 months after the end of the month in which death occurs.

For transfers on death, an account must be rendered within 12 months from the end of the month in which death occurred, or if later, three months from the date on which the personal representatives began to act. Similar rules apply to trustees. There are penalties for failing to deliver accounts, make returns or comply with notices issued by the Revenue requiring information (IHTA 1984 ss 245–253). There are also comprehensive provisions, under which liability for payment can be fastened upon transferors, transferees, and persons taking the property after the transfer (for lifetime gifts); personal representatives; trustees and beneficiaries (for transfers on death); and trustees and beneficiaries (for transfers of settled property).

19.3:2   Determination

Unlike income tax, inheritance tax is not chargeable by reference to specific years of assessment. The equivalent of an 'assessment' is a 'determination', that is a notice in writing sent to the transferor, or other person liable, stating the value transferred and the amount of tax chargeable (IHTA 1984 s 221).

19.3:3   Appeals

Like an assessment, a notice of determination can conclude the issue unless an appeal against it is made in writing within the stipulated time limit, which is 30 days (IHTA 1984 s 222). An appeal against an inheritance tax determination lies to the Special Commissioners (see section **19.2:3**), from whose finding either party may appeal to the High Court (Chancery Division) by a case stated procedure on a point of law (IHTA 1984 s 225). There is a procedure for omitting the Special Commissioners, and appealing direct to the High Court on matters of importance. From the High Court, appeals lie to the Court of Appeal and thence to the House of Lords.

There are also procedures for late appeals; for land valuation disputes to be heard by the Lands Tribunal; to enforce recovery of tax and generally to secure the inflow of tax to the Exchequer. Two features of this system are of special relevance to farmers and landowners.

19.4   PAYMENT OF AND INTEREST ON INHERITANCE TAX

19.4:1   Introduction

Because the sums involved can be large, and the effect on a continuing business or estate correspondingly significant, the rules for dates of payment of inheritance tax assume considerable importance. On death, tax is payable six months after the end of the month in which death occurs. (This includes tax on failed potentially exempt transfers.)

19.4:2   Dates of payment

For chargeable lifetime gifts, a special table of dates of payment is prescribed, under which tax becomes payable not less than six months, nor more than 12 months, from the end of the month in which the transfer was made, depending on whether it was made after 5 April and before 1 October. The table is as follows (IHTA 1984 s 226):

Month in which transfer made	Payment date from which interest runs
January	31 July same year
February	31 August same year
March	30 September same year
April to October inclusive	30 April following year
November	31 May following year
December	30 June following year

The interest rate is varied to keep in line with interest rates generally.

However, in certain cases (IHTA 1984 s 227), tax may be payable in ten equal yearly instalments over the ten years commencing on the date when the whole tax bill would otherwise have been payable. The question whether exercise of this option creates liability for interest on unpaid tax during the instalment period is an important one, and this is considered below (see section **19.4:3**). However, the option is only exercisable, in the event of certain transfers of specified classes of property. The transfers when the option is permitted are:

(a) transfers on death;
(b) lifetime transfers where tax is payable by the transferee;
(c) charges on settled property, where the property remains in trust, or the tax is borne by a beneficiary.

The specified classes of property are:

(a) land or buildings, freehold or leasehold, wherever situated, and howsoever used (it is the inclusion of this item, which makes the instalment system seem so relevant);
(b) shares in limited companies, where one of three separate sets of conditions are satisfied:
    (i) Shares in either quoted or unquoted companies, which immediately before the transfer gave the transferor 'control'. In this context,

control is secured by a majority of voting power, on issues affecting the company as a whole.

(ii) Shares in unquoted companies, the sale of which would cause hardship, on the assumption, if a lifetime transfer, that they are to be retained by the person liable. Alternatively, if the transfer is on death, at least 20% of the tax, for which the same person is liable, is attributable to assets (including the shares in question) which qualify for instalment treatment.

(iii) Shares in unquoted companies, exeeding £20,000 in value, and representing at least 10% of the nominal value of the company's ordinary share capital if ordinary shares, or 10% of total share capital if not ordinary shares.

The object of these various sets of rules is to give relief where the shares constitute a substantial block and sale to pay tax might jeopardise the future of the company, or not be a practicable step. Whether the rules always succeed in that objective is an open question.

(c) The net value of a business or an interest in a business, that is assets less liabilities.

19.4:3   Payment by instalments

When an election to pay by instalments has been made, the unpaid balance becomes payable on the occurrence of certain events, which are: sale of the property or business, payment under a partnership deed, a further charge on a second lifetime transfer, or property ceasing to be held in settlement. The principle here is that these events are likely to produce the cash needed to pay the unpaid tax bill.

In some cases and subject to an overall limit these instalments are interest free if paid on time, and only bear interest if an instalment date is not met. These cases are:

(a) property which qualifies for agricultural property relief (see section **8.5**);
(b) shares in section **19.4:2** (b), other than shares in a holding company or a property company (for this purpose a property company means one holding land and receiving rents, or one dealing in land);
(c) business or interests in a business;
(d) woodlands.

19.4:4   Conclusion

Agricultural land and buildings did not originally qualify for interest free treatment, but this was given by FA 1981 s 92(2) for transfers on or after 10 March 1981. There was an overriding limit of £250,000 of value (FA 1975 Sch 4 para 16(5)) qualifying for interest free instalments, which was repealed in relation to chargeable transfers on or after 10 March 1981 (FA 1981 s 91).

19.5   FALLS IN THE VALUE OF LAND

Generally, the value of an estate on death is the total price the property might be expected to fetch in the open market as at the date of death. However, relief is available where land, including buildings, when ultimately sold, does not realise an amount equal to the open market value at the date of death. To qualify for relief, such a sale must occur within three years of the death (IHTA 1984 s 191). For sales after 16 March 1993, the period has been extended to four years (FA 1993 s 199). Where there is more than one sale, the results are aggregated, and relief is limited to the net loss if any.

There is also a *de minimis* rule. Sales are disregarded, if the price realised differs from the value at death by less than £1,000 or 5% of the value at death, whichever is the lower (s 191). The relief given for land is separate from a similar relief given on quoted shares. That is, sales of land and shares are not aggregated to arrive at a net profit or loss.

A further set of rules limits the relief where the post-mortem sale was to a beneficiary or one of his near relatives (s 191). The detailed provisions need study by executors and administrators since the timetable of estate realisation may need adjustment to take them into account.

Appendices

APPENDIX I: FORM OF GRAZING AGREEMENT

AN AGREEMENT made the   day of   19
BETWEEN   of   (hereinafter
called 'the Owner') and   of
(hereinafter called 'the Grazier') WHEREBY the Owner agrees to
grant unto the Grazier and the Grazier agrees to take ALL THAT
right to graze [or mow] all those pieces or parcels of land (hereinafter called 'the said land') comprising   acres or there-
abouts and situate at   in the County of being OS Nos
                    on the OS Map for the district   Edition, upon the
following terms and conditions:

(i)
(see below)

1   The Grazier shall have the right to occupy and graze [or mow]
the said land from the   day of   until the
                    day of   , and shall have the use of the said
land only for grazing [or mowing].

(ii)
(see below)

2   The Grazier shall pay to the Owner the sum of   pounds
in respect of the period of occupation mentioned in Clause 1 above
such sum to be payable on or before the said   day of

3   The Grazier shall use the said land for the purpose only of
grazing [or mowing] the same.

(iii)
(see below)

4   The Grazier shall use only cattle or sheep for the purpose of
grazing the said land and shall not allow the said land to be entered
upon or in any way used by horses ponies donkeys asses goats pigs
poultry or any diseased animals.

(iii)
(see below)

5   The Grazier agrees to the following conditions:
   (a) that he will not permit any trespass upon the said land;
   (b) that he will keep the said land clean and free from Spear
        Thistle, Creeping or Field Thistle, Curled Dock, Broad-
        leaved Dock and Ragwort;
   (c) that he will keep the gates fences and ditches in good
        order;
   (d) that he will not depasture on the said land any but his own
        cattle or sheep;
   (e) that he will graze and use the said land in a good and
        husbandlike manner.

6   The Owner shall have a lien upon all the Grazier's animals for
the time being depastured on the said land for any sum owing or
expense incurred for which under this Agreement the Grazier is
liable and this lien may be enforced by the sale of any animal or
animals belonging to the Grazier for the time being depastured upon
the said land.

7   If the Owner shall require the whole or any part of the said land
for any purpose whatsoever he shall have the right to resume possession at any time of either the whole or any part of the said land upon
giving either by himself or through his agent one month's notice in
writing and deducting a proportionate sum from the amount herein-
before agreed and without paying any compensation whatsoever to
the Grazier.

8   This Agreement is not a contract of tenancy for the purposes of the Agricultural Holdings Act 1948.

9   It is expressly agreed and understood that the Owner does not undertake to repeat this grazing [or mowing] licence for another period but if he agrees to do so a fresh agreement will have to be entered into by the Grazier to operate from a date subsequent to the agreed period such fresh agreement to operate as a new and distinct contract.

Signed by the Grazier . . . .

In the presence of . . . . (Name, address &
. . . .   occupation)
. . . .

Signed by the Owner . . . .

In the presence of . . . . (Name, address &
. . . .   occupation)
. . . .

Notes

 (i) Should be a period of 364 days or less.

 (ii) Or: '. . . such sum to be payable in two instalments.
The first payment of £   to be made on the   day of
              19   (or: on the signing hereof) and the second
payment of £   to be made on the   day of
              19   .'

(iii) Delete or amend any words or sentences as necessary (in these paragraphs only.)

APPENDIX II: MAKING A CLAIM FOR CONDITIONAL EXEMPTION OR DESIGNATION

1 Claims should be addressed initially to the Capital Taxes Office in London, Edinburgh or Belfast, as appropriate. But it should be noted that, in practice, all claims for heritage exemption are dealt with by the *London office*.

2 The prospective ten-yearly charge on certain heritage property in discretionary trust apart, claims for designation or exemption can be considered formally only when a charge to CTT or IHT has arisen or where there is evidence (such as a draft conveyance) that a transfer will occur as soon as exemptibility is confirmed. However, some of the advisory bodies, like the Countryside Commission, the Countryside Commission for Scotland, the Historic Buildings and Monuments Commission for England, the Scottish Development Department (Historic Buildings and Monuments Directorate), the Historic Buildings Council for Scotland and the Nature Conservancy Council are prepared to offer informal advice on the prospects of securing exemption, *at their discretion and in so far as this is possible within limited staff resources*. The Historic Buildings and Monuments Commission for England is unable to make site inspections for the purpose of reaching an informal view, and the advice which it can give on this basis is limited to offering a view, on the basis of photographs and a brief description, of whether a building is of outstanding architectural or historic interest. *It must be emphasised that any opinion offered in this way is preliminary and informal in nature and does not in any way commit the Inland Revenue*, with whom the statutory responsibility for designation rests.

3 When making a claim the information itemised below should be provided. It is important for the claim to be complete and in the correct form. Otherwise, it may lead to delay.

(A) WORKS OF ART AND OTHER OBJECTS

  (i) Full details of the property (photographs may occasionally be required).
  (ii) The address or addresses at which the object or objects may be inspected.
  (iii) Details of any previous exemptions.
  (iv) The measures proposed for providing for reasonable public access.

(B) OUTSTANDING LAND

  (i) Particulars and description of the landscape, identifying those features considered to be of outstanding merit on account of the scenic, scientific or historic interest.
  (ii) Details of the transfer in respect of which the claim has arisen and the statutory provision under which the claim is made.
  (iii) Name, address and telephone number of the person with whom the advisory body may arrange a visit.
  (iv) Six copies of a map of 1:10,000 (or 1:25,000 for very large estates) on an Ordnance Survey base, clearly marked with:
    (a) land claimed;
    (b) so far as practicable, all buildings which, though not eligible in their own right, are considered to make some positive contribution

to the qualifying interest of the land on which they are situated (please also provide a supporting schedule indicating their location (by grid reference, farm or village name, or by cross reference to symbols on the map supplied), approximate age and construction materials);

(c) all public rights of way, differentiating between footpaths and bridleways;

(d) any scheduled ancient monuments (quoting the relevant County Site and Monuments Record reference number, if possible) and listed buildings (with grades);

(e) any Sites of Special Scientific Interest or in Northern Ireland any Areas of Special Scientific Interest;

(f) any nature reserve;

(g) any woodlands on the Nature Conservancy Council's Inventory of Ancient Woodland (describe their age and species and indicate whether subject to any Forestry Commission scheme);

(h) any other contiguous land in the same ownership; and

(i) any land subject to tenancy or other burden.

(v) Details of the measures proposed for providing reasonable public access.

(C) BUILDINGS OF OUTSTANDING HISTORIC OR ARCHITECTURAL INTEREST AND SUPPORTING PROPERTY

(i) Particulars and description of the property, including any essential amenity land and any historically associated objects for which exemption is also being claimed. In particular:

(a) Up-to-date photographs of the main building to show the principal elevations of the exterior and interiors of the principal rooms. Black and white or coloured photographs are acceptable but not transparancies. (Good photographs are important in advancing a claim; submission of uninformative photographs can lead to delay in processing a claim.)

(b) Photographs of the exteriors of all other buildings included in the claim with their identification marked on the backs.

(c) Photographs which show clearly the relationship between any essential amenity land for which exemption is being claimed and including the principal views to and from the main building concerned.

(ii) Six copies of an appropriate scale Ordnance Survey base map with the information as listed in sub-paragraph (B)(iv) above.

(iii) Details of the measures proposed for providing for reasonable public access to the outstanding building and land (if any).

(iv) Where the claim is for essential amenity land and 'supportive undertakings' are required in respect of other property – the outstanding building (and possibly other essential amenity land) – appropriate details, as outlined in sub-paragraphs (i) to (iii) above, of that other property.

(v) In cases where historically associated objects are detailed in catalogues, please indicate clearly for which items exemption is being sought.

APPENDIX III: GUIDELINES AS TO THE TAX TREATMENT OF HISTORIC HOUSES AND GARDENS OPEN TO THE PUBLIC

Introduction

1   The following notes have been prepared in consultation with the Board of Inland Revenue, for the guidance of owners on the treatment for taxation purposes of houses and gardens open to the public.

2   Liability to tax is based, not on the full amount of the admission fees, but on the balance of profits remaining after deducting from the receipts any allowable expenses. The expenses which can be deducted and the ways in which relief is allowed for a loss, if one is incurred, differ according to the treatment of the showing of the property for tax purposes.

Houses maintained solely or mainly as show places

3   If an occupier is carrying on a trade of showing his house or garden to the public – that is, if it is 'managed on a commercial basis and with a view to the realisation of profits' – the profits will fall within TA 1988 s 53(3) and will be taxed under Schedule D Case I. The occupier will be entitled to claim as a deduction in calculating his profit so much of any expenditure which he incurs on the upkeep of the house, its contents and gardens as is referable to the trading activity. Capital expenditure incurred on the provision of machinery or plant for the maintenance, repair or management of the house, its contents and gardens may qualify for capital allowances. Any grant under the Historic Buildings and Ancient Monuments Act 1953 s 4 which is used wholly or partly to meet expenses attributable to the opening of the property to the public will be taken into account in computing profits.

4   If there is a trading loss in any year, relief from tax on the amount of the loss is allowed either by setting it against other income for the year or against income from all sources for the following year (TA 1988 s 380ff). In so far as the loss has not been allowed in these ways it may be carried forward and set off against any assessable profits from the same trade for a later year (TA 1988 s 385).

5   As to the meaning of the words 'managed on a commercial basis and with a view to the realisation of profits', the Board of Inland Revenue has no power to lay down rules which have any binding force, but what follows represents in general the Board's views on the application of the law which would be followed by Inspectors of Taxes in dealing with particular cases. Failing agreement with the Revenue the taxpayer has the right to appeal to independent tribunals, namely the General Commissioners or the Special Commissioners and, if he thinks the Commissioners have gone wrong on a point of law, from them to the courts.

6   Subject to this we are informed by the Board of Inland Revenue that the matters which they for their part take into account in considering whether the property is managed on a commercial basis are:

(i) the extent to which the property is likely to attract visitors having regard, inter alia, to its historic, architectural, and in the case of gardens, horticultural interest;

(ii) how much of the property is set aside as a show-place; a substantial part of the property should be open to visitors but appropriate allowance will be made for utility and other rooms of little interest to the public, and for those houses where the delicate condition of the fabric prevents part from being shown;

(iii) the number of days on which the property is open to the public. This would usually have to be a substantial number of days in the year but must be compatible with the aim of making a profit from opening. For example, where opening on 75 days or less might be expected to show a higher return than, say, 125 days, then the former figure would satisfy this requirement. Days on which the house is open by appointment to groups and parties can also be taken into account;

(iv) the amount of organisation for the attraction and reception of visitors, eg adequate advertising and publicity, the provision of ticket offices, car parks, refreshments and guides, the sale of postcards and guide books; it must be shown in general that a definite organisation has been set up for attracting and dealing with visitors.

7   It must also be shown that the showing is with a view to the realisation of profits. As the then Chancellor of the Exchequer, Mr R A Butler, said in reply to a Written Question in the House of Commons on 14 July 1954, it must be shown that 'the whole activity is undertaken with the intention of making a profit and not for purely altruistic motives or with a view to getting relief from tax'. If these conditions are fulfilled the Board does not object to the enterprise being treated as a business, just because the receipts are less than the expenses.

8   Where a property is opened to the public for the first time, the 'realisation of profits' test will be regarded as prima facie satisfied where a sufficient number of visitors is attracted to suggest that there is a reasonable prospect of profits being made in the foreseeable future. A property receiving 15,000 visitors a year from regular opening will be regarded as satisfying this test in the years when the property is first opened to the public. This is not, however, a minimum figure of visitors which every house must achieve in order that the opening can be regarded as a trading activity. A lesser figure would be appropriate where the circumstances of the property do not permit this level to be achieved, for example, on account of its size, accessibility or the delicate condition of its fabric.

9   The continuation of the enterprise in face of prolonged losses would, however, make it necessary to consider whether the property was really being managed 'on a commercial basis and with a view to the realisation of profits'. It does not follow that because a title to relief has been established in one year it has been established for all time. The Inspector of Taxes is required, just as he is under TA 1988 s 397 in respect of farming losses, to review the results periodically, and continued substantial losses over a reasonable period, with no apparent prospect of ever showing a profit, might point to the conclusion that the enterprise is not conducted with a view to the realisation of profits.

10   The investment of a substantial amount of capital to provide improved or new facilities for sightseers, eg a new car park or refreshment rooms would, in general, be regarded as evidence of an attempt to attract more visitors and make the enterprise profitable.

Other receipts

11   In practice, the net proceeds from special attractions, events, tea-rooms, sales of brochures and souvenirs which can be associated with the showing of the property to the public will be taken into account in determining whether the 'realisation of profits' test is satisfied and will not be separately assessed to tax.

Houses not maintained solely or mainly as show places

12   If the house or gardens are not maintained wholly or mainly for making a profit from the admission of the public, eg if there is no commercial organisation or simply the receipt of fees from casual visitors, profits will normally fall under Schedule D Case VI. In computing profits for assessment under Case VI, deductions are normally allowed only for the additional expenses incurred as a result of the opening, eg wages for a man to collect entrance fees, extra expenditure on cleaning, making good damage done by the public and so on.

13   Relief for any loss so computed is allowed not against income generally but only against profits from any other transactions taxed under Schedule D Case VI either for the same or future years.

14   In a few instances profits strictly fall within the provisions of Schedule A (TA 1988 s 15). This would be so where the admission fee merely gave access to a viewpoint or empty building (where the attraction lies substantially in the contents of the house or in amenities provided by the occupier Case VI is appropriate). Under Schedule A only the additional expenses attributable to the showing are allowed as a deduction. Any loss is allowed only against receipts from like transactions in that or future years.

APPENDIX IV: JOHN BACON AND FAMILY:
1993 TAX-PLAN

Each earlier edition of this book included a comprehensive tax-planning exercise, to provide a worked example, showing the value of financial planning applied to reduce contingent death duties and to preserve the value of a farm or estate for future generations. Each exercise was designed to illustrate practical ownership rearrangements amongst members of a family, which either reduced tax or deferred tax or provided the cash necessary to pay tax. Schedule II shows the benefits to be secured by this process.

The new business and agricultural property reliefs enacted in FA 1992 appear to make this form of tax-planning redundant. In the example which follows, John Bacon's estate, worth in total £1.3m, would be relieved, so that only some £195,000 would remain chargeable, an amount almost wholly exhausted by first slice exemption. This result is illustrated in Schedule III, included for comparison with Schedules I and II.

It might have seemed reasonable to have omitted this example of comprehensive tax planning as no longer worthwhile. That, however, is not the true position. The conclusion which emerges is that the survival of Northwold now depends exclusively on the application of these reliefs. Because of their overwhelming importance, it is necessary to satisfy – and to continue to satisfy – all the conditions set out in sections **8.3** and **8.5** above. Failure to pass the Revenue's examination of these requirements may lead to loss of critical reliefs and the imposition of a burdensome tax liability.

It is worth adding, that should these reliefs be withdrawn at some time in the future, the vulnerability to inheritance tax will dramatically increase.

Finally, ownership rearrangements do not depend only on taxation factors. Family and farming considerations may make partnerships or alternative profit sharing arrangements necessary to reflect respective contributions to the business. John Bacon and his advisers had these considerations well in mind, when they prepared his 1991 tax-plan, and will continue to do so in future.

Facts

John Bacon is 50 years of age. His wife Ann is a year younger. They have one son, Peter, aged 27 years, who in turn has two young sons.

John Bacon farms about 476 acres at Northwold professionally valued at £2,000 per acre. His working capital, including stock, plant, machinery and equipment is valued at £150,000. In addition, John owns some 90 acres of tenanted land, at Southwold, which has been in the family for some time, and is farmed by a neighbour. Although he has contemplated obtaining vacant possession, no opportunity has ever presented itself, and what he now wishes is simply to maximise the value of Southwold, in the hope that at some time landlord and tenant law will somehow be changed.

Unlike many farmers, John Bacon has been determined not to commit all resources to the farm. He has built up a portfolio of investments, which is professionally managed for him, and he has become a collector of English eighteenth century watercolours including a very fine example of Ambrose Pastelle, valued at £40,000. The remainder of his investments divided between himself and his wife, are valued at £130,000. His personal effects and contents of his home are valued at £50,000 of which some £20,000 belongs to his wife, Ann.

Northwold is mortgaged to the AMC for £40,000 and John has a bank overdraft of £30,000. The overall Balance Sheet looks like this:

Schedule I – Pre-planning exercise (pre F(2)A 1992)

ESTATES AND INHERITANCE TAX

		JB £	Mrs B £	IHT £
Farm 476 acres @ £2,000 per acre		952,000		
Stock		150,000		
		1,102,000		
Tenanted land		90,000		
Investments/cash/precious chattels		120,000	50,000	
Personal effects		30,000	20,000	
		1,342,000	70,000	

		JB £	Mrs B £	IHT £
Mortgage	40,000			
Bank overdraft	30,000	(70,000)	—	
Net estates		1,272,000	70,000	
Assets passing to widow on death of JB		(1,272,000)	1,272,000	
			1,342,000	
Inheritance tax on death of JB		—	—	NIL
Inheritance tax on death of Mrs B			(249,600)	£249,600
Net assets passing to successors after second death			£1,092,400	

Note:

Agricultural relief at 50% has been given on £952,000 and at 30% on £90,000. Business relief at 50% has been given on £150,000. The mortgage and overdraft were paid off on JB's death.

One more important consideration is that Peter has worked successfully on the farm since leaving Wye, and shows every sign of wanting to succeed. Ann is also active on the farm, and John is anxious to provide for her separately from his son, since it is clear that the two wives will never be close . . .

Finally, John would like to make direct provision for his grandchildren's education and maintenance during their 'teens. After detailed consultations with his comprehensive tax-planning advisers, John agrees the following seven recommendations:

(I) LIFE POLICIES

John and Ann each pay £3,000 per annum premiums on policies for the benefit of their grandchildren. These gifts will be potentially exempt transfers but would be applied against the £3,000 annual exemptions, one on his own life and one on Ann's life. This is the first step.

(II) GIFT TO WIFE

John gives Ann 171 acres. There are no tax liabilities on the gift. The reservation of benefit rules do not apply to it for inheritance tax purposes.

(III) PARTNERSHIP

John agrees to create a farm partnership between himself, Ann and Peter. However, he decides after careful consideration not to create a tenancy agreement or licence between himself as landowner, and the partners as joint tenants. The partners are advised that if the business occupies each partner's land and each takes a commercial share of the profits of the trade, there will be no reservation of benefit for inheritance tax purposes on the land given by John to Peter.

(IV) MORTGAGE

The mortgage against Northwold is switched to Southwold so that agricultural relief is obtainable on whole value at Northwold, not the net amount after deducting the mortgage debt. The effect is to produce an extra £8,000 of relief, if Ann dies before John.

(V) NATIONAL HERITAGE DESIGNATION

John gives to Peter his water colour by Ambrose Pastelle. If John dies within seven years Peter will apply for the picture to be 'designated' as of outstanding artistic merit. He had contemplated making a similar application for part of his land as being of outstanding scenic importance, but was advised not to do so, because of the lock-in effect capable of being so created. Peter may apply, if he wishes, after his parents' deaths.

(VI) GIFT TO SON (PET)

John gives Peter 134 acres of in-hand land. Peter takes out a seven-year level term insurance on his father's life to pay inheritance tax if he dies within seven years. John's chargeable capital gains are held-over so that no immediate liability arises on this gift and that in (v) below.

(VII) WILLS

John and Ann both rewrite their wills, so that:

(a) John: gives a specific devise of 100 acres of land in hand to his son bearing its own tax, with the residue to Ann, his widow.
(b) Ann: if John survives her, he is to get residue after a specific gift of 171 acres to Peter, bearing its own tax. If not, her estate goes to Peter.

Schedule II – Post-planning exercise (death within three years)

	JB £	Mrs B £	Son and grandchildren £	IHT £
Net estate	1,272,000	70,000		
Less: gift to son	(268,000)		268,000	
Initial IHT	—	—	(NIL)	NIL
	1,004,000	70,000	268,000	
Gifts to son and grandchildren				
Annual	(9,000)	(9,000)	18,000	
National heritage	(40,000)		40,000	
	955,000	61,000	326,000	
Gifts to wife – 171 acres	(342,000)	342,000		
	613,000	403,000	326,000	
On JB's death				
Assets to wife (IHT exempt)	(413,000)	413,000	—	
	200,000	816,000	326,000	
IHT on PET and land passing to son on JB's death (paid by son)	(37,600)			37,600
	162,400			
Net assets passing to son	162,400		162,400	
Proceeds of policy to meet tax on PET			13,600	
On Mrs B's death IHT thereon		(161,200)		161,200
		654,800		
Net assets passing		(654,800)	654,800	
			1,069,000	286,200
Add: proceeds of policies on lives of JB (£60,058 less £9,000 premiums)			59,058	
On Mrs B (£75,620 less £9,000 premiums)			66,620	
			£1,282,478	
Cost in IHT				198,800
IHT per Schedule I				249,600
Net improvement in IHT position				£50,800

Notes

(1) If JB's death occurs three years after the gift to the son, the inheritance tax on the lifetime gift will be reduced by taper relief.

(2) For the post FA 1992 computation see below.

Schedule III – Post Finance Act 1992

	JB £	*Mrs B* £	*IHT* £
Net	1,272,000	70,000	
To widow	(1,272,000)	1,272,000	
	—	1,342,000	1,342,000
APR & BPR farm		1,102,000	
less 100%		1,102,000	1,102,000
		Nil	240,000
APR (tenanted)		90,000	
less 50%		45,000	45,000
		45,000	195,000
Less nil rate band			150,000
Liable to IHT			£45,000

Index

Alternative land use – *contd*
crops, 17.1:12
finance, 17.1:12
generally, 1.1
income tax, 17.1:1–3
inheritance tax, 17.1:1–4, 17.1:11
loss of tax reliefs, 1.1
nature of new activity, 17.1:12
potentially exempt transfers, 17.1:4
presentation of accounts, 17.1:12
property development, 17.1:5
rental income, 17.1:12
scale of activity, 17.1:12
set aside scheme, 1.1, 17.1:10–11
specialised enterprises, 17.2
stock, 17.1:12
tax considerations, generally, 17.1:1–4
tax strategy, 17.1:12
timing, 17.1:12
trade or business, 17.1:12
value added tax, 9.4:2, 17.1:1, 17.1:2

Animal. *See* FARM ANIMAL

Bee keeping
uniform business rate exemption, 11.4

Benefit in kind
employee, given to. *See* EMPLOYEE

Buildings
See also AGRICULTURAL BUILDINGS;
NATIONAL HERITAGE
agricultural property relief, 8.5:1
glass house, 5.2:2
land, as, 7.3:6(C)
new or partly completed, sale of, 9.6:14
non-residential, sale of, value added
tax, 1.1
plant, difficulty of distinguishing, 5.2:2
protected,
meaning, 9.2:3
substantially re-constructed, 9.6:6
value added tax, 9.2:3, 9.6:6
reconstruction, conversion, alteration
or extension, 9.6:14
redundant, alternative uses, 17.1:12
value added tax, capital goods scheme,
9.6:15

Business assets
capital gains,
hold-over relief, 7.5:5, 7.5:6
retirement relief, 7.6:2
meaning, 7.6:2

Business assets – *contd*
sale of, value added tax, 9.6:1
sporting rights, 9.1:3

Business development
acquisition, additional,
buildings, of, 5.2:1, 5.2:5
land, of, 7.4:1
plant, of, 5.2:1, 5.2:2
acquisitions and new activities,
companies, use of, 17.1:1
development, 17.1:5
tax planning, aims, 17.1:6
value, addition of, 17.1:6
alternative land use. *See* ALTERNATIVE
LAND USE
assets, acquisition of, 17.1:6
'Boden' scheme, 17.3:2
borrowing, cost of, 16.2
contract farming,
agreement, drafting of, 17.4:1
nature of agreement, 17.4:1
profits, division of, 17.4:1
share farming, 17.4:3
herd basis and, 17.4:4
tax consequences, 17.4:2
deferred shares, transfer of interest
using, 17.3:3
diversification. *See* ALTERNATIVE LAND
USE
erosion of farming interests, 17.3
estate management company,
flexibility of, 17.5:4
function of, 17.5:2
introduction, 17.5:1
remuneration, limitation of,
17.5:3
retirement annuity premiums,
deductibility, 17.5:4
structure, 17.5:2
taxation of, 17.5:2, 17.5:4
tax liability,
capital gains tax, 17.5:5(B)
inheritance tax, 17.5:5(A)
father, reduction in working time,
17.3:2
finance, additional, 7.4:1
generally, 17.1:6
inheritance tax,
contract farming and, 17.4:2
reduction of, transfer of interests to
younger generation, 17.1:5,
17.1:6, 17.3:1
limited company, deferred shares,
17.3:3
partnership, transfer of shares in,
children, to, 17.3:2

Rent – *contd*
value added tax, charge to, 9.2:4
yield from tenanted land, 1.1

Rent a room relief
bed and breakfast accommodation,
5.6:6
generally, 5.6:6

Residence
company, non-resident, use of, 17.6:3,
17.6:5
domicile, meaning, 17.6:2
double taxation relief, 17.6:3
emigration, 17.6:2
farming abroad, UK resident, by,
17.6:3
foreign property, rents received from,
UK resident, by, 17.6:3
meaning, 17.6:2
non-resident,
sale of property, 17.6:2
taxation of, 17.6:2
transfer of property by, 17.6:2
overseas buyers,
capital gains tax, 17.6:4(B)
corporation tax, 17.6:4(A)
income tax, 17.6:4(A)
inheritance tax, 17.6:4(C)
meaning, 17.6:4
tax avoidance, 17.6:5
test for, Revenue practice, 17.6:2
trade carried on in UK, taxation of,
17.6:2

Retirement
agricultural property relief inapplicable
to transfers after, 8.5:5
capital gains tax relief. *See* CAPITAL
GAINS TAX

Revenue practice
animals, farm bred, valuation, 3.1:3
capital expenditure, 2.3:2
capital gains tax,
companies, private, special roll-over
relief for, 7.4:2(G)
retirement relief, partnership,
7.6:6
roll-over relief,
part-use of land, 7.4:2(J)
time limit, discretion, 7.4:2(M)
tenancy-at-will, surrender of, 7.7:3
tenancy, rack-rent payable, 15.4:3
value of tenancy, 7.7:8
domestic expenditure, apportionment,
4.4:1

Revenue practice – *contd*
family partnership, grant of tenancy to,
associated operations rule, 15.3:2
death of partner, 15.3:5
pre-10 March 1981, 15.2:1
retention of benefit, 15.3:7
farm cottages, occupation by farm
workers, 4.2:3
growing crop, valuation, 3.3:1
historic buildings open to the public,
hobby-trading, 4.4:2, 14.5:2(F)
house opened to public, 4.4:2
apportionment, 14.5:1, Appendix III
land, sale of, 5.7:2
losses, hobby-farming, 2.6:5
partnerships, 6.1:4
residence, test for, 17.6:2
retirement relief, 7.6:3, 7.6:6
share farming and herd basis,
17.4:4
stock valuation, 3.1:2
tenancies, family, granted pre-10
March 1981, 15.2:2
tenancy, valuation for capital taxation
purposes, 7.7:8

Royalties
mineral exploitation, 5.3:2

Schedule A
annual, meaning, 4.2:2
assessment,
current year basis, 4.2:4
provisional, 4.2:4
sale of property, 4.2:4
background,
pre-1963 tax law, 4.1
taxation of owner-occupied property,
4.4:2
capital allowances. *See* CAPITAL
ALLOWANCES
charge to tax, 4.2:2
deductions, allowable, 4.3:1
entitled, meaning, 4.2:2
exceptions to, 4.2:3
excess allowances, relief for, 4.3:3
excess expenditure, relief for, 4.3:3
feu duty, meaning, 4.2:2
furnished lettings, 5.6:2
ground annual, meaning, 4.2:2
houses open to the public, 14.5:2(B)
income charged to tax under, 4.2:2
incorporeal hereditament, meaning,
4.2:2
incorporeal heritable subject, meaning,
4.2:2